SPEAKING OF PEASANTS

ESSAYS ON INDIAN HISTORY AND POLITICS IN HONOR OF WALTER HAUSER

Group photo of participants in the Hauserfest symposium at the University of Virginia in May 1997.

Front row, left to right: Ruhi Grover, Dharma Kumar, Philip McEldowney, Anand Yang, Richard Barnett, Harry Blair; *Second row, left to right:* Arvind Das, Harold Gould, Paul Brass, Walter Hauser, Ajay Skaria, Edith Turner, Wendy Singer, Prem Shankar Jha, Majid Siddiqi, Ian Barrow; *Back row, left to right:* Peter Reeves, Christopher V. Hill, Tom Tomlinson, Peter Robb, James R. Hagen, Ronald Herring, Vijay Pinch, Kailash Chandra Jha, John Echeverri-Gent. Photo credit: Deej Baker

SPEAKING OF PEASANTS
Essays on Indian History and Politics in Honor of Walter Hauser

Edited by
WILLIAM R. PINCH

MANOHAR
2008

First published 2008

ISBN 81-7304-746-4

Published by

Ajay Kumar Jain for
Manohar Publishers & Distributors
4753/23 Ansari Road, Daryaganj
New Delhi 110 002

Typeset at

Digigrafics
New Delhi 110 049

Printed at

Lordson Publishers Pvt. Ltd.
Delhi 110 007

Contents

Contributors

Harry Blair is Associate Chair, Senior Research Scholar and Lecturer in Political Science at Yale University.

Stuart Corbridge is Professor of Development Studies at the London School of Economics.

Frederick H. Damon is Professor of Anthropology in the Department of Anthropology at the University of Virginia.

Arvind Narayan Das (1948 – 2000) was an activist, social scientist, writer, and the founding-editor of *Biblio*.

Peter Gottschalk is Associate Professor of Religion at Wesleyan University.

Harold A. Gould, is Visiting Scholar, Center for South Asian Studies, University of Virginia.

Ruhi Grover is currently a Project Manager for Mencap, a national charity in Britain that deals with adults and children who have learning disabilities.

James R. Hagen (1941 – 2006) was Professor of History at Frostburg State University.

Ronald J. Herring is Professor of Government, Cornell University.

Christopher V. Hill is Professor of History at the University of Colorado at Colorado Springs.

Sho Kuwajima is Professor Emeritus of South Asian Studies, Osaka University of Foreign Studies.

Philip McEldowney is a Librarian at the University of Virginia, selecting materials for the Anthropology and Religious Studies and South Asia Departments.

William R. (Vijay) Pinch is Professor of History at Wesleyan University.

Peter Robb is Pro-Director and Professor of the History of India at SOAS (University of London).

Mathew N. Schmalz is Associate Professor of Religious Studies at the College of the Holy Cross, Worcester, MA.

Majid H. Siddiqi is Professor of History at the Jawaharlal Nehru University and currently Senior Fellow, Nehru Memorial Museum & Library.

Ajay Skaria is Associate Professor at the University of Minnesota.

Preface

This volume honors Walter Hauser, since 1995 Professor Emeritus of History at the University of Virginia. Walter is many things to many people. For the contributors to this volume, he is first and foremost an eloquent and energetic promoter of Bihar. Some of us work, or have worked, on Bihar for no other reason than the simple fact that Walter somehow persuaded us to do so. Bihar's reputation as—to put it gently—the 'wild west' of India is evidence enough that Walter can be very persuasive. Walter also introduced Bihari peasants and their struggles—as well as their remarkable leader, Swami Sahajanand Saraswati—to the academy, both in India and the West; he built from scratch the University of Virginia's Center for South Asian Studies; and he trained a small army of graduate students, some of whom are represented in this volume.

In 1997, two years after Walter's retirement from full-time teaching, the Center for South Asian Studies hosted a celebration of Walter's career. Most of the contributors to this volume presented their essays in lecture form at that gathering, held between 23 and 25 May. As is always the case in Charlottesville, the weather was perfect, the food delicious, and the libations abundant. It was a happy time, made profoundly bittersweet in retrospect by the remembered presence of Rosemary, Walter's wife, who left this world in 2001. This volume also honors her memory.

The 1997 'Hauserfest' and the current volume, though much delayed, were the products of considerable individual and institutional labor. Richard B. Barnett in History at Virginia organized the gathering, and Daniel J. Ehnbom in Art History has offered patient encouragement of the volume over the past ten years. The conference was made possible with institutional support from the Office of the Dean of the Faculty of Arts and Sciences (Raymond Nelson), the Center for South Asian Studies, the Office of International Studies, and the Bhatta Urdu Studies Fund. Cindy Benton-Groner at the Center for South Asian Studies provided key administrative support on occasions too numerous to mention. More recently, the production of the volume was made possible by Manohar in New Delhi, led by Ramesh Jain, by the editorial labors of Justin Schaeffer Duffy, and by generous funds from the Office of the Vice President for Research (Professor Ariel R. Gomez) at the University of Virginia and the Deans' Fund (Professor J. Donald Moon) at Wesleyan University. The in-house editor and copy editor at Manohar deserve special recognition for their painstaking and perspicacious work. Philip McEldowney, South Asia & Middle East Librarian at the Alderman Library of the University of Virginia, prepared the bibliography at the end of this volume and responded graciously to too many stray bibliographic queries over the past two years, often late at night. The photograph of Walter that graces this volume was taken by Florence Hauser; the group photo from the 1997 gathering is provided courtesy of Deej Baker. I thank all of these individuals and institutions for their help, encouragement, and support.

Thanks are due as well to the additional participants beyond those listed as essay authors in the table of contents, who served as discussants and paper givers. They include, from the University of Virginia, Murray Milner, Jr., and Sukirti Sahay, Sociology; Edith L. B. Turner, Anthropology; and John Echeverri-Gent, Government. From farther afield came Anand Yang, formerly in History at the University of Utah, presently Director of the Jackson School of International Studies at the University of Washington; the late Dharma Kumar of the Delhi School of Economics, Delhi University; Ian Barrow in History at Middlebury College; Paul R. Brass in Political Science at the University of Washington; Kailash C. Jha in the Political Section at the U.S. Embassy in New Delhi; Wendy Singer in History at Kenyon College; Peter Reeves, formerly of the Curtin Institute of Technology, Perth, Australia, and now Coordinator of South Asian Studies at the National University of Singapore; Prem Shankar Jha, distinguished columnist with *The Hindu* and *Business Standard*; and Tom Tomlinson, formerly in History at the University of Strathclyde, now at the School of Oriental and

African Studies, London. Bernard S. Cohn in History and Anthropology at the University of Chicago, was unable to attend at the last minute; Frederick H. Damon served as a discussant in his stead.

Four contributors to the volume were not among the original presenters, but the relevance of their work to Walter's wider concerns prompted the solicitation of their contributions. Peter Gottschalk in Religious Studies at Wesleyan University and Mathew Schmalz in Religious Studies at The College of the Holy Cross kindly agreed to author a reflection on their remarkable teaching and research tool, 'The Virtual Village', http://virtualvillage.wesleyan.edu/, which enables web-users to wander through a living and breathing rural hamlet in south-western Bihar. Stuart Corbridge in Development Studies at the London School of Economics graciously allowed us to include an essay on the politics of 'reservations' in Jharkhand. Frederick H. Damon, who (as noted above) took part in the conference as a discussant, was inspired by the proceedings (and by the late James R. Hagen's paper in particular) to probe the cultural-ecological connections between Bihar and Melanesia for a later gathering in Patna. I am pleased that he has allowed us to include his elegant and stimulating essay in the volume as well.

Finally, for permissions to publish previously committed essays, I thank Oxford University Press, Delhi (for Peter Robb); *The Indian Economic and Social History Review* (Ajay Skaria); *Indian Social Science Review* (Harold Gould); *The New Zealand Journal of Asian Studies* (Ruhi Grover); *The Journal of Asian Studies* (Stuart Corbridge); and *Past & Present* (William R. Pinch).

As will be evident from the shifting institutional ties of many of the 'Hauserfest' participants and volume contributors, much has changed since 1997. Some of us are no more. In addition to Rosemary Hauser, we mourn the loss of three conference participants: in 2000, Arvind Narayan Das, journalist, social scientist, activist, and founding editor of *Biblio*; in 2001, Dharma Kumar, Professor of Economic History at the Delhi School of Economics; and in 2006, James R. Hagen, Professor of History at Frostburg State University. Clearly too many years have come and gone while this volume was gestating. Hopefully it will prove to have been worth the wait. What matters in the end is not the delay, but the fact that the names and institutional origins of the conference participants and essay contributors are evidence of the wide-ranging—and continuing—impact of Walter's energy, good will, and intellect. We are, each of us, indebted to him in different ways.

Walter prepared the ground—always figuratively, often literally—upon which many of us have trod on our own intellectual journeys. And those of us who came to Walter after coming to Bihar now see Bihar in a new, brighter light. On behalf of all of us, I offer him our collective thanks.

21 January 2007 VIJAY PINCH

Introduction: Walter and Friends

William R. Pinch

The essays in this volume range widely, in terms of scope and approach as well as temporal and geographic coverage. Some, such as Das and Kuwajima, and Hill and Corbridge, deal directly with Bihar. Others do not limit themselves to matters Bihari, but have much to say to Bihar nonetheless. Damon sees the imprint of landlocked Bihar in maritime South-East Asia; Hagen compares the agrarian ecosystem of Bihar (and India) to China; Blair compares social and economic development in Bihar to Maharashtra and Bangladesh; Grover investigates the business of timber in what is now Uttarakhand; Siddiqi and Gould take us on very different tours of peasant politics in India; Pinch begins and ends in Bihar, with interludes in religio-intellectual retreats in Ayodhya and London; Herring introduces us to the rise and demise of land reform in Kerala; and Skaria takes us inside the mind of a sometime Gandhian Gujarati peasant activist. Corbridge and Hill's Jharkhand was in earlier days a large part of Bihar. Much of what Gottschalk and Schmalz tell us about south-western Bihar is true as well for the wider Bhojpur region extending into eastern UP. And Robb offers us a magisterial theoretical reflection that applies equally to Bihar and India and Britain, and their collective engagement with the modern, 'colonial' state.

It must be emphasized that all the essays illuminate, each in its own way, the world of the peasant in South Asia. That world that has been central to the thinking, writing, and teaching of Walter Hauser since the 1950s. A quick glance at the 1991 census reveals why: nearly 70 per cent of India's population then derived its livelihood from farming, fishing, hunting, logging, or related work with the land and its products. Of that population, the vast majority, well over 90 per cent, was directly engaged in agriculture.[1] These figures have not changed dramatically since 1991. In the 2001 census, nearly 75 per cent of India's population was classed as 'rural'.[2] Nearly 60 per cent of the total workforce was listed either as 'cultivators' or as 'agricultural labourers'. In Bihar, that figure was over 77 per cent.[3] Each contributor to this volume weaves his or her way through a series of investigations to uncover and, to some degree, explain some dimensions of the history that mattered to that 'rural', agriculturalist majority of India's population, living in village, forest, or in *ashram*—and sometimes even in cities and towns.[4] Each of the authors heeds, I think, Herring's advice to balance the desire to generalize about a 'peasantry' against the reality that the 'peasantry' is beset with class stratifications and 'multiple identifications'—not least among them, caste and religion. Several of the essays explore the question of leadership and its cultural and religious dimensions; others investigate commerce and commercialization, agrarian struggle, religious belief and practice, artisanship and human ecology, and colonial-imperial epistemology. What glues these essays together is the conviction, for the most part unstated, that it is the world of those who extract sustenance from the land that we should be trying to understand.

This was the central problematic that preoccupied Walter Hauser for nearly half a century. Happily it preoccupies him still. My most vivid image of Walter is of him exhorting us around the seminar table to probe more deeply: to understand what precisely, religion, nationalism, imperialism, socialism, capitalism, caste-ism—and any other analytical abstraction, whether suffixed with an 'ism' or not—meant for the people on the ground who put the tiller to the soil. And for Walter, the person who best articulated the implications of those 'isms' for India's *kisan*s was Swami Sahajanand Saraswati, the 'Hindu' ascetic-turned-caste-reformer-turned-socialist-radical. Indeed, since the early 1960s and the completion of his Chicago PhD dissertation on the Bihar Provincial Kisan Sabha, it has been Walter's quest to present Sahajanand Saraswati's struggle—ideological, political, social, and, it should be said, religious—to the English-speaking and reading public. That quest was a long one, interrupted in the late 1960s by a sudden illness that robbed Walter of two or three years and much bodily strength. However, the wait was worth it: we have, since the mid-1990s, begun to see the fruits of his painstaking labours. It is no exaggeration to say that historians of the Indian subcontinent are in Walter's debt for *Sahajanand on Agricultural Labour and the Rural Poor* (1994) and *Swami Sahajanand and the Peasants of Jharkhand* (1995). We know too that Kailash Jha was instrumental not only in the successful delivery of those books, but to their production and gestation—so we are in Kailash's debt as well. However, the capstone of the Hauser–Jha partnership is yet to come: their forthcoming translation of Sahajanand's autobiography, *Mera Jivan Sangharsh*, 'My Life Struggle'. This work is eagerly awaited. It will make an excellent primary source text for modern Indian history, to supplement, and in some ways correct, Mohandas K. Gandhi's *The Story of My Experiments with Truth*.

'The Swami' presides over this volume in the same way that Walter does. The convictions that drove Sahajanand, and transformed him from a Saiva *samnyasi* to social reformer to socialist radical, are not far removed from those that have transformed the discipline of history over the course of the twentieth century and drew Walter and many others into the study of peasants and peasant politics. That such a large proportion of our scholarly resources could be aimed at the uncovering of the history and culture of ordinary agrarian 'subalterns' in India speaks, in the final analysis, to the degree to which the political and intellectual concerns of Marx remain central to Western social science. That said, the varied nature of the essays here demonstrates that the frameworks brought to bear, and the understandings and explanations offered, go beyond (and sometimes against the grain of) Marx.

Given the legacy of the Swami as a tireless organizer on behalf of peasants, and given the nature of Walter's pioneering work on the Swami (and as a tireless institutional rainmaker, and mentor of students), it is not surprising that many of the essays that make up this volume are concerned in one way or another with mobilization. Majid Siddiqi offers a typology of peasant mobilization and concludes that the 'historicity of peasant insurgency in modern India has come full circle'—from the caste and religious networks that produced the more modern political associations like the Kisan Sabha of the 1930s, to the caste and communal and class warfare that bedevils the Indian present. This cycle reappears in various forms in the essays that follow, though there will doubtless be disagreement as to whether Indian agrarian activism is simply running in circles or spiralling upward—or, for that matter, downward. Where the historian Siddiqi proposes a schematic outline, the political anthropologist Gould retraces the regional evolution of north-Indian peasant politics, both as those regional movements evolved but also as they were inflected through the national political positioning of leaders like Mohandas Gandhi and Charan Singh. Gould is particularly interested in the problem of class formation, and sees the rise of Charan Singh and analogous figures in the late 1960s and 1970s as a 'breakthrough point' for the 're-classification' of the middle castes. For Gould, there is much to celebrate here, since caste and religious divisions seem to be giving way to a variety of regional, class-oriented unions. They may not have produced a 'single class thesis' for all of India, but they did evince common class 'threads'.

For Arvind Das, who covered similar temporal ground but focused primarily on peasant radicalism in Bihar, beginning with the Swami and ending with the rise of the 'Naxalite Movement' and its aftermath, the picture was less rosy. The agrarian armies on the right and left, and the language of violence that emerged with a vengeance in the 1970s and thereafter, seemed to reinforce the sharp caste divisions on the ground. Das still managed to end on an optimistic note, however: if violence has become the language of peasant politics, at least those at the bottom are now better armed. These stories share much with Ron Herring's, particularly when it comes to the combustible tension between the 'conservatizing' beneficiaries of land reform and those agricultural labourers for whom land reform always remains just out of reach. One lesson to be taken from Herring's account is that land reform, depending on how it is enacted, can take the radical wind out of agrarian politics. Herring's arena of investigation is the objectively successful (especially in comparison to Bihar) history of communism and land reform in Kerala; of particular concern for him is the history of the religious and caste dimensions of class division, and what they mean in terms of agrarian structure and individual agency.

Herring argues, *contra* much classical 'peasantist' theory, that the personal political theory of individual leaders matters, that structure cannot be understood independent of agency. We get an up-close-and-personal look at individual agency coming to terms with agrarian structure in Sho Kuwajima's compelling account of the 1939 Reora Satyagraha in Gaya District, based on the writings and speeches of a wide array of activists and leaders, including Sahajanand, Jayaprakash Narayan, Rahul Sankrityayan, A.N. Sinha, and, most importantly, Jadunandan Sharma, the leader of the movement. Kuwajima provides a fascinating transcript of an interview with Sharma conducted in Gaya in 1966, in which the latter describes the behind-the-scenes maneuvring of key players. And Ajay Skaria introduces us to the ambivalences and ambiguities of personal agency, as on public display in the life of that conflicted Gandhian, the erstwhile Kisan Sabha leader, Indulal Yagnik. Yagnik's 'homeless ness', which is enacted in the no-man's land between ideological 'transcendence' and pragmatic 'neighbourliness', or leadership and fellowship, is a homelessness felt by many if not all the political radicals described here (certainly it is evoked in Jadunandan Sharma's remarks, quoted in Kuwajima's essay, and as Skaria suggests it emerges at multiple levels in Sahajanand's writings)—and perhaps by those who write about them as well. Hence Skaria's call to 'engage more seriously with the subaltern politics that we have often failed to even recognize in our midst'.

Where there is mobilization and political radicalism, and the angst of homelessness, the state cannot be far behind. Ruhi Grover and Christopher Hill seek to bring the state out of the shadows and show how it managed (whether in its imperial or national incarnation) to control, manage, and understand local communities. Hill focuses on the experience of the Santals in what is now the state of Jharkhand, and examines in particular the ways that European understanding of 'nature' and 'the wild' structured British assumptions about the non-sedentary people with whom they were dealing. If the Santals—and 'adivasis' generally—were seen as different, Hill argues, it was not because the British simply constructed them as such in a desire to displace them from the forest resources for which they (the British) hungered. Rather, it was because they *were* different: they were wild. And to be wild was to be wasteful, in the European way of thinking. Hence they had to be either eradicated or transformed. If Hill's lens is focused on the ways in which the British managed forest populations, Grover is focused on the state's efforts (in the Forest Department) to manage the forest. What is remarkable here is the ability of some timber merchants to, in effect, manage the state. Unsatisfied with the 'resistance' model, Grover argues for the existence of a shadow economy, 'nestled within' and overlapping with the official, state-run economy. We are left with a more complex understanding of both state and society—each responded to subgroups in the other, and in so doing were 'mutually constituted'. Reading Grover after Hill prompts questions about whether the British construction of tribalism and nature was simply European. To what degree was the discourse, and the epistemology that sustained them, also Indian?[5] And what does that say about the nature of the 'colonial' state?

The relation of state to society and the ways in which the 'colonial' context informed and structured social, economic, cultural, even eco-systemic change—and agrarian struggle—are concerns close to the heart of Peter Robb's powerful and wide-ranging reflection on imperial state-formation and the production of knowledge. In seeking to relate the British understanding of India to the evolution of the Indian identities, political organization, and ultimately the state, Robb makes clear that an interactive British-Indian 'govern-mentality', intent on improvement and regulation, laid the ontological foundation for peasant politics, even as that 'govern-mentality' aided in the exacerbation of the harsh agrarian realities of the nineteenth and twentieth centuries that necessitated those politics. Whereas many of the essays focus on specific examples of peasant mobilization, Robb's essay shows how the very possibility of that mobilization depended upon an evolving colonial understanding of rights, status, and profit. Thus, Robb argues, Sahajanand was remarkable not because his agrarian-political diagnoses were original, but because of the degree to which his goals, theories, and tactics emerged out of the circumstances of the colonial state. Indeed, Robb shows that to understand Sahajanand's significance we should see him as a product of his times: Because he was embedded in, and largely produced by, the British–Indian intellectual climate, Sahajanand was able to be an effective mobilizer and ideologue whose pleas for justice, whose 'diagnoses', resonated at the highest echelons of state power. Robb cautions against privileging either external (colonial) or 'internal' (indigenous) categories in understanding Indian social, cultural, and political change, and argues instead that it is more productive to see the ways in which borrowings occur to produce new understandings.

The desire to avoid primordialism and an essentializing of either British or Indian understandings is also at the heart of my own essay on *bhakti* and empire. But while I am only too willing to agree that Indian understandings drank deep from the well of British (and European) systems of meaning, I endeavour to show that the reverse was often true as well: British understandings were themselves transformed by the British-Indian interaction, however unequal it may have been. More broadly, the long interpenetration of Hindu and Christian religious thought in the nineteenth and twentieth centuries calls into question the utility of the term 'colonial' for describing the political, social, and cultural formation that was British India. Given that George Grierson, of *Bihar Peasant Life* (Calcutta 1885) fame, was one of those engaged in the act of interpenetration, it stands to reason that this dialogical evolutionary process was not irrelevant to the world of the north Indian peasant. Possibly Robb would agree that the term 'colonial'—and all that it implies—confounds more than it clarifies with respect to the period 1757-1947. What term we should then use to characterize India's British experience remains an open question. Clearly, however, true understanding can only be achieved if it is grounded in semantic precision: words have a way of leading us astray.

Where the term 'colonial' clearly possesses functional utility, however, is in the *longue durée* context of Indian agriculture and its environmental constraints. This is where the steady macro-historical hand of James R. Hagen enters, to paint for us a portrait of the distinctive features of 'agricultural intensification' as it was undertaken on the Gangetic plain from western UP to Bengal over the very long term. Hagen argued that intensification here was achieved mainly through a gradual extension of cultivation *in tandem* with biomass (including forest) depletion, and an increase in labour inputs from the rising population. In retrospect, the beginning of the eighteenth century may be seen to have witnessed the initiation of a range of agricultural practices that signaled increasing stress on the system; the point of no return seems to have been the late nineteenth century, when, Hagen argued, population began a rapid growth phase just as new cultivable lands were no longer available. Peasants found themselves up against a resource wall, as it were, which created the conditions for the stressed agrarian relations of the early twentieth century and the rise, especially in Bihar, a zone of particular vulnerability because it shared features of its wet- and dry-agriculture regions to its east and west respectively, of contentious peasant movements. If, as Robb argues, Sahajanand was a product of the colonial times in which he lived, right down to the language of rights that he deployed on behalf of peasants, he was also, for Hagen, a product of shifts in long-term patterns of human agricultural resource exploitation and population change.

Central to Hagen's thinking is the symbiotic connection between forest biomass and agricultural production. Damon too focuses on the ecosystem production/resource nexus, and—inspired by Hagen's essay and subsequent conversations with him—draws particular attention to shared botanical meanings evinced by ancient Biharis, especially as articulated through the flora of Buddhism, and modern Melanesians, as enacted in the culture of boat production. There is an important lesson here, Damon suggests, about religion: that it is embedded in things that the modern academy has long tended to regard as ordinary and mechanistic, particularly (in the case of Melanesians) in boats and in the tools and trees used to construct them. In so far as Indian understandings adapted themselves to and were displaced by 'colonial' norms, *pace* Robb, including modern post-Industrial (and post-Enlightenment) European religious norms, the deeper meanings embedded in things retreated into the shadows of history. Closer attention to the quotidian and mechanistic affords startling continuities—or, at least, the possibility of continuities (Damon is reluctant to make narrative claims that smack of the 'dispersal' school of Austronesian studies)—that link southern Asia (Bihar and Kerala especially) to the western edge of Oceania, and enable us to cross our own oceans of understanding. We should not, Damon argues, discuss religion simply in terms of belief and practice, and as something opposed to 'science', but in terms of production—the production of things and of people, nested in a watered-landscape, whether oceanic or agrarian. Our inability to appreciate Melanesian understandings, as both ethnobotanically religious and scientific, has more to do, Damon suggests, with the failure of our own words—disfigured as they are by the rise of disembodied technical language over embodied thought-action—than with any failure on the part of Melanesian culture. Once again, our words have led us astray.

Damon's essay traverses immense geographic as well as temporal ground. As such it serves as a useful transition to the three concluding essays in the volume, by Corbridge, Blair, and Gottschalk and Schmalz, which bring us firmly into the present with three distinct visions of social, religious, and economic reality in Bihar, and beyond Bihar. Corbridge investigates the fate of tribal people in Jharkhand, and tracks in particular the expanding influence of a 'tribal elite' that has benefitted disproportionately from the positive discrimination programmes known generically as 'reservation'. Corbridge does not dispute that the state has deployed an 'invented' category of *adivasi* and 'tribal' for development purposes, but he does caution against the notion that such classifications only serve to further embed inequalities in Indian society. To the contrary, he argues that a new 'tribal middle class' has emerged in Jharkhand, even if its fate is tied to a continued insistence on difference and a resistance to assimilation and 'normalization' into the broader body politic. In other words, reservation works, even if it works unevenly. While there is good reason, then, to feel optimistic about social development in Jharkhand, Bihar itself makes us less sanguine. Blair compares the track record of rural development in Bihar with Bangladesh to the east and Maharashtra (and to some extent Gujarat) to the west, and asks why rural development has proceeded so successfully in western Maharashtra in particular, whereas it has failed in Bihar and, to a large extent, in Bangladesh. For answers Blair turns to history, caste demography, political culture, and social relations; his narrative is engaging and is sure to be provocative—nowhere more so perhaps than when he suggests that western Maharashtra has a martial culture of resistance to foreign rule (e.g. Shivaji) that seems lacking in Bihar.

Development is more than electricity, roads, jobs, and politics. Gottschalk and Schmalz afford us a different and perhaps more comforting image of Bihar, and of that 70 per cent of India that is 'rural', as seen from the ground up via their 'Virtual Village' website (http://virtualvillage.wesleyan.edu). Their essay, and the website, are graceful reminders of the artificiality of the scholar's analytic categories. We are afforded, in the 'virtual village', a glimpse into the richly contextualized lives of ordinary people, and the ways in which they navigate their way through religion, economics, politics, identity, history, and gender. A particular concern of the authors has been to challenge received notions of Indian religion, on two levels: first, that India is a place that is defined, in some core, essential way, by its religious traditions; and second, that Hinduism and Islam are mutually exclusive and antagonistic religious traditions, hermetically sealed off one from the other. The website offers a way out of the all-too-familiar heuristic challenge that many of us have faced when seeking to complicate our students' understanding of religion in the lives of ordinary villagers, namely, that one is constrained at the outset to point to the fact of difference: that one person, party, or group is Muslim, while the other is Hindu. As they put it, 'It has proven difficult to directly emphasize interrelations without emphasizing Hindu and Muslim identities.' The 'virtual village' circumvents this problem by allowing the visitor to gradually get to know the residents of 'Arampur' through a series of interviews, by wandering around and seeing the sights. One is never presented with a decontextualized view of religion, in isolation.

*****

Gottschalk and Schamlz make a larger hermeneutic point in

their essay, that assumptions about the world in which we live govern the kinds of questions we ask about it. This is reminiscent of Robb's argument concerning the evolving concept of rights and its deployment by Sahajanand and others in the work of agrarian reform. It hardly need be said that the lesson here, that the explanatory narratives that result from scholarly inquiry should not be read independent of the complex intellectual-cum-institutional-cum-epistemological structures that produce and enable them, is one that Edward Said urged upon the Western academy nearly three decades ago. Gottschalk and Schmalz's answer to this lesson is twofold: first they foreground the problem of their 'authority' as Western academics as a 'perspectivalist' 'teaching moment', based upon which students (and teachers) are prompted to reflect not only on the designers' inherited biases, whether conscious or unconscious, but also on their own—perhaps more raw—assumptions as they attempt to come to grips with 'the other' that confronts them on their computer screens; second they relinquish control of the camera, and the 'virtual village', to the inhabitants of 'Arampur', so as to begin to hear and see them on their own terms. This latter move is only a momentary 'turning of the tables', true, but a valuable one nonetheless, not least because it allows us—as viewers—to see ourselves (and the designers) through new eyes. Thus Gottschalk and Schmalz cut a postmodern escape from the thicket of deconstructionist irony.

It is partly in this reflexive spirit that the final section of the volume is presented to the reader. The academic world that we, the authors, inhabit is an immensely powerful and privileged one, even if it occasionally finds itself under siege. In order to fully appreciate the fruits of our intellectual labors, it is necessary to be cognizant of not simply the power of the institutions that stand behind us, but the enormous power of the institutions, and governments, that stand behind them. And we must also be cognizant of the long years of individual and collective labor that went into shaping those institutions and governments. The chapter on 'South Asian Studies at Virginia' seeks to do precisely this work. Together with Philip McEldowney's bibliography, it constitutes a professional (auto)-biography of Walter Hauser; but this individual story is also emblematic of an important chapter of the larger, collective institutional biography that all' 'Asianists' working in the West—even the West in the East, and especially in the USA—possess. In a sense, this section *of Speaking of Peasants* may be read as a coda to the obligatory first footnote or preface that distinguishes much scholarly writing, concerning the funding agencies and institutional support that made such writing possible. As such, the hope is that it will afford a more thoughtful reading of the intellectual projects on display in the volume. It is also a way of affirming the obvious, namely, that without the institutionalization of Asian Studies, and South Asian Studies as its most lively theoretical and methodological corner, and without the generosity of spirit that distinguished the generation of scholar-builders to which Walter belonged and which made such institutionalization possible, the American academic world would be a flat, dull, and colorless place to work.

Notes

1. Table C-1, *Census of India 1991*, Part B19(F)—Economic Tables, and Part IIB—Primary Census Abstract. Portions of the Indian census may be viewed online at <http://www.censusindia.net/cendat/index.html>.
2. 'Urban' and 'rural' are, of course, terms that denote the two ends of a spectrum. Indian 'towns' are defined as 'places with a municipal corporation, municipal area committee, town committee, notified area committee, or cantonment board'—as well as 'places having 5,000 or more inhabitants, a density of not less than 1,000 persons per square mile (390 per sq km), pronounced urban characteristics, and at least three fourths of the adult male population employed in pursuits other than agriculture.' John F. Long, David R. Rain, and Michael R. Ratcliffe, 'Population Density vs. Urban Population: Comparative GIS Studies in China, India, and the United States', paper presented in session S68 on 'Population Applications of Spatial Analysis Systems (SIS)' at the International Union for the Scientific Study in Population Conference, Salvador, Brazil, 18-25 August, p. 6.
3. *Census of India Online* <http://www.censusindia.net/results/wrk_statement2.html>, 'Statement 2—Total workers (main +marginal) and their categories—India: 2001 (Provisional)'.

4. Over seven million cultivators and agricultural labourers were classed as 'urban' in the 2001 census.
5. I attempt an answer to this question in *Warrior Ascetics and Indian Empires*, Cambridge: Cambridge University Press, 2006.

PART I

Empire and Ideology

From Law to Rights: The Impact of the Colonial State on Peasant Protest in Bihar*

Peter Robb

Walter Hauser is concerned with political and protest movements. His perspective being that of the underdog, over many years he steeped himself in the society and life of Bihar (as well as its records) in order to explore its history. By contrast, I have focused my attention on the colonial state, also often enough in regard to Bihar. True, I have long argued for attention to different voices and for history from below, and against 'directive interpretations',[1] and I have extensively studied agrarian society. But state policy has been my starting point. Can the two perspectives meet? This paper will argue that they should, and specifically that the colonial state played a crucial part in shaping identity and politics, not least in the areas of peasant activism that Hauser has examined.[2]

I

My starting assumption is that identities in Bihar took different forms and had a different basis before and after colonial rule.[3] One may take up this question towards the end of the early modern era by interpreting colonial reports, such as those of Buchanan-Hamilton. But it is quite hard to discern any change.

* This paper is a version of material also published in Peter Robb, *Empire, Identity, and India: Peasants, Political Economy and Law* (2007) and is reproduced here with the permission of Oxford University Press.

We might look, in Marxian terms, for unfree and then landless labor, and primitive and then capitalist accumulation; we might expect, following the work of C.A. Bayly in particular, that the colonial state's successful drive for secure (landlord) property and settled agriculture was a necessary prerequisite for the evolution of a range of agricultural classes, at least beyond the gentry and merchants for whom Bayly ascribes an earlier existence.[4] However, in Purnea, for example, Buchanan had already reported a fairly clear range of socio-economic categories in the early nineteenth century.[5] First came the dominant and independent rural elite, the zamindars, augmented by area intermediaries: the zamindari *dewan* and other agents, and revenue-farmers (*mostajirs*). Next came village elites, people outside the *mostajirs*' authority (those occupying unassessed land, paying low rents in perpetuity, or paying directly to the zamindars; and all high castes, Hindu and Muslim, 'exempted from rent for their houses and gardens'). Such elites, and perhaps some other landholders, expressed their dominance by employing and controlling labour, including one specialist ploughman for every six cattle. In another category were village officers, the watchmen and messengers. Then came other cultivators (*adhiyars*) who held land through *mostajirs* or other agents. Last, there were the slaves and poor labourers who at least 'procured room for their houses from those for whom they work'. Within this broad pattern, different types of tenure also certainly existed, their names and character briefly recorded by Buchanan—various kinds and degrees of fixed-rent tenants, tenants in perpetuity, short-leaseholders and so on.[6] Such categories (not being wholly invented by Buchanan) must imply degrees of power and wealth, and solidarities perceived by people themselves.

On closer examination, the much-cited findings of Buchanan indicate a general fluidity, ambiguity, and contingency of status. He may have missed social structures, either for want of information or because of his presuppositions. Yet it does seem that, for every tenurial categorization or social layer, there were many other connections and identities that overlapped. In Purnea, first, there were large numbers of servants and hired workers, but outsiders found it very difficult to obtain labour: workers could not escape the vertical control provided by debt bondage. Second, broader identities were expressed, but possibly, like caste and community, cut across the economic strata: 'more than half the Hindus', reported Buchanan, 'consider themselves as belonging to foreign nations, either from the west of India or Bengal, although many of them have no tradition concerning the time of their emigration and may have no knowledge of the particular part of the country from whence they came'. Third, among such broad categories, caste was plainly fluid. For example, as 'Hindu law' was strongly enforced, the numerous high-caste families found 'great difficulty in procuring proper marriages for their daughters'. Should they fail before the onset of puberty, as often they did, daughter and parents risked disgrace. Some then would convert to Islam, according to Buchanan, and some be 'lowered to an inferior degree' of society.[7] Fourth, castes were also ambiguous as occupational categories. Buchanan records many that were not confined to their 'proper profession'. Only 10 per cent of Mithila Brahmans 'stud[ied] more or less, and reject[ed] service', some 'carr[ied] arms', and more than two-thirds 'occup[ied] lands . . . and attend[ed] chiefly to their cultivation'. Lavana Brahmans lived 'entirely by commerce'. Rajputs would not 'condescend to such drudgery' as to hold the plough, except that one in eight did so, while others were traders or went for service in other districts. Mithila Kayasthas still adhered 'to the proper duties of their caste, being writers and accountants, but many rent[ed] land' without cultivating it themselves. Many Telis (oilmen) worked as traders. Finally, nonetheless, considerations of 'purity' did matter. Buchanan refers to the many castes of 'pure cultivators' and others apparently confined in practice to their ritual occupation. Small sections, such as Malis who worked as garland-makers, were 'admitted to be a very pure order of Sudras', and similar positions of relative prestige seemed to adhere to potters, blacksmiths, and barbers, all of whom 'generally confine[d] their labours to their profession'. Similarly, impure and 'vile' castes identified by Buchanan reflected their actual occupations, though also, apparently, 'aboriginal origin'.[8] There are echoes of supposed Hindu decline in Buchanan's account; but we may assume that he described conditions that had long been fluid.

All these distinctions affected the rights and perceptions, and hence divided the body, of tenants and cultivators. Above all, although stable bands of people can be discerned amidst the diversity, and though some 'types' were becoming richer or poorer, yet an unambiguous class identity for 'cultivators' was unlikely. This was because of non-'class' distinctions, such as the avoidance of physical labour that was so important for the higher castes, who generally paid lower rents, and might hold their household plots free. Because social categories were of mixed basis, caste, tenure and occupation were each important but not decisive. Moreover, they usually derived from hierarchical and dependent relationships more than from horizontal commonalities. Into this setting came the colonial state, and with it not only legal and administrative change but also the priorities of aggressive international trade. There were two known outcomes: a discourse of the 'peasant', and organized 'peasant' protest.

II

The evidence of Buchanan-Hamilton implied that notions of 'peasant' characteristics, rights or solidarities, insofar as they have appeared in India, required to be constructed—just like all the other modern identities that have been analysed by scholars. Even at the end of the nineteenth century in Bihar, it was reported, Indians tended to emphasize their caste and ritual status before their occupation. Stevenson-Moore remarked of Champaran district:

> No person will state his chief means of livelihood to be other than the recognized occupation of his caste. Thus a very large number of Brahmins, who live entirely by cultivation, assert their main occupation to be that of a priest. Again, a barber, who lives mainly by cultivating his land, asserts his hereditary profession to be his chief means of livelihood. Conversely a *Koiri*, who has been mulcted of his land and lives by labouring for others, still claims to be a cultivator . . . .[9]

The echo of Buchanan-Hamilton is not surprising. Stevenson-Moore's evidence was of identities apparently being asserted irrespective of status, and of caste as immutable. But we also know that very many attempts at upward mobility were already being made, including ones which involved a change in 'hereditary occupation' as well as in *varna* standing. For the purposes of the present discussion, the real issue was raised when, according to Stevenson-Moore, the Koiris, the 'backbone of the Bihar peasantry', were determined to assert their status as peasants. Would they do so, in common with non-Koiris, even in contradistinction to Koiris who were not cultivators, and thus accept modern definitions of 'peasants' and 'peasant rights'? Or were the misconceptions of definition self-fulfilling—did they prevent the creation of peasants *as a class*, a process different from the regionalization of *jati* that was also occurring?

Stevenson-Moore was writing of a region where agrarian interests were hotly contested, because of indigo disputes. As yet, he suggested, the raiyats did not like indigo but their attitude remained one of 'passive acquiescence'. He attributed the apathy to a want of competition where villages were held entirely by one influential zamindar. There also may have been less need of contestation in a district described as having relatively sparse population, low rents, abundant cultivable waste, uncertain measurement, and few petty proprietors, and where survey disclosed 'large excess areas in the holdings of the tenants for which no rents were paid'.[10] But more to the point, the circumstance was that raiyats were 'ignorant of the value of their rights' and that 'Assistant Settlement Officers often had great trouble in inducing them to understand a question sufficiently to give an intelligent answer'.[11] In short, it may be inferred that such 'apathy' as existed was no necessary reflection of lack of intelligence of self-assertion; the problem was that the raiyats did not recognize the (Western, external) frame in which the questions were asked, or their rights conceived.

That was to change quickly enough, not least through the settlement operations. These too were not undisputed. Even in the Champaran of the 1890s there were some tenants thought less ignorant and less 'apathetic' than others. In two places raiyats already 'united to assert their rights'. On the estates of the Madhubani Babu (Tappa Duho Suho, *thana* Alapur) the landlord claimed a rent of between 8 and 9 rupees per *bigha*, and the raiyats denied that it was more than 3 to 6. In Tappa Bahas in the same *thana*, where the raiyats were more independent and better off than elsewhere in the district because of the great richness of the soil, they were also on bad terms with their effective landlord, the Murla indigo factory. Collectively they denied holding excess area when the factory sued for increased rents, and most of the Duho Suho raiyats won their case before the settlement officers. The Murla raiyats also won, as no prior measurement could be proved.[12] Was this class action, or one orchestrated by local leaders? It is unclear, but such claims, successfully prosecuted, may be assumed to have encouraged an awareness of the possibilities people now enjoyed as 'tenants', say, rather than as Koiris or Rajputs—even in a situation in which high castes might still enjoy favourable rents.

On average about a third of all holdings in the district were subject to fair-rent suits during the settlement operations of the 1890s. Mostly the outcomes disadvantaged tenants, but as a process the record was expected to stabilize rents somewhat and to 'retard the advancement of rent-rates enormously, and so secure to the tillers of the soil a larger share of the unearned increment'.[13] The status of land also was contested, and rights of possession. For the latter there were 122 cases between landlords, 1,298 by landlords against tenants, 217 by raiyats against landlords, and 572 between raiyats. In all only about 3 per cent of holdings were subject to dispute, but these totalled 12,432 in number (there were 364,659 raiyati holdings). Such statistics indicate a substantial, even 'modern', involvement of subjects with the state. This has significance in a region where, investigations revealed, there had been no general custom of measuring land even at transfer: a new tenant accepted the *jama*, irrespective of the actual area of the land.[14] It means that the state was promoting particular views of people's interests: not only introducing ways of resolving disputes but also, before that, defining their nature.

Peasant consciousness is notoriously difficult to gauge, but it may be assumed from peasant actions. If so, then J.A. Sweeney's revision report on Champaran, prepared between 1913 and 1919, reveals a change.[15] The munsif's court at Motihari (covering Champaran) entertained considerable civil litigation between 1907 and 1917: except for 1907 with 4,763, the total number of cases instituted ranged between about 3,000 and 4,000 a year, but rose to 6,033 in 1916 and 7,690 in 1917, 'swollen' by settlement and indigo disputes.[16] In preparing his revision, Sweeney found disagreements far more numerous than expected, on average 19 per square mile; and suits for the enhancement of rents affected nearly 40 per cent of all tenancies in the district.[17] This was partly because landlords and their agents were using the system even more vigorously than before in order to extend their power. But, Sweeney concluded, it was also attributable to the bad relations between landlords and tenants, especially with regard to indigo, dating from at least 1907/8. He commented on this at length. The murder of one factory manager arose out of an 'isolated' dispute, but also 'there was a general feeling of uneasiness. . . . Continual meetings of the Muhammadan raiyats were held in the Sathi area under the guidance of one Shaikh Gulab. Acts of violence were committed on factory servants by raiyats who refused to labour for the factory after they had received advances [obliging them to do so]. . . . Arson followed and, most significant of all, the mowing down of the raiyat's own crops in the . . . fields set aside for indigo. . .'. The dispute was prosecuted through the courts, and with the government. 'A common fund was raised for contesting cases and petitions were put in against the factory.' Arenas for resolving the argument were also provided by an official investigation and report, involving the planters' association. The remedies were equally generalized. They included an agreed increase in the price paid to the raiyats and a local by-law reducing the area to be set aside for indigo cultivation. The terms of the raiyats' complaints themselves anticipated these procedures and bases for a solution. They referred to the failure of due process (damages taken for not growing indigo although no *sattas* or agreements had been executed); they alleged illegal cesses; and they claimed that payment was not made for labour and services.[18]

One 'remarkable effect of our operations', observed P.N. Gupta in his revision report for Saran district, was 'the large increase in the number of suits for arrears of rent . . . in every district in North Bihar'. The average more than doubled in Saran and Champaran, and 'in many villages where serious rent disputes existed, the raiyats combined during the process of the settlement operations and withheld payments of rent altogether'. 'The raiyats', Gupta went on, 'or the more intelligent of them, now understand that the [earlier] enhancements and the methods of realising them were illegal.' He regarded this as a 'revolution from a system . . . where the landlord kept no proper rent accounts, and issued no receipts, but collected as much as he could from raiyats who paid as little as they could, to a system where every man's rent is accurately known'.[19] Friction was inevitable during such a change, but so too, surely, was combination, based on an appreciation of common experience and collective force.

I do not want to be chronologically prescriptive. Some features evident in this account had occurred earlier in other agrarian disputes, and perhaps had parallels over very long periods. As a package, however, I suggest that these conditions were distinctive. They contributed to a context in which there seems an inevitability about peasant agitations, such as those led by Gandhi or the Bihari kisan leader, Swami Vidyananda. With the experience of the new laws at work and the consciousness that they spread of new kinds of rights, it begins to seem less remarkable that peasant associations emerged, despite the ambiguities of social and economic conditions as they affected different groups. These were not just caste associations by another name. They came complete with a partly-imported anti-landlord rhetoric and an armoury of tenant rights conceived as 'property'—both *for* peasants, and defining them.[20] In the past, rural people had tried to resist or avoid oppressors by a variety of means. It is uncertain that these too constituted a frame for class identity or formal organization, as 'peasants' or 'tenants'.

III

'Peasant' protest thus implied the establishment of 'modern' bounded categories. There could be no rights without definition, and both derived from the legal and administrative acts of an interventionist state. In other words, peasant activism was part of a very general process in colonial India. This section will give some illustrations. The most familiar example concerns the delineation of space and sovereignty, a process (I suggest) of the same kind as that which created 'peasants'. Changes at many levels produced the concepts of 'India' and 'nation', and the new meanings of 'state'. Again, it is a challenge to define the precise nature of the change. It is not easy to conceptualize pre-colonial concepts of territory, because they evidently were not devoid of measurement or certainty or 'ownership', except on superficial examination, just as modern ideas and practices have inherited aspects. But, broadly speaking, it does seem, for pre-modern states (as for estates or villages), that frontiers were more likely to be zones of overlapping or intermixing sovereignty. Jurisdiction was stronger at the centre than on the periphery (geographically or in terms of function). There were segmentary states, in which jurisdiction and functions were divided, though often replicated in ever-smaller arenas; or military states dependent on booty and personal allegiance to a strong leader; or 'feudal' states; and so on. By contrast, the British attempted to apply 'modern' principles of boundaries. Nineteenth-century writers and rulers were explicit about what the frontier indicated about the different stages in the evolution of states. In the most primitive cases, there might be personal allegiances but there was no impersonal citizenship within a particular territory. In an influential article on India's transition from frontiers to boundaries,[21] Ainslie Embree showed that the modern state has exact, known and permanent external borders, and within them there is an undivided sovereignty, and laws to which even the state itself is subject. In effect it is a nation embodying all the people—the *responsible* state.

Colonial and pre-colonial practice were much more complicated and in some ways more similar than this simple comparison suggests. Nonetheless, we should not underestimate the impact on South Asian peoples, to this day, of the outer limits, the larger units and the claims for control, established during the colonial period. Most of all, it mattered that effective central authority was consistently extended within territories. British colonial notions of the state contained within them impulses for evolution. Thus by small steps in a continual process even provincial British–Indian governments edged towards the independent sovereignty which they were to be partially granted in 1919. For example, they had long bought and sold land for various purposes (subject to sanction), using such powers very extensively in the interest of railway construction and other public works. Governments, even the supposedly feeble one in Bengal, were ready and indeed often felt constrained to use their 'property' (powers, land and income) as an instrument for broader changes—that is, not merely to follow rules and consult the legal niceties, but to construct a view of the ultimate public good. This meant that, just as land and classes were ranked, so too were priorities and benefits, which it was the job of the state to decide. There were rules and responsibilities that expressed a *special* need to bend India to the colonial will, but also (and by the same means) a *general* need to adhere to 'proper' forms and goals of 'civilized' government under the rule of law. By the 1930s, such exercise of local sovereignty was very largely in local hands (Indian, or British colonial) and imperial authority was reserved only in such areas as monetary and constitutional policy or military security.

Here was presented a united, hegemonic and potentially benevolent state. And so the colonial administration often took on popular significance. Borders were significant and contested. Especially among educated contemporaries, they generated loyalties.[22] It was the new roles and expectations of the state that consolidated popular and rhetorical identifications with defined lands and jurisdictions. Of course it helped that, in colonial India, deliberate efforts were made for most estates and districts to stick with 'natural' and 'historical' borders, on principle and for convenience. Even during British rule boundaries tended increasingly to be legitimized according to cultural rather than administrative traditions—a discourse more appropriate for nationalist than colonial ideology. In the same way the British favoured what they took to be legitimate indigenous taboos and norms. On the other hand, many divisions, provinces and presidencies were too coloured by accident and political expediency for their boundaries to be altogether consistently drawn. By the same token, the British imposed their own ideas of social categories. Thus the actions of the state were of varying novelty, but always helped generate identifications within defined space.

By the later nineteenth century, even the limits of Commissioners' divisions (intermediate groupings of districts introduced in 1829 as part of important bureaucratic reforms) were recognized to be sensitive. On a proposal to change divisional boundaries, splitting Patna Division, H.H. Risley wrote in 1906: 'The question is not merely one of administrative efficiency and convenience. We have also, especially at the present time [during the anti-partition agitation in Bengal], to reckon with popular feeling . . .'.[23] Patna Division was certainly over-large: its population was thought to be 15,514,987, whereas that of Bombay Presidency, excluding Sind, was 15,304,677. In itself Patna division reflected no particular regional or cultural identity of long standing. The suggestion that it might be cut in two at the Ganges was sensible in physical and cultural terms. Then, a little less plausibly, it was thought that districts might also be reallocated westwards (Monghyr to Patna division, and Birbhum or Murshidabad to Bhagalpur division), thus relieving pressure on Presidency and Burdwan divisions. Support for the changes was given by the Government of India on the assurance of the Bengal government that there would be no local opposition, but later the Secretary of State for India refused extensive boundary changes because of the political climate.[24] Why should administrative divisions have had such significance? They still present major problems in India as elsewhere in the world.[25] Risley underestimated the 'reality' of sentiment (as also in the 1905 partition of Bengal), but he was right when he went on to notice that it was bolstered by self-interest, in this case including those likely to be affected by resultant changes in the jurisdictions of the courts.[26]

Another paradigm of new kinds of border was the standardization of language. Knowledge of the English language by Indians from different regions played a part in generating and creating the sense of a nation in India. The use of English in administration was advocated for efficiency and to reduce fraud. A typical example of this impulse is the request by the Collector of Champaran district in 1893 to be permitted to keep the estates ledger account in English, making use of an English-knowing treasury clerk: this would, the Collector argued, 'check many evils, facilitate inspection and not cause any inconvenience'. The change was approved.[27] However, the direct influence of English was small on the population at large.[28] Far more important was the role of the state in promoting developments in Indian languages.[29] There have been several studies of this, but I will draw some conclusions, mainly from the effects on Bihar.

In the early stages, state translations of official documents promoted orthography and influenced vocabulary; state printing presses, when used for non-official purposes, played a major part in developing public literary culture. Later the government was influential in further defining linguistic boundaries, which, as remarked by G.A. Grierson, the great linguistic expert and earlier a Bihar officer, was 'not always an easy matter' because Indian languages tended gradually to 'merge into each other'. Grierson's 'mostly uneducated' enumerators could not distinguish 'Bihari' and Hindi.[30] The contradiction is poignant: the linguist operated with separate, labelled languages, whose speakers could not tell them apart.

Definable languages had undoubtedly existed, in several senses, yet they had not been exclusive or standardized, even in formal versions and for 'high' purposes. The British helped decide which were languages and which dialects, as in the case of Oriya and Bengali. There was a dispute in the mid and late nineteenth century about the status of Oriya, and pressure for it to be replaced by the superior and mutually intelligible Sanskritized Bengali; the pressure was resisted, on practical and political grounds, by officials who wanted to recognize an equally standardized and Sanskritized, printed Oriya.[31] Colonial rule linked each language to a distinct written form, to a region, and in some cases to 'race' or religion. In Bihar, for example, in the 1870s Hindi written in Kaithi script had been proposed as the standard. The Persian script was also proposed, in the interests of consistency, in 1876.[32] According to Grierson, Kaithi was used from Bihar to Gujarat 'alongside the more complete and elegant Devanagari'. 'Practically speaking, the former may be looked upon as the current hand of the latter, though epigraphically it is not a corruption of it as some think.'[33] Sir Steuart Bayley, then Commissioner in Patna, declared Kaithi to be 'more suitable to the wants of the people' (a significant choice of criterion), though he agreed that the Nagari script was sometimes used by zamindars.[34] However, in the same year,

1872, Sir George Campbell, Lieutenant-Governor of Bengal, had required that all notifications and processes be in Nagari, and that *amla* and police officers learn the script within six months. This practice was followed after 1875 for all printed materials and returns, though hand-written entries were commonly made in Kaithi. The alternative use of the Persian script was abolished in 1880. Hindi written in the Kaithi script continued to be used for court proceedings, but in the 1890s Sir Charles Elliott's government ordered that, though plaints might be presented in any language, all summons, reports and other official documents should now also be written in Nagari (when not in English). It was further proposed that Nagari should be introduced in all primary schools.

Thus standardization proceeded, under government sponsorship, though it remained controversial in Bihar: many local officials favoured Kaithi even in the 1890s. In 1892 Antony MacDonnell, temporarily inheriting the issue, proposed to withdraw Elliott's order (to some extent foreshadowing his own policy later in the north-western Provinces).[35] MacDonnell had been convinced by a quick survey of signatures and documents in the Patna Registration Office, and in Muzaffarpur, that Kaithi was used overwhelmingly by the few Biharis who could write.[36] Again it was indigenous usage that was supposedly to prevail. But in 1896, Grierson advised that Nagari had been 'systematically taught for some years past in all but the lowest classes of the schools'. The Government of India, convinced that MacDonnell was exaggerating, instructed that Elliott's order should be enforced as far as possible. The local interests of the people had vanished, or been reinterpreted by an 'expert'; the change had all the hallmarks of linguistic imperialism of the kind experienced in Britain or France. Value and political judgements abounded. Elliott thought Kaithi 'rough and savage', so that Nagari could be seen as part of a civilizing force. Muslims opposed Kaithi, it was said, in the hope of an advance for the Persian script. Hindus supported Kaithi for the opposite reason. Nagari was presumably 'superior' to Kaithi partly by virtue of its association with the Sanskrit past. It was also 'Hindu', and widely intelligible as 'Hindi'. These were pregnant combinations. Unities, once enunciated in one sphere, might be assumed for others.[37] Stereotypes were not only necessary to definitions and understanding, but also contagious, as when Islam came, in India between 1917 and 1947, to be equated with Muslim politics through a range of political issues.

Today there are recognized languages of Bihar—Maithili, Bhojpuri and so on—all regarded, more or less, as variants of Hindi and written in Nagari. Over two or three generations, old revenue and other records, in Kaithi, have become increasingly inaccessible. Such language controversies, which were repeated in every part of British India, reflected the standardization that was inherent in the empire's 'civilizing' mission. The arguments mainly concerned the units that were to be consolidated. The spread of 'civilization', economic and political linkages, and administrative convenience all required the units to be large: in this spirit, many officials wanted to remove barriers, and imagined hierarchies of languages and dialects, of localities, regions and overarching, national identities, the greater in each case subsuming the lesser. As regards the Punjab, the 1961 Census of India marked another transition: 'there was a move to return the two main mother tongues on the basis of religion' (Hindi by Hindus, and Punjabi by Sikhs), though 'the population returning Punjabi as mother tongue was more than the population returning themselves as Sikhs'.[38]

Some of the colonial standardization was beyond doubt shallow or imposed. Accordingly, in Bihar in recent years there have been some attempts by regional or linguistic 'nationalists' to replace Nagari by Kaithi or other distinctive scripts.[39] The re-emergence of the local languages at the expense of Hindi was noticed in the 1961 Census; and, in the 1921 Report for Bihar and Orissa, P.C. Tallents had remarked that 'the smaller dialects are taking an unconscionable time over dying'. On the other hand, more recent and popular linguistic claims depend upon the same criteria of defined historical languages and associated peoples and cultures, as assumed by Grierson. In his categorization, the Bhojpuri, Magadhi and Maithili 'languages' were grouped as 'Bihari', and regarded with Bengali and Oriya as belonging to an eastern Indo-Aryan group derived from Magadha Apabhramsa.[40] Hence 'Bihari' was a rather artificial term, influenced by political nomenclature; by itself it was a language claimed by very small numbers of speakers. Though Grierson held that Bihari languages were originally of the same family as Bengali, he admitted the connection had been severed, since Bihar had been 'for centuries much more closely connected politically with the United Provinces of Agra and Oudh than with Bengal'. One might regard this last point as placing a limit on the influence of colonial rule, given Bihar's inclusion in British Bengal from 1765 to 1912; on the other hand, Bihar was always considered distinct, culturally and administratively. The languages of Bihar were affiliated to Eastern Hindi, and debates continued into whether Bhojpuri, for instance, was not really very close to Awadhi. In the language schedule to the Indian Constitution the Bihari languages were included under Hindi (or Urdu). The post-colonial state also had a vested interest in large and consistent categories. They were sometimes the same as and sometimes different from those employed under colonial rule; they were not necessarily differently constructed or more 'legitimate' or 'indigenous'. Moreover, like administrative structures, the linguistic boundaries plainly generated interests. They did so because they were categories with intent: they existed to allow control and interference; and they too permitted a rhetoric of rights and well-being.

IV

Having outlined experiences under colonial law and government, I now return to peasant identity and consider the spread of ideas that gave the experiences meaning. I shall examine two unpublished tracts of the 1940s, recovered, translated and edited by Walter Hauser,[41] written by the Bihari kisan leader, Swami Sahajanand Saraswati. They provide striking case-studies of attitudes and arguments that also contributed to the construction of peasant identities. I will suggest not only that Sahajanand was a product of his time, in his understandings and his goals, but also that it is possible to observe in him a direct response to the colonial conditions that we have just been considering.

The first text is *Khet Mazdoor* (Rural Labour), a treatise on agricultural labour. Its political message is that landless labourers and poor peasants share a common oppression, though their roles and status are analytically distinct. The three main elements in the argument are a scientific, evolutionist approach using ancient texts as well as interpretive reasoning; a Marxist class-based analysis of economic factors and power; and the deployment of statistical data and other empirical evidence. The second text is *Jharkhand ke Kisan*, a tract on the condition of and remedies for the peasants and especially the Santhals of Jharkhand. This uses similar means, but elaborates the measures needed to improve conditions, a significant list that equates with the many demands for rights or reforms set out by protesters.

Khet Mazdoor takes a long and pessimistic view of the origins of the problems of twentieth-century Bihar. Sahajanand started in ancient times, with everyone engaged in agriculture, in an age of equality. (That word itself is his own, arguably 'modern' addition to his sources, though they do talk of a lack of social differentiation.) In the second phase, Sahajanand explained, occupational specialization developed through population growth and warfare. As a result, though even Brahmans (say) might continue to cultivate, cultivation was not their defining role; instead they sought to use the labour of others, and so a new class emerged. 'Vaishya' ceased to mean the people at large but instead signified the section that cultivated. 'Sudras' appeared, those who undertook physical work. The third and current phase in this evolution, according to Sahajanand, was characterized by full land use, and hence by four classes among the cultivators: rich, middle and poor peasants, and the laborers (*khet-mazdoori*), all defined effectively by access to land and the means of production. The rich employed labor, middle peasants mostly used family resources, the poor had to sell their labor, having insufficient land, and the landless relied wholly on finding work. Sahajanand produced a predictable pedigree for this analysis: Marx had argued that slaves were themselves sold, but laborers sold some or all of their labor. Serfs did so as tribute for the landholder; others did so for payment or subsistence. Russian sources and examples were cited.

In India as elsewhere, according to Sahajanand, the rush for private property and the subdivision of holdings over the generations deepened the social differentiation. Finally, more recently, the interrelated factors of loss of industries, growing dependency on agriculture and excess labour-supply led to increasing numbers and proportions of landless agriculturists. Sahajanand argued that daily-wage labour was inherently precarious and that total wages, whether in cash or in kind, could readily fall below the minimum needed for subsistence. Since the First World War, debt bondage had been increasing and real wage-levels had dropped sharply, having been more or less stable since the early nineteenth century. Behind this interpretation, even though Sahajanand was writing in prison, was a host of statistics from census and other reports—not all of them accurate. Some were taken indirectly from the writings of the Marxist, Palme Dutt, the calculations of the agrarian economist, Radhakamal Mukerjee, the studies by the British official, Harold Mann, and the findings of the Commission of Agriculture chaired by Linlithgow.

Workers' interests obviously diverged from those of their 'peasant' employers. Sahajanand called for solidarity among the oppressed groups, noting that it was an oppressor's ploy to divide the oppressed against each other. He considered that only plantation workers could be described as proletarian, in Lenin's sense, and that otherwise class-formation was interrupted by rivalries and occupational distinctions (such as for ploughmen) as well as by caste and religion. His take on the perennial importance of intermediaries and the minute distinctions within Indian society was that everything was *ek ke upar ek*, one above the other. He objected to those who focused on socio-religious disadvantage (as he interpreted the use of terms such as dalit or *harijan*), arguing that they missed the common oppression of which untouchability, say, was only a part. More, they implied that there was a problem in terms of fixed classes, whereas there was an ever-growing body of the dispossessed and impoverished. The main point of Sahajanand's evolutionary explanations was to show that oppression was dynamic.

Where did these kinds of explanation come from, and lead? Sahajanand's analysis was socialist and *à la mode*, spiked with specific calculation, given that he sought political co-operation between labourers and kisans (or at least those who were not effectively landlords). He had access to the ideas of Marx, Lenin, and even Stalin, as well as to now-printed Sanskrit texts and the accounts of some of the officials, experts, and nationalists who had investigated agrarian conditions in India. In short, he had both an ideology and a methodology with which to develop his ideas and inform his politics. For him, oppression was due to competition for land and surplus labour. More land or the effect of it through greater productivity would bring social improvements. Sahajanand favoured the confiscation of zamindari land. He held up as an example Lenin's support for the poorest peasants and workers on model farms, though he did not propose collectivization. He felt the capital for economic improvements would have to come from the state, both for practical reasons and to break the cycle of oppression by landlords and capitalists. But change would only be achieved through popular organization and action. Initially it was realistic to expect separate movements for kisans and for labourers, but a merged public movement would be more effective, and should be achievable eventually through informed co-operation and enlightened self-interest.

For Jharkhand, Sahajanand's verdict was less historical and more specific, though again dependent in part on colonial statistics, gazetteers, and inquiries, this time the evidence of the recent Santhal Parganas Inquiry Committee, set up under a British official by the Congress government of Bihar. Sahajanand thought *adivasis* were at the mercy of exploiters and let down by the very measures designed to protect them. He discussed different kinds of tenure provided in custom and law, and the impact of British legislation. He believed that landlords were looting the country, and that *adivasis* were 'literally trapped by the law',[42] unable to defend themselves under a system operating in the English language and with English concepts. He considered forest reservation another exploitation by law as well as greed. He noted the problem of debt; this too related to contract law and to the spread of money-lending and commercialism. He did not blame the British—that would be a weak excuse. Moreover, his remedies were remarkably similar to theirs, by type if not in every detail. His principal demands were as follows. Protect kisans from landlords by regulating rents and fixing them for five-year periods. Relate rent to the land revenue; and provide safeguards for tenants in rent-arrears proceedings. Enforce zamindari responsibilities. Unify the region's tenancy acts, with special protection for *adivasis* and 'backward' tenants. Ensure 'traditional' rights to forest and other products. Provide pure drinking water, and irrigation. Furnish kisans with government loans. Introduce compulsory education. Improve various aspects of the administration. These sound like the goals of a colonial policy minute, or the promises of a modern election manifesto. Sahajanand was demanding reform of the land-tenure system, despite the imperfections he had identified in the operations of the law. He was calling for education as a public good, arguing that Hindus should follow the example of Christian missionaries and empower the downtrodden (though he did not quite use those words). His assumption was of a modern state, in a world conceived as it had been by colonial power: a world of forests and agrarian land, of landlords and tenants, of tribals and Hindus; a modern state concerned with legality and transgression, with citizen-subjects, and with rights, responsibilities, and the public interest.

Nothing in Sahajanand's diagnoses was particularly original, and very little would have been possible except under the circumstances that colonialism helped create—especially the access to intellectual trends, theories and methods, some of it through the English language. All of it was politically important at the time and influential since, not just because Sahajanand was a significant figure but because some of these ideas influenced policy well after Independence (not least zamindari 'abolition'). More than this, however, the explanations related specifically to the circumstances of British colonial government: its agrarian laws, its belief in development through capital (partly to face a perceived demographic crisis), its use of categories and collection of statistics, its construction of a specific form of responsible and managerial state. These were not just taken for granted by Sahajanand; they were central to his explanations and prescriptions.

My conclusion is that in the twentieth century a different vocabulary became widely available to Indians agitating for agrarian and other rights. This can be traced to official categorizations and policies, as well as to political theorists and leaders. It represented an available identity, though not of course an exclusive one, or one invariably chosen. (This is not intended to revive the old debates *between* class, caste or faction as guiding principles of Indian society and politics.) My argument is that colonial categorizations (and also capitalist practices, another subject) engendered contested politics of rights; they helped create politico-economic classes, and their organization *as interests*—indicated for example in the Landholders' Association of 1838 or the British Indian Association of Awadh, the peasant protests against indigo, opium or outside moneylenders of the nineteenth century, or the kisan sabhas and peasant parties of the twentieth century.

In the end, apparent 'classes' were showing considerable solidarity. As is well known, peasants in general were repeatedly involved in movements claiming tenurial and latterly political rights. Among more general explanations of these developments we may place the property laws and agrarian policies of the colonial state. They provided concepts to describe felt economic and social disabilities. They were related to a number of different ideas of political economy: land-ownership, property in and from work, and village community. Indigo cultivators for example had rights, and were entitled to state protection; it was in large part these rights and entitlements that defined the active category of 'indigo raiyat'. Such ideas were influential, partly because exemplified in real measures of government and law.

Many groups identified themselves through class interests that also drew on policy debates, and the broader European discourse to which they had been indebted. As said, the zamindars came first, with societies defending their political interests and seeking to reduce their liabilities. In Bengal in the 1870s and 1880s both additional local taxation and tenancy laws were resisted as a 'confiscation of property'. On the other hand, as a deliberate official defence of property, land revenue was repeatedly reduced as a proportion of incomes and of total tax during the colonial period and rural taxation has remained comparatively low since Independence. Later, each formation of a kisan sabha, for example, also reflected a complex indigenous and colonial inheritance. Where a society was active, there were usually more successful agriculturists operating within a market economy, and new rivalries as a result of that upward mobility. And there were always claims about fair tenancy and enjoyment of property, concepts that had been embedded in colonial laws, and transmitted through administration, courts, surveys, and settlements.

Colonial rule's generalizing features helped to direct or limit indigenous processes, and thus to influence change. In part, the social classes, a 'definite organization of the labour of society', were created, as Marx explained, by 'the separation of the labourers from all property in the means by which they can realize their labour'—by a capitalist division of labour that 'seizes upon, not only the economical, but every other sphere of society'.[43] At the same time new forms of social association were created in India by colonial law, policies, and assumptions, in advance of economic and social transformation, and despite a limited penetration of capitalist modes of production.

In short, agrarian policies engendered assumptions that nowadays are scarcely questioned. More than that, they may be traced in the very fabric of society. Take the case of Calcutta. It has long been dominated by upper-caste literate service and professional elites, the *bhadralok*. These were not the direct descendants of the mixed bag of landed magnates, merchants, bankers and office-holders that ran the eighteenth-century city. They were the product of a society made in large part by the permanent zamindari settlement. After an upheaval in which some great families were dispossessed, the settlement permitted the emergence of secure and increasingly wealthy landed classes. It allowed them to live away from the land in the city; to build houses, temples, schools and hospitals; and to sponsor societies, printing, and other civic goods. True, it created many smaller and subordinate landed interests that were less secure, indeed insufficient. But it also demanded a range of lesser employees, the managers, agents, and clerks who worked the system in practice, plus a host of professionals, especially lawyers. The permanent settlement was based on regulation and then on statute, implying top-heavy and centralized private and public bureaucracies, regulated by the law-courts, rather than on dispersed day-to-day hands-on administration by landholder and state. Calcutta's concentration of writers and literate workers was the result, and they in turn required and manned Calcutta's offices, schools, newspapers and associations.

V

My purpose has been to show how much flowed from definition, in particular from the law as it affected agrarian classes. Processes of categorization encouraged the politicization of issues including those of poverty and oppression. The same lesson may be applied to almost any category, as shown in a brief discussion of political and administrative boundaries and of bounded languages. Many more instances could be given. They are parallel in their character and effects. Under colonial rule, India experienced a politicization of the everyday.

This is not to deny that alternative senses of peasant community existed, for example as identified by William Pinch. He has claimed, in apparent contrast with the story just told, that peasant assertiveness arose out of religious and social attitudes and change.[44] He described peasants thinking of themselves as ksatriya rather than sudra, and of *sadhus* articulating Vaisnava and hence relatively egalitarian ambitions to underpin agrarian radicalism. It is certainly true that where there were active agrarian movements, there was often also evidence of social mobility—among Vellalas, Ezhavas and Mapillas in the south, Patidars in the west, Jats in the north, and so on. In Bihar, there were religious and social movements drawing on older texts and traditions, and making claims to status within an increasingly generalized *varna* hierarchy. But in addition, I suggest, the forms and vocabulary of such alliances and struggles were strongly influenced by the legacy of colonial rule: not so much by its own versions of legal-political relations (for it was never able to achieve what it proposed), but by the working of its categorizations upon existing and continuing relations, both in practice and in terms of ideology and understanding. The ambitions Pinch identifies swam in a sea of other influences. Hence, upward mobility for an agrarian caste within a Hindu hierarchy (for example) could be *of a type* with demands for rights as a tenant, honor as a cultivator, and profit as a producer.

In the end, debates about the degrees of colonial or 'external' influence on 'indigenous' processes of change are less interesting than examinations of the logic of the processes themselves. Because social forms evolve continually in conjunction with historical and rhetorical forces, so the distinction between internal and external features continually dissolves. The key questions concern how the actors in each drama fashion events and identities out of the variety of components available to them. This makes it unsatisfactory to privilege the 'external', as in versions of modernization theory. By the same argument one also should not privilege the 'internal' as if it were immutable, essential, or wholly autochthonous.

In that spirit, it *is* worth asking once again what was the role in peasant mobilization of several old stalwarts—the evolution of the state and its standardizations; the emergence of new institutions, professions and expectations; the growth, increased speed and reduced cost of communications, through transport, language and print; the increasingly shared economic and political experiences; the awareness of Western ideas and examples in regard to the nation and to class, to individual or equitable 'rights'. It cannot be that such influences played no part, for example in peasant mobilization or consciousness. Nor did indigenous or religious forces operate in some kind of pristine arena. As others have noticed, to assume that they did is merely to produce a new Orientalism.[45] How, then, did the religious and inherited elements emphasized by Pinch combine and react with selective borrowings from other traditions and reactions to new circumstances?

In principle, that is the question that I have tried to examine. A Bihari might be a Kurmi, an indigo raiyat, an occupancy tenant, or a kisan. The choice was not unlimited, however, and it was not only self-defined. Nor was it the same at different periods of history. Colonial Indians were subjected to a 'modern' view of their society. Acts of state, in defining the quality and borders of classes and types, gave definite rights to, and encouraged the political representation of, sections of society that the law itself had defined. Then, after that, Indians were still not objects but actors. On the one hand, therefore, I have not succumbed to the view—paralleled by colonialism's own faith in Indian primordialism—that 'popular culture' in India was a 'storehouse' that 'preserved an enormously rich collection . . . of forms of popular protest'. Nor have I said that 'the domain of legal-political relations constituted by the state' *had* to be the 'exclusive . . . site of peasant struggle'.[46] I have suggested that Indians did not just preserve and draw on their own culture, but engaged in a *process* and a *negotiation*. I have suggested that the allegiances and vocabulary of India were strongly influenced by colonial rule, even though the state alone never wholly 'constituted' the legal-political domain. Colonial rhetoric emphasized given identities of language, tribe, caste or community, and British policies also helped define class interests. European categorizations worked upon continuing relations; while pre-colonial inheritances channeled Western influence.

NOTES

1. P.G. Robb, *The Evolution of British Policy towards Indian Politics, 1880-1920: Essays on Colonial Attitudes, Imperial Strategies and Bihar*, New Delhi: Manohar, 1992, chap. 10. My position was not always understood, even in respect of this paper, though it argued (originally in the 1970s) against the notion that 'popular agitations were brought into being by agitators', against attributing Shahabad cow-protection riots to 'positive leadership' without attending to the 'self-assertion' of so-called followers, and against Judith Brown's idea that pre-Gandhian Champaran was politically 'latent'.
2. This essay is drawn from my forthcoming book, *Empire, Identity and India*, parts of which were in turn developed from the original paper I presented to the 'Hauserfest' in Charlottesville.
3. Richard M. Eaton's characterization of Muslim 'conversion' (*The Rise of Islam and the Bengal Frontier, 1204-1760*, Berkeley: University of California Press, 1993) is suggestive here, as are other works on syncretism.
4. C.A. Bayly, *Rulers, Townsmen and Bazaars: North Indian Society in the Age of British Expansion 1770-1870*, Cambridge: Cambridge University Press, 1983; see p. 30: 'It is easy for us to assume that the state was the only political organization in pre-colonial Indian society, and that the peasant family farm was wholly predominant as an economic form. But in this period the state was only one of the political formations which existed, and a large part of the population subsisted through petty carrying, plunder and pastoralism'. Thus

for the ensuing period Bayly focuses on 'the triumph of the state, both Indian and British, over its competitors, and the settlement of the agrarian and commercial economy'—though without taking up the 'class' attributes of pre-colonial peasants.

5. Francis Buchanan, *An Account of the District of Purnea in 1809–10,* ed. V.H. Jackson, Patna: Bihar and Orissa Research Society, 1928, pp. 117-19.
6. Ibid., pp. 438-43.
7. Ibid., pp. 121-3.
8. Ibid., pp. 202-57. There are some exaggerated accounts of the 'invention' of caste under colonial rule. What seems to have occurred was a development of the nature of caste.
9. C.J. Stevenson-Moore, *Final Report on the Survey and Settlement Operations in the Champaran District, 1892 to 1899*, Calcutta: Bengal Secretariat Press, 1900, p. 16.
10. Ibid., p. 63.
11. Ibid., p. 58.
12. Ibid., pp. 58 and 72-3.
13. Ibid., p. 76.
14. Ibid., p. 71.
15. J.A. Sweeney, *Final Report on the Survey and Settlement Operations (Revision) in the District of Champaran (1913-1919)*, Patna: Superintendent, Government Printer, Bihar and Orissa, 1922.
16. Ibid., p. 12.
17. Ibid., pp. 35 and 82.
18. Ibid., pp.18-25.
19. Phanindra Nath Gupta, *Final Report on the Survey and Settlement Operations (Revision) in the District of Saran (1915-1921)*, Patna: Superintendent, Govt. Printing, 1923, p. 186.
20. This is one of the arguments more fully developed in Peter Robb, *Ancient Rights and Future Comfort: Bihar, the Bengal Tenancy Act of 1885, and British Rule in India*, Richmond: Curzon, 1997.
21. A. Embree, 'Frontiers into Boundaries: From the Traditional to the Modern State', in R.G. Fox, ed., *Realm and Region in Traditional India*, Durham: Duke University Program in Comparative Studies on Southern Asia, 1977, pp. 255–80.
22. I have discussed this in Robb, *Evolution*, pp. 72-4 and 90-5.
23. See Government of India, Home Department, Establishments Branch proceedings, National Archives of India (hereafter H Est), A 1-3 (May 1907) and 139-42 (September 1907), pp. 1-3 and 139-42.
24. 'Notes by G. Fell, 20 June, H.A. Stuart, 20 June and 8 August, and E.N. Baker, 11 August 1907, H Est A (September 1907), pp. 139-42.

25. Obvious examples are the 'linguistic' re-drawings of state boundaries in independent India, and continuing problems over 'Sikh' Punjab or 'non-Bengali' Assam.
26. Risley note, 11 March 1906, H Est A 113-17 (December 1906).
27. See Robb, *Evolution*, Chap. 2. See Collector of Champaran to the Patna Commissioner, 16 May 1893, and reply, 29 May 1893, in the Records of the Commissioner of Patna, Bihar State Archives (hereafter PCR) 359, 12/22 (1893/4).
28. There is no doubt that English has been one of the 'cosmopolitan' languages (Sheldon Pollock's term) of India, but it was not a core language in the way that Sanskrit was. Arguably, it is not even (yet) as influential a language of culture as Persian—though see R. Snell, 'The Hidden Hand: English Lexis, Syntax and Idiom as Determinants of Modern Hindi Usage', *South Asia Research*, vol. 10, No. 1, 1990, pp. 53–68.
29. This brief section is intended as a small accompaniment to B.S. Cohn's important article, 'The command of language and the language of command', in Ranajit Guha, ed., *Subaltern Studies IV*, Delhi: Oxford University Press, 1985, pp. 276–329. As it was beyond his scope to discuss the 'results of the first half-century of objectification and reordering' upon 'Indian thought and culture', Cohn was content merely to insist that Indians were not 'passive' in their response (p. 329). On the one hand, he suggested, Indians '*took over*' that control of 'social and material technologies' which the British had tried to exercise (and thus ousted the British); but, on the other hand, Indian consciousness 'at all levels in society was transformed as they *refused* to become specimens in a European-controlled museum of an archaic stage in world history' (my emphasis). This unresolved ambivalence is central to my discussion here.
30. Census of India 1901, vol. 1, India, Pt. 1, Report, chap. VII, paragraphs 373, 535 and 537 (written by Grierson, then in charge of the linguistic survey; see p. xvii).
31. See Pragati Mohapatra, 'The Making of a Cultural Identity: Language, Literature and Gender in Orissa in [the] Late Nineteenth and Early Twentieth Centuries,' PhD Dissertation, London University (SOAS), 1997.
32. See 'Officiating Collector of Gaya to Patna Commissioner', 6 November 1876, PCR 335, 19/2 (1876) wrongly filed with 14/7. On this question more generally see Christopher King, *One Language, Two Scripts: The Hindi Movement in Nineteenth-Century North India*, Delhi: Oxford University Press, 1994, and 'Forging a

New Linguistic Identity: The Hindi Movement in Banaras, 1860-1914', in Sandria Freitag, ed., *Culture and Power in Banaras: Community, Performance and Environment, 1800-1980*, Berkeley: University of California Press, 1989, pp. 179–202.

33. *Census of India 1901*, vol. 1, India, pt. 1, Report, chap. VII, Paragraph 543.
34. Unless otherwise stated this and the next paragraph draw on H Judicial Branch D 1-4 (August 1893).
35. See Francis Robinson, *Separatism among Indian Muslims*, Cambridge: Cambridge University Press, 1974, pp. 43-4, 69-78, 83, and 135. MacDonnell first proposed joint use of Persian and Nagari scripts in NWP, and later, while approving the more general use of the latter, did not think it necessary to hasten the change in practice, even after the Nagari Resolution of 1900.
36. In Patna the figures for documents were Persian 43, Kaithi 82, Nagari nil; and for witness statements, Persian 161, Kaithi 327, English 5, Nagari nil.
37. See King, 'Forging', on scripts and 'pure' and (socially) superior Hindi. Shahid Amin has spoken (at SOAS in April 1997) of notions of a 'Hindu' agriculture derived from a 'Hindu' past as expressed in 'Hindi' words.
38. Census of India, 1961, vol. 1, part II-C (ii), p. xii.
39. Information from Subhajyoti Ray, 18 November 1993.
40. See Census of India 1961, vol.1, part II-C (ii), passim.
41. Walter Hauser, ed., *Sahajanand on Agricultural Labour and the Rural Poor*, New Delhi: Manohar, 1994, an annotated Hindi and English edition of *Khet Mazdoor*, written but not published in 1941; and, in the same format, W. Hauser, ed., *Swami Sahajanand and the Peasants of Jharkhand: A View from 1941*, New Delhi: Manohar, 1995. Sahajanand was a Bhumihar Brahman who began his political career as a supporter of Bhumihars. In the 1920s and 1930s he was involved in political activism with the Kisan Sabha; it included upper-caste tenants and also those of lower status. In the late 1930s, under the Congress ministry, his concern was mostly for those of lower standing, including landless labourers.
42. Hauser, *Jharkhand*, p. 4.
43. Karl Marx, *Capital*, tr. F. Engels, S. Moore and E. Aveling, New York: Modern Library, 1906, pp. 389, 400 and 785-6.
44. William R. Pinch, *Peasants and Monks in British India*, Berkeley: University of California Press, 1996.
45. Hauser has made a parallel point about assumptions that the 'subaltern' school alone has recovered the extent of dissent and

resistance among Indian subordinate classes. He has questioned the privileging of colonial discourse but also the existence of 'official history'. For this and other relevant comments, see *American Historical Review* 96 (February 1991), pp. 241-3, and 97 (October 1992), pp.1269-70, and *Journal of Asian Studies* 50, 4 (November 1991), pp. 968-9.

46. The quotations come from Partha Chatterjee, *The Nation and its Fragments*, Princeton: Princeton University Press 1993, pp.170-1.

Power, Agrarian Structure, and Peasant Mobilization in Modern India

Majid H. Siddiqi

It is an enormous privilege to have been allotted the very pleasant, though for me formidable task of reading the keynote address to an audience consisting, as it does, of colleagues with large reputations. As I endeavor to rise to the task, let me also say how happy I am to be among friends and with Walter and Rosemary Hauser.

When Walter Hauser wrote his Chicago thesis, peasant studies hardly existed, peasant movements were almost unknown to the academy, and agrarian structures were expressed solely in the reigning idiom of British policy or economic history. The very face of social science history has itself changed since the early 1960s, in some cases (and it must be added not necessarily to our advantage) entirely beyond recognition. But the history then inaugurated abides.

While Walter Hauser's thesis on the Bihar Kisan Sabha was the first in peasant movement histories in South Asia, the subject had indeed been broached in writings by nationalist leaders during the colonial period itself. Rajendra Prasad, Jawaharlal Nehru, Mahadev Desai and tens of other nationalist leaders had written accounts directed at the iniquities of the Indian agrarian social order but mainly directed at the fact of British rule. Simultaneously, in those very years of the nationalist movement, peasant movements had arisen that weakened the symbiosis of the power of the landed elite with the contingencies of the requirements of British rule. In a word, peasant movements and nationalist politics pressured policy making towards, first, modifying and then ending the era of landlordism in colonial India. Agrarian power at Indian Independence stood redefined. But the process of the making of the Indian nation had many complexities of character, not the least of which was that of the agrarian class struggle that underpinned it. But, as students of history would know, class struggles are never simple if at all they are, when they are, class struggles.

Let us first consider how the history of rural political mobilization had been written, mainly in the 1960s. In one significant area of scholarship peasant movements were viewed as peasant wars. Within each of the six major upheavals of the twentieth century the middle peasantry was supposed to have played an initially revolutionary role. The idea of evaluating the role of the peasantry in social revolutions came from the political texts of the Russian and Chinese revolutions and it made its impact in the form of the 'middle peasant theory' in the writings of Hamza Alavi and Eric Wolf. Modifications of this idea, whether in empirical refutation or as a qualified redefinition, were applied to India. Usually the answers sought were to affirm (or deny) this middle peasant thesis.

The history of peasant protest was also, following Eric Hobsbawm, divided into 'political' and 'prepolitical'. Thus the major question implicit in such a treatment of the subject proved to be: were the peasants political? If so, how did the mobilization actually occur? This question had a longer and more lasting impact as over the years it was modified, to assert the case, albeit in structuralist terms, peasant insurgency against the social order as a whole, of which social order it was itself a part. To this theme we shall return.

The questions that became dated pertained to the role that peasants played in the transformation of the social order. They were: Which section of the peasantry played a revolutionary/reactionary role? As a political peasantry must be led from the outside, it was also asked: what was the nature (class origins/ideology) of this outside agency? Was it a revolutionary movement which heralded the consolidation of the bourgeois state (Zapata in Mexico) under an urban leadership? Or did the peasantry serve through rebellions to break up the existing state polity (the Russian Revolution)? Or did the peasants provide the social basis (and an area for tactical retreat) for a working-class revolution (Cuba, China)? Were peasant movements millenarian? Did they exhibit in their struggles an alternative 'moral economy' (Burma, Vietnam)? The theoretical armoury of scholarship on rural political mobilization began to be reconstituted. By the 1990s the questions had indeed changed. But the anguish remained: peasants were either tricked or bullied or led under false pretensces into a modern world, which, given its need for development, was (and is) heavily tilted against their interests. Their cultures are dominated, never dominant, their futures always at the mercy of an unrelenting progress in which town dominates country, burghers, rural folk, the bourgeoisie the peasantry.

We can neither undo the past nor alter the course of the future in this regard. Yet, within social science concerns, we can try and reformulate some of our questions on lines which do not presume a preordained social reality. To do this we restrict our reflections to an outline of peasant movements in modern India, 1860–1950, and examine this outline anew in light of existing scholarship. We also try and reformulate some of the questions by specifying those features of agrarian society which make more for discontinuity than change and which demonstrate cultural and ideological disjunctures as opposed to presumed continuities, especially when these latter have connoted success and failure.

Beginning at the middle of the nineteenth century, which also corresponded with the end of the stage of direct plunder, British policy in India increasingly became one of support for landlords through whom the officialdom of empire sought to protect their dominions. Every now and then there was a deviation from this policy to accommodate the pressure generated by an unequal agrarian society which, under the impact of the market, produced peasant movements. Between 1860 and 1950, with the exception of half a decade between 1930 and 1935 when prices of agricultural produce did indeed fall, there was an overall rise in prices. The single greatest impact which such a rise in prices produced was manifest in a developing struggle between landlord and peasant for control over the increased value of agricultural surplus. The landlord raised rents. Tenants protested. The landlords asserted their proprietary rights, by emphasizing their power to evict tenants while the latter claimed, and were occasionally and with increasing frequency granted, occupancy rights. Over the century, the peasants' ability to resist landlord control of rent and produce increased and the structure of landlordism stood considerably weakened by the end of British rule.

It is hardly necessary to state that our preceding remarks present an oversimplified picture of the background to the emergence of peasant movements. Many peasants who won tenancy and property rights against the landlords themselves became rent-receivers. They rented out the land rented in (or acquired after a struggle) from superior proprietors. Many others became rich cultivators. Still others, and these were most numerous, continued to lead their lives within the framework of a landlordism which became top-heavy. While the agrarian structure remained unequal and indeed skewed, the greater stratification of rights in Indian rural society both within the category of 'landlord' as well as within the category of 'tenant' altered the relationship between different agrarian social classes. In the various peasant movements which emerged, we find that the actual mobilization was carried out in a myriad ways. Some of these may be reproduced as an elementary typology thus:

1. The Blue Mutiny, 1859-62

Poor peasants and small landlords opposed indigo planters in Bengal. In this they were helped by moneylenders whose own credit resources stood threatened by the structure of the monopsonistic rights of the planters.

2. The Pabna and Boora Uprisings, 1872-5

Rich cultivators, benefiting from the commercialization of agriculture and producing cash crops, protested to secure further their occupancy rights, granted nominally in 1859. In this they succeeded by 1885 when the Bengal Tenancy Act was passed. Later, by the middle twentieth century, such tenants were transformed into rent-receivers.

3. THE MAPPILLA REBELLIONS, 1836-1921

Poor peasants in Malabar (Kerala) protested for security of tenure. This was granted in 1887 and 1929. But only rich tenants benefited. This tenantry itself acquired afresh and consolidated further its rights as rent-receivers *vis-à-vis* the larger landlords. Peasant protest fed into the assertion of rentier claims of one section of rural society against another.

4. THE DECCAN RIOTS, 1875

Up against a heavy land revenue demand of the state, 1840-70, cultivators lost their lands to moneylenders from the towns. The symbiosis of peasants with rural moneylenders was upset as a dependence development of these latter on the moneylenders of the towns. The protest against the structure of legal authority which allowed such land transfer took the form of anti-moneylender riots. The state intervened to legislate in favour of the 'agriculturists' in 1879. The state's pro-landlord stance therefore could also become pro-peasant the framework within which it realized its land revenue did not alter to its disadvantage.

5. PUNJAB AGRARIAN RIOTS, 1907

The state intervened to prevent alienation of land from peasants to moneylenders in 1900, but urban middle classes protested, in nationalist idiom, against government intervention. Riots broke out against moneylenders. The government appeared pro-peasant, as the peasants rioted against 'agriculturalist' moneylenders, who were landlords. Landlords, we might recall, were over the long term supported by British rule.

6. PEASANT MOVEMENTS IN OUDH, 1918–22

The peasants of eastern Uttar Pradesh defied large landlords through a tenants' movement for security of tenure. Oppressive traditions of forced labour were attacked through fierce agrarian riots. Small landlords and the rural poor supported and led the movement. Statutory rights of occupancy were secured in 1921. This movement marked a phase of retreat for landlordism.

7. Peasant Protest against Indigo Cultivation in North Bihar, 1860-1920 and Champaran, 1907–9 and 1917–18

Moneylenders and rich peasants voiced the grievances of indebted small peasantry and agricultural labourers. Planters of indigo were put to rout but the rural hierarchy was left undisturbed. The movement signified the emergence of the peasant as a symbol in a nationalist ideology.

8. Agrarian Unrest in Uttar Pradesh, 1930–2

When prices slumped, peasants could not pay rents to landlords nor landlords revenue to the state. The Indian National Congress launched a no-rent no-revenue campaign of middle and rich peasants, supported by the rural poor, and small property holders. The movement marked a simultaneous retreat for landlordism and an attrition of the political domination of the colonial state.

9. Peasant Agitations in Kheda, 1917–34 and Bardoli, 1928

In Bardoli a proletariat in traditional agrestic servitude protested against an increased land revenue valuation alongside a dominant and (in relation to the 'serfs') exploitative peasant community. The 'serfs' were partly convinced of the validity of nationalist ideology as represented to them and were in part coerced into joining the movement. In Kheda rich and pauperized peasants with shared cultural traditions and kinship alignments agitated against higher revenue rates, resorting to the relinquishment of holdings and migration *en masse* to other neighbouring regions as a form of protest.

10. Peasant Struggles in Bihar, 1933-42

When prices fell in 1930, the rents to which tenants had agreed in a period of rising prices (1900–20) became too heavy to bear.

Peasants were evicted by landlords as the latter attempted to increase their power and control. The tenants' movement that developed sought to regain control over the lands from which the peasants had been evicted. The popular force of these struggles was provided by rich and middle peasants and occasionally poor peasants. Agricultural labourers were not even formally included in the programme of the Peasants Association till 1944.

11. Sharecroppers Agitation in Bengal, 1938–50

The sharecroppers were mostly poor peasants with very small holdings, who fought landlords for security from eviction and a right to at least two-thirds of the produce. This demand originated from the government's Land Revenue Commission of 1938 and was propagated by the Communist Party in 1946–7. Sharecroppers were joined in their movement by small peasants with occupancy rights, small impoverished landlords, and a few rich peasants. In legislation in 1950 and in 1978-79 these rights were recognized and pushed through despite landlord opposition by various governments in independent India.

12. The Telengana Rebellion, Hyderabad, 1946–51

A movement involving sustained armed struggle of rich peasants and the rural poor. The peasantry sought to destroy the political power of large landlords while the agricultural labourers opposed forced labour. The political consequences of the movement may be appraised at two levels. The popular unrest provided the basis for the absorption of Hyderabad State into the Indian Union. The communist leadership of this movement made for electoral victories in the early 1950s for party members from this region.

A glance at the preceding synopsis suggests two ideas for discussion:

1. While each of the movements, and all together, may well be said to be in some way to represent anti-landlord tendencies in the colonial agrarian society as a whole, no single one of these

exhibits any such features. Among the more remarkable conundrums of our schema, poor peasant protest has strengthened rentier structures, anti-moneylender riots have stood opposed to the nationalist political idiom, and movements under a communist leadership have served (however inadvertently this may have come about—here we are not concerned with intentions) to strengthen the domination of the rich peasantry, and, at a remove, even the post-colonial state.

2. Leaving aside the question whether or not we can or ought to infer any one tendency merely because all such instances of protest 'add up' to, finally, a single development, we find remarkable the extreme disjunction between the politics of each episode against rentier landlordism. There was absolutely no common leadership for these instances of protest; no organization except the All-India Kisan Sabha (1936) spoke for the entire Indian peasantry. Even when the Kisan Sabha in Bihar or the Communist Party in Bengal and Telengana did formulate demands for the peasantry, demands that would have an all-India character, the very specificity of each local variant of the agrarian structure as well as the sheer diversity of peasant communities in India prevented any generalized acceptance of their programme. While, therefore, the agrarian structure did indeed consist of unequal peasant and landlord holdings and the economy reflected a dominant landlordism and, temporally, an emerging process in which the stratum of richer peasantry proved ascendant, the ideological distance between the ultimate act of zamindari abolition (and other land reforms of the 1950s) and the series of peasant agitations over a hundred years of British rule was never bridged. Consequently, while it may be possible for us to say that in the colonial Indian economy a backward capitalism emerged plagued with all the evils characteristic of under-development, and in the nationalist struggle against British rule, representatives of the Indian middle classes as the urban counterparts of the peasantry came ultimately to dominate and even determine the politics of peasant protest, the gap between this statement and another with which one might highlight the cultural dimension of the mobilization process would still remain. (A cultural dimension that would take into account the lived

and experienced little traditions of the peasantry in simultaneity with the articulation of the agrarian class structure and not merely presuppose the domination of such traditions by 'nationalist' political mobilization, notwithstanding the number of instances one might be able to record of this nationalist mobilization never having been, as it were, 'complete'.)

In order to move towards a more credible version of the political mobilization process, we need to disaggregate our story of peasant struggles. We might use the same sources but shift the focus towards one main aspect: an evaluation of the cultural moorings of the leadership of the peasantry which, we would argue, came from the ranks of the *mofussil* middle classes and from *éléments déclassés*. This leadership had little link, and a highly tenuous one when it did, with the over-arching spread, control, and domination of the modern state as that came to evolve, in its institutional form during the period of British rule and in its political expression in the decades since. Nor can its origins be defined in any simplistic 'social class' terms, given its culturally heterogeneous, socially stratified, and temporally disjunctive character. Yet, it stood on the rural-urban continuum in its many manifestations, and while it aided the process of mobilization through its strategic relevance to the peasantry, it simultaneously reinforced these self-images of culture and community which served to widen the distance between town and country and further the ideological disarticulation of Indian political society.

The process of political mobilization among the Indian peasantry did not, as may be expected, respond to the secular formulae of class struggle while the latter was indeed carried on and developed in some of the forms of the social class alignments we have just described. Instead, much of this mobilization was the consequence of those features of Indian society which, in their customary rooting, did not share the modernity of the urban 'social contract'. In this, religious belief played no small role. In Champaran (Bihar, 1917) and northern Oudh (Uttar Pradesh, 1922) the sanction of village deities was considered necessary for determining the membership of the peasant associations and for the success of the movement. The reluctance of those who did not wish to join in with the peasants' protest was compared to the sin of having violated food taboos as laid down in Hinduism and Islam (Bihar, 1917; Uttar Pradesh, 1921). Stories of Gandhi's non-violent success in South Africa, commonly told in the Champaran movement, tapered into the regard of the laity for the ascetic and the renouncer; indeed, Gandhi's presence in Champaran also often led his followers towards a deification of his person. The Congress leader Sardar Vallabhbhai Patel invoked the message of God, as did Gandhi, in the Bardoli (1928) campaign. The use of religious beliefs and symbols in the mobilization process overlapped with the social identity of the community, strengthening thereby caste and communal identities. In Uttar Pradesh (1918-22), Bardoli (Gujarat, 1928), Bihar (1920-35), and Bengal (1938-47), caste and community associations provided many of the symbols for protest. In Malabar (1836-1921), Islam was a source of cohesion among the poor peasantry and for the linking up of this community with the urban-based *sabhas* of the richer Muslims. There is no evidence in this latter experience of any rift or tension between poor peasant protest, born of and in identification with the Islamic community to which they belonged, and their subservience to and acceptance of their richer, socially dominant, counterpart. The necessity of preserving Patidar (Gujarat, 1917-34) and Kurmi (Uttar Pradesh, 1918-20) traditions of endogamy was emphasized as an element in mobilization. Even Sanskritization, the cultural emulation of Sanskritic practices for upward social and ritual mobility, which confirmed the distinctions between castes, was reinforced during popular unrest. The Bhumihar-Brahman Sabha in Bihar (1910-35), Hari *sabhas* and Kshatriya *sabhas* in Bengal (1938-47), and the Kurmi-Kshatriya *sabha* in Uttar Pradesh (1920-40) are all instances of the simultaneous reinforcement of caste values and peasant mobilization. Peasants marginal to Hindu society converted to Christianity (Sardari Larai, Chota Nagpur, 1880-5), or Vaisnavite Hinduism, which strengthened the purity-pollution opposition (Tana Bhagats, Chota Nagpur, 1915-19), or to Islam (Malabar, 1870-90).

The propensity of many a peasant movement leader to be peripatetic, a fact hardly explicable in the simple-minded terms of wanderlust, was a remarkable feature of political mobilization.

Baba Ramchandra of Oudh, Swami Sahajanand Saraswati, Rahul Sanskrityayana and Yadunandan Sharma of Bihar, Motilal Tejawat and Vijay Singh Pathik of Rajasthan, Janardan Sharma of Gujarat, and scores of others roamed the Indian subcontinent, in and out of sects, religions, towns and villages, schools and monasteries, but hardly ever from one peasant movement to another. Each of such individuals experienced multiple identity crises—the stories are too many for us to narrate—as they protested against the social process from which they had all emerged: usually one of the pauperization of a traditional village-level elite. They looked for answers to the mysteries of life in holistic terms, moving as they did between the world and its renunciation, often several times in a single lifetime. Several of such leaders who knew as many languages as they did their many worlds could be observed in swarms, dotting the political landscape in 1921. With its eternal fear of Bolshevism, government thought these leaders to be 'political emissaries disguised as Sadhus or Fakirs . . . fomenting discontent and antagonism to government especially in Bengal, Bihar, Assam and the United Provinces'.[1] Moreover, they changed their names several times, leaving behind them a trail of aliases, designed as often to evade arrest as to escape from and obliterate traces of their own earlier selves. It was altogether this ubiquitous presence on the rural-urban continuum of such individuals which allowed others, who were not itinerant wanderers, to pose as these persons, to switch roles, as it were, with roles discarded by others. It was this process of moving in and out of one's self and in and out of others' selves which made for the multiplex potential of Gandhi's message(s) which could be transformed to suit the occasion.

Between the mercurial character of the lower level leadership and the working out of high politics was a stratum of a 'rurban' intelligentsia, firmly rooted in the various regions. The members of this intelligentsia derived their livelihood from a combination of an increasingly diminishing rental income from small holdings and professional earnings as small town lawyers, school teachers, lower-rung government officials, and employees and editors of the Indian languages press. Such an intelligentsia, though itself 'traditional' in that it did not represent the interests of any 'fundamental' group or class, produced a spate of mobilization literature for the peasantry—whose demands it helped to shape and whose interests it represented in the nationalist press. The politics of this intelligentsia, crucial as it was for the peasant masses as a whole, was not related in the same way to the peasant classes as it was to Indian nationalism. The proliferation of regional vernacular papers in the 1920s and 1930s—*Tarun Rajasthan, Gana Bani, Langal, Pratap, Abhyudaya*—served more to integrate the little traditions of the peasantry with Indian nationalism (variously understood, variously defined) than promote the interests of any single stratum, rich or poor, among the peasantry. The attitude of the peasantry towards this intelligentsia was itself ambivalent, suspicious, and trusting at the same time. This attitude lent itself very well to the subsequent exploitation of peasant beliefs by electoral politics in Independent India. However, to see in this latter process only a cynical manipulation of the rural masses by urban-dominated constituencies is to miss the historic roots of populism: the historically specific character of the mobilization process as that came to be structured over a century.

The historicity of peasant insurgency in modern India has come full circle. The deeper sinews of community economies, traditional moralities, and customary bindings has transmuted, through land reform and in a strange marriage with the social contract of political democracy, into becoming a mix of casteist movements, communal politics, and class struggles. On this we have little perspective.

Postscript

This address was written in 1997. The perspective of a half-century since the end of colonial rule affords certain new insights and raises issues pertinent to the historiography of peasant movements both before and after Independence.

There are three issues deserving of reflection. The first is that the very peasant movements that fought against landlordism and rentier domination have turned into engines of oppression. Numerous small armies of the middle castes of the Yadavas, Kurmis, Koeris, and others, now, after the abolition of zamindari, at least and specially in northern India, traverse the land. These caste groups, as militia as well as dominant castes in everyday roles, bully, intimidate and coerce those who do not belong to their affinities. They lay claim to be the peasants who have the legacy of the anti-landlord struggles behind them. This indeed they do. They are at the forefront of agitations based largely now on the demand for cheaper power rates, agricultural subsidies on fertilizers, and the setting by the state of prices for their products that are remunerative to them. It is from this perspective on 'urban' society that the divide between 'Bharat', a deprived rural hinterland and 'India', the chief beneficiary of Independence, has been articulated. This, paradoxically, is the peasant populism that unites the dominant rural interest with the truly downtrodden and mercilessly exploited. The 'progressive' peasant movements of yesteryears have turned conservative, both politically and socially, in fifty years.

The second issue worth noting is that the independent Indian state is now strong and to be defended by the nation, and by the peasant nation within, from which it derives its sinews, the *jawan* from the *kisan*. More than anything else it is this that has marginalized the militant radical movements of the rural poor and the tribals, of the 'Naxalite' Maoist groups (where these have appeared at all) in the minuscule pockets of rural Andhra Pradesh and Bihar.

The third issue that strikes the eye is that much of the writing on peasant movements before Independence had derived its ballast from the rhetoric of a mainly Marxian Left, in a conception of social change in which the ascendance of peasant radicalism was ever expected to act as a partner to revolutionaries of all hue in bringing about a just social order. Suddenly, in the batting of an eyelid, this perspective has vaporized.

These three points, have important implications for the writing of peasant history. A problematic must now be developed that unites the (as much seeming as real) disjunction between the past before Independence and the years since. Contemporary concerns can no longer be read back into peasant history. Historical categories must necessarily be thought out afresh. In two instances, for the Ramanandi sect for the eighteenth and nineteenth centuries and for the Bhartiya Kisan Union in the late twentieth century this has been done with much ingenuity.

But these are monographic accounts that lie within peasant society but outside a universalizing framework.[2]

We might feel justified in asking if there will ever be a universalizing framework again. It seems not. The peasant has arrived, now forever a part of history.

NOTES

1. 'Report on Political Emissaries Disgnised as Sadhus and Fakirs', Home Poll, File No. 118 of 1922, National Archives of India.
2. David Ludden, Bibliography on South Asian Agrarian History. http://www.sas.upenn.edu/~dludden/aha-bib2.htm. See also Dipankar Gupta, *Rivalry and Brotherhood: Politics in the Lives of Farmers in Northern India*, Delhi: Oxford University Press, 1997; William R. Pinch, *Peasants and Monks in British India*, Berkeley: University of California Press, 1996; and Tom Brass (ed.), *New Farmers Movements in India*, London: Frank Cass, 1995.

Gandhi, Marx and Charan Singh: Class and *Gemeinschaft* in Peasant Mobilization*

Harold A. Gould

When Mahatma Gandhi returned to India in 1915 from his long sojourn in South Africa, he was a man with a revolutionary idea but no political vehicle through which he could put it into practice. That idea, of course, was Satyagraha, the application of the concept of *ahimsa* (whose conceptual roots lay in both the Hindu and Buddhist traditions) to political action. The logical setting for promulgating his doctrine was the Indian National Congress, the only major political organization in India which was under the control of local leaders. However, the Indian National Congress, since its inception in 1885, had, up to the point where Gandhi entered the Indian political scene, failed to evolve an ideology and mobilization strategy capable of generating a genuinely mass-based political movement to cut across the vast congeries of cultures, nationalities, castes, classes, and religions into which the people of India were subdivided. While not exerting a negligible influence on British policies toward India, Congress had remained essentially an instrumentality of the country's urban and professional classes. It seemed reluctant to go beyond trying to exert 'gentlemanly persuasion' on the colonial power in the form of resolutions urging increased scope for native participation in the political process.

* This essay was previously published in *Indian Social Science Review* 3, 1 (2002), and is reproduced here with permission.

True, there were times when Congress immersed itself in real political agitation of sufficient magnitude to put the Raj on the defensive, as during the furore over the Partition of Bengal in 1905. But such confrontations were rare and of comparatively short duration. Jawaharlal Nehru, in fact, had scoffingly characterized the pre-Gandhian Indian National Congress as essentially a 'debating society'![1]

Once he achieved a dominant position in the Indian National Congress, Mahatma Gandhi successfully transformed it into a mass-based organization able to translate his ideology into political action on the grand scale. The main reason he was able to make this transition was Gandhi's imaginative invention and manipulation of symbols that resonated in the minds and hearts of Indians from all walks of life. Especially important in this regard was the ability of Gandhi's charisma and symbolic creativity to draw the country's peasantry into the political arena and persuade them that their increasingly vocal demands for social and economic justice would be fostered by the political party in whose name the Mahatma spoke. To achieve this connectedness with the country's rural masses, Gandhi essentially took on the persona of a political sadhu. It was an imagery that successfully captured the imagination of so-called *sadharan janata* (ordinary folk) in the countryside whose social consciousness was pervaded by the morality and mythology of rustic Hinduism.

This was a fundamentally important linkage not merely because it was the way political discourse had always been expressed in the *dehat*. It was also fundamentally important at this juncture—from the end of World War I into the 1920s—in Indian political history because there were pockets of agrarian unrest simmering in many parts of the subcontinent. These had been generated by fluctuating economic conditions in the aftermath of the war, as well as by social stress and the country's various agrarian problems. These 'contradictions', in Marxist parlance, were always present in India's caste-structured, rigidly hierarchical social system. But they were especially significant in the early stages of the transition from East India Company rule to the establishment of the Raj. In their pursuit of land revenues to finance the imperial enterprise, the British steadily undermined the stability of the traditional agrarian systems (i.e. the *jajmani-*

like interdependence between landholding elite-pure castes, cultivator castes, artisans and menial-impure castes) by commodification of land which then changed hands in response to market forces.[2]

The rapid acceleration of modernity intensified the processes of class differentiation. By the time Gandhi came onto the scene, however, they had still not reached the level of 'class-conscious' conflict that would have met the criteria for class formation adumbrated by Marx. (That would come later and only then for a very specified period of time, as we shall see.) On the contrary, the socio-political eruptions that had thus far occurred had few universal features; they were confined within the administrative and cultural ambit of princely states and regional territories directly under the suzerainty of the Raj. In terms of political expression, their ideologies and mobilization styles displayed a mélange of both 'modern' and nativistic or chiliastic characteristics. This ambiguity played into the Gandhians' hands, of course, by enabling the Mahatma's symbolisms to resonate with traditional imagery, such as *Ram Raj*, which had historically legitimized collective action among the peasantry.

There were many pockets of agrarian discontent of this half-way-house variety in every part of India that may be characterized as simmering insurrections waiting to happen, ripe to be catalysed by higher-order organization with political legitimacy. Thus, when Gandhi entered the picture there was social unrest everywhere and he had a mix of symbolic material with which to address it. Equally important, from the standpoint of agrarian radicalism, there were, despite the verticalities of regional cultural diversity, some basic structural properties which the various agrarian systems throughout the country shared. By whatever vernacular name they were designated, there were 'landlords' who owned and/or controlled most of the land; there were partially or wholly tenureless cultivators (kisans) who grew the crops on modest plots of land which they rented from or share-cropped for these land-controllers; and there were landless labourers who performed the most menial agricultural tasks for pittances. And tensions always existed between them at the grass-roots level.

These 'class-categories' closely approximated the traditional caste hierarchy of elite, backward and scheduled castes, which added continuity and legitimacy to their antipathies. And with the growing commoditization of land, wide fluctuations in the market economy, the frenzied pursuit of revenue by the colonial government, and the equally frantic pursuit of rents by landlords in order to stay ahead of government revenue demands, these differing relationships to the means of production and the sources of power, all against the background of escalating nationalism, everywhere provided ample bases for political confrontations.

Through Gandhi, Congress had successfully established a political image that quickly encompassed the entire subcontinent. The party was able to make major inroads into the peasantry through the 1920s and early 1930s by taking advantage of existing patterns of agrarian unrest. As a national organization, it could provide local and regional grass-roots peasant agitations with a body of organizational and ideological raw material upon which local peasant leaders could draw. Gandhi, as noted, with his 'political-holy-man' style, functioned as the role model for this scalar amplification of agrarian ferment.

The problem for both Congress and the kisan agitations during this Gandhian phase, as it turned out, was that the overarching goals of the two were not wholly congruent. The former were groping for ways to move the Freedom Movement from the parlour to the streets. The latter were groping for ways to call attention to their economic plight. The former's agenda was primarily political—building a national consensus against the perpetuation of British rule—and only nominally economic. The latter's agenda was primarily socio-economic—achieving social and economic justice—and 'political' only in the sense of wanting to arouse as much public support as possible for agrarian reform. For the peasantry, their struggles were driven by implicit class concerns (kisans versus landlords), even though at this stage of their struggle, little more than incipient 'class-consciousness' had as yet crystallized. For the Congress, their struggle was not only lacking a class thesis but indeed was antithetical to it. Under Gandhi, the Congress *modus operandi* was to incite so-called non-violent resistence to the Raj wherever possible by co-opting whatever peasant restiveness was 'out there' regardless of its class/caste locus. Once co-opted, however, the peasantry were dissuaded from pursuing any class-specific (i.e. anti-landlord) interests they might have and instead urged to focus their energies on supporting Congress's nationalist agenda. The message of the Gandhi-led Congress to the peasantry was that they were made for each other as long as the peasantry eschewed class conflict in favour Gandhi's concept of 'trusteeship'.[3]

As a prelude to our analysis of this pivotal aspect of Indian political development at the start of the inter-war years, it is interesting to see how the developing convergence between peasant and non-cooperator was perceived by those who were on the spot. A letter written by J.C. Faunthorpe, the Commissioner of Lucknow District, to the Chief Secretary of UP on 14, January 1921, illustrates official perceptions of what was taking place. Having returned from home leave, he declares:

> I am not well informed on the history of the non-cooperation movement, but I have formed the opinion that the non-cooperators, finding their efforts to stir up trouble among students and the general public unsuccessful, had to look round for some more promising field for their operations . . . They have succeeded in stirring up the cultivators of Oudh to a state of considerable excitement because the cultivators have in many cases considerable grievances against the landlords.[4]

Although accurately depicting the magnitude of agrarian unrest in Awadh at this time, and even hinting at the disparity between the motives of the parties involved, Faunthorpe's conception of cause and effect was too simplistic. Nehru understood the situation better. While he saw that non-cooperation was 'reaching the remotest village', he also realized that Congress was by no means the instigator of agrarian unrest. While *Swaraj* 'was an all-embracing word to cover everything', he wrote, 'the two movements—non-cooperation and the agrarian—were quite separate, though they overlapped and influenced each other greatly in our province', and indeed everywhere else as well.[5]

At the grass-roots interface between these two streams of political ferment there was by no means either an identity of ideological intent, or clarity as to who was co-opting whom. This came out clearly in the famous Bardoli satyagraha of 1928 that followed a number of what Dhanagare calls 'small-scale dress rehearsals' that 'involved only local grievances'. These were the Champaran movement of 1917, the Kheda satyagraha of 1918, the Ahmedabad mill workers' strike of 1918, and the Rowlatt satyagraha of 1919. These were 'the chief landmarks in Gandhi's preparation for a massive but non-violent anti-imperialist struggle throughout the length and breadth of the country'.[6]

What is important about them, particularly as prelude, is that each (except for the Rowlatt agitation) was an event with distinct economic overtones which the Gandhian Congress tried to transform into a predominantly political expression of its nationalist agenda. In each instance, Dhanagare rightly declares: 'More fundamental questions relating to land control and antagonistic class relations, whether in Champaran district of Bihar or in the Kheda district of Gujarat, were carefully left untouched by Gandhi.'[7] One major result was that by playing down the class implications of these situations, Gandhi, in order to maximize support and public visibility for his cause, ended up implicitly favouring the economic interests of the landholding classes (and thus of the higher castes to which most of them belonged) at the expense of the middle and lower castes (as tenants and menials) who suffered greatly at the hands of the landholding classes. At whatever point his agitations threatened to unleash the forces of class-conflict (i.e. address the economic inequities inherent in the structure of India's agrarian systems), Gandhi would back down, 'compromise with the authorities (and) . . . terminate the movement just when it began to gather momentum'.[8] Under these conditions, understandably, '. . . the main support to Gandhi came primarily from the better-off sections of the Indian peasantry'.[9] What induced the less privileged sections of rural society to remain loyal to Gandhi was not any significant improvement in living standards or a right to the unencumbered enjoyment of the fruits of their labour, but his charismatic status as a political saint and his appeal to their religious sensibilities.[10]

The Bardoli satyagraha illustrates these points well, because in the end the principal beneficiaries of this movement were the local Patidar megacaste in that *taluq*, who were the largest group of landholders and, along with Brahmans and Banias, among the richest. Their complaint had nothing to do with economic exploitation, rack-renting or absence of secure tenures. It pertained to increased revenue demands which the government had instituted following a land reassessment in 1925. Revenue demand, which had been steadily rising for years anyway, underwent a further jump of 30 per cent following the resettlement. This set-off protest and resistence among the Patidars and other elite castes which escalated into a 'no-rent' campaign. Patidars took the lead because they were the numerically dominant caste, because, as landholders, it was predominantly their ox that was being gored, and because several Patidars had participated in Gandhi's South African satyagrahas. They were schooled in the technique and, of course, had special entree to the Mahatma himself. In this sense, Gandhi and the Bardoli Patidars were made for each other.

There is another sense in which Gandhi's choice of the Patidars fitted well into his evolving style of political mobilization. By focusing on a category of 'victims of the system' whose grievance was revenue demanded by government and not rent demanded by 'landlords', he was recruiting into the Congress' those sections of rural society who would be the most amenable to the party's nationalist agenda—those most willing to make the Raj the target of their non-violent resistance to 'tyranny' because it was in their economic interest to do so, rather than others whose economic interests lay in demanding major structural changes in the agrarian system itself.

Patidars and other high castes in Bardoli were themselves essentially landlords who exploited the labour of lower castes. Dhanagare notes that in Gujarat there was what we would call today a racialist distinction drawn between *Ujla lok* (the fair complexioned upper castes) and *Kaliparaj lok* (the dark lower castes, untouchables, tribal people, etc.). This cleavage was particularly significant in Gujarat where a high proportion of the peasant population was owner-cultivators. There were proportionately fewer 'intermediary classes' such as sub-proprietors and cultivating tenants and thus proportionately more landless agricultural labourers than in many other parts of India. The gap between 'haves' and 'have-nots' was therefore especially pronounced.[11] Most of the latter (especially the *Dublas*) lived in virtual slavery, so much so that Gandhi himself pressured the land-controlling castes in Bardoli to pursue his 'constructive programme' for improving the lot of the downtrodden sections of rural society as a condition of his supporting the no-rent agitation. However, while he did successfully induce his Patidar followers to undertake some improvements in the lot of the *Kaliparaj lok*, structural change in the underlying agrarian system formed no part of the final settlement between the government and the peasantry.

It will be recalled that Sardar Vallabhbhai Patel rose to national prominence on the wings of the Bardoli satyagraha. He and Kunvarji Mehta of the Patidar *Yuvak Mandal*, were major forces in developing the no-rent campaign and then melding Patidar class interests with the Gandhi-ized Congress. It was 'Kunvarji Mehta and other workers of the Patidar Mandal', according to Dhanagare who 'formed a cadre of leaders at the grass-roots level, and were mainly responsible for forging alliances with the *Kaliparaj lok*'. Otherwise, these segments of rural society might have been mobilized as class enemies of the Patidars. This linkage was achieved by conveying 'the new urban and elitist political culture' to the 'politically docile (tribals, untouchables, and other backwards in Bardoli) in a moral and religious idiom'.[12]

Dhanagare concludes that the Bardoli satyagraha 'symbolized agrarian class alliance against the government . . . only insofar as it did not give rise to consciousness along class lines, and *only to the extent that it did not disturb the traditional social structure.*' (The emphasis here is mine.) The aim was to establish a '. . . *gemeinschaft* solidarity among the various castes and classes' as an anti-imperialist device. Finally:'The whole range of agrarian or peasant movements of the Gandhian variety must be seen partly as an ingredient of Gandhi's power politics and partly as an instrument used by rich and middle-caste peasants to maintain their power in the rural hierarchy while collaborating with the urban bourgeoisie and middle-class intellectuals who led the national movement.'[13]

This process of selective co-optation and ideological manipulation is, key to understanding how Congress interfaced with agrarian unrest in the Gandhian phase—'roped the peasantry in', as it were—but then risked losing its hold on the peasantry had the Congress Socialist faction not forced the party leadership to at least tacitly adopt a semblance of a Marxist orientation to peasant mobilization.

Babas, Non-cooperators and Revolutionaries

Let us turn now to agrarian unrest among the Awadh and Bihar peasantries. As elsewhere in India, political dissent from the turn of the century through the rise of the Gandhi-ized Congress typically had taken on nativistic overtones, a sort of class warfare pursued in the name of *Raja Ram* instead of Karl Marx, against the economic rapacity of taluqdars, and zamindars mainly of the elite Brahman, Rajput (Thakur), Bania and Bhumihar castes.

Since 1919, the Awadh and Bihar countrysides had fallen into forms of political turmoil which the landed elite and many government officials perceived as threatening to the social order. A typical array of economic and demographic factors were feeding into this turmoil.

Agricultural prices were experiencing serious oscillations at a time when population was rapidly increasing and land values were consequently rising. To take advantage of this inflationary situation, the land-monopolizing taluqdari and zamindari classes (mainly Thakurs, Brahmans, Banias, and Kayasthas, plus high-status Muslims and a smattering of castes later known as 'Backwards') were searching for ways to increase their rents and cesses. The pressures they put on their tenants in pursuit of the quest for income-maximization threatened even further the already shaky hold which the cultivating peasantry enjoyed on the land they tilled. Simultaneously, market conditions were causing the prices of the coarser food grains consumed by the tenantry and the landless laborers to rise more rapidly than those of the refined food grains consumed by the elite. Such distress at a time when the country was experiencing rapid and disruptive social change intensified the normal distrust which the peasantry felt toward the pattern of feudal relations in the countryside. Prior to these latter day market- and demographic-driven aberrations there had existed for a long time a modicum of stability in the rural social order, exemplified by the pattern of religiously sanctified *jajmani* relationships to which we alluded in discussing the background of the Bardoli satyagraha. However, even by the turn of the century, as far as Awadh at least was concerned, factors were at work which laid the foundations for social destabilization. By this time, declares Siddiqi, 'the agrarian structure itself stood changed . . . as a result of proprietary mutations, the intrusion of the *thekedar* (contractor or long-term lease-holder of the land), the impoverishment of small zamindars and the changing nature of the landlord's relationship with the under-proprietors and the tenantry. These were fundamental social changes which in the course of time came to upset the rather precarious relationships of class and caste and, finally, also of power within the colonial framework.'[14]

Emergent post-war conditions simply exacerbated this situation until it led to grass-roots political upheavals throughout the region. As Siddiqi puts it, 'By 1920 . . . the development of social tension in Oudh had taken the form of an economic conflict between the different interests of the agrarian classes.'[15] In other words, prototypical class warfare had broken out and was playing a tangible role in political relations between landlords and tenants in a region where tenantry constituted the most pervasive form of economic dependency and social insecurity.

In Awadh particularly, *kisan* uprisings produced an interesting grass-roots leadership whose imagery and *modus operandi* had, as suggested, drawn for political expression upon precedents contained in the rich folk mythologies. Its leaders presented themselves to the rural masses as *babas* or what may be termed 'political sadhus'. They legitimized their political messages by infusing them with a religious content and presenting themselves, the 'messengers', in the saffron garb of holy men. In this sense, the Awadh agitators stood a cut above the oppressed sections in Bardoli taluq in their degree of organizational sophistication and 'class consciousness'. The reason, of course, is that the former were more socially advanced than the landless labourers of Bardoli; the Awadh tenantry were middle-caste cultivators (Kurmis, Koeris, Yadavs, Muraos), in terms of traditional status comparable to the Patidars, with some measure of ethnic pride and self-awareness and with strong emotional attachment to the land they tilled, despite the fact that (unlike the Patidars) they lacked secure title to it. When the Gandhians 'discovered' them, the tenantry already had upward-evolving proto-organizational resources to interface with the downward devolving Congress political apparatus.

Babas sprang up throughout the Lucknow, Faizabad, and Gorakhpur divisions of Awadh during this period.[16] They rallied large gatherings of peasants who flocked to their standard with cries of *Ram Chandra ki jai* and *Sita-Ram ki jai* and with readings from Tulsi Das's *Ramayana*. Employing the traditional panchayat as their structural model, they organized so-called Kisan Sabhas to articulate grievances with the landlords and press for reforms in the agrarian system.

The most famous of these early political babas was Sridhar Balwant Jodhpurkur, born in Neemuch district of Bombay Presidency.[17] He became an *awara* (wanderer) at age thirteen, and found his way to Fiji at eighteen where he changed his name to Ram Chandra Rao in order to disguise his Maharashtrian Brahman origins (because they were politically suspect). He returned to India in 1904 to avoid prosecution for his agitational activities among the indentured workers in Fiji, became a sadhu in Ayodhya in 1909, settled at Pratapgarh in 1919, and, in the words of the police records of the day, 'almost immediately started spreading disaffection among the peasantry'. By the time he reached Awadh, Ram Chandra had a political agenda and a wealth of experience for carrying it out. Significantly, Jodhpurkur married a woman of the Kurmi caste (one of the major middle castes of this region) and commenced calling himself 'Baba Ram Chandra'. Moving around the region with a copy of the *Ramayana* under his arm, he blended readings from this epic, which combined allegorical denunciations of both the Raj and the landlords, with appeals to the peasantry to act in concert against their exploiters. A legend in his own time, Baba Ram Chandra became the model *par excellence* of the indigenous peasant politician. He was a major force in broadening the political impact of the first formal Kisan Sabha that had been established in 1917 by Jhingury Singh and Sahdev Singh at an underproprietary village in Gorakhpur district named Rure. V.N. Mehta, the Deputy Commissioner of Pratapgarh district, and a native official with strong sympathies for the plight of the peasantry, includes in his famous *Report* of 11 November, 1920, an excellent depiction of the elemental conceptualization which went into the formation of this prototypical peasant body of Rure. Inaccurately attributing its founding to Baba Ram Chandra, he states:

The people of Rur[e] were suffering from no disabilities nor had they any grievances. The cause of the selection of Rur[e] as the headquarters of the Sabha is rather interesting. When Rama and Laxmana attended Sita's *Swayamvara*, Tulsidas described them as follows: "In the assembly of the Rajas the two brothers shown like two moons in the galaxy of stars. [*Raj Samaj Virajat Rure*]"

"Rur[e]" means beautiful. "Rure" was constructed to mean "in Rur village."[18]

It was into this rural ferment that the Congress entered, much as it had done in Bardoli and elsewhere. As noted above, however, differences in agrarian structure between Bardoli and Awadh made for differences in how it entered the fray even though from a doctrinal standpoint the approach to the class aspects of the situation was essentially the same.

Because land-control in Awadh was predominantly in the hands of taluqdars and zamindars who, on the one hand, were strongly allied with the Raj and, on the other, had a reputation for rapacity which even the colonial authorities recognized was to be a catalyst for tenant unrest, the non-cooperators made the rent-paying tenantry instead of the revenue-paying land-controllers (as in Gujarat) the principal target of their mobilization efforts. Clearly this posed problems that were much more delicate than in Bardoli. The dilemma was how to cope with a multi-tiered agrarian stratification system where the principal mobilizational target was a class composed of 'lower' castes who were already in rebellion against the party's preferred coalitional target, the revenue-paying class above them, without violating the party's rejection of class warfare. This dilemma haunted the Congress throughout its pre-Independence efforts in many parts of the Hindi belt, not only in Awadh, to harness agrarian unrest to the nationalist cause.

As elsewhere in rural India, the non-cooperation movement initially appealed to broad spectra of the peasantry not because the Congress was in sympathy either with the aims or tactics of those sections of rural society who sought confrontation with the landholding classes in the name of social and economic justice. They emphatically were not. Indeed the Congress leadership seemed to lack much insight into the class aspects of the agrarian social order, mainly because most of them were from urban and small town backgrounds. Their identification with Congress came from the fact that in the eyes of the peasantry Congress was synonymous with Mahatma Gandhi. To the *sadharan janata* Gandhi himself, not his message, was the message. He was seen as the penultimate political saint, a grand-scale holy man whose *darshan*, purported supernatural powers, and promise of *swaraj* was all that mattered. He was a larger than life manifestation of the political sadhus who were already driving the kisan movement. His ubiquitous presence in every corner of Indian society infused struggles against landlords with a millenarian energy and conferred upon such struggle an overarching legitimacy, even though Gandhi himself had never intended to confer any legitimacy whatsoever upon the votaries of class confrontation.

Shahid Amin, in his masterly study of Mahatma Gandhi's impact in Gorakhpur district in 1921, clearly documents this:

> . . . what people thought of the Mahatma were projections of the existing patterns of people's beliefs about the 'worship of the worthies' in rural north India. As William Crooke has observed, the deification of such 'worthies' was based among other things, on the purity of the life they led and on 'approved thaumaturgic powers'. The first of these conditions Gandhi amply satisfied by all those signs of saintliness which a god-fearing rural populace was prone to recognize in his appearance as well as his public conduct. As for thaumaturgy, the stories [which] attribute to him magical and miraculous powers which, in the eyes of villagers nurtured on the lore of Salim Chishti and Sheikh Burhan, put him on a par with other mortals on whom peasant imagination had conferred godliness.[19]

There are two senses in which the Gandhi-factor was important to the Kisan Sabha movement. The revivalist atmosphere he generated enabled the numerous babas who sprang up throughout the countryside to wrap themselves in the symbolic mantle of both baba and non-cooperator. 'The "power of a name" was evident again in Awadh in the first years of the 1920s', declares

Gyanendra Pandey, as both Baba Ram Chandra and Gandhi came to 'acquire an extraordinary appeal'. Ram Chandra appeared to develop a 'multiple personality,' says Pandey: '. . . he was reported to be in Bahraich on the 5th [January 1921] by Nelson, to be in Bara Banki at the same time by Grant, and in Fyzabad by Peters.'[20]

The other sense in which the Gandhi factor was important is that it drew Congress field workers toward the kisan movement despite the misgivings of Gandhi and other high ranking, urbanized party magnates about its class warfare proclivities. Baba Ram Chandra led a delegation of 500 followers from Gorakhpur to Allahabad in early June of 1920 (allegedly to coincide with a holy bath at Prayag on a *Saptami* day) in an effort to broaden the movement by putting it in touch with 'Mahatma Gandhi and other educated urban leaders'. They were unable to meet Gandhi and Nehru disparaged Baba Ram Chandra's 'lack of a programme'. However, in Kumar's words, 'For three days the marchers propagated their woeful tales in the city.' And most important, I think, 'They came in touch with the U.P. Kisan Sabha people who arranged for their stay.' Despite this, however, 'The urban leadership was . . . somewhat reluctant to take up the cause of the Pratapgarh peasants.' But in the end it was agreed that P. D. Tandon, Gauri Shankar Mishra, K.K. Malaviya, and Nehru would visit their villages.[21]

This was a breakthrough that helped pave the way for the development of a significant interface between the class-driven concerns of the tenantry and the nationalist concerns of the Congress. It would lead to the incorporation of the agrarian question (i.e. a class agenda) into the designated ideological tasks of the Congress, at first only tentatively, indeed ambivalently, and then much more decisively once the Congress Socialists entered the political picture in the mid-1930s as an organized force. At this time, however, the effect was to catalyse the interplay between the babas in the Kisan Sabha cells scattered throughout Awadh and the local-level operatives in Congress who came in contact with the peasantry at the grass-roots level. It soon led to attempts to create Congress-sponsored peasant organizations designed to encompass and co-opt the spontaneous Kisan Sabhas and exploit their political energy for the party's benefit.[22] The manner in which this occurred, however, exposes the daunting issue of how this could be accomplished in a manner that would reconciled the Gandhian preoccupation with national unity and the tenantry's materialistic preoccupation with radical change in the agrarian system.

In 1920, two separate Kisan Sabhas were established within the ambit of Congress. The *Oudh Kisan Sabha*, created by Jawaharlal Nehru, embodied the younger, more radical section of the party that wanted to follow a class thesis in its approach to peasant mobilization. The other, established by Purshottamdas Tandon, represented the more conservative wing of the U.P. Congress that supported Gandhi's reluctance to endorse any type of peasant protest that threatened to radically disturb the agrarian *status quo*. The conflict that developed between these two factions resulted, by 1921, in the Congress leadership trying to re-establish party unanimity on agrarian issues by creating a new, consolidated U.P. Kisan Sabha with Motilal Nehru as its president. The Tandon faction lost the most in this transition because Motilal's son, Jawaharlal, and his younger Marxist-oriented followers, gained the upper hand in the new sub-party, and used it to pit the tenantry against the taluqdars and zamindars.[23]

In this 'proto-political' stage of Congress's entree into the countryside, many if not most of the party workers who were championing the party's cause at the grass-roots level were not easily distinguishable in their demeanor, dress, and educational level from their non-Congress counterparts. In Faizabad District, for example, there were two highly active Congress field workers, Kedar Nath Arya and Deo Narain Mishra, who exemplified this blurred line. After one of Deo Narain's agitational escapades, the Commissioner of Faizabad Division, was prompted to declare to his boss, Sir Harcourt Butler: 'Deo Narain is a person of at best unbalanced mind if not actually tinged with insanity.'[24]

Despite the fact that Congress had come round to some kind of organized attempt to co-opt the kisan movements, and that the presence of their grass-roots workers had consequently increased throughout the countryside, strains and disenchantment between Congress and the proto-political kisan leaders soon began to surface. Partly this was because after 1921 '. . . the

Congress interest had shifted away from the rural areas'.[25] It was also because the U.P. Kisan Sabha's more radical leadership was never able to completely free itself from the constraints imposed by the powerful Gandhian faction. They, of course, continued to take a dim view of class-conflict and did whatever they could to inhibit it.

These divisions opened the way for the Raj to step in and forcefully crush this initial round of peasant unrest in Awadh. As Pandey puts it:

> By the winter of 1921-2, the peasant movement in Awadh had overcome many, though by no means all, of its own traditionalist limitations. Yet, its localism and isolation remained. To get over these it needed an ally among other anti-imperialist forces in the country. But the chief candidate for this role, the party of the growing urban and rural petty bourgeoisie [i.e., Congress], had turned its back on the peasant movement long before that time.[26]

Final Phase: Birth and Death of the Class Thesis

An eventual merger of sorts between non-cooperation and agrarian revolution finally did occur for a limited period. But more than a decade had passed before both sides were ready for each other. This came with the formation of the Congress Socialist Party in 1934. It was now that the younger generation of Congressmen who had imbibed Marxism and Fabianism in their student days abroad or on the campuses of Banaras Hindu University, Allahabad University, Lucknow University, and Kashi Vidyapith had emerged as a force to be reckoned with. This new breed included Jawaharlal Nehru, Acharya Narendra Dev, Rafi Ahmad Kidwai, Jayaprakash Narayan, Ram Manohar Lohia, Raghukul Tilak, Sarvjit Lal Varma, and many others. They had been especially effective in UP and Bihar where many young leaders had grown up and had cut their agitational teeth under the tutelage of some of the more noteworthy political sadhus who had built followings among the peasantry in their home districts.

Acharya Narendra Dev is a type-case of this maturation process. The asthmatic son of a rich, Arya Samajist merchant in

Faizabad city, he had become radicalized while a law student at Banaras Hindu University, had returned to the district to become a follower of Lallanji, a founder of the Congress peasant strategy in Faizabad (through his association and identification with Deonarain, Kedar Nath and other rustic revolutionaries), and in turn became one of the founders and principal intellectuals of the Congress socialist movement by the 1930s. Similarly in Bihar, Hauser has shown how the fusion of the cultural, political, and agrarian was quintessentially expressed in the remarkable career of Swami Sahajanand, which was then confirmed at the political level through the formal coming together of the Kisan Sabha and the Congress Socialist Party upon the founding of the CSP at Patna in 1934.[27]

The turn toward more explicit and aggressive class-conflict actually began in 1930 in the United Provinces and Bihar. Ironically, it occurred in the context of what was perhaps Gandhi's most spectacularly successful nation-wide non-co-operation campaign which included the 'Salt Satyagraha'. It also drew economic impetus from the impact of the Great Depression on rural society, and ideological inspiration from Nehru's identification with what he perceived to be the revolutionary dynamism he witnessed in the Soviet Union during a visit he made there in 1927.

In this period, the better off sections of the peasantry (the middle caste cultivators) were the worst affected by the Depression because they produced for the market, and market prices for food grains were on a roller-coaster. Increasingly unable to either pay their rents or repay the loans they owed to landlords they were ripe for class-based mobilization. And the landlords, in their turn, facing their own financial difficulties, pressed ever harder for settlement of arrears for both. 'By 1932', says Dhanagare, 'only 25 per cent of short-term and 7 per cent of long-term loans had been repaid, and lands therefore passed steadily into the hands of creditors (landlords and moneylenders) as mortgages were foreclosed.'[28]

In the face of these circumstances it proved relatively easy to involve the tenantry in a 'no-rent' campaign against the taluqdars and zamindars. Technically it was initiated by Rafi Ahmad Kidwai in Rae Bareilly district with Motilal Nehru's blessings.

Jawaharlal Nehru had kicked the campaign off with public addresses around the district urging tenants to withhold their rents from landlords, and both landlords and tenants to refuse to pay their taxes to government. This rather mixed message was consistent with the cleavage that persisted in Congress over the class issue, because it placated the Gandhians by offering the landlords as well as the tenantry the chance to commit themselves to the nationalist cause. When the landlords expressed their 'loyalty' to the Raj by paying their land revenues while the tenantry expressed their commitment to the Freedom Movement by refusing to pay rent, this got the Congress socialists off the hook, so to speak, and enabled them to push ahead with their class-struggle agenda. By rendering the 'no-tax' aspect of the agitation moot, 'The "no-tax" campaign boiled down to a "no-rent" campaign.'[29] Henceforth, the Gandhian faction could not oppose it on the grounds that it violated their injunction against pitting one indigenous class against another. By their refusal to go along, the taluqdars and zamindars had shown that they were in the pocket of the Raj. This became even more apparent by 1934 after the government encouraged the landlords to form their own party, the National Agriculturalists Party,[30] in order to counter the political inroads the Congress socialists were making with the tenantry. For their part, the Congress had employed a class-criterion to accord the middle-caste tenantry of Awadh a structural status equivalent to that which the Patidars occupied in the Bardoli satyagraha. The ultimate standard for recruitment was not so much whether a given class were tenants or landholders, i.e. revenue-payers or rent-payers, as whether or not their economic situation could be exploited for the benefit of the Non-Cooperation Movement.

Moreover, all of the developments in the agrarian sector during the first half of the 1930s must be understood in the context of a major change in constitutional structure that was in the wind and would consummate in the Government of India Act of 1935. In many ways, this piece of legislation was the final chapter in the pattern of constitutional reforms that had provided progressively wider scope for native participation in their own governance at both the central and provincial levels of government. The Morley–Minto Reforms of 1909 had created legislative bodies based on the elective principle and, most importantly, had formally introduced the ethnic factor into Indian electoral politics by creating separate Muslim constituencies. The Montagu–Chelmsford Reforms of 1919 had considerably expanded both the size of the electorate and the number of both general and Muslim constituencies. In the United Provinces, a total of 60 open seats were set aside for 'non-Mohammedans' (52 rural and 8 urban) and 29 for 'Mohammedans' (25 rural and 4 urban), plus six 'special' seats for landlords, Christians, and others, and 23 for government nominees. The 1935 Act not only enormously enlarged the size of legislative councils but significantly altered the demographic structure of the electorate, as well as patterns of party participation in elections and government. In India as a whole, the 1935 Act created an electorate of 35 million for legislative assembly seats and 90,000 for legislative council seats. Most importantly, it also facilitated party structured competition for assembly seats and party-structured government by legislative majorities.[31] In UP the legislative assembly was expanded to 228 seats (140 General and 64 Mohammedan, plus the usual variety of special seats) and the franchise from 3 to 14 per cent.

These changes in constitutional structure paved the way for what was one of the most purely class-based confrontations that has ever occurred in pre-Independence electoral politics. By the time the first election took place under this Act, Congress had

TABLE 1
Agrarian Categories in UP during the 1930s

Agrarian Category	*Number*	*Per cent*
Non-cultivating owners	245,789	1.6
Cultivating owners	1,301,389	8.6
Non-cultivating tenants	167,193	1.1
Total rentiers	1,714,372	11.3
Total cultivating tenants	8,618,814	56.8
Total agricultural laborers	3,138,667	20.7

Source: *Census of India 1931: Provincial Tables: United Provinces*. Allahabad: UP Government. (See endnote 23) Adapted from Table 5.1 in Gould 1994.

had almost seven years to draw the tenantry into the fold with its 'no-rent' campaign. The landlords had had three years to organize themselves into a countervailing political organization, the NAP, designed to defend their class interests. But most of all, for the first time in the country's constitutional history, large sections of the middle-castes who in Awadh and Bihar comprised the tenantry, would have the vote. Two social groups with differing relationships to the means of production and power, which through party-structured mobilization had developed a significant measure of class-consciousness, would for the first time confront one another at the ballot box.

The demographics are striking, as Table 1 indicates. Prior to the 1935 constitution, franchise restrictions limited voter eligibility in the UP countryside, primarily to persons in the first four categories (non-cultivating owners and cultivating owners, non-cultivating tenants and total rentiers), i.e. the landholding class, who together constituted at most 22.5 per cent of the agricultural population.[32] Small wonder that Congressmen were, on these grounds alone, rarely able to get elected to provincial legislative councils.

After 1935, however, the rules of the game had been radically altered. A huge proportion (numbering 8.6 million, or more than 56 per cent of the rural population) of those towards whom the Kisan Sabha and the Congress socialists had targeted their 'no-rent' campaign, had now been enfranchised. Their presence in the electorate clearly was the difference in the 1937 elections. In the United Provinces, Congress swept to power in 125 of the 140 General constituencies where middle-caste tenants normally outnumbered all other categories combined. By contrast, the landlord party (NAP), whose pool of potential support came primarily from the mostly Brahman, Rajput, Bania, Kayastha, and Khattri landholding section of rural society (the upper 22 per cent) were annihilated, garnering a total of only 8 seats. A similar pattern prevailed in most of the other provinces where the 1935 Act was in force.

Only cross-cutting ethnicity disrupted the class-structuring of the vote in UP in 1937. In the 64 Muslim constituencies, the communal factor predominated, although there was evidence that class-specific economic issues still played some role in the outcome. The Muslim League, the most outspoken advocate of Muslim separatism, garnered only 33 per cent of the total vote in these constituencies and less than half (27) of the 64 seats, and proportionately more of these in the urban (48.2 per cent) rather than in the rural constituencies (28.7 per cent). Independents won only one less seat (26) than League candidates, while Muslim landlords running on NAP tickets won more than half as many seats (11) in the rural Muslim constituencies as did the League (19).

Thus the foundation for the powerful support which Congress received from the middle-caste cultivators in the United Provinces and Bihar (the heartland of the Hindi Belt) from the 1930s to Independence and thence onward until the mid-1960s was laid when the party augmented the purely *gemeinschaft* style of political mobilization propounded by Mahatma Gandhi with a class thesis. The impetus for this lay with the emerging, younger Congress activists who had come under the sway of Marxist and Fabian doctrines during their university days and consequently were less convinced than the 'fundamentalist' Gandhians that a purely political agenda was a sufficient basis for attracting the less privileged segments of Indian agrarian society. The Gandhians supplied the energy Congress needed to successfully co-opt the rustic Kisan Sabhas (substituting khadi-capped, dhoti-clad 'field workers' for saffron-clad babas), absorb them into the corpus of its own overarching, more sophisticated peasant organization (Kisan Sabha), and culminate the process of class-based agrarian mobilization through the mechanism of a sub-party structure, the Congress Socialist Party, which one might say was specifically tailored for the purpose.

After Independence

The success of the Congress Socialist Party in bringing the UP and Bihar tenants into the Congress fold enabled them, in UP at least, to become the dominant faction in the provincial party.[33] However, that dominance was short-lived, because their doctrinal naiveté got in the way of political practicality, and because of the hostility of the right wing dominated by Sardar Patel to their Marxist orientation. The refusal of leaders like Acharya Narendra

Dev to accept high political office in the UP government handed over control of the party apparatus to their factional opponents.[34] The subsequent passage in 1948 by the Patel-dominated national party of an edict banning sub-parties within the organization was specifically aimed at the socialist group and had the desired effect of driving the most militant of the young socialists out of the Congress. Before this happened, however, the socialists had, as far as UP and Bihar were concerned at any rate, successfully committed the Congress Party to a land reform policy whose centre pieces were the elimination of landlordism and the distribution of agricultural land to the tiller. This commitment held even though the Congress socialists as an organized intra-party force were gone, largely due to Nehru who stayed behind, as it were, and shepherded much of the CSP social agenda through Parliament.[35] Because of Nehru's intra-party clout, especially from late 1950 after Sardar Patel's death, the Zamindari Abolition Act was passed by the UP Vidhan Sabha in 1951 (and similar legislation was enacted in other provinces), just in time to benefit the Congress in the first General Election held in 1952. From that point on, Yadavs, Kurmis, Jats, Koeris, and other middle or 'Backward' castes, who now, thanks to the Congress, had ownership rights in the lands they had rented from zamindars and taluqdars, became one of the party's most stalwart sources of support at election time. This had been achieved first by co-opting the old, originally nativistic Kisan Sabha movements in the name of Mahatma Gandhi and then, contrary to Gandhi's wishes, gradually transforming the tenantry, for a time at least, into a class bent upon forcing (and indeed eventually achieving) a major restructuring of the agrarian system.

Ironically, the political success of the kisan movement laid the groundwork for the eventual demise of the class thesis that drove it. With the implementation of Zamindari Abolition, the erstwhile tenant's class enemy had been eliminated. For the next fifteen years this fact did not seriously weaken the ties of the middle-castes' to the Congress, however. There was gratitude for the role that Congress had played in liberating them from the onus of landlordism and enabling them to own their own plots of land. Once they became landowners, however, they were transformed into a conservative force in the countryside who were resistant to further radical changes in agrarian structure such as collectivization. In the post-taluqdari/zamindari agrarian social order, the middle-caste former tenantry (Yadavs, Kurmis, Jats, Koeris, etc.) shared the status of land-controllers at the individual village level with those sections of the elite castes (in UP primarily Brahmans and Thakurs) who had retained title to the modest plots of land which they themselves cultivated. This emergent conservatism, coupled with the departure of the socialists from the party, cleared the way for Congress to build its post-Independence rural political machine around these new categories of intra-village landholders. This was the key to the party's ability to amass huge majorities in the Lok Sabha and in most of the country's major provincial legislatures until well into the 1960s.

This admixture of loyalty to the Congress as their class benefactor and attachment to the lands they now owned was clearly exemplified by the former tenantry's reaction to the 1948 by-elections in UP. Following their dissolution as a sub-party and subsequent institutionalization as the Socialist Party of India, the UP branch of the party believed that political integrity required their members who currently held seats in the legislative assembly as Congress MLAs to resign and seek a fresh mandate from the people. Thus a series of by-elections were held in 18 UP assembly constituencies commencing in late June of 1948. The most important and dramatic contests occurred in the nine assembly and one legislative council constituencies. The outcome was a disaster for the Socialists. They lost all of these elections by huge margins. Over the ensuing two years, they lost seven of eight by-elections. Even the single seat they won came later after the by-election held on 11 October 1950 to fill the vacancy created in the Muslim General constituency in Faizabad district by the departure of its Muslim League incumbent, Faiyaz Ali Khan, for Pakistan to become that new nation's first Advocate General.

The question is, why did this happen? The answer is that erstwhile tenants no longer had a collective grievance against the existing *status quo*. They had become part of it. These by-elections were conducted under the rules of the 1935 Government of India Act whose eligibility requirements implicitly limited the franchise to members of the landed and tenant classes. Virtually none of the more than 3 million landless agricultural laborers (mainly from the Scheduled Castes, and who might on these grounds conceivably have been the most amenable to proletarian ideologies) were qualified to vote.

As socialists, the 18 former Congressmen depicted themselves as the true champions of the kisans. The reason they gave for leaving the Congress party was that it was dominated by leaders who favoured the rich and would never bring real socialism to India. 'Freedom has been won and now we have to establish Socialism', declared Acharya Narendra Dev. 'Congress cannot perform that task. We have to do it.'[36] Although land-reform had not been implemented in 1948, Congress candidates presented themselves to the peasantry as the party which had brought freedom, which had led the fight against agrarian oppression, and would implement promised land reforms.

As the party in power that had indeed ended colonialism, they had assured both the elite castes that they could keep the land they cultivated themselves and the middle-caste tenantry that they would soon own the land they heretofore had rented from the landlords. In the ten constituencies contested in June 1948, Congress received a total of 1,41,096 votes to the Socialists' 47,439, i.e. about 75 per cent of the votes cast. What this means is that under the 1935 Act's franchise rules, Congress received the same proportion of tenant support as it had in 1937. The tenantry as a class had not been permanently radicalized by the Freedom Movement or by the Congress socialists' impact.

What the cultivating elite and middle castes wanted was not the Marxist millennium but that which the tenantry had consistently wanted since the original spontaneous Kisan Sabhas arose in the 1920s: title to the lands they cultivated. Henceforth, the Socialists in all their subsequent manifestations[37] struggled to achieve a mass following for democratic socialist agendas that never really materialized. The cultivating peasantry no longer meaningfully responded to their appeals of Marxist-style class conflict. Even after the universal franchise was adopted with the ratification of the 1950 Constitution, the lower or Scheduled Castes never rushed to their standard either. Until the 1980s, the latter remained with the Congress, it had won their allegiance during the Freedom Movement through Gandhi's untouchability-removal campaigns and had retained their loyalty through 'affirmative action' programmes, democratic decentralization, and inclusion in the party's patronage system. The greatest successes with the class-conflict thesis, and these never on a national scale, were achieved by the various Communist parties in selected parts of India, such as the CPI (ML) in Bengal and Bihar, the CPM and CPI in Bengal and Kerala, and for a time in the late 1940s and early 1950s the Andhra CPI in Telengana.

Once Congress had extruded the Socialists from its ranks and withstood the challenge of the Left to its political authority and legitimacy, it found itself in virtually exclusive control of the political centre. For almost two decades, all the major interest formations (caste, religious, regional) in the country were encompassed and nurtured by what Kothari termed 'the Congress system'.[37] One could say that Congress was able for this period of time to be all things to all classes, a vast democratically structured patronage machine which successfully created and distributed material and status resources with sufficient equity to deter defections and organized political challenges by the major interests it served.

While this broad consensus lasted, class-based competition for the material and status resources which Congress controlled gave way to competition on ethnic lines. The so-called 'casteism' that beset Congress once it was transformed from a movement to a political machine concerned with acquiring and remaining in power, reflects this fact. Once Congress had removed the 'class-enemy', viz., the landlords, with zamindari abolition there was no longer any motivation for the former tenantry to maintain class cohesion. They abandoned the 'lateral integration' that facilitated common action and reverted to the 'vertical integration' of caste differentiation. Under the Congress umbrella this became ethnic competition—Yadavs, Kurmis, Jats, or Bhumihars competing against each other, and against Brahmans, Rajputs, and even Chamars as hereditary status groups attempting to maximize their political and economic advantage.

Toward the end of the 1960s, however, changes in the agrarian system were generating new forms of class-consciousness among the middle-caste former tenantry. Now designated Backward

Castes, the middle-castes had consolidated their position as smaller-scale proprietors producing for the market, to an important extent as the principal beneficiaries of the Green Revolution. Growing crops for an increasingly more dynamic market with increasingly more sophisticated technologies, Jats, Yadavs, Kurmis, and Koeris, were beginning to translate their improved economic status into political clout. This was a process that was abetted by a combination of the effects of democratic decentralization (Panchayati Raj) and demographic reality. It was in *gaon panchayats* and *block samitis* that Backward castes first discovered that numbers count in electoral politics, and here that they discovered there were fundamental interest-differences between them and the elite castes. At the village level, The higher castes were numerically weaker, but proportionately stronger in economic terms. The average intra-village land-holdings of upper-caste families were normally several times greater than the average holdings per family among The backward castes—who, however, vastly outnumbered Brahmans, Thakurs, Kayasthas and Vaishyas in most villages. In the village the elite caste households, therefore, behaved as much like landlords as cultivators; they had high ritual status; they had surplus land to rent; they had more money with which to buy political access. Moreover, most higher-level Congress politicians were from such backgrounds which created an implicit affinity between them and the most powerful segment of intra-village landholders. Through local-level elections, a type of class cleavage began to appear again, based this time on the status discrepancies between these two types of agricultural proprietors. This gradually percolated upward through the political system, as more and more politicians from the backward castes were able to use the power of ethnic solidarity and numbers to gain access to the halls of legislative power and to positions of power in the party apparatus, and from these vantages challenge the authority of the long-entrenched upper-caste establishments.

This new class-cleavage began to show up at the ballot box commencing with the fourth General Election in 1967. The strength of the Congress in the Lok Sabha declined dramatically in that election. Having won 76 per cent of the parliamentary seats in 1952, 78 per cent in 1957, and 74 per cent in 1962, their share of seats shrank to 55 per cent in 1967. The Congress had lost power in several provinces mainly because major segments of the old Congress coalition were beginning to carve out separate political identities for themselves. In many of these instances it was the middle-caste cultivators or their structural equivalents who took the first steps. Between 1967 and 1969, Congress governments fell and were replaced by opposition coalitions in Bihar, Haryana, Orissa, Punjab, Uttar Pradesh, Kerala, Tamil Nadu, and West Bengal. The UP case is seminal in this regard because the principal architect of middle-caste 'reclassification' in that state was the Jat leader Charan Singh.

For years, Chaudhuri Saheb, as he was known, had been a persistent spokesman within the UP Congress for the small cultivators whom he regarded as the productive heart of the post-Independence agrarian system. In the 1950s he had alienated Jawaharlal Nehru by vigorously opposing his efforts to introduce 'joint-farming' (a kind of half-way house toward collectivization) as part of his announced determination to achieve a 'socialist pattern of society' for India. He wrote books analysing India's agrarian situation whose main thesis was that small-scale agriculture performed by peasant proprietors, not mechanization and collectivization, was suited to India's man-land ratios. Like Japan, the scarcity of agricultural land in relation to population required labour-intensive methods of cultivation. This could only be achieved by facilitating in every way possible the productivity of peasant farms by cultivators bound by sentiment and secure tenures to their lands and prepared to employ the labour of family members on an intensive basis to cultivate crops. For the problem in India with its huge population and limited amount of agricultural land, Charan Singh declared, was not productivity per worker but productivity per acre. 'Mechanization helps a farmer in cultivating or controlling a large area of land, rather than increasing per acre production (which is what has to be aimed at in India).' The correct policy, therefore, should be to '... emphasize those elements in modern technology which do not displace labour ... and those forms of capital formation which use a great deal of manpower. ...'[38]

Charan Singh's formulations regarding the nature of the contemporary Indian agrarian system and the policies which government should pursue toward it, were essentially an argument for recognizing and institutionalizing the structural position which the cultivating peasantry (the former tenantry and their middle-caste equivalents elsewhere) had, in his opinion, come to occupy in the agricultural economy. In political terms, of course, it was an implicit call for Backward Castes to demand representation in the system of power consonant with their numbers and economic importance. In other words, it was once again a call for class mobilization.

The first breakthrough came following the 1967 general election. The UP Congress failed for the first time to obtain an absolute majority of seats in the legislative assembly and was compelled to scramble for support from independents and splinter groups in order to retain power. At the point where the C.B. Gupta faction representing the old guard seemed to have succeeded in assembling the necessary support, Charan Singh formed his faction of 16 MLAs into a sub-party called the Samyukt Vidayak Dal (SVD) and threatened to secede from the Congress unless the Gupta faction made concessions to his group. Overtly the demands were for a more equitable distribution of cabinet posts, which the SVD claimed had been 'biased' in favour of the Gupta group. Underlyingly this was a coded statement implying that elite castes had received the lion's share of posts at the expense of the middle and lower castes.

When no solution was found, Charan Singh and his SVD faction left the Congress, thus bringing down the government. All the opposition groups then combined with the SVD to form the first non-Congress government UP had ever known. Charan Singh was chosen by the coalition as UP's first non-Congress and first Backward Caste Chief Minister.

The social composition of this opposition coalition reflected the nascent class-differentiation that was taking place. Although it cut across parties and castes, the leadership demonstrated an interest in affording special recognition to the Backward and Scheduled Caste members in their midst. This was clearly reflected in Charan Singh's cabinet selections. The C.B. Gupta cabinet had 8 (73 per cent) elite caste, 2 (18 per cent) middle caste, 1 (9 per cent) lower caste and 1 (9 per cent) Muslim members. In the Charan Singh cabinet there were 6 members from Upper Castes. But these constituted only 38 per cent of the total because there were also 6 (38 per cent) middle-caste members, 3 (18 per cent) from the lower castes and one (6 per cent) Muslim.

I consider this the breakthrough of the 'reclassification' of the middle castes. From this point, not only in UP but in many other parts of India, the class attributes of the middle-castes became an increasingly self-conscious basis for differential political mobilization. In Karnataka, for example, Devraj Urs initiated a comparable restructuring of the agrarian social order by enabling peasant farmers and labourers outside the megacastes to enter the Congress system instead of leaving it. In the overall, however, the decline of the party has much to do with this process. From the 1970s onward, the upper castes gravitated toward the BJP for reasons that have definite class implications. This trend facilitated the attempts by the V.P. Singh government to implement the recommendations of the Mandal Commission in the 1980s. Middle-castes have provided the principal class-ingredient in the United Front formations that have attempted to stem the rise of the elite caste-driven socio-religious agenda of the Hindu Right. Gradually these processes of class-differentiation have assumed all India proportions that are evolving as I write. Non-Congress governments have become common place in the Indian states and indeed have manifested themselves with increasing frequency at the centre as well. Their political core has almost invariably been class-structured coalitions of ethnically differentiated, middle-range megacastes which like the former tenantry of Oudh have found their strength in numbers, but unlike the former tenantry have been able to augment their demographic weight with real power over the lands they cultivate. The Jats of Haryana, the Jats, Yadavs, and Kurmis of UP, the Yadavs and Kurmis of Bihar, the Kammas and Reddis of Andhra, the Vokkaligas and Lingayats of Karnataka, the Ezhavas, Christians and Muslims of Kerala are all instances of non-elite groups whose political behaviour acquired class implications. The same is true of Other Backward groups who have entered the political arena.

Another form of 'post-Marxist' agrarian mobilization that has arisen in various parts of India in response to the increased 'marketization' of the agricultural economy has been termed 'rural unionism' by Dipankar Gupta.[40] Structurally as well as ideologically, rural unionism differs both from Marxist styles of peasant mobilization and the Charan Singh mode of Backward Caste politicization in that it purports to be 'apolitical'. Instead of appealing to the peasantry as a general class, such movements focus almost exclusively on a single category within the peasantry, the farmers. They function as pressure groups and target specific economic grievances like taxes, electricity rates, and other measures affecting farmers' productivity, prosperity, and labour relations. We have seen that by contrast Charan Singh and others who followed him pursued essentially conventional political agendas. That is, their strategy was to form parties, or factions within existing parties, among Backward Caste communities, for the purpose of achieving systemic power for kisans writ large. Their purpose was to infuse non-elite castes if not with a sense of class-solidarity then at least a willingness to politically co-ordinate their pursuit of common interests arising from their relationship to the means of production and the system of power. Through this 'classification' process, the goal was to enable middle-castes in the Hindi belt—Jats, Yadavs, Kurmis, Koeris, and Gujars—to parlay their demographic preponderance and productive capabilities in the agricultural economy into a major political force. Their original venues were Haryana, Uttar Pradesh and Bihar. Their coalitions challenged elite caste dominance in the Congress; they formed the heart of V.P. Singh's United Front alliance; they filled the ranks of regional parties which spun off from Congress (and from each other!). Along with Charan Singh, they spawned leaders like Mulayam Singh Yadav in UP, Laloo Prasad Yadav in Bihar, and Devi Lal Singh in Haryana.

Rural unionism in the Hindi belt began to emerge as a new variation of peasant mobilization toward the end of the 1970s. In the Hindi heartland it took the form of an organization called the Bharatiya Kisan Union (BKU). All over the country comparable formations emerged such as Shetkari Sangathan in Maharashtra and the Rajya Ryota Sangha in Karnataka. The BKU arose as a more or less spontaneous resistance group by Jat farmers in the Haryana village of Kanjhwala who were angry about the granting of 120 acres of land to the village's Harijans. This in itself indicates the limited range of economic and status interests which the originators represented—viz., non-elite peasant farmers, mainly Jats. It was the organizational talent and charisma of Mahender Singh Tikait, a Jat farmer from western UP, who by the 1980s had transformed the BKU, for a time at least, into a major agrarian force. Gupta refers to this phenomenon as 'narrow unionism' which confines itself to a single category of producers, the farmers. It has rarely engaged in 'vertical outreach' as the more typical kisan parties have done. As Gupta phrases it, 'Like most other unions the BKU is not very sympathetic to the inclusion of demands other than its own.'[41]

In terms of social impact, the BKU's style of rural mobilization reached its climax between 1987 and the early 1990s. During that period a number of mammoth gatherings were organized. In March 1987, Tikait organized a *gherao* (sit-in) at Karmukhera power station by 50,000 farmers to protest against electricity rates. Says Gupta, 'The sheer spectacle of all this immediately gave national prominence to both the BKU and to Tikait.'[42] It was followed by a 'grand show' in Meerut city in which 'tens of thousands' of protesters camped outside the District Collector's office for three weeks without engaging in any violence or disruption.

What was singular about Tikait's unionism is that it was able to reach across caste and communal lines to incorporate Muslims and those members of other castes who fit the definition of farmers. It was also able to be thoroughly non-violent without being 'Gandhian', that is, without engaging in the type of religiosity that would arouse communal sentiments. It could successfully impel huge numbers of supporters to assemble and focus their collective energies on pressuring government over very specific bread-and-butter issues. In this sense, it was at its height penultimately secular. However, in the end, it would seem that the BKU under Tikait's leadership could not sustain its unionist universalism, and edged toward the threshold of politicization. As it did so it began to acquire a casteist and communalist hue. This process commenced when Tikait decided to '. . . take a more serious interest in elections'[43] and came out in support first of the Janata Party in 1989 and then the BJP in 1991. The latter decision was the most crucial because after the destruction of the Babri Masjid in December 1992, Muslims were alienated from the BKU. It sacrificed some of its universalistic, apolitical appeal. The process went deeper as the BKU struggled with its own identity—i.e. whether to remain apolitical or adopt more inclusive strategies which made immersion in conventional politics inevitable. In the end, it was Tikait's decision to move back from politicization. But doing so required resort to some other organizational basis for mobilizing support. His solution was to fall back on a 'traditional' social structure. He employed the Jat caste's clan or *khap* structure as '. . . the central organizing principle'.[44] The effect of this was to 'parochialize' the BKU, to limit its scope almost exclusively to Jat farmer-cultivators.

This indicates to me the fact that in the culturally multiplex world of Indian society, perhaps more than any other place on earth, no attempts at interest-based mobilization, no matter how 'universalistic' they purport to be, can forever escape enmeshment in the particularizing power of the ethnically structured social formations that prowl the country's democratically structured political arenas. This is a reality which seems not have been lost on the Shetkari Sangathan in Maharashtra. While manifesting many of the same unionist characteristics as the BKU, its leader, Sharad Joshi, himself neither a Maratha nor a farmer-cultivator but a Brahman intellectual, imparted a political dimension to this organization by defining it as appealing not only to farmer-cultivators, or *kheduts*, but to *shetkaris* a term embracing all persons who work on the land in any capacity—landless labourers, owner-cultivators, or anyone else, regardless of caste. This, of course, suggests, as my own thesis would indicate, a further variation within the corpus of unionizing patterns of mobilization wherein, unlike the BKU, the pursuit of narrowly constructed economic issues can be combined with more conventional class mobilization principles.

Such differences notwithstanding, I think the importance of these formations is that, on the one hand, they further demonstrate the point that 'class mobilization' in India has never been a monolith. Its forms and consequences have reflected historical time, social context and, indeed, systemic economic factors for the simple reason that in a socio/cultural/political world as large and diversified as India, no single, uniform 'class thesis' ever has provided or ever will provide basis for understanding these processes.

On the other hand, the Backward Caste mobilizational procedures of the Charan Singhs and the unionist mobilization procedures undertaken by the Mahender Singh Tikaits and Sharad Joshis are indicative of how far rationalizing and marketizing tendencies in the Indian economy, and most particularly their impact on the agrarian system, have gone since the inception of the Green Revolution. If Marxism pertains to class mobilization in relation to the 'means of production', then unionism reflects the changes that have taken place in the relationship of agricultural producers to the rapidly burgeoning post-Cold War industrialization and globalization of the Indian economic system.

Conclusion

We may conclude that there has never been a single class thesis that can be applied to a world as large and socially complex as India. There have been periods of class-formation in specific places at specific points in time. The Kisan Sabha movements in Oudh and Bihar from the 1920s until Zamindari Abolition, which spawned indigenous leaders like Baba Ram Chandra and Sahajanand, were one such manifestation. The Bardoli satyagraha in Gujarat in the 1920s was another. So were the Moplah Rebellions in Malabar in the nineteenth and twentieth centuries. Even the uprising of 1857 had prototypical class aspects which, I hope to show in a subsequent study, deserve more recognition than they have received. None of these events produced a single class thesis that could be applied to the whole of India. But there have been certain common threads that have run through all the manifestations of agrarian unrest that have occurred in India at least in modern times. Caste hierarchies have everywhere correlated with differing relationships to the means of production. Land controllers have been concentrated in the higher castes, small-scale cultivators and tenantries have come from middle-range castes, and landless labourers have come from the lower castes. Therefore, everywhere and at all times there has been the potential for class formation and class conflict whenever inequities in wealth, social condition, and status deprivation have reached critical levels of intolerability. The names of the oppressors have varied depending upon which regional culture and agrarian system one is talking about. But the structural relationships which have led to class-formation and conflict remain underlyingly the same.

NOTES

1. Jawaharlal Nehru, *An Autobiography*, New edition, London: The Bodley Head, 1936 (reprint 1953), p. 57.
2. For an early, trenchant analysis of the sociological impact of the introduction of market forces into India's agrarian economy, see Bernard S. Cohn, 'Political Systems in Eighteenth Century India: The Banaras Region', *The Journal of the American Oriental Society*, vol. 82, 1952, pp. 312-20. As Dhanagare notes, '. . . the land belonged to the peasant who enjoyed hereditary occupancy rights under the Mughal rulers. Land was seldom sold or purchased as a commodity and so long as the peasant paid his rent or revenue (cash or a share of the produce) he could not be evicted by anybody. Cultivation of land was considered a socially vital function, and hence, the peasants' occupancy rights were always respected. There was some zamindari oppression of the peasantry but since the rights of landed aristocracy were not absolute, it was limited to extortion of revenue.' (p. 27) Dhanagare continues: 'In the decades following the 1857 Mutiny . . . the landowning and moneylending classes gradually rose to power in the rural areas.' This process cut across all regions, says he: '[It] was a pan-Indian development irrespective of the system—zamindari, raiyatwari or wahalwari. It had immediate and direct social consequences: the courts, police and petty revenue officials now safeguarded the interests of the usurers—the moneylending and rich landowning classes. The new alliances also worked against the interests of small landowners, raiyats and sharecroppers who constituted the poor peasantry.' (D N. Dhanagare, *Peasant Movements in India, 1920-1950*, Delhi: Oxford University Press, 1986, p. 39.)
3. The belief that each varna must perform its hereditary duties with integrity and responsibility toward the others.
4. UP Archives, General Administrative Department, File 50-3, 1921.

5. Jawaharlal Nehru, op. cit., 1953.
6. Dhanagare, op. cit., p. 88.
7. Ibid.
8. Ibid.
9. Ibid., p. 89.
10. In Dhanagare's words: '. . . we must note that Gandhi did not completely alienate the poorer sections of the peasantry and the landless. Rather through his "constructive programme" he always maintained a semblance of relief for these sections of rural society. Whether latently or manifestly, Gandhi's "constructive programme" helped the Congress sustain it basic liberal, political and economic reformism and to prevent any potential revolutionary activity at the grass-roots level.'
11. Dhanagare presents statistics showing that in Surat district 24 per cent of the agricultural population were owner-cultivators while landless labourers constituted 67 per cent. This contrasts with Faizabad district in Oudh where zamindars and taluqdars were the principal land-controllers. In 1931, agricultural laborers in Faizabad comprised only 19.4 per cent of the agricultural population, owner cultivators comprised a mere 6.0 per cent, and tenants comprised 63.0 per cent.
12. Ibid., p. 95.
13. Ibid., pp. 107-8.
14. M.H. Siddiqi, *Agrarian Unrest in North India: The United Provinces (1919-22)*, New Delhi: Vikas, 1978, p. 17.
15. Ibid., p. 103.
16. Lucknow Division: Kheri, Sitapur, Hardoi, Lucknow, Unnao, Rae Bareilly; Faizabad Division: Bahraich, Gonda, Bara Banki, Faizabad, Sultanpur, Pratapgarh; Gorakhpur Division: Basti, Gorakhpur, Azamgarh.
17. Kapil Kumar, *Peasants in Revolt: Tenants, Landlords, Congress and the Raj in Oudh, 1886-1922*, New Delhi: Manohar, 1984, provides detail on the career of Baba Ram Chandra both prior to and after his arrival in Awadh. In the context of the discussion that follows, Kumar shows that Ram Chandra could not have been the founder of the Rure Kisan Sabha for the simple reason that he did not reach the area until at least a year after its founding. However, his role in publicizing it and ramifying its influence cannot be denied.
18. V.N. Mehta, 'Report to the Commissioner of Fyzabad Division', Pratapgarh, dated 11 November 1920, p. 2.
19. Shahid Amin, 'Gandhi as Mahatma' in Ranajit Guha and Gayatri

Chakravorty Spivak, ed., *Selected Subaltern Studies*, New York/ Oxford: Oxford University Press, 1988, p. 316.

20. Gyanendra Pandey, 'Peasant Revolt and Indian Nationalism: The Peasant Movement in Awadh, 1919-22' in Guha, and Spivak op. cit., p. 255.
21. Kumar, *Peasants in Revolt,* p. 92.
22. Somewhat prior to this, Pandit Madan Mohan Malaviya had organized a kisan sabha in Allahabad district that was supposed to address peasant grievances. But Malaviya was even more conservative than Gandhi on agrarian issues and did not promote any agitation that embraced the broad spectrum even of the tenantry. In Dhanagare's (1986) words, '. . . Malaviya's interest in the agrarian situation was essentially a by-product of his involvement in the Home Rule campaign . . . although its aim was to advance the political interests of the peasantry as a whole, its actual appeal was limited to high-caste Brahmin and Rajput tenants and small zamindars. Hence there was little grass-roots activity. . . .' (p. 117)
23. Their success in this regard prompted the U.P. government to try and counter this type of class-oriented mobilization by undertaking to mobilize the landlords as a more coherent, 'loyal' opposition to what was perceived as a radicalizing Congress. See Peter Reeves, 'The Politics of Order: "Anti-Non-Cooperation" in the United Provinces, 1921', *Journal of Asian Studies*, vol. XXV, no. 2, 1996, pp. 261-74—on the *aman sabhas*, or 'anti-revolutionary leagues'. See Harold A. Gould, *Grass-Roots Politics in India: A Century of Political Evolution in Faizabad District*, New Delhi: Oxford & IBH Publ. Co., 1994. Chaps. 4 and 5 dealing with landlord politics are especially pertinent.
24. UP Archives: Commissioner of Faizabad to Sir Harcourt Butler, 24 January 1921.
25. Dhanagare, op. cit., p. 117.
26. Pandey, op. cit., p. 281.
27. See the Introduction to Walter Hauser, ed., *Sahajanand on Agricultural Labour and the Rural Poor*, New Delhi: Manohar, 1994. See also the review by Peter Reeves of Hauser's *Sahajanand on Agricultural Labour and the Rural Poor*, in *South Asia*, vol. XIX, no. 1, 1996, pp. 103-6.
28. Dhanagare, op. cit., p.120. Dhanagare found that: 'Evictions for arrears of rent were an added burden for tenants. In 1930-1 there were 31,383 suits for eviction in Oudh districts, compared with 24,061 in 1926-7.' He obtained these data from the *Report on the Administration of the U.P., 1926-27*, Allahabad.

29. Ibid., p. 121.
30. Actually, two parties were formed: The National Agriculturalists Party of Oudh and the National Agriculturalists Party of Agra. This reflected the somewhat different agrarian systems that existed in each of these sections of the United Provinces. In Oudh, the taluqdars were the defining landlord class. Agra was a *raiyatwari* area where zamindars were interspersed with peasant cultivators who had alienable ownership rights over their land. In this sense, Agra bore a closer resemblance to the tenurial pattern in Bardoli. For the purposes of this essay, however, it is sufficient to refer to the National Agriculturalists Party as if it were a single entity for which I use the abbreviation NAP.
31. The latter was more a *de facto* than a *de jure* arrangement since technically the provincial governors had the power to veto legislation of which the government did not approve. But a 'gentlemen's agreement' was arrived at whereby the government pledged not to exercise this power in the name of political harmony and responsible representative government. The process worked reasonably well until Congress boycotted the assemblies following the breakdown of negotiations with the British government over India's participation in World War II. See M.V. Pylee, *Constitutional Government*, Bombay: Asia Publishing House, 1960.
32. In actuality the politically relevant landholding group were a much smaller proportion of the agricultural population than this, but no means are available to differentiate them within this pool from minor land-controllers.
33. See Gould, op. cit., especially chap. 7, and Paul Brass, *Factional Politics in an Indian State: The Congress Party in Uttar Pradesh*, Berkeley: University of California Press, 1965.
34. In the legislative assembly, it went to Pandit Pant who belonged to the anti-CSP Patel faction. See Brass, op. cit.
35. However, Nehru's refusal to leave Congress with his fellow Socialists following the Patel edict left a legacy of bitterness among leaders of the democratic left which lingers to this day. They accused him of opting for expediency over principle—of choosing the power and celebrity he could enjoy by remaining within Congress over the political risks and challenges that would have to be faced by leading his leftist flock into the wilderness, as it were. An old Congress Socialist from Faizabad district once complained to me: 'Jawaharlal Nehru is not a political leader; he is a political star!' See Gould, op. cit., Brass, op. cit., and Myron Weiner, *Party*

Politics in India: The Development of a Multi-Party System, Princeton: Princeton University Press, 1957.

36. *Pioneer,* Lucknow, 22 March 1948.
37. After the first General Election, the Socialist Party merged with the Krishak Mazdoor Praja Party (KMPP) to form the Praja Socialist Party (PSP). The KMPP was another party-ized group of defectors who broke away from Congress in 1951 in order to contest the first General Election as a separate party. They were a loose alliance of politicians who characterized themselves as 'socialist' but not 'Marxist'. Their president was Acharya J.B. Kripalani, a self-styled Gandhian, who had once been President of the Congress until forced out of office by the Patel group over issues of both ideology and party authority. Brass and Franda say of them: They were largely 'non-Socialist faction leaders who had been defeated at the all-India level and in several states in struggles for power in the Congress. . . .' In 1955, a more militant anti-Congress section of the PSP, led by Ram Manohar Lohia, broke away from the PSP and re-formed the Socialist Party. Brass and Franda continue: 'The two Socialist parties retained a separate existence until 1964, when they merged into a new entity called the Samyukta Socialist Party (SSP). In January 1965, however, some dissatisfied PSP members split off and revived the PSP, leaving the bulk of the Socialist members in the new SSP. In August 1971, the SSP and PSP leaderships merged the two parties once again into a united Socialist Party (SP) . . . the SP was the only Socialist group with significant national strength in India in 1972.' (Paul R. Brass and Marcus F. Franda, eds., *Radical Politics in South Asia*, Cambridge: MIT Press, 1973, p. 10.)
38. Rajni Kothari, *Politics in India*, Boston: Little, Brown, 1970.
39. For a detailed analysis of this process, see Gould, op. cit., and Brass, op. cit.
40. Charan Singh, *India's Economic Policy: The Gandhian Blueprint*, New Delhi: Vikas, 1977, p. 104. See also his original major work on this subject: *Joint-Farming X-Rayed: The Problem and its Solution*, Bombay: Bharatiya Vidya Bhavan, 1959.
41. Dipankar Gupta, *Rivalry and Brotherhood: Politics in the Life of Farmers in Northern India*, Delhi: Oxford University Press, 1997.
42. Ibid., p. 19.
43. Ibid., p. 32.
44. Ibid., p. 34.
45. Ibid., p. 157.

Bhakti and the British Empire*

William R. Pinch

Love God, Government and goodness
Rupkala, 1923[1]

PROLOGUE

A government official named Sitaramsharan Bhagvan Prasad was travelling through a rugged section of Bhagalpur District in rural Bihar, deep in northern India, on his way to conduct the inspection of a school. His route took him across a stream in the middle of a dry riverbed. So that his Kahars (carriers) could navigate the stream more easily, Bhagvan Prasad decided to alight from his palanquin and cross on foot. When he had

* I am grateful to Phillip Wagoner, Sumit Guha, and Ronald Inden for their comments on an early version of this essay; also to Christian Novestke, Richard Elphick, and the anonymous readers for *Past & Present*, for their detailed responses; and to Kailash Jha for facilitating contacts in New Delhi. I also extend thanks to the children of Sarjoo Prasad, son of Brajendra Prasad, who welcomed me into their New Delhi home and generously granted permission to reproduce the family photograph of Rupkala-ji. The research for the essay was supported by a variety of funding agencies since about 1986, including the Fulbright-Hays Program of the U.S. Department of Education; the Joint Committee on South Asia of the American Council of Learned Societies and the Social Science Research Council with funds provided by the National Endowment for the Humanities and the Ford Foundation; and the Office of Academic Affairs at Wesleyan University. I am grateful to these organizations for their support. The essay was previously published in *Past & Present* 179, 1 (2003), and is reproduced here with permission.

reached the middle of the stream, however, a sudden torrent of water began to swirl up around him. The Kahars watched from the shore as the water level rose precipitously. Despite the water's great depth, Bhagvan Prasad did not sink below his waist. He remained suspended in the river for many hours; when the flood finally subsided, he completed his crossing. As he recounted the incident, 'I don't know who or what grasped me firmly by the waist, but I wasn't able to move forward nor was I permitted to sink and drown.' One of his devotees would conclude the story thus: 'It is said that on that day people came to realize that his constant love for God (*ishvar*) sanctified the very ground of India (*bharat bhumi*).'[2]

According to the Census of British India, about 100,000 Britons and 287,000,000 Indians lived in the country in 1891.[3] This paper is about two of those people, Bhagvan Prasad (1840-1932), whom we have just met, and George Abraham Grierson (1851-1941). More precisely, it is about the interpenetration of their religious worlds, and what that tells us about their understanding of British India and, by extension, the British Empire. I argue that the lives and thoughts of these two men encourage a rethinking of recent post-colonial depictions of British India as a site of unidirectional mental colonization by a rationalizing, scientific Europe on a pliable, pre-modern Orient.[4] Such descriptions, while politically compelling in the present, do not explain how it was that nearly three hundred million Indians could be governed by, and gradually govern themselves with, one hundred thousand Britons. I argue, *inter alia*, that we need to pay more attention to religion and religious belief if we are to arrive a fuller understanding of what Empire meant to the individuals who lived it.

The overlapping religious worlds of Britain and India at the height of empire have attracted increased scholarly attention in recent years.[5] Much of this work is inspired by a desire to better understand British India in terms of its intersecting British and Indian cultural arenas, and situates itself in particular in the broad rubric of 'post-colonial studies'.[6] As such, it parallels and occasionally overlaps with developments in the historical investigations of women and gender, in which the imperial periphery is brought to the metropole and examined in a unified

Figure 1: Rupkala Sitaramsharan Bhagvan Prasad 1840-1932. From a photograph held by the descendants of Sarjoo Prasad, son of Brajendra Prasad, New Delhi. By permission.

Figure 2: George Abraham Grierson, 1851–1941. From Grierson's obituary notice in *Proceedings of the British Academy*, xxviii (1942), 282. By permission.

analytical frame.[7] The extension of this unified frame to the study of imperial religion is welcome, especially in so far as Western historians of empire 'turn the searchlight inward', to quote Gandhi,[8] to reexamine European—and especially British—secularism from the inside out, and rediscover in the process much that is religious. Particularly important in this context is the work of Talal Asad, and the insight that 'the universalization of the concept of religion is closely related to the coming of modernity in Europe and to the European expansion over the world'.[9]

However, certain myopias are evident. One is a tendency to overstate the impact of Protestant Christianity and the agency of an undifferentiated West.[10] Another is a related desire to attend too fervently to a narrowly conceived 'zone of contact',[11] in which central importance is given over to religious meanings that emanate from the metropole and reverberate through the periphery. This results in an overemphasis on syncretistic (and demographically limited) religious movements, such as the Ramakrishna Mission and the Theosophical Society, and on politically embattled figures such as Swami Vivekananda and Annie Besant. As Philip Lutgendorf has noted, following C.A. Bayly, 'the scholarly focus on the activities of a handful of reformers, based mainly in the Punjab and Bengal where foreign influence was strongest, has tended to overshadow the complex pattern of mainstream Hindu activity both in the same regions and in the vast, largely Hindi-speaking Gangetic plain'.[12] Both Bayly and Lutgendorf were directing attention to the emergence of a high-caste neo-Hinduism, known as *sanatana dharma* or 'eternal faith', that was taking root in northern India in the late nineteenth century and would play a prominent role in Hindu nationalism in the coming decades. This essay, however, is concerned with a devotionalist sentiment that existed, and exists still, among the middle and lower castes and classes of northern India. This devotionalist sentiment is rarely glimpsed and even less frequently discussed in historical literature concerning India. It did not occasion political controversy but, rather, seemed to enjoy widespread recognition and support, particularly as we retreat from the major Presidency centres of Bombay and Calcutta. And it paralleled a devotionalist ethic that had evolved in late Victorian Britain. These interpenetrating devotions produced the overarching religious values that sustained the imperial age.

This essay should be read, then, as an attempt to widen the 'zone of contact'. Firmly situated in the devotionalist topography were Bhagvan Prasad and Grierson. As both Bayly and Shahid Amin have noted, Grierson was a leading member of a generation of linguistically accomplished ethnographer-folklorists educated at Trinity College, Dublin.[13] He is known to many Indian historians as the author of the encyclopaedic *Bihar Peasant Life*[14] and to linguists for his monumental nineteen-volume *Linguistic Survey of India*.[15] Grierson entered the Indian or 'Covenanted' Civil Service in 1873 and was posted over the next two and half decades in the province of Bihar in the Bengal Presidency. After 1898 he lived in Camberley, a quiet suburb of London, and devoted himself primarily to completing the *Linguistic Survey* and related interests, including scholarly-religious reflections on the place of Christianity in Hinduism. In recognition of his many intellectual accomplishments, he was awarded a knighthood in 1912.

Bhagvan Prasad was also a servant of the empire, but in the 'Uncovenanted' or Provincial Civil Service, and worked for thirty years in the Bihar Education Branch of the Bengal Presidency, where he rose to the rank of Sub-Inspector of Schools. Bhagvan Prasad came from a family of respected scholar-exegetes in the Vaishnava *bhakti* tradition, about which I will have more to say below. During the later years of his life he attracted a sizeable following as *Rupkala* (art-form), a mystic-devotee, poet, and guru. In 1893 Bhagvan Prasad retired to a quasi-monastic existence in the pilgrimage centre of Ayodhya, where he devoted himself entirely to God, to his followers, and to hagiographic exegesis.[16]

Bhagvan Prasad and Grierson were acquainted, though it is not clear how well. They probably met during their government work in the Bihar education service, where Grierson had temporary mid-career postings in the early 1880s as Inspector of Schools. Bhagvan Prasad would then have been his immediate subordinate. Even if theirs was only a passing acquaintance (which I doubt), they were well aware of each other's deep interest in Ram-centered Hindu religious devotion. But Grierson and Bhagvan Prasad shared more than a scholarly devotion to *bhakti* and Vaishnava hagiography. The lives of both men reflect, their individual perceptions of imperial obligation. Each took refuge in the world of *bhakti* in a way that reflected his relative place in the British empire. For Grierson, this point is clear and unambiguous. He says as much in both public lectures and writing about the historical relationship between Hinduism and Christianity. Bhagvan Prasad is less forthcoming, in fact almost silent, on the question of empire. Is this is a reflection of his subordinate (though not entirely colonized) position? Did the political inequality built into British India not concern him? His actions, I believe, speak louder than words.

We know more about Bhagvan Prasad's inner spiritual world than Grierson's, primarily because Bhagvan Prasad had a wide following among government servants of the upper and middle ranks in Bihar and the United Provinces. One of these, Brajendra Prasad (1880-1947, a Sub-Judge of Patna), committed his guru's recollections to paper, which were published posthumously as *Shri Rupkala Vak Sudha*, or *The Nectar Discourse of Rupkala*.[17] The story that introduces this essay is one of several that Brajendra Prasad told in which God (Ram) assists in carrying out the work of Empire. Indeed, at one point God actually stands in for Bhagvan Prasad and does the work himself. I shall return to these tales by way of conclusion, but the key message that they transmit is that Bhagvan Prasad loved God and he loved the government—and that these two loves were connected. These interconnected loves suffused his existence. They formed the inspiration for the motto that he lived by, which introduces this essay and which he sought to communicate to his numerous followers in an English-language leaflet that he had printed for easy distribution:

By God's Grace
The chief three subjects of teachings are:

(1) Loving Communion with God;
(2) Liberal brotherhood among ourselves;
(3) Time more Valuable than money;
And the motto of Rupkala is —
Love God, Government and goodness (virtue).

There are many ways to interpret religious love in the context of imperialism. One response that has generated much attention and support among historians of India in recent years (including the 'post-colonial' strand already noted) is to situate it, following Gramsci, in a framework of domination and resistance. Ranajit Guha, to take the main exponent of this approach, sees *bhakti* as a made-to-order mental colonization of the worst kind—as an 'ideology of subordination *par excellence*'.

> If the politics of collaboration was informed by the Humean idiom of Obedience—however uneasy that obedience might have been under the hushed, almost hopeless, urge for enfranchisement among the colonized—it drew its sustenance, at the same time, from a very different tradition—the Indian tradition of *Bhakti*. All the collaborationist moments of subordination in our thinking and practice during the colonial period were linked by *Bhakti* to an inert mass of feudal culture which had been generating loyalism and depositing it in every kind of power relation for centuries before the British conquest.[18]

For his part, Partha Chatterjee has suggested that the retreat into *bhakti* by the colonial *babu* may be read as an expression of cultural anxiety as he struggled to dig a moat around the self (the 'home') to protect it from invasion by a Westernized public (the 'world').[19] The hegemony of the colonial state is held thus in abeyance: indeed, it fails (in Gramscian terms) to be hegemonic, and in that failure are sown the seeds of national resistance. And, as Dipesh Chakrabarty and others have noted, *bhakti* as a generalized sentiment of loving devotion became the basis for political unity in the thinking of many nationalist authors.[20] For Chakrabarty, however, *bhakti* (as all religious attitudes) has a both a larger and smaller role to play: as an 'ontic' way of holding reason at bay, religion is reduced to a thoroughly individualized habit, little better than superstition, a way of being quirkily human amid the totalizing tyranny of the modern ('the narrative of Capital').[21]

These scholars are able to gesture at such conclusions because they cohere with what they know about the nature of the 'colonial' state and conflicted subaltern responses to its hegemony. According to such understandings, all Indians who took part in Empire did so under duress, either conscious or unconscious.

This is an attractive proposition in the post-colonial moment. But buried in their interpretations is a desire to explain religious devotion in terms of subaltern failure and colonial displacement. Left unsaid is that the religious devotion of Indians living under British rule could not be what they claimed it was, namely, a response to God's intervention in human affairs. Either it was a twisted mental technique to justify to themselves their own oppression at the hands of others (Guha); or a kind of psycho-cultural therapy for dealing with that oppression and, ultimately, finding a way to resist it (Chatterjee, Chakrabarty); or one side of 'a dialogue between two contradictory points of view'—the other being modernity—held forever in abeyance (Chakrabarty). In sum, the effusion of *bhakti* religiosity in Bengal was simply a series of 'strategies devised within a relationship of dominance and subordination, and they take on doctrinal or ritual attributes and acquire different values according to the changing contingencies of power.'[22] If God has a role to play in all this, it is an exceedingly small one.

The subordination of *bhakti* to a world of power, of domination and resistance, is not limited to scholars writing in the subalternist mode; indeed, it is a subset of a general analytical reductionism that pervades the study of religion in social science. There is much to unlearn here. But unlearning reductionism in the study of religion does not necessarily mean crafting an approach that relies on undemonstrable claims. As Brad Gregory has noted, historians should maintain a strict agnosticism when working on religion and the religious in history, since neither God's existence nor non-existence, let alone intervention or non-intervention in human affairs, is susceptible to proof. If we slip into reductionist, 'confessional' explanations (whether church or secular), we risk distorting much and missing even more—the former because the discrediting of the mental world of people in the past renders the interpretive slate blank, and therefore open to the projection of our own particular desires, the latter because that same act of discrediting prevents us from being interested in the broader historical implications of what those people had to say. What is called for is a 'thicker description' than has been permitted by reductionist approaches, that allows the discernment of key points of 'human disagreement' (and agreement) that, potentially, offer clues to change (and continuity) over time.[23] In the case of Bhagvan Prasad and Grierson, and by extension India and Britain, what is needed is a fuller investigation of religious culture in the late nineteenth and early twentieth centuries. Only then can we begin to understand the interpenetrations, religious and otherwise, that inevitably occurred between them, and between India and Europe.

Monologues or Dialogue?

Bhagvan Prasad's life was built around his powerful love for a loving God. That love did not emerge in a vacuum, nor was it devoid of disciplinary roots. Bhagvan Prasad was a member of a family that had produced at least two other nineteenth-century religious intellectuals who, like himself, were well known for their literary contributions to hagiographical exegesis in the *bhakti* tradition.[24] He joined, at the age of eighteen, a vast spiritual network of devotional aestheticians known as *rasikas* that had spread across northern India in the seventeenth and eighteenth centuries from monastic centres near present-day Jaipur, west of Delhi. In 1881 he took a second initiation from one of the most prominent *rasikas* of Bihar, Ramcharandas Hanskala, who bestowed upon him the name 'Rupkala'. Bhagvan Prasad's *magnum opus*, a critical edition of the *Bhaktamala*, which he published in instalments between 1903 and 1909, reflected his commitment as both an aesthetician and a hagiographer. Originally composed in 1600 and supplemented with commentary and additional material in 1712, the *Bhaktamala* corpus is a collection of Braj (medieval Hindi) verse, some of it exceedingly cryptic, containing anecdotes about the lives of numerous Hindu saints and devotees. Bhagvan Prasad's 1000-page critical commentary of the *Bhaktamala* provided modern Hindi translations, as well as extensive interpretation of the poetic corpus in terms of *rasa* (aesthetic) theory.[25] As such, Bhagvan Prasad's *Bhaktamala* edition became the major constitutive text for north Indian *rasika* devotionalism, at a time when the latter was emerging as the theological and ritual foundation of north Indian Hinduism.[26]

Rasika devotion involves elaborate ritual practices and

visualization techniques to recreate on a daily basis the supercharged emotions, presided over by love, occasioned by God's presence among humans. These practices and techniques are more often associated in Western understanding with the ecstatic, and occasionally erotic, worship of Krishna, the cowherd of Vrindaban (south of Delhi) and *avatar* of Vishnu, particularly as developed by Rupa Goswami in the middle of the sixteenth century. Rasika practices and techniques very quickly migrated into the worship of Vishnu's other main *avatar*, Ram.[27] Ram-centered rasikas generally credit the inspiration for this importation to the late sixteenth-century Agradas of Galta (and later Raivasa), near Jaipur, but the rasika approach to Ram is best exemplified in the highly stylized Hindi version of Ram's life as told by the early seventeenth-century Tulsidas of Banaras, known as the *Ramcharitmanas*. By the eighteenth century the epicentre of Ram-bhakti had shifted to Ayodhya, a town widely regarded as the capital of Ram's kingdom—and the town to which Bhagvan Prasad retired in 1893. Indeed, Bhagvan Prasad took up residence in Kanak Bhavan, the oldest and arguably most important rasika institution in Ayodhya.[28] 'Kanak Bhavan' means 'House of Gold' and is considered the abode of Sita; as we shall see, it was an appropriate location given the particular devotional posture adopted by Bhagvan Prasad as Rupkala, but also because Sita was from the kingdom of Janakpur, not far from Bhagvan Prasad's birthplace in north Bihar.

The rasika tradition has deep roots in the devotional soil of north Indian Hinduism. It is impossible to imagine its spread without the lavish patronage bestowed upon it by royal households associated with the Mughal imperial era. The seventeenth and eighteenth centuries in particular saw widespread Ram and Krishna-temple construction in towns throughout northern India, including most notably the major pilgrimage centres of Amer (Jaipur), Mathura-Vrindaban, Banaras, and Ayodhya.[29]

What is perhaps less well recognized is the degree to which the expansion and consolidation of British rule in northern India actually advanced this process. Partly this had to do with the catholic social appeal of *bhakti*, which had been a factor as well in the earlier period.[30] Partly it was due to the fact that the quietist, private nature of *bhakti* compared favourably with other strands of Hindu activity from the perspective of a modernizing state seeking the ready extraction of agrarian revenue.[31] But the accelerated appeal of *bhakti* in the nineteenth century benefited from long-term social and economic changes as well. The rise of Hindu mercantile families, whose fortunes were tied to British rule and who were eager to institutionalize their wealth in religious expression, guaranteed a continued source of financial support for the construction of temples and the maintenance of religious communities devoted to Ram or Krishna in important provincial towns like Banaras and Allahabad, despite the declining influence of the old order.[32] At the same time, the expansion of the state's bureaucracy was opening up a whole host of opportunities for a widely dispersed professional literati who had served earlier regimes, prominent among whom were Khatris in western UP, the area around Delhi, and the Punjab, and Kayasthas in central and eastern UP and Bihar.[33] Bhagvan Prasad is emblematic of this class: he was himself a Kayastha, as were many of his early followers. Particularly significant here, however, are the links between socially ambiguous Kayasthas and Khatris and communities of slightly lower social and economic status—peasant cultivators, artisans, and labourers. Again Bhagvan Prasad serves as a good example: as a child in the village, he learned religion at the feet of a Koiri, a member of an influential, if socially stigmatized, community of cash-crop cultivators. In later years, while in government service in Patna, Bhagvan Prasad gained some local notoriety for providing religious ministration to Kahar and 'untouchable' Chamar labourers.[34]

Given Grierson's own concern for the plight of landless agricultural labourers in rural south Bihar, it is possible that he knew about Bhagvan Prasad's ministry among the downtrodden in Patna.[35] He was certainly aware of Bhagvan Prasad's labors as a hagiographer. In fact, Grierson's scholarly attentions were in no small measure responsible for the subsequent esteem in which Bhagvan Prasad's *Bhaktamala* commentary has been held in Western understanding. Grierson himself authored a series of essays on the *Bhaktamala*, published in the *Journal of the Royal Asiatic Society* in 1909–10, which derived in large measure from an examination of Bhagvan Prasad's writings.[36] As with Bhagvan Prasad, Grierson's interest in the *Bhaktamala* was not simply scholarly. His translations inspired him to comment at length on the shared religious ground occupied by Hinduism and Christianity. Grierson's work on the *Bhaktamala* thus represented the beginnings of yet another level of commentary, in so far as he discoursed at length on many key hagiographic and aesthetic nuances found in the work. Perhaps to repay the compliment, and to acknowledge Grierson's own ecumenical commitments, later editions of Bhagvan Prasad's commentary included references to Grierson's 'Gleanings from the *Bhakta-Mala*'.[37]

Like Bhagvan Prasad, Grierson did not write in a vacuum. And like mainstream north Indian Hinduism, British Christianity in the nineteenth century was also tending towards a devotional aestheticism, toward what Owen Chadwick has called 'Victorian devotion'. These evolutionary shifts occurred for different reasons, and at a different pace—so care should be taken in asserting any kind of simplistic comparative symmetry. Nevertheless, there were important similarities, productive of a kind of cultural convergence by the late nineteenth century. The 'infinite diversity' of Victorian devotion included, in the wake of the Oxford Movement and rising Anglo-Catholicism, an increased fascination with the historical Jesus and an increasingly idiosyncratic use of ritual and symbolic ornamentation in worship. As Samuel Wilberforce, Bishop of Oxford, observed in an 1865 letter to the Archbishop of Canterbury, 'There is, I believe, in the English mind a great move towards a higher ritual.' Closely tied to this was the intellectual shift, the 'unsettlement of minds', brought on by textual-historical study of the Bible, the increasing knowledge of and respect for other religious traditions (especially in South Asia), and the scientific study of nature.[38] The Victorian response to this mental unsettlement was not to give up on a search for religious truth, nor even necessarily to abandon Christianity. Rather, Christian thinkers focused their attentions on God in history embedded in the details, a God of love incarnate among men in the world. The distant, transcendant creator God—the God of atonement—retreated to the background.

Deprived of the basic supports of prophecy and miracle,

Victorian Christians looked to religious experience to aid them in arriving at a deeper, more global sense of faith. And Empire gave them the wherewithal to look beyond the confines of Christianity. Today the best known of the new breed of comparative religionists are the Oxford scholars Monier Monier-Williams (1819–99) and Friedrich Max Müller (1823–1900). Though he himself was ambivalent about evangelical Christianity and the missionary enterprise, Müller's translations of the *Rigveda* were celebrated as 'the greatest gifts which have been bestowed on those who would win to Christianity the subtle and thoughtful minds of the cultivated Indians'.[39] Müller's own view was that all great religions contained the essential seed of love and that it was the duty of Christians to simply nurture its growth. As he put it, there was no need to 'transplant . . . Christianity in its full integrity from England to India, as we might need to transplant a full-grown tree'.[40] Like Müller, Monier-Williams saw much that was good in ancient Indian religion and resented the use of the term 'heathen' to describe Hindus. Unlike Müller, however, Monier-Williams saw a strong link between his scholarly work and missionary aims, a posture that was in keeping with his occupancy of the Boden Chair in Sanskrit.[41] Less well known today than these two, but equally if not more important in shaping official attitudes on the ground in India, were John Muir of Banaras (1810–82) and F. S. Growse of Mathura (1836–93). Unlike Monier-Williams and Müller, these scholars possessed long professional experience in India. Their respective responses to the apparent doctrinal, and devotional, commonalties between Christianity and Hinduism are instructive in so far as they reflect the shift from the confident evangelism of the first half of the nineteenth century to the later more comparative posture. Whereas Muir in the 1830s and 1840s argued the Biblical origins of the *Bhagavad Gita*, Growse in the 1860s and 1870s sought to de-emphasize discussion of origins and was content to simply note the fortuitousness of the shared religious sentiments in devotion to Krishna and Christ, not to mention the orthographic similarities of the two names.[42]

All four of these men were dead by 1901, but their views seemed to live on in an amalgamated form in Grierson. In 1906 Grierson expressed himself on the subject of Christianity and

Hinduism in the journal *The East and the West* and again in a lecture on 15 January 1907 to the Royal Asiatic Society of Great Britain and Ireland (subsequently published in the April issue of the journal of that body).[43] The timing is significant, since he was also translating portions of the *Bhaktamala* into English.[44] Grierson's view in 1906–07 was that modern Hinduism, and particularly the historical rise of *bhakti*, owed its origins to the spread of early Christianity into India. He acknowledged that he was not the first European scholar to posit the Christian origins of bhakti: 'The subject . . . has been much discussed by Sanskrit scholars, and to many here I have been telling no new thing'.[45] Grierson cited the German Sanskritist Albrecht Weber (1825–1901) as 'the leader of those who maintained the Christian origin of this bhakti', and relied heavily on Weber's booklet, *Zur Indischen Religionsgeschichte—Eine Kursorische Uebersicht* (Stuttgart, 1899), for his own account of the early impact of Christianity.[46]

Grierson argued that *bhakti* was the product of early Nestorian influence on the theology of Ramanuja in the twelfth century. 'Ramanuja taught that God was personal, and that by His prasada or "grace" the faithful after death obtained undisturbed personal bliss "near the Lord"'—but he 'taught all this as a system of philosophy, couched in Sanskrit'. It was not until the north Indian Ramananda walked the earth in the fourteenth century that the loving approach to God found full expression as a popular creed. As a student and, later, teacher in the Ramanuja tradition, Ramananda 'drank afresh at the well of Christian influence'. He broke with caste exclusivity, attracted to himself twelve disciples (the significance of the number is not lost on Grierson) of varying statuses, including an untouchable and a woman, and pronounced the famous phrase, 'Let no one ask a man's caste or sect; whoever adores God, he is God's own.' Ramananda's rejection of both Sanskrit and Brahman privilege resulted in 'the greatest religious revolution that India has ever seen, a revolution the effects of which are still the moving force of the spiritual life of millions upon millions of Hindus'.[47]

The immediate response to this historical portion of Grierson's lecture may be described as a genial skepticism. The retired missionary scholar James Kennedy questioned the trajectory of Christianity's spread into southern Asia and emphasized instead northern connections via the North-West Frontier. Both Kennedy and the young Sanskritist and legal scholar Berriedale Keith (1879–1944) questioned the degree to which a borrowing actually occurred, with the former noting that 'Devotion to a particular deity is a universal feature of religious life, and had been known in India since Vedic times'.[48] Before long Grierson would soften his argument that *bhakti* owed its origins to Christianity and would agree, as his biographers put it, 'that the Indian bhakti was far older than Christianity'.[49] He seems to have been moved in particular by the arguments of R.G. Bhandarkar, who would soon demonstrate the existence of a theology of *bhakti* in the pre-Christian era.[50] By 1908 Grierson was beginning to revise his views,[51] and in his note to the Third International Congress for the History of Religions held at Oxford, September 1908, he acknowledged the important ongoing work of Bhandarkar and others.[52]

Grierson's apparent abandonment of the Christian origins argument did not weaken his deep conviction regarding the importance of *bhakti* in the context of Christianity. What was significant about Grierson's approach, as his critic Kennedy noted, was his focus on and fascination with religious belief in the medieval Indian past.[53] Grierson invited his Royal Asiatic Society audience to accompany him 'into a strange land—strangest of all to those who have studied Indian religions only in the light of Sanskrit literature. We shall visit, for far too brief a space, a land of mysticism and rapture. We shall meet spirits akin, not to the giant schoolmen of Benares, but to the poets and mystics of Mediæval Europe, in sympathy with Bernard of Clairvaux, with Thomas à Kempis, with Eckhart, and with St. Theresa.'[54] Grierson was himself spending considerable time in that 'strange land' as a result of his ongoing work on the *Bhaktamala*. 'In those early days the north of India was filled with wandering devotees, vowed to poverty and purity. Visions, trances, raptures, and even reputed miracles were of common occurrence. Rich noblemen abandoned all their possessions and gave them to the poor, and even the poorest would lay aside a bundle of sticks to light a fire for some chance wandering saint.'

Story after story offered, for Grierson, striking parallels to the message of God's love for humanity contained in the New Testament—of 'being born again', of turning the other cheek, of self-blinding and amputation to cast away sin. 'Much that we read', Grierson allowed, 'is insipid and perhaps even childish to our Western minds, but the student who possesses sympathy with the naïve joy of an Oriental nation that has discovered divine love for the first time will never regret the hours spent in its study.'

Grierson's particular fascination with *bhakti*, and by extension the *Bhaktamala*, stemmed from his interest in it as the product of Hindu–Christianity, or Christian–Hinduism.[55] His views were not the unconscious, discursive product of post-Enlightenment assumptions about religion, but the strongly argued assertions of a late Victorian convinced that Christian Europe's tolerant engagement with Hindu India would enable the latter to fulfil itself religiously.[56] The 'fulfilment' sentiment was not a new one. Inklings of it can be seen in the early seventeenth-century writings of the Jesuit missionary to south India, Roberto de Nobili. It became increasingly popular with many late Victorian Christians uneasy with the heavy-handed dismissal of Hinduism by many Protestant missionaries, and unsettled by the post-Darwinian realization that Christianity itself 'taught what was not true'.[57] Grierson's own profession of faith in the idea emerges in his 1906 essay for *The East and The West*, a missionary quarterly published by the Society for the Propagation of the Gospel in Foreign Parts (an organ of the Church of England). In this essay Grierson rehearsed many of the same points he argued in the Royal Asiatic Society lecture, but from an openly Christian posture. 'Too often', he observes, 'we are asked to look upon the many Hindu religions as being wholly evil, wholly pagan, wholly anti-Christian. I believe, on the contrary, that many of them contain elements due to Christianity, and that it is our duty to foster and purify these elements rather than to destroy them.'[58] He wrote candidly of 'our own religion . . . founded in Palestine', of 'our Lord's birth', of 'our Lord's time', and of how 'our Lord Jesus Christ was born in the little village on the outskirts of Jerusalem.' These are turns of phrase that are conspicuously absent in his Asiatic Society lecture, and probably are as much a reflection of his Anglican audience as his own personal religious convictions. As Kennedy put it, responding to the lecture, 'We admire the extent of his learning and the goodness of his heart, his large sympathy with religious feeling wherever he meets it, and his exhilarating enthusiasm.'[59]

Grierson's sympathies extended only so far, however. He drew the line when it came to what he termed the 'extremist phase' of Krishna-bhakti, 'based on the love of a man for a woman'. This was, for Grierson, a corruption of true Christian bhakti: 'Krishna's legendary exploits as an incarnate God were far from edifying. He is said to have divided the days of his youth between dallying with the herd-maidens among whom he grew up, and destroying demons. . . . Our religion has only been debased by association with [Krishna-bhakti] lewdness.'[60] By contrast, he applauded Ram-bhakti as based on the pure love between father and child. 'There was nothing licentious in the character of Rama. . . . There was nothing ignoble or sensual in the worship directed to him.' He elaborated at length in terms that combine the Christian manliness of Charles Kingsley with the martial romanticism of Rudyard Kipling:[61]

> The contrast between the Rama worshippers of northern India and the Krishna worshippers of Bengal is most marked. The northern Indian is brave, sober, and hard-working. We recruit our armies from his villages. It was the sepoys of northern India who had the courage to stand up against the sahibs in the great Mutiny. It was the villagers of northern India who, in that same Mutiny, gave asylum to hundreds of Englishmen and women fleeing for their lives, and who refused under all temptations to give them up. . . . Rama worship has made a nation of men.[62]

Catalogue

For Grierson, the Christian underpinnings of bhakti had urgent implications for the British in India and, more particularly, for their understanding of India. Consequently he had advice for missionaries, administrators, and scholars. His comment to the former was that 'the Spirit of God does not confine itself to this [the missionary] channel of grace. Christianity is still "in the air" in India as it was in the time of Tulasi Dasa.' In a passage that is an elaboration of Müller, Grierson urged his missionary audience to 'see how, to become the religion of India, Christianity must necessarily grow. As long as it is an exotic, something from a foreign land, and preached by foreign missionaries who impose upon their converts Western thoughts and Western systems of theology unsuited to an oriental mind, it cannot hope for wide acceptance.' Only an *Indian* Christianity, based on *Indian* principles sprung from within, could have hope of 'eventually becoming the national religion of our Indian Empire'.[63]

> Our task must be not to plant full-grown trees but to sow the seed. . . . When it is sprung up our duty begins again—not to force it into the artificial growths of our Western life, but to guide it and guard it from grafting itself on to other trees of baser origin. . . . What may we not hope from it, if the shoot grows strong and vigorous—a true product of Indian soil—free from the contamination of the West and of the East alike?

More significantly, Grierson also had advice for British officials. At the end of his Royal Asiatic Society lecture, he made a plea 'for the serious study of the Indian vernacular literature by all interested in our great Eastern possession, whether as administrators or as missionaries'.[64] He bemoaned the emphasis on Sanskrit in British understandings of India: 'Fashion decrees that we must study Sanskrit or else books written by scholars, great scholars I freely admit, whose linguistic horizon is bounded by that language. . . . No one would pretend that a knowledge, however complete, of the glories of Latin literature would enable anyone to understand or describe modern Italy; and yet it is thus that we seem to think that we can act toward India.' Though 'a knowledge of the old dead language' might 'win respect and admiration' from Indians, it would not earn their love. 'Believe one who has tried it', Grierson urged, 'the quotation of a single verse of Tulasi Das or of a single pithy saying of the wise old Kabir will do more to unlock the hearts and gain the trust of our Eastern fellow-subjects than the most intimate familiarity with the dialectics of Sankara or with the daintiest verse of Kalidasa.' Unlike his arguments about the Christian origins of bhakti, these sentiments were wholeheartedly endorsed by the audience.[65]

Grierson's views, and the views of the scholars, officials, and retired missionaries gathered in the London meeting room of the Royal Asiatic Society, ran counter to and were openly critical of the stream of European knowledge production so often invoked by historians of India, the Orientalism that looked only to Sanskrit knowledge to distil Indological understandings and facilitate, consciously or unconsciously, British imperial power.[66] Grierson eschewed Sanskrit understanding as emblematic of a dead past, utterly irrelevant to the reality of contemporary India. This was a critique in which some Sanskritists shared. Berriedale Keith, who would follow Henry Maine (1822–88) in combining classical Sanskrit with constitutional scholarship, was in the room, and there is no record of his having raised an objection to the anti-Sanskritist sentiment in Grierson's address. Two decades earlier, Müller, the most respected Sanskritist of his day, had found Grierson's position compelling. The two had become acquainted after the publication of Grierson's encyclopedic *Bihar Peasant Life* in 1885. Praising Grierson's efforts, Müller declared that 'Language lives in dialects, and dies in classical languages'.[67] Both Müller and Monier-Williams would become staunch supporters of Grierson's campaign to convince government of the merit of the *Linguistic Survey of India* project.

Grierson's critique of British knowledge did not lead him to eschew British power in India. Rather it was axiomatic for him that, as an obligation of British rule, British administrators should understand India as it is, not as it was—and that Indians in the present were equivalent to Europeans in the present, and that that equivalence was based on a shared set of core religious values in the present and a comparable (and relatively recent) religious past. Like his Sanskritist colleagues, Grierson understood religion, particularly Hinduism, to be fundamental to any understanding of India and Indians, past or present. But unlike them, Grierson decried what he perceived as the tendency of Britons to distance themselves from Indians, to resist intimacy with them, and he saw Sanskrit literary and linguistic study as factor in this distancing syndrome. His was, in this sense, an anti-Orientalizing sentiment—if we understand the term 'Orientalize' in the way it has been deployed in recent scholarship, as displacement and decontextualization. He did not understand this critique to be contradictory to Empire, but rather an obligation of Empire—built out of a personal religious desire for communion with his 'fellow-subjects'.

Given his stature in the British academy, and the thoroughness with which he approached the subsequent task of the *Linguistic Survey of India*—the intellectual outgrowth of his passion for the vernacular—it is not an overstatement to suggest, as Bayly has, that Grierson 'reversed a hundred years of official thinking'.[68] But in needs to be emphasized that he did so because of his Christianity. Furthermore, to understand the full significance of what Grierson was saying in 1906–07, we need to recognize that in so far as he actually believed in the Christian significance of bhakti (and, later, the potential significance of bhakti for Christianity) he may have also believed himself to be, in some vague way, a Hindu. This is not as uncommon as it may seem. Even the missionary-inclined Oxford Sankritist Monier-Williams used to remark off-handedly that he was 'half a Hindu'.[69] Unfortunately, Grierson gives us little on which to proceed. One can only surmise that his acceptance of the view that bhakti predated Christianity only opened him up further to a fluid sense of religious identity. In any case, it would appear that he was perceived as a Hindu–Christian long after he had retired from active scholarship. The American Methodist E. Stanley Jones (1884–1973), author of *The Christ of the Indian Road,*[70] wrote to Grierson twice in 1930 begging for his autograph.[71] Jones would become famous for his use of simple ashram settings to conduct missionary work and for his view that Christianity, to be embraced by India, needed to be stripped of its Western institutional trappings and presented in terms of Christ alone.[72] Grierson seems, in retrospect, to have been an inspiration.

It is possible to read too much into Jones' devotion to Grierson, and it does not in any event offer conclusive evidence of the precise nature of latter's religious convictions. Nevertheless, it is difficult to think of someone who can author the following unpublished passage as someone spiritually unsympathetic to the worship of Ram:

. . . and yet [having acknowledged the persistence in India of the belief in minor 'spirits hungry for oblations', in 'so-called gods' and 'uncounted demons'] there is also Râma,—Râma looking, as they say, down from his lattice-window,—placing each in his state of life, guarding him, rewarding him according to his work,—Râma, the giver of all to all alike, to the fluttering sparrow, even to the creeping snake, and how much more to man,—Râma, who, when man's day's work is done and he stands lonely and shivering on the bleak shore of the ocean of existence before taking the last great plunge, stretches out his arms to him and cries in loving accents, 'come, I will ferry thee across'.[73]

ANALOGUE?

Grierson's views resonated with late nineteenth and early twentieth-century religious responses to British imperialism. How different was Grierson's plea to missionaries to nurture a homegrown Christianity in India from Keshab Chandra Sen's earlier call for an 'Asiatic Christ', in the 1870s? As Partha Chatterjee has noted, 'To Europeans, (Keshab) had this to say: "if you wish to regenerate us Hindus, present Christ to us in his Hindu character. When you bring Christ to us, bring him to us, not as a civilized European, but as an Asiatic ascetic, whose wealth is communion, and whose riches prayers."'[74] And soon after Grierson's essays appeared, Mohandas K. Gandhi began fashioning a response to Empire that called upon Britons to be better Christians. 'We believe', he wrote in *Hind Swaraj*, 'that at heart, you belong to a religious nation. We are living in a land which is the source of religions. How we came together need not be considered, but we can make mutual good use of our condition.'[75] It hardly needs to be said that Gandhi came to this conclusion after long and intimate contact with Christians in England and South Africa.[76]

The overlapping ground of Hinduism and Christianity represented for Grierson (and Sen and Gandhi) a religious topography—'a strange land'—full of opportunities for self-discovery, for arriving at a new sense of imperial subjecthood. It bears asking whether such a topography was visible to individuals more firmly embedded in the religious community that was, for Grierson at any rate, the embodiment of nascent Christian-bhakti values. Unlike Grierson, Bhagvan Prasad did not take up either Christianity or the British Empire in his devotional scholarship in any explicit way. Like Grierson, however, Bhagvan Prasad was open to other religious world-views. According to his early twentieth-century biographer, Sivanandan Sahay, Bhagvan Prasad believed that while 'it is certainly important to place your faith in one religion or point of view and to develop a sentiment for a particular conception of God . . . it is no sin to know and experience the wisdom of other religions as well; it is foolish to erect barriers between any religions or points of view.'[77] Bhagvan Prasad's 'particular conception of God', Sahay explained, was the *yugalsvarup* or 'divine couple' Sita-Ram; and his approach to the coupled Sita-Ram was via the feeling of *shringar-ras* (erotic love). Bhagvan Prasad utilized rigorous role-playing and visualization techniques to recreate the sensory and emotional bliss of the just-married Ram and Sita.[78] Bhagvan Prasad's particular role was that of a female attendant to the young couple, and he is often pictured as such, attired in a white sari with a generally feminine appearance, as in the photograph that accompanies this essay. It was in this connection, Sahay noted, that Bhagvan Prasad was known as *Rupkala*.

The *shringar-ras*-erotica of Bhagvan Prasad seems a far cry from the Ram-worshipping 'nation of men' envisaged by Grierson in 1906–07—based 'on the pure love between father and child'—and closer to the corrupting 'lewdness' that Grierson decried in the 'extremist phase' of Krishna-bhakti. It is unclear whether Grierson fully appreciated the gender dimension of Bhagvan Prasad's religious identity. (Nor, for that matter, do we know whether Bhagvan Prasad knew of the gender dimension in Grierson's understanding.) But Grierson was well acquainted with *rasika* aesthetics and their potentially erotic overtones. In 'Gleanings from the *Bhakta-Mala*', Grierson included a lengthy 'Note on the Employment of the term "Flavour" (*rasa*) in Connection with the Bhakti Religion', in which he observed that 'Every religious attitude depends upon an objective Dominant Emotion, *sthayi bhava*, considered as an abstract condition', which were five in number, and that 'Each of these Dominant Emotions . . . produces a corresponding subjective psychic condition or feeling, technically called *rasa* or "Flavour" in the person subjected to it.' The highest of these is the 'Passionately

Loving Flavour, *srngara rasa* or *madhurya rasa*'. Grierson noted as well the various emotional effects produced by the excitement of the *rasas*, including temporary paralysis, trembling, disturbed speech, change of color, crying, sweating, thrills, unconsciousness, fluster, pining, involuntary gesturing, and rapture.[79] In a concluding comment he underscored his earlier emphasis on the shared ground between Hinduism and Christianity: 'From the above it will be seen that the Hindu love for systems of classification has been carried even into the province of religious emotion; and a very little consideration will show how closely Indian religious experiences, and especially the phenomena attendant on what we should call "conversion", agree with what we know to be prevalent in Christian England.'

Sahay, Bhagvan Prasad's contemporary biographer (writing in 1908), explained Bhagvan Prasad's gender crossing in terms of Christian spirituality, attributing to one 'Newman Sahib' the assertion, 'If thy soul is to go on into higher spiritual blessedness, it must become a *woman*, yes, however manly you may be among men.'[80] Though I have yet to track down the quote, it appears likely that the 'Newman Sahib' referred to was John Henry Cardinal Newman, whose very public conversion to Roman Catholicism from the Church of England created enormous controversy in mid-nineteenth-century Britain. The readership of Sahay's biography of Bhagvan Prasad consisted primarily of Hindus employed in the middle rungs of the provincial administration in Bihar and the United Provinces—civil-service-minded Hindi literati who possessed some English-language fluency as well.[81] So it might seem remarkable that he would look to Newman's words—or what he thought were Newman's words[82]—to explain this aspect of the spiritual life of his subject. On closer inspection, however, Christianity emerges as more than an occasional blip on Bhagvan Prasad's spiritual radar screen. Sahay reported, for example, that one of Bhagvan Prasad's closest friends was one 'Padre Reverend J. B. Archer' of Bhagalpur and Purnea.[83] Though little is known about Archer, he was probably connected to the Anglican Diocese of Bhagalpur, which dates to the late seventeenth century. The Church Mission Society Boy's School at Bhagalpur (dating to the 1840s) and the

Leper Home (established in the 1890s) in the same town were two of its most notable institutions, and it may have been in the schools connection that Bhagvan Prasad met Archer.[84]

More direct evidence of Bhagvan Prasad's interest in Christianity appears in Brajendra Prasad's spiritual memoir of his guru, written forty years after the publication of Sahay's biography. According to Brajendra Prasad, his guru often used 'New Testament language' (*injil ki bhasha*) in his presence, and pasted the walls of his room with numerous English 'mottos' such as 'Love is God, God is Love', 'Remember God', 'Remember Death is Sudden but Sure', and 'Prayer is the key'.[85] Brajendra Prasad also observed that his guru kept a kind of religious diary. Pasted onto a page of the 1929 volume of this diary was the following literary notice from the 4 November, 1928 issue of *The Indian Daily Mail* (the awkward phrasing is due to poor typesetting in Brajendra Prasad's work):

> A European writer has recently written that India has given us three great words: *Bhakti*, Sanyas and Yoga, *but the greatest of these is Bhakti* [86]— 'Calamus' writing in the London 'Inquirer' referring to Mr. J. C. Winstows [*sic*] 'The Indian Mystic'[87] writes about *Bhakti* as under: This is the way of Devotion. *Bhakti* is a beautiful and rich term, as Dr. Stanlay [sic] Jones points out in the 'Christ of the Indian Road' and Mr. Winstows shows us something of its beauty and richness. *Bhakti* is that loving devotion to God which has proved the most dynamic force in the religious life of India. It is good to learn from a Christian book that [in] India a noble conception of God 'as one who loves mankind and thirsts for the response of man's love' and that 'His most characteristic name is Bhagwan the Adorable one, the Supreme Lovable, who gives Himself in love to Man.'
>
> This book (*i.e., Bhaktmal* of Nabhaji) contains a large number of the lives of those who have loved God and their love has been known to be reciprocated.
>
> . . . There are numerous examples which show how people have loved their God—and how through thick and thin they have always been saved by Him.[88]

This news clipping brings the narrative full circle. Bhagvan Prasad's edition of the *Bhaktamala* (the publication of which began in 1903) had enlivened Grierson's passionate commentary on Hinduism and Christianity (1906–07), which in turn seems to have inspired E. Stanley Jones's *The Christ of the Indian Road* (1925), a favourable mention of which in turn finds its way into *The Indian Daily Mail* (1928) and, ultimately, into Bhagvan Prasad's diary (1929). Bhagvan Prasad probably kept the news clipping because it spoke glowingly of a text close to his own heart, the *Bhaktamala*, as emblematic of the common ground shared by Hindus and Christians. But it is worth noting that both English-language books referred to in the notice, Jones' *Christ of the Indian Road* and Winslow's *The Indian Mystic*, emphasize the lessons that bhakti holds for a deeper Christian relationship with God. Jones in particular saw in bhakti 'utter self-abandonment', where the 'Other becomes the life of our life, the very centre of our being', and added: 'This was doubtless Paul's conception of faith, but the word has lost some of its deep original meanings and has become more or less identified with belief or trust. Self-committal is not its principal content. India will restore this through Bhakti.'[89] It would not be an overstatement to suggest, then, that while Grierson hoped that Christianity would fulfil Hinduism in the future, Bhagvan Prasad may have sensed an alternative possibility, namely, that Hinduism was fulfilling Christianity in the present.

The *Indian Daily Mail* clipping may have held a second, more personal meaning for Bhagvan Prasad, captured in the phrase, 'There are numerous examples which show how people have loved their God—and how through thick and thin they have always been saved by Him.' Bhagvan Prasad's experience in the river comes to mind. As it turns out, God had come to the rescue on other occasions. Indeed, these other episodes form a prominent part of Brajendra Prasad's own introduction to his guru's teachings—not least of all because they explain Bhagvan Prasad's 1893 decision to retire from his post as a Sub-Inspector of Schools.[90] The first transpired while Bhagvan Prasad was on an inspection tour near Bihta, a small town about fifty miles west of Patna. At that time, the then director of the Bengal Education Department, Sir Alfred Kraft, had come to Bankipore (the 'civil lines' of Patna city). Bhagvan Prasad's superior, one Inspector Martin, sent a letter to Bhagvan Prasad directing him to return to Bankipore by a certain date to confer with Kraft prior to the latter's departure for Calcutta. Unfortunately the letter was delayed and only arrived fifteen minutes before Kraft's train was set to depart. Distraught at not being able to obey Martin's order, Bhagvan Prasad went to his inspection bungalow and fell asleep. He suddenly awoke to the sound of a bell, and was surprised to see himself sitting in the Bankipore Station waiting room, wearing his work clothes, with the necessary papers in his pocket. He walked out of the waiting room, saw the Director, and immediately proceeded to discuss the important departmental business. After the Director's train departed, Bhagvan Prasad returned to the waiting room and fell back to sleep. When he awoke he was back in the inspection bungalow near Bihta, in his work clothes, with the relevant papers, and with the memory of the miraculous meeting and conversation 'painted upon the canvas of his memory'.

According to Brajendra Prasad, a second and more radical intervention occurred in 1893. On a particular day in October of that year, Bhagvan Prasad was scheduled to take the evening train with Mr. Stag, the Inspector of Schools, to conduct an inspection in a small town south of Patna. However, Bhagvan Prasad missed the appointment because he was engrossed in meditation. When he broke the meditation, he noticed the time and realized that the train must have left without him. Nevertheless he put on his work clothes and rushed to the station, only to have his fears confirmed by the stationmaster that, indeed, the train had departed on schedule. When Bhagvan Prasad later appeared before Mr. Stag, the 'inspector sahib', to apologize, the latter acted surprised and insisted that Bhagvan Prasad had accompanied him on the trip and even 'signed the inspection register'. Stag summoned his orderly, who confirmed that the '*babu* was always with *hazur* and did indeed put his signature in the register'. Upon hearing this, tears welled up in Bhagvan Prasad's eyes; he joined his hands together and declared, 'henceforward I am unable to work',[91] indicating his intention to resign then and there. The inspector was even more surprised and, believing Bhagvan Prasad to be unwell, intimated that he would not accept the resignation, but would have no objection if Bhagvan Prasad wished to take a vacation. Bhagvan Prasad took his leave and returned home. Meanwhile, the Head Clerk of the office, who was a great admirer of Bhagvan Prasad, came to learn of the latter's precipitous act. He urged Bhagvan Prasad to file the appropriate application for pension, and even prepared the necessary papers above Bhagvan Prasad's signature. Bhagvan Prasad replied that, 'pension or no pension, I am going to Ayodhya.' Two or three days later he left for Ayodhya, and he remained there to the end of his life. 'By the grace of Ram, the Head Clerk submitted all the papers for the pension.'[92]

How do we interpret all this? Some would choose to read into these stories a host of hidden meanings that stem from the calculus of colonial domination and resistance, or see Bhagvan Prasad's recourse to Ayodhya as a retreat to a cosseted world, sheltered from the epistemological invasions of the British. Or perhaps Bhagvan Prasad's miraculous encounter was a retreat from Time and History altogether—hence the significance of railway platforms, alarm bells announcing the departures of trains, and stone-faced stationmasters. In this context, it is worth noting that in the decade prior to his retirement, Bhagvan Prasad had lost his father (1885) and wife (1890); his mother passed away two years after his retirement, in 1895.[93] In other words, he was coming face to face with the ravages of time. But such interpretations, whatever glimmers of truth they may contain, reveal more about modern doubt than they do about Bhagvan Prasad's reality, and the reality of his devotees. Recourse to these requires the construction of alternative explanatory scenarios—for example, that Bhagvan Prasad simply forgot to show up for work one day in October of 1893, that his boss, the 'inspector sahib', gently suggested his retirement, and that his friend the head clerk arranged for signatures to be affixed on both the inspection register as well as the pension papers. Or, alternatively, that his memory was playing tricks on him—that he attended all these appointments, but simply forgot and remembered the circumstances differently. In our haste to provide a reasonable (and tragicomic) history situated in colonial anxiety, we would deprive the past of its voice, the central claim of which is that Ram performed miracles on behalf of Bhagvan Prasad. We would lay that claim aside and allow it to gather dust because it bothers us in an age of reason.

Brajendra Prasad the sub-judge and devotee anticipates this

unease and assures his readers that even he had his doubts. He reports that Bhagvan Prasad insisted to him that events occurred in precisely the way he had related them, namely, that he had had no recollection of going on the inspection tour but that the inspector had insisted he had done so.[94] If we are to allow Brajendra Prasad to speak for his guru, we must focus on *his belief* that, on one occasion in history, Ram transported Bhagvan Prasad to a distant railway platform so that he could attend an official meeting, and that on another Ram stood in for him altogether and performed his duties on a routine school inspection. Ram's timely assistance, and his guru's tearful resignation from government employment in response, would have had added meaning for Brajendra Prasad, because it recalled many similar crises in the lives of Ram-worshippers. One such crisis that is particularly instructive occurred in the life of Tulsidas, the early seventeenth-century author of the *Ramcharitmanas* and paradigmatic devotee of Ram. As Bhagvan Prasad described it in his commentary on the *Bhaktamala*, a group of thieves had repeatedly attempted to rob Tulsidas' house, only to be thwarted at every turn by a beautiful, blue-skinned youth armed with bow and arrow. Finally, after a long night of matching wits with this intrepid watchman, the thieves approached the poet and asked, 'who is this brave, blue-skinned boy with bow and arrow that guards your house?' After hearing all the details, tears began to flow from Tulsidas' eyes. Overcome with remorse at the thought that his beloved Ram had taken to guarding his house at night, Tulsidas gave all his possessions to the thieves. They in turn, softened by having gazed unwittingly for so long at Ram, and moved by the love of their intended victim, became pure of heart.[95]

This remembered moment in Tulsidas' life does not aid in explaining the mystery of Bhagvan Prasad's signature on the school inspection register (if any explanation were necessary), but it does (in my view) help us to understand it free of reductionism. The tears that Bhagvan Prasad wept were not tears of humiliation at the prospect of his boss and his underling conspiring to protect his job and pension, nor were they the tears of a colonial babu trapped in the no-man's-land between East and West. They were tears of remorse at the thought that

Ram had intervened to save his reputation. In this sense, his decision to resign on the spot was no different from Tulsidas' abandonment of all his possessions: each act was geared to free Ram from having to bother with such lowly tasks, and each catapulted the actor into a life of blissful asceticism. Some may read in this mixed feelings toward the British—as thieves who come in the night—on the part of Bhagvan Prasad or his devotee Brajendra Prasad. This would not be surprising given the social, economic, and political hierarchies of British India. But the overarching message of Tulsidas' encounter with the thieves is that the roles of victim and victimizer recede into insignificance when confronted by loving devotion to Ram.

EPILOGUE

History is, in large part, a conversation with the past. If we listen to the voices from the British Indian past—if we suspend disbelief and enter that 'strange land' inhabited by the saints and devotees of the *Bhaktamala*, not to mention Bhagvan Prasad and George Grierson—our understanding of the British empire is prodded in a new direction. We are forced to contend with Grierson's call for a trusting love between the fellow subjects of empire, British and Indian alike. We are forced to make intellectual room for Bhagvan Prasad's desire for 'liberal brotherhood among ourselves', and his admonition to 'Love God, government and goodness'. These sentiments, uttered in distant mental retreats, suggest that the British–Indian experience cannot be reduced to colonial antipathy enacted in racism, violence, anxiety, and displacement.

Reading bhakti into British Indian history renders it more imperial and less colonial. This is as it should be. India was not a British colony: to refer to the British domination of India as 'colonialism' suggests that Indians did not take part, but simply watched from the shrinking sidelines while Britons appropriated to themselves the wealth and territory of the subcontinent. Such descriptions may assuage a wounded national pride, or serve some narrow political interest in the present, but it silences a wide range of important voices and meanings. The historiographic logic of 'colonialism' for India, which has produced post-colonial theory globally, creates a mythology of the past where Indian participation in empire never happened. And this is tantamount to saying imperialism itself did not happen.[96]

This is a past with which some historians may not wish to converse. After all, where amidst all this religious love is there room for the violence and inequalities and injustices the British brought to India? To ask this question, however, misses the point. Attending to religious understandings does not mean that we should downplay violence and displacement in our understanding of empire, colonial or otherwise. To the contrary, violence and displacement must be understood alongside, and in terms of, their antonymns, non-violence and embeddedness. Herein lies the significance of Grierson's reference to 1857 where, in one breath, he praises Ram-worshippers for having 'the courage to stand up against the sahibs' *and* for giving 'asylum to hundreds of Englishmen and women fleeing for their lives', for refusing 'under all temptations to give them up'. The hate is meaningless without the love; the love lacks pathos without the hate. The analytical suspension of disbelief aids in joining intimacy (as productive of both love and hate) to inequality, and allows us to understand the political formation that was British India in its entirety.

The *Bhaktamala* puts a premium on love between unequals, between servant and master.[97] This message is conveyed in many ways, but perhaps most powerfully by the example of Nabhadas, the author of the original early seventeenth-century verse. An 'untouchable' orphan adopted into the Ramanandi order, Nabhadas lived a life of such exemplary devotion in service to his brother-devotees that his guru chose him above all others to sing the glory of the *bhaktas*.[98] His was a selfless love that Christians would have found appealing. It is a love that enabled both Grierson and Bhagvan Prasad, on opposite sides of the unequal imperial equation, to find personal, and global, meaning. Was this kind of love simply a mentality of colonial enslavement? Certainly bhakti—and all religious devotionalism—is about subordination, though devotees refer to it in slightly different terms. A grandson of Brajendra Prasad prefers the term 'submission', and his brothers agree.[99] Grierson should be seen in this light. He is disconcerting because, despite his enormous stature in the British intellectual and political establishment, he sought a Hindu–Christian religious communion with Indians, his 'fellow-subjects', as fellow servants of empire. Bhagvan Prasad should make historians uncomfortable for a related reason—and, as with Grierson, this discomfort is why we should pay close attention to him. Despite his long years as a middle-rung 'babu', he seems to have found the government of British India worthy of love, however he may have felt about the British. If these are not attitudes that scholars today would associate with a British linguist and an Indian babu, it is because we are too eager to find images of our secular, anti-colonial selves inscribed in the people who inhabit the past.

NOTES

1. From a printed leaflet by 'Rupkala' (also known as Sitaramsharan Bhagvan Prasad), pasted into his 1923 diary, cited in Brajendra Prasad, *Shri Rupkala Vak Sudha* (The Nectar Discourse of Rupkala), New Delhi: Sarjoo Prasad, 1970, p. 374.
2. This story is told in Brajendra Prasad, *Shri Rupkala Vak Sudha*, p. 23. The author cites 'Sarkar ki Jivani,' which is probably Shivanandan Sahay, *Shri Sitaram Sharan Bhagvan Prasad-ji ki Sachitra Jivani* (an illustrated life of Sri Sitaram Saran Bhagvan Prasad), Patna: Khadgavilas Press, 1908. Unless otherwise noted, all translations are my own.
3. *Census of India*, vol. 1, General Tables, 1892–93, London: pp. 391–2. All Europeans taken together came to 166,428; 'Eurasians' added another 81,044, but this did not include Indian Christians, numbering 1,807,092 (many of whom were Goan, see vol. II, Statistics, p. 16). I am grateful to Philip McEldowney for providing and clarifying these data.
4. Most notably, by Nicholas Dirks, *Castes of Mind: Colonialism and the Making of Modern India*, Princeton: Princeton University Press, 2001, and Bernard S. Cohn, *Colonialism and Its Forms of Knowledge: The British in India*, Princeton: Princeton University Press, 1996.
5. Two prominent examples are Peter van der Veer, *Imperial Encounters: Religion and Modernity in India and Britain*, Princeton: Princeton University Press, 2001, and Gauri Viswanathan, *Outside the Fold: Conversion, Modernity, and Belief*, Princeton: Princeton University Press, 1998.

6. The insights of Edward Said, especially *Orientalism*, New York: Pantheon Books, 1978, and *Culture and Imperialism*, New York: Vintage Books, 1994, are foundational.
7. For example, Antoinette Burton, *Burdens of History: British Feminists, Indian Women, and Imperial Culture, 1865-1915*, Chapel Hill: University of North Carolina Press, 1994, and *At the Heart of the Empire: Indians and the Colonial Encounter in Late-Victorian Britain*, Berkeley: University of California Press, 1998; and Mrinalini Sinha, *Colonial Masculinity: The 'Manly Englishman' and the 'Effeminate Bengali' in the Late Nineteenth Century*, Manchester: Manchester University Press, 1995.
8. Bhatgam Speech, given toward the end of the salt march, March-April 1930, in *Collected Works of Mahatma Gandhi*, vol. 43, New Delhi: Government of India, 1958–1984, p. 146, cited in Dennis Dalton, *Mahatma Gandhi: Nonviolent Power in Action*, New York: Columbia University Press, 1993, p. 110.
9. Van der Veer, *Imperial Encounters*, p. 24, paraphrasing Asad, 'Anthopological Conceptions of Religion: Reflections on Geertz', *Man* n.s. 18, 2, June 1983: pp. 237-59; later published with modifications as 'The Construction of Religion as an Anthropological Category', in his *Genealogies of Religion: Discipline and Reasons of Power in Christianity and Islam*, Baltimore: Johns Hopkins University Press, 1993, pp. 27-54. See also Viswanathan, *Outside the Fold*, pp. xv-xvi.
10. For example, Peter van der Veer (ed.), *Conversion to Modernities: The Globalization of Christianity*, New York: Routledge 1996; cf. C. A. Bayly, *Empire and Information: Intelligence Gathering and Social Communication in India, 1780-1870*, Cambridge: Cambridge University Press, 1996, pp. 191-2. As Bayly notes, 'A generation before the modernist Arya Samaj stepped in to defend ancient religion with print, north Indian Hindu scholars were employing their skills of logical debate to refute, rebuff or incorporate the missionaries. This was no simple Hindu "reaction" to western "impact". . . .'
11. See Arjun Appadurai, 'Is Homo Hierarchicus?' *American Ethnologist*, vol. 13, no. 4, November 1986, pp. 748-9; cf. William R. Pinch, *Peasants and Monks in British India*, Berkeley: University of California Press, 1996, pp. 15-16, for discussion.
12. Lutgendorf, *The Life of a Text: Performing the Ramcaritmanas of Tulsidas*, Berkeley: University of California Press, 1991, p. 362, citing Bayly, *The Local Roots of Indian Politics: Allahabad, 1880-1920*, Oxford: Clarendon Press, 1975, p. 113.

13. Shahid Amin, introduction to the reissuing of William Crooke's 1879, *Glossary of North Indian Peasant Life*, Delhi: Oxford University Press, 1989, pp. xxvi-xxxix; and Bayly, *Empire and Information*, pp. 355-7.
14. George Abraham Grierson, *Bihar Peasant Life*, Calcutta: Bengal Secretariat Press, 1885.
15. George Abraham Grierson, *Linguistic Survey of India*, Calcutta: Office of Superintendent of Government Printing, 1903-22.
16. Sahay, *Shri Sitaram Sharan Bhagvan Prasad-ji ki Sachitra Jivani*, pp. 45-60, and Prasad, *Shri Rupkala Vak Sudha*, pp. 16-17.
17. Brajendra Prasad, *Shri Rupkala Vak Sudha*.
18. Guha, *Dominance without Hegemony: History and Power in Colonial India*, Cambridge: Harvard University Press, 1997, pp. 47-50. Guha includes here a brief discussion of *rasa* (aesthetic) theory, particularly the *rasa* of *dasya*, servitude. See also Guha's *Elementary Aspects of Peasant Insurgency in Colonial India*, Delhi: Oxford University Press, 1983, pp. 18-19. The appeal of this view is considerable, partly because it enables scholars to reconcile bhakti with brahmanical orthodoxy. Viswanathan, for example, takes the view that 'the mystical leanings of bhakti are perfectly consonant with the rigid orthodoxies of hierarchical Brahmanism'—and that the latter both appropriates and makes room for the former. Gauri Viswanathan, *Outside the Fold*, p. 130; see also pp. 89 and 274n19.
19. Chatterjee, *A Nation and Its Fragments: Colonial and Post-Colonial Histories*, Princeton: Princeton University Press, 1993, Chap. 3, 'The Nationalist Elite'.
20. Chakrabarty, *Provincializing Europe: Postcolonial Thought and Historical Difference*, Princeton: Princeton University Press, 2000, pp. 231-2, citing Tapan Raychaudhuri, *Europe Reconsidered: Perceptions of the West in Nineteenth-Century Bengal*, Delhi: Oxford University Press, 1988, pp. 88-9.
21. Dipesh Chakrabarty *Provincializing Europe*, Epilogue: 'Reason and the Critique of Historicism'.
22. 'Caste and Subaltern Consciousness' in Ranajit Guha (ed.), *Subaltern Studies VI: Writings on South Asian History and Society*, Delhi: Oxford University Prsss, 1989, p. 194. Chatterjee is describing pre-colonial as well as colonial Bengal.
23. Gregory argues that church or confessional history is 'skewed by substantive, frequently anachronistic religious claims', while 'secular confessional historians assume—based ultimately on a dogmatic metaphysical naturalism—that no religion is . . . what its believer-

practitioners claim that it is'. Both depend 'in a substantive way on undemonstrated and undemonstrable metaphysical beliefs'. Gregory, 'The Other Confessional History', Wesleyan University Snowdon Lecture on the Study and Teaching of Religion, 1 May 2002, pp. 7-9; I am grateful to the author for permission to quote the lecture. See also his *Salvation at Stake: Christian Martyrdom in Early Modern Europe*, Cambridge, Mass: Harvard University Press, 1999, introduction.

24. His father Tapasviram and his uncle Tulsiram; see my *Peasants and Monks in British India*, pp. 55-6.
25. Bhaktamala means 'garland (*mala*) of devotees (*bhakta*)' and is the title of Nabhadas' 214-stanza work (ca. 1600); Bhagvan Prasad's commentary is titled *Bhaktisudhasvad Vartik Tilak*, or 'tasting-the-nectar-of-bhakti hagiographical gloss'. For this essay I have consulted the 1993 edition from the Tejkumar Press, Lucknow. For more detailed discussion of the intertwining texts, see my 'History, Devotion, and The Search for Nabhadas of Galta', in D. Ali (ed.), *Invoking the Past: The Uses of History in South Asia*, Delhi: Oxford University Press, 1999, esp. pp. 367-75.
26. A good example of the importance of Bhagvan Prasad's work is the degree to which it is relied upon by J.S. Hawley and M. Jurgensmeyer, *Songs of the Saints of India*, New York: Oxford Unviersity Press, 1988, the best general introduction to north Indian Hindu devotionalism.
27. See, e.g., Lutgendorf, *The Life of a Text*, pp. 310-29, citing Bhagavati Prasad Sinha, *Ram-Bhakti men Rasika Sampraday* (The Rasika Community in Ram-Worship), Balrampur: Awadh Sahitya Mandir, 1957.
28. Established in the latter half of the seventeenth century. See Hans Bakker, *Ayodhya*, Groningen: E. Forsten, 1986, part I, pp. 145-6.
29. For example, Catherine Asher, 'Authority, Victory, Commemoration: The Temples of Raja Man Singh', *Journal of Vaisnava Studies*, vol. 3, Summer 1995, pp. 25-35; F. S. Growse, *Mathura, A District Memoir*, rev. ed., Allahabad: NWP and Oudh Government Press, 1882, pp. 241-66; Bakker, *Ayodhya*, pp. 125-53.
30. See my *Peasants and Monks*, Chapter 3; and my 'History, Devotion, and The Search for Nabhadas of Galta', pp. 389-99.
31. For instance, in his blanket ban on itinerant (and usually armed) ascetics from traversing Bengal in 1773, Warren Hastings made an exclusion for 'fixed inhabitants' who 'quietly employ themselves in their religious function'. Hastings drew particular attention to Rāmānandis. See Foreign Department, Secret Branch proceedings

nos. 5 and 6 of 21 Jan 1773 (National Archives of India, New Delhi). Followers of the thirteenth-century Râmânand, Ramanandis are the main proponents of Ram-centered rasika bhakti. Agradas, Tulsidas, and Bhagvan Prasad were all Ramanandis.

32. Bayly, *Rulers, Townsmen and Bazaars: North Indian Society in the Age of British Expansion, 1770-1870*, Cambridge: Cambridge Unversity Press, 1983, esp. pp. 386-93.
33. See C.A. Bayly, *Empire and Information*, passim.
34. Shivnandan Sahay, *Shri Sitaram Sharan Bhagvan Prasad*, pp. 17-18, 37-8; see also my *Peasants and Monks*, pp. 73-4.
35. See, e.g., Grierson's *Notes on the District of Gaya*, Calcutta: Bengal Secretariat Press, 1892.
36. Grierson, 'Gleanings from the Bhakta-Mala', *Journal of the Royal Asiatic Society, 1909-1910* (hereafter *JRAS*): Part I. 'Priya-Dasa's Preface, and the First Four Verses,' and Part II. 'The Avatara System of the Bhagavatas,' *JRAS*, July 1909: pp. 607-44; Part III. 'The Auspicious Marks on the Feet of the Incarnate Deity', Part IV. 'The Bhagavata Nishtas', Part V. 'The Twelve Mighty in the Faith,' and Part VI, 'The Sixteen Archangels', *JRAS* January 1910: pp. 87-109; and Part VII. 'The Forty-Two Beloved of the Lord', *JRAS*, April 1910: pp. 269-306. Grierson had earlier published 'A Verse from the Bhaktamala', in the *JRAS*, July 1907: pp. 679-81.
37. See, e.g., *Bhaktamala*, p. 35.
38. The quotes are from Owen Chadwick, *Victorian Church*, New York: Oxford University Press, 1970, part II, pp. 466, 311, 2. See also Edward R Norman, *The English Catholic Church in the Nineteenth Century*, Oxford: Clarendon Press, 1984.
39. E.B. Pusey to Müller, 2 June 1860, cited in Chadwick, *Victorian Church*, part II, p. 36.
40. Friedrich Max Müller, *Chips from a German Workshop*, vol. 4, New York: C. Scribner's Sons, 1876, p. 261; see the discussion in van der Veer, *Imperial Encounters*, p. 110; and Wilhelm Halbfass, *India and Europe: An Essay in Understanding*, Albany: SUNY Press, 1988, pp. 49-52. The plant metaphor would be embraced by many, including Grierson.
41. Chadwick, *Victorian Church*, pp. 37-8. The first occupant of the Boden Chair, H.H. Wilson (1786–1860), also had missionary inclinations, and this was in keeping with the donor's wishes; van der Veer, *Imperial Encounters*, pp. 108-9.
42. John Muir, *The Course of Divine Revelation: A Brief Outline of the Communications of God's Will to Man, and of the Evidences*

and Doctrines of Christianity with Allusions to Hindu Tenets, Calcutta: Baptist Mission Press, 1846; Growse, *Mathura*, esp. pp. 66-70. For a wider discussion of Growse's generation of scholar-officials, including Grierson, see Bayly, *Empire and Information*, pp. 355-7.

43. 'Hinduism and Early Christianity', *The East and the West: A Quarterly Review for the Study of Missions*, vol. 4, 1906, pp. 135-157; and 'Modern Hinduism and Its Debt to the Nestorians', *JRAS*, April 1907, pp. 311-35. A pamphlet by Grierson that has attracted less attention due to its limited availability is 'Hinduism and Its Scriptures, Ancient and Modern', which he wrote for 'The Bible and the World series', (London: Bible House, n.d.). The only copy I have seen is held in the Oriental and India Office Collection of the British Library (hereafter OIOC), Mss.Eur.E223/75. Large portions of this pamphlet are based on a typescript draft by Grierson (Mss.Eur.E223/4), entitled 'The Birth of a Nation's Soul', dated 1908. See also Krishna Sharma, *Bhakti and the Bhakti Movement: A New Perspective*, New Delhi: Munshiram Manoharlal, 1987, pp. 85-7, where Grierson is understood in the context of European Indologists's understanding of *bhakti* according to Christian categories.
44. In his translation and commentary on the *Bhaktamāla*, Grierson relegated the similarities between Christian saints and their Indian counterparts to the footnotes. See, e.g., Grierson, 'Gleanings', parts I and II, pp. 614n.14, 618n.1 (where he notes that 'The whole idea is a remarkable echo of St. Paul's famous passage in his Epistle to the Philippians'), 640n.2.
45. Grierson, 'Modern Hinduism', p. 317. Grierson cited Auguste Barth, *The Religions of India*, trans. Rev. J. Wood, Boston: Trübner, 1882, see 219 ff., as 'one of the most prominent of those who held the opposite opinion', and Edward Washburn Hopkins, *The Religions of India*, London: Ginn & Co., 1898, 428 ff., as occupying 'an intermediate position'. See also the broader discussion of European understanding in Sharma, *Bhakti and the Bhakti Movement*, chap. III, 'Artificial Formulation,' pp. 74-91.
46. Grierson had translated Weber's booklet for the *Indian Antiquary*; see 'On the History of Religion in India—A Brief Review', *Indian Antiquary*, July 1901, pp. 269-88.
47. Grierson, 'Modern Hinduism', pp. 312-22.
48. 'Notes of the Quarter', *JRAS*, April 1907, pp. 483-92. Kennedy allowed the possibility that 'The influence of the Malabar Christians

may be much greater than has hitherto been supposed; but the question will not be solved until Dr. Grierson has laid before us the contents of the Bhaktamala.'

49. F.W. Thomas and R. L. Turner, 'George Abraham Grierson, 1851-1941', *Proceedings of the British Academy*, vol. 28, p. 12.
50. Bhandarkar, *Vaisnavism, Saivism and Minor Religious Systems*, Strassburg: 1913, part I, esp. pp. 1-60; cf. Sharma, *Bhakti and the Bhakti Movement*, pp. 85-9, on the intersections of Grierson and Bhandarkar's ideas.
51. See Grierson, 'The Narayaniya and the Bhagavatas', *Indian Antiquary*, vol. 37, 1908, pp. 251-62, 373-86.
52. 'The Monotheistic Religion of Ancient India and Its Descendant, the Modern Hindu Doctrine of Faith', printed in its entirety in *The Imperial and Asiatic Quarterly Review and Oriental and Colonial Record*, ser. 3, vol. 28, no. 55/56, 1909, pp. 115-26.
53. 'The influence of the Malabar Christians may be much greater than has hitherto been supposed; but the question will not be solved until Dr. Grierson has laid before us the contents of the Bhaktamala.' 'Notes of the Quarter', *JRAS*, April 1907, p. 485.
54. Grierson, 'Modern Hinduism', p. 319; the remaining quotes in this paragraph come from pp. 321-2.
55. Hence his aside (Grierson, 'Modern Hinduism', p. 317n3) that H.H. Wilson 'deals with some of the people (from the Bhaktamala) whom I shall mention, but not from my point of view'.
56. Cf. Sharma's argument about European understanding of bhakti (including Grierson's) as informed by normative assumptions about religion as monotheism. *Bhakti and the Bhakti Movement*, pp. 74-91; and Asad, 'Construction of Religion'. Though the sources are quiet on his religious upbringing, Grierson appears to have been an Anglican. Born in Ireland, he attended Trinity College, Dublin, between 1868 and 1873, which suggests he was by birth a member of the Church of Ireland, a 'province' of the Anglican Communion. His brother Charles became the Bishop of Down, Connor, and Dromore. See Thomas and Turner, 'George Abraham Grierson, 1851-1941'. I am grateful to my colleague Bruce Masters for clarifying the institutional linkages.
57. Chadwick, *Victorian Church*, part II, p. 2. See Halbfass, *India and Europe*, p. 51, on fulfilment: 'Indian religious concepts and convictions were not to be refuted and dismissed, but instead ought to be led beyond their own limitations to a perfection and fulfilment which the Indians themselves were incapable of seeing without being awakened to it by the Christian missionaries.'

Adherents included, for a time, the missionary-Sanskritist Monier-Williams, who would later dismiss it as 'a limp, flabby, jelly-fish kind of tolerance'.

58. Grierson, 'Hinduism and Early Christianity', pp. 135-6. The quotes in the following sentence are from pp. 136-9, and 144.
59. 'Notes of the Quarter', 477.
60. Grierson, 'Hinduism and Early Christianity', pp. 150, 155. The quotes in the remainder of the paragraph are from pp. 151 and 155.
61. For more on Kingsley and Kipling, see Norman Vance, *The Sinews of the Spirit: The Ideal of Christian Manliness in Victorian Literature and Religious Thought*, Cambridge: Cambridge University Press, 1985. This may have appealed to Grierson as a way of combating what was widely perceived by the British as the effeminacy of the Indian (especially Bengali) male; cf. Ashis Nandy, *The Intimate Enemy: Loss and Recovery of Self Under Colonialism*, Delhi: Oxford University Press, 1983, esp. part one, and Sinha, *Colonial Masculinity*.
62. Grierson was not simply engaging in flights of rhetorical fancy. In the same year that Grierson wrote this passage, a memoir of Joseph Alexander Elliott (1852–1905) was published, which included an account of the flight of the young 'Joey' and his mother from the 1857 uprising in Kotah, near Indore, and their having received the protection of their servant, Ram Din Kahar, 'an absolute and obstinate bhagat' (*bhakta*, or devotee). At one point, they were harboured by a Vaishnava *mahant* (abbot) in what appeared (based on Joey's description) to be a rasika establishment. See Padri Elliott of Faizabad, *A Memorial (Chiefly Autobiographical)*, ed. Rev. A. W. Newboult, London: Kelly, 1906, pp. 82-94. Elliott would become an Anglican priest in Faizabad, adjacent to Ayodhya.
63. Grierson, 'Hinduism and Early Christianity,' pp. 156-7.
64. Grierson, 'Modern Hinduism', pp. 327-8.
65. 'Notes from the Quarter', pp. 485-9. Also present was the Tamil scholar and retired missionary G. U. Pope (1820–1908).
66. See e.g. Ronald Inden, *Imagining India*, Oxford: Basil Blackwell, 1990, chapter 3, esp. pp. 109-15.
67. Müller to Grierson, 21 August 1886.
68. Bayly, *Empire and Information*, p. 356; cf. Shahid Amin's introduction to William Crooke's 1879 *Glossary of North Indian Peasant Life*. Amin argues that 'Crooke and Grierson were not expressly concerned with our history, being more interested in

India's timeless past' (p. xxvii), and cites an earlier letter from Müller to Grierson as evidence: 'I expect to find in your book the houses and carts and utensils of the people very much as they are described in the Veda. . . .' The remainder of the passage, however, gives a different impression: '. . . and I hope that your description will often give me a clearer idea of these things than the re altered (sic) notices in the Veda. I wish you could have added always the Sanskrit names when you give the modern names, but in many cases it is easy to see what the original form must have been.' (Müller to Grierson, 5 January 1886, Mss.Eur.E223/299, OIOC; emphasis added.)

69. Chadwick, *The Victorian Church*, part II, p. 38.
70. E. Stanley Jones, *The Christ of the Indian Road*, New York: Abingdon Press, 1925.
71. Mss.Eur.E223/302 (OIOC, London). Grierson ultimately complied, but not without exasperation, suggesting some ambivalence about his reception in evangelical missionary circles.
72. By the late 1930s Jones would be a household name in the U.S.A., and celebrated as 'the world's greatest missionary' by *Time* magazine (12 December 1938, p. 47). For more on Jones and 'the separation of Christ from Western Culture', see Dana L. Robert, 'The First Globalization: The Internationalization of the Protestant Missionary Movement Between the World Wars', *International Bulletin of Missionary Research*, April 2002, pp. 54-6.
73. This particular passage is not to be found in any of Grierson's published writings, but in a draft typescript from 1908 entitled 'The Birth of a Nation's Soul', Mss.Eur.E223/4, OIOC, p. 25. A scaled-down version of the essay found its way into an undated pamphlet, 'Hinduism and Its Scriptures, Ancient and Modern', which Grierson wrote for 'The Bible and the World series', published by the Bible House, London.
74. Chatterjee, *A Nation and Its Fragments*, p. 41.
75. M.K. Gandhi, *Hind Swaraj and Other Writings*, ed. A. Parel, Cambridge: Cambridge University Press, 1997, p. 115. As Parel notes (115n231), 'Perhaps the most important point in Gandhi's critique of colonialism is that it is inconsistent with the teachings of Christianity.' See also Partha Chatterjee, 'Gandhi and the Critique of Civil Society', R. Guha, *Subaltern Studies III*, ed. Delhi: Oxford University Press, 1984, p. 166: 'In fact the moral charge against the West is not that its religion is inferior but that by wholeheartedly embracing the dubious virtues of modern civilization it has forgotten the true teachings of the Christian faith.'

76. Much of Gandhi's religious logic here, it may be argued, derived from his extensive interaction with members of the Keswick movement in South Africa, who sought to make Christians better Christians. See will Cushing, 'Gandhi and the South Africa Keswick Convention, 1893', *Agora* (an online journal for undergraduate research from Texas A&M University, http://www.tamu.edu/chr/agora/), vol. 2, no. 2, Winter 2001.
77. Sahay, *Shri Sitaram Sharan Bhagvan Prasad*, pp. 39-40.
78. Ibid., p. 36. For a detailed discussion of this aspect of the rasika ethos, see Philip Lutgendorf, 'The Secret Life of Ramcandra of Ayodhya', in Paula Richman (ed.), *Many Ramayanas: The Diversity of Narrative Tradition in South Asia*, Berkeley: University of California Press, 1991, pp. 219-28. Rasika devotional practice consisted of a carefully enacted eight-stage daily cycle, at the end of which Ram and Sita engage in dancing and lovemaking on the banks of the Sarayu River. As Lutgendorf describes it (p. 224): 'The climax of this meditative foreplay is said to be the experience of tatsukh (literally, 'that delight')—a vicarious tasting of the pleasure shared by the divine couple in the union, as witnessed by attendant sakhis and manjaris.'
79. Grierson, 'Gleanings', pp. 611-12.
80. Sahay, *Shri Sitaram Sharan Bhagvan Prasad*, p. 36. Emphasis in the original.
81. A sense of that audience can be had from a list of ninety-nine names of 'colleagues, friends, and followers' provided in Sahay, *Shri Sitaram Sharan Bhagvan Prasad*, pp. 97-114.
82. I have it on good authority that 'Newman never wrote the words quoted—nor anything remotely resembling them' (personal communication, Father Ian Ker, 3 March 2002). Such a view may, nevertheless, have been attributed to Newman by critics who vilified him not only as a papist but as effeminate. See, e.g., Vance, *The Sinews of the Spirit*, pp. 38-41; and David Alderson, *Mansex Fine: Religion, Manliness and Imperialism in Nineteenth-Century British Culture*, Manchester: Manchester University Press, 1998, chap. 3: 'Out of Unreality—J.H. Newman'.
83. Sahay, *Shri Sitaram Sharan Bhagvan Prasad*, pp. 39-40. Such openness on Bhagvan Prasad's part was not restricted to Hindu–Christian relations. Sahay tells another story (pp. 47-8), about 1871–2: while travelling by train between Bariyarpur and Barhiya (in Bihar), Bhagvan Prasad showed great consideration and respect for a fellow passenger, a learned Muslim (maulvi) while he performed his prayer (namaz). Though the maulvi had been put

off by Bhagvan Prasad's sadhu-like appearance, they eventually became good friends.

84. See P. G. Horo, 'Christian Missions and Communities in Bihar', in K. K. Datta and J. Jha (eds.), *Comprehensive History of Bihar*, vol. III, part II, Patna: K.P. Jayaswal Research Institute, 1976, esp. pp. 109-30. I am grateful to Avril Powell (personal communication, 8 February 2002) for clarifying Archer's sectarian identity. It is also possible, however, that Archer was a Roman Catholic priest in the Bihari hinterland of what would become the diocese of Patna after World War I. The Catholics had built extensive networks throughout Bihar dating back to the early 1700s. During the latter half of the nineteenth century, the Capuchins and Jesuits, with the assistance of the Calcutta convent of Sisters of the Institute of the Virgin Mary of Munich, had established numerous schools and churches throughout rural Bihar, including Bhagalpur and Purnea.

85. Prasad, *Shri Rupkala Vak Sudha*, p. 49.

86. Emphasis added. This is a reference to St. Paul, in 1st Corinthians, chapter XIII, verse 13, viz., 'So faith, hope, love abide, these three; but the greatest of these is love.' I am grateful to Richard Elphick and an anonymous reader for drawing my attention to this point.

87. Jack C. Winslow, *The Indian Mystic: Some Thoughts on India's Contribution to Christianity*, London: Student Christian Movement, 1926.

88. *The Indian Daily Mail*, Sunday, 4 November 1928, quoted in Prasad, *Shri Rupkala Vak Sudha*, pp. 448-9.

89. Jones, *The Christ of the Indian Road*, p. 197. Appropriately, Jones concluded his book with an image of Christian missionaries as the girlfriends of the bride at an Indian marriage ceremony (pp. 212-13). 'They usher her into the presence of the bridegroom—that is as far as they can go, then they retire and leave her with her husband. That is our joyous task in India: to know Him, to introduce Him, to retire—not necessarily geographically, but to trust India with the Christ and trust Christ with India. We can only go so far—he and India must go the rest of the way.'

90. Prasad, *Shri Rupkala Vak Sudha*, pp. 21–2.

91. In Hindi: '*ab ham se kaam nahin ho sakta hai*'. Literally, 'work can no longer be done by me'.

92. This episode is remembered slightly differently by Brajendra Prasad's grandsons. According to their recollection of the event, 'Roop kala was a school teacher and one day he did not go to school. That day school Inspector visited the school. Roop Kala feared that he must have lost his job. Next day when he went to school, he was

told by his colleagues that he was present and attendence register was signed by him.' Personal e-mail communication, 23 December 2001, Kailash Jha, who met with the family the same day.

93. Prasad, *Shri Rupkala Vak Sudha*, p. 17.
94. Ibid. p. 22.
95. See *Bhaktamala*, pp. 766-7; Bhagvan Prasad quotes Grierson on p. 759: 'I give much less than the usual estimate when I say that full ninety millions of people base their theories of moral and religious conduct upon his (Tulsidas') writings. . . . Over the whole of the Gangetic valley (Tulsidas') great work (the Ramayana) is better known than the Bible is in England.'
96. See Richard Eaton, '(Re)imag(in)ing Otherness: A Postmortem for the Postmodern in India', *Journal of World History*, vol. 11, no. 1, 2000, p. 70 n44.
97. Mohandas Gandhi learned this lesson from Raychandbhai, the Gujarati mystic, who responded to Gandhi's turn-of-the-century query about the purity of the love between Mr. and Mrs. Gladstone with a query of his own: would not the love between the two be more pure if Mrs. Gladstone were her husband's servant? This repartee confirmed Gandhi in his desire to serve the British Empire by forming volunteer ambulance corps during the Boer War and the Zulu Rebellion, which in turn compelled him to adopt strive for sexual asceticism and commit himself fully to public life. Gandhi, *An Autobiography: The Story of My Experiments with Truth*, Boston: Beacon Press, 1993, pp. 204-6.
98. *Bhaktamala*, pp. 40-6.
99. Conversation with Krishan Kumar, 12 March 2002, New Delhi.

PART II

In Bihar

The Raw and the Simmered: Environmental Contexts of Food and Agrarian Relations in the Gangetic Plain*

James R. Hagen

The contrast between early Gangetic agriculture and that of early northern China offers some useful insights for understanding later Gangetic trends and events. Recent works by scholars of china such as Kang Chao, Dwight Perkins, Cho-yun Hsu, and E. N. Anderson, have suggested strong relationships between early high population densities, the creation of intensive farming

* This research has been directly and indirectly affected by my work with a larger project studying changes in land use in South and South-East Asia for the period 1800 to 1980, and supported by Subcontract No. 19X-43361 C with Duke University under Oak Ridge National Laboratory, Contract No. DE-AC05-840R2400 with the Department of Energy. For more details of this project, see J.F. Richards, James R. Hagen, and Edward S. Haynes, 'Changing Land Use in Bihar, Punjab, and Haryana, 1850–1970', *Modern Asian Studies*, vol. 19, July 1985, pp. 699-732. Recent research in India was made possible by grants from the Smithsonian Institution and the American Institute of Indian Studies. I gratefully acknowledge the assistance of Edward S. Haynes for organizing district level numeric data from our larger project into the multi-district, zonal format of this study. Early in the formation of this study, I benefitted from useful discussions with David Ludden and David Washbrook. I also acknowledge the valuable comments of John F. Richards, Elizabeth P. Flint, Judith Dillion, and Nancy L. Zingrone. Since formulating these interpretations, I have been greatly aided and encouraged by extended discussions with Ester Boserup and Vaclov Smil.

techniques, and styles of cuisine.[1] The early large population in the Hwang He River basin and delta of northern China, with its 'self-fertilizing' loess soil, resulted in the deforestation of the Loess Plateau watershed. A long-term historical trajectory was thus set in place of intensive agricultural input management. The early culinary styles of northern China consisted of intensively preparing foods prior to cooking and then, because of a lack of plentiful firewood, rapidly par-cooking in a wok that requires only grass and crop residues to fuel the short fire and cook the near-raw food. The Chinese case is well documented by others. This study proposes a contrasting case for the Gangetic plain: the simmered food.

The Gangetic plain[2] nurtured a less intensive mode of crop input management because of the the early formation of agricultural systems within an abundant forest and biomass context of adjacent agriculture and the absence of the early population pressure that occurred in China. The householder's culinary styles in the early Gangetic plain entailed intensively preparing foods before cooking but then the use of significantly larger requirement of slow-burning fuel than in China, for the steady simmering of pulses, spices, and vegetables with the oil of clarified butter, or ghee, as well as fuel for a preparation of either rice or wheat/millet. The preparation of ghee is itself fuel intensive, in contrast to the absence of milk and milk products in China.[3]

Gangetic cultivators, prior to the nineteenth century, relied on increasing production through the extension of the cultivated area rather than intensifying production per plot as in early northern China. This Gangetic style worked so long as the population remained moderate and adjacent forest and biomass were plentiful.[4] Such extensive systems gave cultivators options and choices as to how much to produce at any one season and this no doubt offered flexibility in their relations with overlords seeking rent/tribute from their surplus. As I will suggest later, the decline in this flexibility during the nineteenth and twentieth centuries would alter the context of agrarian relations.

Prior to the sixteenth century, Gangetic forest and biomass declined imperceptibly as population increased gradually. There was no compelling rise in population density, as in early China, to signal and force a grand system change at that time. However, with the slow decline in adjacent biomass, Gangetic cultivators did begin to change. But without strong signals indicating their changed environmental context, cultivators were lulled into, in a sense, a scavenger-input, and incremental coping version of the former system. Since the seventeenth and eighteenth centuries, there was greater reliance on the short-term, risk-averting strategies that are commonly described in world peasant literature. Cultivators now had only marginal soils left into which they could extend cultivation and were now with their backs against the wall regarding natural resource inputs.

This new mode of agriculture represents the type of agricultural system found on the plain during the past century. When a compelling rise in population density did occur in the nineteenth and twentieth centuries, the resources for inputs were so meagre—as illustrated by the rapid increase in the use of cow dung for household fuel instead of field manure—that when the ponderous agrarian political-tenurial framework of the colonial period combined with these conditions, the total effect weighed too heavily upon the agricultural population to allow for the needed system-level change in the mode of resource input management. As land-use statistics show, the rich adjacent biomass was depleted by the time of the increase in population density during the past century. This historical timing was a fatefully cruel trick and would have tragic consequences for the region. True, these consequences varied throughout the plain and later I will trace the course of changes in three main regions, concluding with Bihar.

Before looking into the details of the story, however, we must understand here that in the history of world agriculture Gangetic India is perhaps incomparable. Over the millennia there was never a 'know-how' problem regarding how to intensify production on the same plot. There was never a time when indigenous knowledge of agriculture was not first-rate in the world. In this context it should be remembered that the transplantation of wet rice first originated during the sixth century BC in the amply watered fields below the Rajgir Hills in Patna District in hundreds of ancient villages such as Nalanda and Aungari. Nevertheless, even with this sophisticated knowledge-base over time, there still needed to be a compelling historical force to redirect the modes of cultivation on a day-to-day level. And that would not happen.

The Distinctive Character of Gangetic Agricultural History

Recent archaeological studies have stressed that early technology may not have radically changed the distribution of vegetation in India as much as previously thought. The early impact of mining and the use of iron tools were often considered as preconditioning the patterns of settlement and state formation during the first millennium BC. This view is now softened with greater emphasis on the critical development of strong social and political institutions.[5] Moreover, Ghosh and Lal have suggested that the process of forest clearance was gradual and in stride with the needs of the patterns of settlement expansion, rather than a process of massive clearance following the introduction of iron tools. Lal views this slow clearance process as the historical norm until the seventeenth and eighteenth centuries, when a faster rate of clearance began.[6] This slower clearance process indicates a relatively large area of forest, woods, and natural vegetation that was inter-patterned with natural topography and human settlements.[7]

To help interpret these land use data, I draw upon a body of literature developed since the 1960s termed 'agricultural intensification theory'.[8] This literature stems from Ester Boserup, who made population change an independent variable rather that one that was dependent on changes in agricultural technology, organization, and production. For Boserup, agriculture responds to demographic changes by adjusting investment in labour, technology, and land use. This is pushed along by declining marginal returns to labour with the increase of population density. Population density, then, is at least one important driver of agricultural change. Therefore, the intensification of agriculture occurs either as (1) increased investments of labour and improved inputs of nutrients, technology, and/or organization on existing plots of land, as in early northern China, or as (2) increased investments of labour, and/or these same inputs of new extended plots of land. I would argue that the latter fits best with the evidence available for the Gangetic plain.

Using statistical data from Mughal records, as interpreted by Irfan Habib and Shireen Moosvi, roughly two-thirds of the Gangetic plain remained under natural vegetation in 1600 (see Table 1). I have discussed elsewhere the ecological benefits, both direct and indirect, from the close juxtaposition of field and forest. One example is that with the decline of forest and woods, and therefore fuel-wood, cow dung became increasingly used for heating fuel and thus potentially diverted from use as cropping manure. Habib notes that in 1600 there was a liberal use of cow dung as crop manure except in the Delhi-Agra area.[9]

The cultivator in 1600 had productive options in his negotiations with overlords which would be unavailable to his modern counterparts. Options of being able to regulate production were virtually eliminated with the decline of the rich biomass environment.

Agricultural Changes since the Eighteenth Century

With the slow decline in the natural area of biomass since the seventeenth century, the following eight changes appeared. The first was the decline in crop nutrition that accompanied less use of manure for cereal grains as well as the decline of indirect manuring within an adjacent, abundant biomass.[10] This affected the general nutrient level, humus content, and moisture level of the plain.[11] The increasingly scarce manure and sweepings were used only for household garden plots and specialty crops such as betel leaf, sugarcane, or opium.[12] The decline of staple crop manuring seemed to follow a spatial pattern of first appearing in the populous wet regions and then throughout the less populous dry zones.[13] By 1945, the lack of staple crop manuring had become so common place that the colonial government cited it as one of the chief reasons for low production, while at the same time not recognizing that it was formerly part of the agricultural system. In the words of the Bengal Famine Inquiry Commission's final report: 'Hitherto the use of manures has been confined largely to the more profitable among the cash crops, such as tobacco, sugarcane, and vegetables, and the amount of manure applied to the land on which the main crops are grown has been very small.'[14]

The second feature was increased intercropping of pulses and

Table 1: Changes in Land Use, 1600–1980

ARABLE PERCENTAGE OF GANGETIC PLAIN AND TOTAL POPULATION

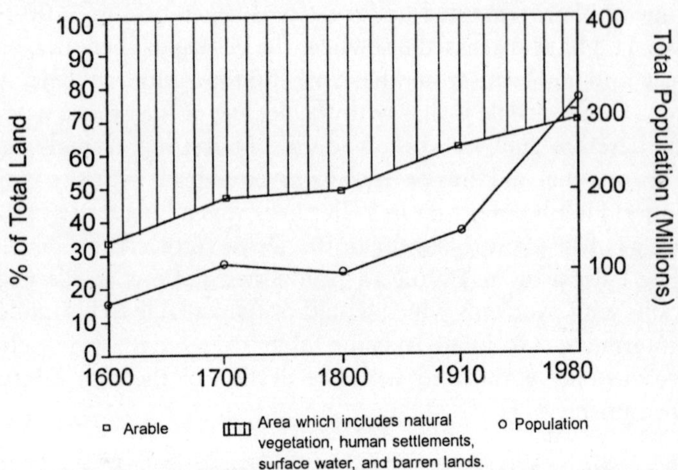

Sources: Irfan Habib, *An Atlas of the Mughal Empire: Political and Economic Maps with Detailed Notes, Bibliography and Index*, Delhi: Oxford University Press, 1982; and Shireen Moosvi, *The Economy of the Mughal Empire c. 1595: A Statistical Study*, Delhi: Oxford University Press, 1987. More recent data were drawn from the various volumes of the *Agricultural Statistics of India* volumes from 1884 to 1974, from parallel provincial and district statistical series after 1947, from the reports on the land revenue settlements of the various disticts, and from the district gazetteers from the mid-nineteenth century through the 1980s.

grains, that is, the mixing of the two crops on the same plot. Intercropping both contributed nitrogen to the soil and also worked as a valuable hedge against total crop failure, since drought resistant pulses would survive when the grain did not.[15] Third, cultivators in the nineteenth and early twentieth centuries also adapted to much greater use of double or multi-cropping, that is, cropping in different seasons, often but not always in the same plot.[16] Although it was a nutrient-draining practice, it was seen as an important short-term hedge against crop failure.[17]

The fourth feature in the new style of agriculture was that livestock was afforded both added importance and less to eat. With the resource base to support livestock greatly reduced,[18] the cultivator turned to marginal lands as a source for special crop manure, and as a source of household fuel.[19]

Fifth, as cultivators tightened their use of manure and sweepings during the nineteenth century, they also decreased their own production of seed grain. Seed production soon lost its urgency in the new agricultural style when the trade-off was some increase in food production. Cultivators with a short-term view now easily took the seed credit offered by their moneylenders and/or landlords, reflecting a widening relationship of credit bonding between these parties.[20]

Sixth, indigenous irrigation fell into disrepair despite an increasing need for crop watering. The primary obstacle to more effective irrigation was the trend of the subdivision of land rights as by then rigidly defined in the new colonial legal regime. The increased number of persons responsible through subdivision caused greater disrepair in the irrigation systems. This was most acute in the deeply structured land systems of the eastern region where irrigation systems had operated within produce rent areas such as in Bihar. Such areas were profit-related to guarantee good irrigation maintenance. When produce rents were commuted to cash in the 1900s, landlords increasingly disregarded their 'traditional' irrigation responsibilities.[21]

Seventh, toward the end of the period, certain regions tended toward crop specialization rather than local mixed cropping.[22] Where formerly there had been a mix in varieties of plants, such as cotton, sugar cane, grains, oilseeds, and pulses, there was now more monocropping determined by how a particular soil type fared under the new low levels of nutrient and organic inputs.[23]

Eighth and finally, the new context of reduced resources and urgent production goals restricted the cultivators' option of leaving plots fallow.[24] This no-fallow trend was heightened at the end of the nineteenth century as the optimal areal extent of cultivation was reached in more and more districts of the plain. Gangetic cultivators, as argued here, had operated their agriculture using the extension of land within a plentiful biomass. They had always worked with the option of building their nutrient and organic soil bases through rotating, resting, and restoring older lands. This systemic was now at an end.[25]

Comparisons among Gangetic Regions, 1600-1980

With the signs of steadily rising population densities and declining biomass, it may be asked why cultivators failed to adapt or intensify—rather than abandon—their styles and systems to meet the challenges described above. The three main regions of the Gangetic plain—the lower wet region (present-day West Bengal and Bangladesh), the middle mixed region (Bihar and eastern UP), and the upper dry region (central and western UP, Haryana, and eastern Punjab)—each experienced these eight trends in quite different, and revealing, ways.

The lower, wet region was the most prosperous and successful in 1600. Gifted with natural moisture, soil fertility, and a thriving sea trade, the wet region was self-described as 'golden Bengal'. Population increased roughly 500 per cent between 1600 and 1980, but this did not compel agricultural changes because of the historical timing of the increases. In 1770 a devastating, entitlement famine over the western areas of the region served as a major disincentive for intensification at a crucial point, namely, the beginning of the colonial period. An estimated one-third of the population died in the affected areas. Cultivation was withdrawn from many lands and long fallow areas were created.[26] The tragic event offered a false signal to cultivators and initiated a new round of arable extension. However this time, tribal labour, mainly that of Santals recruited from nearby uplands, were used to extend cultivation.[27]

For decades to come, the famine of 1770 masked the true conditions in the region. A number of factors continued to hide the effects of biomass depletion and regionally rising population density. The most important was the continuing existence, until about 1900, of additional cultivable land for expansion. A second factor was the continuous string, over centuries, of export-led cash crops. In 1600 these consisted of the famous silky cotton near Dhaka, as well as an export trade in rice, sugar, and ghee. In the eighteenth century indigo became a sensational export, and then jute followed in the nineteenth century. Jute had an additional masking impact. The British introduced a growing demand for jute for their home manufacturing, but such extractive trade did not encourage agricultural intensification. It eliminated fertile land areas of food production and locked tenants and wage labourers into poverty given the heavily structured and inequitable land-access systems in East Bengal. In these circumstances, cultivators had no opportunities to respond to signals encouraging water and land intensification.

In the late nineteenth century the British deforested the Irrawaddy Delta of Burma and very cheap rice came to Bengal. Rather than incite competitive rice intensification in Bengal, the outcome, at this crucial time, was to muffle such urges. Finally, the more plentiful rainfall of this region allowed for quicker regrowth and therefore at least a minimum of grass and scrub vegetation which was very sparse in the other regions.

After 1900, a number of conditions in the wet region seemed compelling enough to perhaps modify the agricultural system. These were the absence of potentially new lands, the dramatic decline in natural vegetation in non-inundated areas that had been more dependent on adjacent use of the landscape, and a decline in the mortality rate which put population pressure on rural society. Why did the systems of cultivation not change at this point? One immediate answer was the escape-valve migration of peasants at this time, especially from Mymensingh District, into the riverine areas of Assam. Another answer is the continued availability of cheap rice from Burma. The main reason, however, may be the heavy burden of institutional commitments to ongoing agricultural practices that by this time existed in the agrarian system and structure in the face of signals to change.[28]

The dry region has had the lowest population density history of the three regions since 1600. It has also had the least to lose by the common trends of the plain. The conventional picture of the dry region is that of a hard-won agricultural surplus derived from the most drought-prone regions of the plain. At least part of this picture may by misleading. Two underlying ecological factors contribute to a somewhat different and balanced assessment. Both factors are indicated from scientific research, but have yet to be integrated into historical explanation. The first is the nature of the different rivers. The silt from high glacier-fed rivers, such as the Ganges and Jamuna, having traversed extensive highland areas, gives greater fertility than do the lower hill or lake fed rivers such as those of Rohilkhand

and Awadh. This high fertility is also the case with the snow fed alluviums of Haryana and Punjab.[29] These factors have softened the impact of the breakdown in the traditional field-biomass system in these areas.

A second factor affecting the dry region is the specific distribution of grasses and livestock. The grass communities in these areas included some of the most advantageous species for livestock found in South Asia. Comparable quality grass distributions are only found in the now dairy-rich district of former Baroda State in Gujarat. Chief among these grasses is the protein-rich, drought resistant *jargu* grass (*Dichanthium annulatum*). Its highly palatable and nutritious companion is *Cenchrus ciliaris*. These important grasses are dominant in the dry region and only found in patches elsewhere in the plain. They can survive down to a bare soil extinction and then reappear as an annual.[30] These grasses provided a buffer against the general trend of biomass depletion. Additional livestock, however, countered this buffer by creating landscapes of erosion.

The millet/wheat cropping pattern of the dry region restricted population density compared to the rice regions. This gave the dry region a stronger position in its response to the general trends, a response that was enhanced still further by the tremendous capital investment by the colonial government since the 1830s in canal irrigation works. A final feature that aided the dry region was the more prevalent kind of agrarian-tenurial systems that were lighter in structure—that is, less marked by subinfendation—and often included owner-cultivators. These light systems reflected the mode of dry grain cultivation with its simpler labour requirements. This may have allowed agriculture to respond more quickly to demographic, market, and environmental forces compared to those of the other regions.

The middle region of Bihar and eastern UP was a mixture of the other regions. This mix made it the most vulnerable in the interplay among the trends of biomass depletion, population change, and arable extension. Its weakness lay in not being consistently wet or dry. Over the past four centuries, rice continued to be the primary cereal crop. However, rice was always highly problematic because of the insecure monsoon climate in the middle plain.[31] Especially in south Bihar, water management has been of critical importance.

Rice production allows more calories per unit area to be made available to encourage an increasing population density.[32] Such a context did not prepare the middle region for the head-on meeting of the general trends of the plain. The social context of agriculture has been a combination of the dry and wet regions. However, because of the primacy of rice, rural society here is more of a reflection of the wet rice agrarian system. Like the wet region, the labour demands encourage a distinction between those who actually ploughed, called *chase*, and those who did not. Like the wet region, most of the mixed region underwent the legal regime of 'permanent settlement' to institute *zamindari* property rights in 1793. Therefore the social context of agriculture for the region represented the very ponderous and thick combination of increasing subdivisions of holdings and the bottom-heavy kind of rural society that stemmed from the labor requirements of wet rice cultivation. However, the middle region seems to have taken this heavy agrarian structure one step further. This was perhaps because of the critical necessity of mobilizing water management. Like the wet region, this ponderous agrarian structure was a primary reason the agricultural systems were not able to respond when population densities began to rise at a faster rate.

Of the three regions, the middle had the most to lose by depletion of natural vegetation. On the one hand, it was not a cattle breeding area with the nutritious grasses of the western plain. The creation of a savannah landscape was more of a strain on rural society compared with the dry region. On the other hand, unlike the wet region, most of the middle region did not have a rapid regeneration of at least a scrubland cover of vegetation. The decline of biomass was particularly severe by the end of the nineteenth century, at which time most districts had reached their optimal extent of cultivated area. Although the middle region began with less depletion of total area than the dry region, my land-use reconstructions indicate that by 1890 the middle region had more of its total area in a degraded condition than the dry region.

As elsewhere in the Gangetic plain, biomass depletion and arable expansion were masked by a continuing supply of cultivable lands. As the availability of these increasingly marginal soils came to an end towards the end of the nineteenth century, the stark picture of rural social distress began to appear. Tenants and sub-tenants, competing over more and more marginal soil types, began to assert their customary rights against each other and against their overlords. Because the middle region had the most to lose by these processes common to the plain, it is not surprising to see that the middle region became the epicentre and most active area of peasant-land conflict in South Asia.[33] Under the former, biomass-abundant, style of agriculture, of say 1600, cultivators had the water and nutrient inputs necessary to adjust production needs. They were thus in a stronger bargaining position in their relations with overlords.[34] However, in the new style of input-poor agriculture, evolving during the eighteenth and nineteenth centuries, their production elasticity virtually vanished and their bargaining position with overlords became similarly affected. This kind of tightening in the productive options, or productive power, in rural society was a general process and effect throughout the entire Gangetic plain.[35] All levels of society were affected and the process raised the level of tensions among competing groups. In the 1920s this was the context at least partly responsible for the creation of South Asia's primary peasant organization, the all-India Kisan Sabha,[36] organized first in the south Bihar district of Patna in the middle region.

In conclusion, there is reason to believe that undetected below our many constructions of Gangetic agrarian history since 1600 there was a significant shift in the productive options of cultivators. If the history of Gangetic agriculture was to extend cultivation to meet the needs of a growing population, then today's lack of prosperity is understandable. Although population increased 430 per cent between 1600 and 1980, arable land was extended only 112 per cent.

NOTES

1. See Kang Chao, *Man and Land in Chinese History: An Economic Analysis*, Stanford: Stanford University Press, 1986; Dwight H. Perkins, *Agricultural Development in China, 1368-1968*, Chicago:

Adline, 1969; Cho-yun Hsu, *Han Agriculture*, Seattle: University of Washington Press, 1980; E.N. Anderson, *The Food of China*, New Haven: Yale University Press, 1988, pp. 1-45.

2. For descriptions of Gangetic culinary traditions see Aninda K. Chakravarti, 'Diet and Disease: Some Cultural Aspects of Food Use in India,' in Allen G. Noble and Ashok K. Dutt, eds., *India: Cultural Patterns and Processes*, Boulder: Westview Press, 1982, pp. 305-26.
3. For example, see Paul Wheatley, 'A Note on the Extension of Milking Practices into Southeast Asia during the First Millennium A.D.', *Anthropos*, vol. 60, 1965, pp. 577-90; and also Frederick J. Simoons, 'The Traditional Limits of Milking and Milk Use in Southern Asia', *Anthropos*, vol. 65, 1970, pp. 547-80.
4. In this study, I prefer to use the term 'biomass' because it encompasses both plants and animals, or 'total dry weight of all living organisms in a given area', rather than a term for plants only such as 'phytomass'. This more inclusive term is important because as vegetation declines or increases in geographical area so is there also change in density and diversity of animal life. See G. Tyler Miller, Jr., *Living in the Environment: An Introduction to Environmental Science*, Belmont: Wadsworth, 1988, p. A-40.
5. See D.K. Chakrabarti, 'Concept of Urban Revolution and the Indian Context', *Puratattva*, vol. 6, 1973, pp. 27-32; 'Beginning of Iron and Social Change in India', *Indian Studies: Past and Present*, vol. 14, 1973, pp. 329-38. Also A. Ghosh, *The City in Early Historic India*, Simla: Indian Institute of Advanced Study, 1973; and George Erdosy, 'Settlement Archaeology of the Kausambi Region', *Man and Environment*, vol. 9, 1985, pp. 66-79. I thank the palaeobotanists K.S. Saraswat and Vishnu-Mittre, at the Birbal Sahni Institute of Palaeobotany, Lucknow, for stimulating discussions of these points during my 1985 visit.
6. For example, see D.P. Agrawal, *The Copper Bronze Age in India*, Delhi: Munshiram Manoharlal 1971; N.R. Banerjee, *Iron Age in India*, Delhi: Munshiram Manoharlal, 1965; and R.S. Sharma, 'Material Background of the Origin of Buddhism', in *Das Canitai Centenary Volume*, (Delhi, 1965), re-issued in Bhairabi Prasad Sahu (ed.), *Iron and Social Change in Early India*, Delhi: Oxford University Press, 2006, pp. 42-48.
7. For the extension of this direction of argument toward the process of forest clearance, see N.R. Ray, 'Technology and Social Changes in Early Indian History: A Note Posing Theoretical Question,' *Puratattva*, vol. 8, 1978, pp. 132-8; and Makhan Lal, 'Iron Tools,

Forest Clearance and Urbanisation', in Makkan Lal, *Settlement History and the Rise of Civilization in the Ganga-Yamuna Doab*, New Delhi: B.R. Publ. Corp., 1984.

8. For some of the applicable literature regarding agricultural intensification, see Ester Boserup, *The Conditions of Agricultural Growth*, London: Allen & Unwin, 1965; Ester Boserup, 'Environment, Population, and Technology in Primitive Societies', *Population and Development Review*, vol. 2, 1976, pp. 21-36; Ester Boserup, *Population and Technological Change: A Study of Long-Term Trends*, Chicago: University of Chicago Press, 1981; H.C. Brookfield, 'Local Study and Comparative Method: An Example from Central New Guinea', *Annals of the Association of American Geographers* (hereafter *AAAG*), vol. 52, 1962, pp. 242-52; H.C. Brookfield, 'Intensification and Disintensification in Pacific Agriculture', *Pacific View Point*, Vol. 13, 1977, pp. 30-48; B.L. Turner II, Robert Q. Hanham, and Anthony V. Portararo, 'Population Pressure and Agricultural Intensity', *AAAG*, vol. 67, 1977, pp. 384-96; J. Adams, and B. Bumb, 'Determinants of Agricultural Productivity', *Economic Development and Cultural Change*, vol. 27, 1979, pp. 705-22; Edison Dayal, 'Agricultural Productivity in India: A Spatial Analysis', *AAAG*, vol. 74, 1984, pp. 98-123.

9. The baseline date for this study is 1600, the approximate date of the great survey (for purpose of taxation), directed by Abu-al-Fazl ibn Mubarak, an agent of the Mughal Emperor Akbar (1542–1605). On this, see the important sources: Abu-al-Fazl, *Ain i Akbari*, tr. H. Blochmann, Lahore, 1975, reprint of 2nd edn., originally published. 1927; Irfan Habib, *An Atlas of the Mughal Empire: Political and Economic Maps with Detailed Notes, Bibliography and Index*, Delhi: Oxford University Press, 1982; and Shireen Moosvi, *The Economy of the Mughal Empire c. 1595: A Statistical Study*, Delhi: Oxford University Press, 1987. I have used Moosvi's analysis and estimates for both arable and population. Her sources were the statistical tables in the accounts of individual provinces in the third book (*Murk abadi*) of the *Ain i Akbari*. I have also used her methodology with the land use numbers reported by Habib for the Aurangzeb period *ca.* 1700. For this, see John F. Richards, James R. Hagen, Elizabeth P. Flint, and Judith B. Dillon, 'Environmental History of the Gangetic Plain, 1600-1980', paper presented at the symposium, 'The Earth as Transformed by Human Action', Clark University, Worcester, Mass., 25-30, October 1987.

10. See J.E.M. Arnold, 'Wood Energy and Rural Communities', *Natural Resources Forum*, vol. 3, 1979, pp. 229-52.
11. S. Kolade Adeyoju, 'The Future of Tropical Agroforestry Systems', *Commonwealth Forestry Review*, vol. 59, 1980, pp. 155-61.
12. See Irfan Habib, *The Agrarian System of Mughal India (1556-1707)*, Bombay: Asia Publishing House, 1963, p. 56, where he draws on the observations of the Seventeenth-century travelers, Pelsaert and Ovington. Francisco Pelsaert, 'Remonstrantie', *c.* 1626, tr. Moreland and Geyl, *Jahangir's India*, London: Cambridge University Press, 1925, p. 4; J. Ovington, *A Voyage to Surat in the Year 1689*, ed. H.G. Rawlinson, London: Oxford University Press, 1929, p. 183; also see P.N. Deogun, 'Punjab and Colonization', *Indian Forester*, vol. 68, 1942, pp. 74-81.
13. Staple manuring declined in the wet zones in the 1810 while light staple manuring was still taking place in the drier zones in 1838. For the dry zones, see Donald Butler, *Outlines of the Topography and Statistics of the Southern Districts of Oudh and of the Cantoment of Sultanpur-Oudh*, Calcutta: Bengal Military Orphan Press, 1839, p. 56. For the wet zones, see R. Montgomery Martin, *The History, Antiquities, Topography, and Statistics of Eastern India*, London: W.H. Allen and Co., 1838, vol. 3, pp. 267-8; vol. 2, pp. 216, 532; vol. 1, pp. 293 (though Martin elides the point, the author of these pages is Francis Buchanan).
14. Government of India, *The Famine Inquiry Commission: Final Report*, Madras: Government Press, 1945, pp. 144-50, esp. 144.
15. For descriptions of intercropping, see George A. Grierson, *Bihar Peasant Life*, 1885, Reprint ed., Delhi: Cosmo, 1975, pp. 246-51; Francis Buchanan, (afterwards Hamilton), *An Account of the Districts of Bihar and Patna in 1811-1812*, Patna: Bihar and Orissa Research Society, 1928, vol. 2, pp. 522-5, 776; W.W. Hunter, *A Statistical Account of Bengal*, London: Trübner and Co., 1875–1877, vol. 11, pp. 140-65; F. N. Wright, *Memorandum on Agriculture in the District of Cawnpore, Allahabad: Northwestern Provinces and Oudh*, Calcutta: Government Press, 1877, p. 23; Hifzur Rahman, and Azimuddin Qureshi. 'Pulses in Indian Agriculture', *Geographer*, vol. 30, 1983, pp. 75-81; Tapan Raychaudhuri, 'The Mid-Eighteenth-Century Background', in Tapan Raychaudhuri and Dharma Kumar (eds.), *The Cambridge Economic History of India*, vol. II, Cambridge: Cambridge University Press, 1982, pp. 3-35, esp. 16-18; Birendranath Ganguli, *Trends of Agriculture and Population in the Ganges Valley*, London: Methuen & Co., 1938, p. 103.

16. The consequent depletion of the soil may have contributed to the increased incidence of famine reported under British rule. For this line of reasoning, see William Digby, *Prosperous British India*, London: Unwin, 1901; B.M. Bhatia, *Famines in India*, Bombay: Asia Publishing House, 1963; and Ira Klein, 'Population and Agriculture in Northern India, 1872-1921', *Modern Asian Studies*, vol. 8, 1974, pp. 191-216.
17. For examples, see Radhakamal Mukerjee, *Fields and Farmers in Oudh*, Madras: Longmans, Green and Co., 1929, p. 13; H.M. Leake, 'The Trend of Agricultural Development in the United Provinces', *Agricultural Journal of India*, vol. 18, 1923, pp. 10-22; P. Dayal, 'The Agricultural Geography of Bihar', PhD dissertation, London University, 1947, p. 263; Birendranath Ganguli, *Trends of Agriculture and Population in the Ganges Valley*, London: Methuen & Co., 1938, pp. 42-57, 103, 150-68; and S.R. Bose, *A Study in Bihar Agriculture*, Calcutta: Firma K.L. Mukhopadhyay, 1967, p. 8.
18. See Grierson, *Bihar Peasant Life*, p. 243.
19. For examples, see John Augustus Voelcker, *Report on the Improvement of Indian Agriculture*, 2nd edition, Calcutta: Superintendent of Government Printing, 1897, pp. 191-207; J. MacKenna, 'Notes on the Fodder Problem in India', *Agricultural Journal of India*, vol. 11, 1914, pp. 38-58; Government of India, *The Famine Inquiry Commission*, 1945, pp. 19, 176-93; W. David Hopper, 'Seasonal Labour cycles in an Eastern Uttar Pradesh Village', *Eastern Anthropologist*, vol. 8, 1955; H. Martin Leake, *The Foundations of Indian Agriculture*, Cambridge: W. Hefter 1923, pp. 39-69; N. A. Mujumdar, 'Cow Dung as Manure', *Economic Weekly*, vol. 12, 1960, pp. 743-44; R. B. Venkatraman, 'The Indian Village, Its Past, Present, Future', *Agriculture and Livestock in India*, vol. 7, 1938, pp. 702-10.
20. In 1890 John Voelcker, after touring the Gangetic Plain, observed that '. . . the root of the mischief lies in the system by which the cultivator is not his own seed merchant, but is entirely dependent on the baniya, mahajan, or similar individual of the money-lending class. These men supply the raiyat with seed, charging interest at an exorbitant rate, for they know that he must have seed or else he cannot grow his crop. The accounts between merchant and cultivator, thus begun over seed transactions, are seldom allowed to lapse, and often assume enormous proportions, leading to mortgaging of land and other evils.' Voelcker, *Report on the Improvement of Indian Agriculture*, p. 236, see also pp. 237-40. For

additional examples of the decline of cultivator seed production, see C.E.R. Girdlestone, *Report of Past Famines in the North Western Provinces,* Allahabad: Northwestern Provinces and Oudh Government Press, 1868, p. 11; *The Famine Inquiry Commission*, 1945, appendix iii, 'Rural Credit and Indebtedness,' pp. 459-69; Government of Bihar and Orissa, *The Bihar and Orissa Provincial Banking Inquiry Committee*, 1929-30, Patna: Government Press, 1930, vol. 2, pp. 501-19.

21. Francis Buchanan, *An Account of the District of Shahabad in 1812-13*, Patna: Bihar and Orissa Research Society, 1934, p. 321; Nirmal Sengupta, 'The Indigenous Irrigation Organization in South Bihar', *Indian Economic and Social History Review*, vol. 17, 1980, pp. 157-87; B. B. Chaudhuri, 'Movement of Rent in Eastern India, 1793-1930', *Indian Historical Review*, vol. 3, 1978, pp. 33-64; Government of India, *Report of the Indian Famine Commission (1878-80)*, Calcutta: Government Printing, 1880, chapter 5; Government of India, *Report of the Indian Irrigation Commission*, 1901-03, Calcutta: Government Printing, 1904, pp. 162-3; Great Britain, *Royal Commission on Agriculture in India*, vol. 13 (Evidence taken in Bihar and Orissa), London: H.M.S.O., 1927-28, p. 289.
22. See the description of the geographical distribution of crops for Patna District in 1811 in James R. Hagen, 'Indigenous Society, The Political Economy, and Colonial Education in Patna District: A History of Social Change from 1811 to 1951 in Gangetic North India', PhD Dissertation, University of Virginia, 1981, pp. 130-200.
23. In recent decades, the World Bank has consistently encouraged this trend, which usually involves increasing the cultivation of exportable cash crops in Third World lands as the most 'rational' development policy despite the very risky consequence of losing lands that had produced subsistence crops. The history of Gangetic agriculture indicates how this monocropping trend can be partly the product of growing soil impoverishment. Export-led, cash-monocropping is facing growing criticism due to the strong shift toward concern for sustainability in both the economic and environmental dimensions of development. For example, see Michael Redcliff, *Sustainable Development: Exploring the Contradictions*, London: Methuen & Co., 1987, p. 57.
24. Bose, *A Study of Bihar Agriculture*, p. 8; see also Habib, *Agrarian System*, p. 53.
25. Butler, *Outlines of the Topography and Statistics of the Southern*

Districts of Oudh p. 56; Voelcker, pp. 36-7, 232-4; Ganguli, *Trends of Agriculture and Population in the Ganges Valley*, p. 6; W.H. Moreland, *The Agriculture of the United Provinces*, Allahabad: Government Printing, 1910, pp. 13-26.

26. See Hemendra Prasad Ghose, *The Famine of 1770*, Calcutta: Book Co., 1943; Nani Gopal Chaudhuri, 'Some of the Results of the Great Bengal and Bihar Famine of 1770', *Indian History Congress, Proceedings* 12, 1949, pp. 239-49; Kali Charan Ghosh, *Famines in Bengal, 1770-1943*, Calcutta: India Associated Publishing Co., 1944; N. K. Sinha, 'The Famine of 1769-70 (b.s. 1176-1177)', *Bengal Past and Present*, vol. 77, July-December 1958, pp. 120-31.
27. See Binay Bhushan Chaudhuri, 'Agricultural Growth in Bengal and Bihar, 1770-1860: Growth of Cultivation Since the Famine of 1770', *Bengal Past and Present*, vol. 95, 1976, pp. 290-340.
28. See James K. Boyce, *Agrarian Impasse in Bengal: Institutional Constraints to Technological Change*, Oxford: Oxford University Press, 1987.
29. See Mohammad Shafi, *Agricultural Productivity and Regional Imbalances: A Study of Uttar Pradesh*, New Delhi: Concept, 1984.
30. R. O. Whyte, *The Grassland and Fodder Resources of India*, New Delhi: Indian Council of Agricultural Research, 1964, p. 117; N. L. Bor and George Taylor, *The Grasses of Burma, Ceylon, India and Pakistan (Excluding Bambuseae)*, New York: Pergamon Press, 1960, p. 31; P.M. Dabadghao and K.A. Shankarnarayan, *The Grass Cover of India*, New Delhi: Indian Council of Agricultural Research, 1973; J.S. Singh, Yang Hanxi, and P.E. Sajise, 'Structural and Functional Aspects of Indian and Southeast Asian Savanna Ecosystems', in J. C. Tothill and J.J. Mott, eds., *Ecology and Management of the World's Savannas*, Canberra: Australian Academy of Science, 1985, pp. 34-51.
31. See Buchanan, *An Account of the Districts of Bihar and Patna in 1811-1812*, vol. l, p. 547.
32. For an expression of this idea, see Tom G. Kessinger, *Vilyatpur 1848-1968: Social and Economic Change in a North Indian Village*, Berkeley: University of California Press, 1974, p. 151.
33. See Walter Hauser, 'The Bihar Provincial Kisan Sabha, 1929-1942: A Study of an Indian Peasant Movement', PhD Dissertation, University of Chicago, 1961; Walter Hauser, 'From Peasant Soldiering to Peasant Activism: Reflections on the Transition of a Martial Tradition in the Flaming Fields of Bihar', *Journal of the Economic and Social History of the Orient*, vol. 47, 2004, pp.

401-34; Arvind N. Das and V. Nilakant, eds., *Agrarian Relations in India*, Delhi: Manohar, 1979; Manoshi Mitra, *Agrarian Social Structure: Continuity and Change in Bihar, 1786-1820*, New Delhi: Manohar, 1985.

34. See Girish Mishra, *Agrarian Problems of Permanent Settlement: A Case Study of Champaran*, Delhi: People's Pub. House, 1978.

35. See David Ludden, 'Productive Power in Agriculture: A Survey of work on the Local History of British India', in Meghnad Desai, Susanne H. Rudolph, and Ashok Rudra, eds., *Agrarian Power and Agricultural Productivity in South Asia*, Berkeley: University of California Press, 1985, pp. 51-99.

36. See Anand A. Yang, *The Limited Raj: Agrarian Relations in Colonial India, Saran District, 1793-1920*, Berkeley: University of California Press, 1989; Anand Yang, 'Peasants on the Move: a Study of Internal Migration in India', *Journal of Interdisciplinary History*, vol. 10, 1979, pp. 37-58; and Amit Bhaduri, 'A Study in Agricultural Backwardness under Semi-Feudalism', *Economic Journal*, vol. 83, 1973, pp. 120-37.

Of Nature and Nurture: Sedentary Agriculture and the 'Wandering Tribes' of Jharkhand*

Christopher V. Hill

> The *kisans* are victim to a continuing series of exploitations. For example, if they were able to meet their needs of woods from the jungle, then what would be left for the forest officials, great and small to do? In fact these 'rangers', 'foresters', 'patrolmen', and others seek out any opportunity to oppress the people, very much like beasts of prey. If they are not bribed, their sole object is to harass the poor. My blood begins to boil when I recall the many stories told to me by the Adivasi *kisans* of the harassment they have had to endure at the hands of forest officers.[1]
>
> —Swami Sahajanand Saraswati

In earlier works I have argued at some length that the subjugation of nature was part and parcel of the legitimizing aspect of imperialism in India. Just as the Western concepts of social and cultural superiority provided the rationale for Eurocentric approaches to the issues of politics, education, and economy, so did European notions of the purpose and usefulness of nature result in Western forms of land control, public works, and forestry management in the colonial period.[2] Sir Arthur Cotton, the director of the Mahanadi River Management System in the 1850s, made this point quite clear in arguing to dam the river.

* I thank Walter Hauser, Kailash Jha, and Anand Yang for assistance in locating sources for this essay.

He said, 'In [any] district where our Western knowledge and energy have been brought to bear, the people freely acknowledge that it is to Europeans and Christians that they are indebted for benefits which they never received from their own Government, and their own gods.'[3] While Cotton's comments revolve around the tired clichés of imperial justification, they are still a telling example of the link between social and environmental attitudes brought forth by the colonial infrastructure.

In this essay, I look at the other side of this equation, moving away from the contention that colonial ideology, which defined the role of government in 'civilizing' the Indian population, also defined the function of nature. I shall instead argue that the colonial construct of the *proper* function of nature affected European perceptions of the relative cultural 'sophistication' of certain ethnic groups, especially non-sedentary ones. The prevailing colonial view of the characteristics that defined civilization and modernization led the Raj to view swidden agriculture, along with hunting and gathering, as economically backward and socially dangerous. Given that philosophy, the government was determined to eradicate these means of subsistence, always under the guise of British trusteeship. I intend to use the Santals of the Jungle Mahals of Jharkhand to exemplify the evolution of this practice.

My understanding of this process has been clarified by the reading of two intriguing articles by Ajay Skaria and Sumit Guha.[4] Both deal with colonial perceptions of tribal people and how such views evolved, and why they were consequential to Adivasis in colonial and independent India. While Skaria and Guha look at this question from different spectra, their arguments not only add insight to the issue of the treatment of Adivasis in contemporary Indian politics and society, but also open new doors to understanding the categories to which Adivasis have been assigned, both before and after 1947.

Ajay Skaria concentrates on the concept of 'wildness'. By looking at the different legal attitudes towards punishment of castes as opposed to that of tribals, Skaria argues that the colonial construct of ideal tribal society differed from imperial notions of 'civilized' peoples, and hence caused justice under the rule of law to be differentiated between caste and tribe. So, for instance, sentences tended to be much lighter for a tribal killing of a witch than for *sati*, which was a preserve of caste Hindus.[5] Skaria describes this situation as anachronism. He notes, 'different societies were . . . ranked according to how much behind the time of Europe they were'.[6]

Skaria then addresses the question of why tribes fell under the construct of 'primitive'. One factor, he argues, is that of race. The colonial ethnographers took it as a political given that the Aryan invasion resulted in Aryan castes in contradistinction to indigenous tribes, which explained the division of labour and racial groups in India. The other issue that Skaria claims was decisive in deciding wildness was modes of subsistence. It is this aspect that attunes itself best to the colonial practice of using the utilization of nature as a litmus test for social and economic sophistication, when legitimizing control of South Asia.

Sumit Guha covers much of the same intellectual territory, but he does so by looking almost exclusively at colonial views of race as the decisive factor. He argues that geology provided the construct for race; just as stratification of rocks indicated their age, so too did it explain racial variance in India. Guha quotes a report from 1865: 'The ethnology of this part of the Dekhan has a great resemblance to its geology. First of all, and older than all, are the remnants of tribes that originally peopled the continent of India. . . . [W]e may liken them to the granite rocks that underlie the trap, and crop out here and there from among the overlying strata.'[7]

This belief had a nice, mythic, legitimizing ring to it. The British were simply the second coming of the Aryans, here to finish the civilizing project begun by the first Aryans millennia ago. Guha concludes by noting the irony that such a view of Indian ethnicity was lapped up by Indian elites as well: 'The mythic history of clashing races . . . took shape when brown sahibs and white sahibs sought to escape their fears about the instability of social hierarchy by giving it a biological basis and projecting it into the past—thus covering extant hierarchies with the mantle of the natural and the primordial.'[8]

Both Skaria and Guha are dealing with the colonial construct of 'tribalism'. Skaria argues that the concept of 'wildness', which includes modes of subsistence, race, and definitions of 'civility' as its major components, is the defining factor. Guha concentrates on the issue of colonial constructs of racial categorization. I would add that in all colonial definitions of Adivasi ethnicity there is also an aspect of 'the noble savage'. Thus, tribals could not be punished for murder in the same manner as Brahmans, for killing was part of tribal society.

This construct of primitivism is a nice paradigm for colonialism, for it justifies imperialism as nothing more than a Kiplingesque duty. There is, however, one more factor that I would like to add to this equation, and that is the colonial connection made between civilized people and controlled nature.

The Jungle Mahals of Jharkhand provide a fascinating arena for studying colonial views of migratory peoples. This area bordered the conjunct of Bihar and Bengal along the Ganga river to the north, and moved south to include the Santal Parganas, as well as the districts of Birbhum, Bankura, Burdwan, and Midnapur in Bengal. The Mahals were included in the original *diwani* that the East India Company received in 1765, and yet were not really incorporated into the empire until the vicious repression of the Santal Uprising in 1855. In 1772 Warren Hastings appointed Captain Brooke as military governor of the *thanas*, charging him 'to subdue the hill robbers and rebellious zamindars, re-establish order and induce them to adopt *settled ways of peace*'. Brooke was replaced in 1774 by Captain James Browne, whose report on the area provides early evidence of the colonial view of migratory Adivasis.[9]

Browne admired the Adivasis of the Jungle Mahals immensely, in the sense that any conqueror admires the doomed noble primitive: 'What are these people? Not wretched, spiritless, unarmed Bengalees, inhabiting a plain central country, neither formidable by character or situation; but an armed people, martial, proud, and independent, and constituting, by their situation, the only barrier we possess against that [Maratha] enemy.'[10]

Browne urged that these Adivasis should not be disarmed, leaving them instead as a buffer against the Marathas. Rather than taking their weapons away from them, he argued, the Adivasis should be given waste land to cultivate in return for military service. In short, they were to be settled.

> This is the plan, I beg permission to offer for consideration and it is, as I elsewhere said, an improvement, not an abrogation of the ancient Government; the feudal soldiery are not only preserved, but supported by the troops of Government, who at the same time will much more effectually answer the end of control over these Jungle chiefs, than their former feudal lords possibly could.[11]

Such a plan offered several advantages. It brought the Adivasi militia under the control of the East India Company. It allowed them to continue to be a buffer against the Marathas. And, of equal importance, it made them sedentary. They could now easily be kept under the watchful eye of the government. Within the Jungle Mahals, this policy of settling Adivasis, by force if necessary, became law. The evolving attitude toward the Santals in the northern regions of the Mahals provides another example.

While the origin of the Santals is wrapped in myth, we do know that they practised both swidden and sedentary agriculture in the hilly, forest-covered terrain of the Jungle Mahals. When the British came upon them, however, they categorized them as primeval hunters. By the beginning of the nineteenth century the Santals began moving to the Damin-i-koh, which comprised the hilly area of what would become the Santal Parganas. They continued to exist on the same modes of production they had before the advent of colonialism, but this was soon to change.

Between 1838 and 1851, some 80,000 Santals were encouraged by the East India Company to migrate to the Damin-i-koh, clear the forests, and settle the land. They did this in clusters since they were a communal society, and always settled as a body and with a headman. Sedentary agriculture almost immediately proved unsuitable for them, for under the aegis of the emerging world economy, the Santals were now fixtures in a settled, commercial, cash enterprise. Never having been involved in cash ventures, the tribals soon found themselves in debt to the local landlords and *mahajans* or moneylenders. The *mahajans* were usually Bengali, collectively referred to by the Adivasis as *dikkus*, or outsiders. As W.W. Hunter noted, the Santals were ignorant of adjudication regarding commercial revenue, while the *mahajans* were well-versed in the letter of the law. Hunter's understanding of the consequences of capitalism in this tribal community, although imbued with colonial rhetoric, is nonetheless sophisticated, and as such his views need to be quoted to some extent:

> The law of supply and demand operates in the long-run as effectively, although more tardily, in the valley of the Ganges as on the banks of the Mersey or the Clyde. . . . Hindu merchants flock thither every winter after harvest to buy up the crop, and by degrees each market-town throughout the settlement had its own grain dealer. . . . They cheated the poor Santal in every transaction. The forester brought his clarified butter for sale; the Hindu measured it in vessels with false bottoms; the husbandman came to exchange his rice for salt, oil, cloth and gunpowder; the Hindu used heavy weights in ascertaining the quantity of grain, light ones in weighing out the articles given in return. . . . The fortunes made by traffic in produce were augmented by usury. A family of new settlers required a small advance of grain to eke out the produce of the chase while they were clearing the jungle. The Hindu dealer gave them a few shillings worth of rice, and seized the land as soon as they had cleared it and sown the crop. . . .
> Year after year the Santal sweated for his oppressor. If the victim threatened to run off into the jungle, the usurer instituted a suit in the courts, taking care that the Santal should know nothing of it until the decree had been obtained and the execution carried out. Without the slightest warning, the poor husbandman's buffalos, cows, and little homestead were sold, not omitting the brazen household vessels which formed the sole heirloom of the family. Even the cheap iron ornaments, the outward token of female respectability among the Santals, were torn from the wife's wrists. Redress was out of the question; the court sat in the civil station perhaps a hundred miles off. The English judge, engrossed with the collection of the revenue, had no time for the petty grievance of his people. The native underlings, one and all, had taken the pay of the oppressor; the police shared in the spoil. 'God is great, but He is too far off', said the Santal; and the poor cried, and there was none to help them.[12]

Given the ruthlessness of the new market economy pressed upon them, the Santals were soon alienated from their land, with few options for pursuing their traditional means of livelihood, and thrown against the harsh reality of a commercial economy. In the summer of 1855 they rebelled. Venting their anger at the government, landlords, and moneylenders, the Santals attacked *dikku* and policemen.[13] Some thirty thousand of them took up their bows and arrows; they were met by fourteen thousand well-armed government troops. In the ensuing conflict, over ten thousand Santals were killed.

This bloody encounter eventually led to administrative reform for the Santal homeland. In late 1855 'the district called the Damin-i-koh and other districts which are chiefly inhabited by the uncivilized race of people called the Sonthals were incorporated into the Santal Parganas'.[14] Two stipulations of the covenant with the Santals need to be emphasized. The agreement was not retroactive in terms of loss of land, and it did not cover the Jungle Mahals of Birbhum, Bankura, Burdwan, and Midnapur, all of which were located south-west of the Santal Parganas.

The exclusion of the Jungle Mahals was made all the more pertinent by the provisions for revenue administration in the Santal Parganas. Under the provisions set forth in 1855 (and amended in 1886) the Adivasis within the Santal Parganas received specific protection for their agrarian enterprises. Within the district there were to be no under-raiyats, nor could rents be raised arbitrarily. Rather, the peasantry could petition the Deputy Commissioner of the district to settle the rent directly. Of primary importance, however, was the clause that exempted the raiyat from liability to eviction except by the direct order of the Deputy Commissioner.

None of these protections applied to the Jungle Mahals, which were instead guided by the provisions of the Bengal Tenancy Act. Under the Bengal Tenancy Act, as Swami Sahajanand Saraswati noted, 'an occupancy tenant is considered to be the owner of his land. He has the right to plant trees and bamboos on this land, to make bricks and tiles and dig wells and tanks. . . . But non-occupancy tenants have no such rights.'[15] The Santals, of course, were considered non-occupancy tenants. Furthermore, instead of protecting the land rights of these Adivasis, the government argued that local customs, which effectively put the control of land into the hands of powerful zamindars, must prevail. This policy was ludicrous; as Sahajanand noted, 'the very idea of local customs involving zamindars is meaningless', since the Adivasis were on the land well before zamindars appeared on the scene.[16]

Given the fact that colonial officials knew full well that

zamindari rights historically did not prevail in Jharkhand, why would the government put forth such an obvious charade? It is here that I come to the heart of my argument: colonial actions were guided by an inherent suspicion of mobile groups.

As I will argue later, however, colonial distrust of unsettled ethnic groups did not germinate in India; it was imported from Europe. The basic misgivings towards wandering clans were carried to India on the shoulders of physiocracy and utilitarianism. Once there, two policies immediately reinforced the distrust of Adivasi modes of subsistence: The Permanent Settlement Act of 1793, and the Criminal Tribes Act of 1871.

The Permanent Settlement, with its policy of an unchanging revenue on fixed estates, had no place for shifting cultivation. Indeed, the very rationale behind the act was to provide a steady, predictable source of income for the Company. There was, not surprisingly, a philosophical rationale behind the Permanent Settlement as well. Lord Charles Cornwallis, the instigator of the Act, epitomized the English gentleman farmer. He envisioned an agrarian society with contented, sedentary peasants (the raiyats), basking in the good fortune provided by the lord of the manor (the zamindar). Wandering cultivators not only had no place in this scenario, they upset the delicate balance between lord and peasant; they were 'dangerous'. An example of the perceived dangers of shifting cultivation can be found in the colonial reaction to the traditional farming of alluvial land along shifting rivers. For the best part of two hundred years the government in India tried to make permanent the mode of production (and thus the population) along these rivers. They never succeeded. The implementation of the Permanent Settlement led to numerous survey and settlement operations, and thousands of lawsuits, some of which are still active today.[17]

The Dangerous Tribes Act of 1871 provided an enormous amount of leeway for dealing with wandering tribes. As Anand Yang has noted, 'the Act empowered local governments to designate "any tribe, gang, or class of persons" a "criminal tribe" if they were "addicted to the systematic commission of non-bailable offences." Once officially notified, groups had no recourse to the judicial system for removal of this designation.'[18] Once a tribe was legally labeled criminal, local officers had many sanctions to use against its members. The government could resettle them forcefully, restrict their movements, conduct roll-calls, or arrest members without a warrant, and incarcerate them for as long as six months if they were caught traveling without a pass.[19]

One of the main purposes of the Act was to keep tabs on the tribals. As such, wandering tribes were considered especially dangerous. As Yang has further noted, 'The official judgement on criminal tribes was also shaped by the fact that so many of them were identified as "gipsies", "wandering tribes", or "vagrant tribes". This view was consistent with the contemporary notion that vagrancy was the "nursery of crime".'[20] Thus the Act had several purposes, among which were the identification of non-sedentary groups, the act of defining them in monolithic terms, and the forced settlement of tribes in the name of civilization and progress.

In the Santal Parganas, these tasks were made considerably easier by the provisions of the Santal Land Alienation Regulations, which put all aspects of Santal subsistence exclusively in the hands of the Deputy Commissioner. Revenue Officers could force sedentary agriculture upon them in the guise of 'civilizing' the backward tribes. If the Adivasis refused to accept the beneficence of the Raj, they were labeled a Criminal Tribe and dealt with by the law. Other tribes were treated much the same way in the southern districts of Jharkhand.

This process can be seen more clearly in confrontations between the Adivasis and the Forest Service. Mahesh Rangarajan has detailed this conflict in the Central Provinces during the period from 1860 to 1920. The Forest Act of 1878, essentially, changed the way the government looked at the woods. As forest products became increasingly commodified, the authority of the Forest Officers grew, increasing the conflict between revenue officers, who wanted the forests cleared for cultivation, and the Forestry Service which wanted the timber reserved for revenue. In most cases the Forest Officers won. These men, trained as silviculturalists, knew little or nothing of the customs of the Adivasis, nor did they care. They instead concentrated on production, by excluding cattle grazing from the forests and increasing the proportion of 'superior' trees, such as teak and sal. This meant a complete change in life for the swidden agriculturalists as well as for those who made their living from hunting and gathering wood.[21]

In Jharkhand the implementation of forest policy was carried out in several ways. One was to turn to the zamindars to help establish commercial forestry. Land was increasingly settled by *dikkus*, under the provisions of the Bengal Tenancy Act, with the stipulation that forests were to be managed and lumber was to be sold to the government. In the early days there was an abundance of work for the Santals, for they were given the task of clearing the forests of undesirable trees. Employment opportunities quickly disappeared, however, once the forests were replanted. Faced with the extermination of their traditional lifestyle, Santal leaders turned to the Deputy Commissioner. The response of the government was simply to wait until the Santals ran out of room. Revenue Officer M.C. McAlpin noted as much: 'The Sonthals are on the verge of the purely Dikku areas, where reclamation is drawing to a close, and where there is jungle possessing any terror for the mahajan. . . . The Sonthals have been reduced to the status of a raiyat or under-raiyat rack-rented on a large produce rent or . . . [are] being reduced to the position of a labourer.'[22]

This is precisely the state in which the government wanted them. The Revenue Department soon realized that the Santals would never practise settled agriculture in the way it was performed in Britain. They also recognized the skills of the Santals at clearing jungle and reclaiming land. And so the government was able to kill two birds with one stone. On the one hand they could put the land in the hands of the *dikku*, who would practice orthodox cultivation, while on the other, they now had a disenfranchised group to work on clearing the land in other districts so that they too could be brought under settled cultivation. In the last decades of the nineteenth century, thousands of Santals were encouraged to migrate to other areas either to clear the jungles or work on plantations. With few alternatives, large numbers often complied.

The economic and social state of Jharkhand that the Swami found in 1941 was largely a product of the policies explicated above. Santals in Jharkhand found themselves completely disenfranchised from their lands. They either worked as labourers, or migrated, or starved. This was a fate that affected Sahajanand deeply. After seeing the circumstances in Jharkhand, the Swami put forth a list of demands, including fixed rates of rent only after five years of cultivation; no restrictions on the use of jungle products; Paharias to be allowed to continue swidden agriculture; and one uniform tenancy act for all of Jharkhand.[23]

Of doubtless little surprise to the Swami, none of the demands were addressed. As Sahajanand later concluded, 'the law in practice is neither that of the Chotanagpur Tenancy Act nor the inherited experiences of Adivasi culture . . . but rather . . . "it is the zamindar's will which is the law."'[24] The plight of the peasant in Jharkhand has changed little since the Swami wrote those words.

CONCLUSION

The major question that needs to be addressed here is why the government was so adamant about changing the culture of the Adivasis. From the advent of British rule, Adivasis were dealt with separately from the rest of India. They came under a special administration; their boundaries were marked on ethnicity rather than geography. They were flooded with hordes of missionaries, unlike that seen in other parts of India. What made the Adivasis different in the eyes of the Empire?

The answer to this, I think, lies in the fact that the Adivasis *were* different. The only comparable group the British had dealt with in the past were the gypsies. Just as the British relied on European (rather than local) knowledge in dealing with the ecosystems of India, so too did they rely on their parochial sense that vagabonds were dangerous and untrustworthy. They were unfamiliar and uncomfortable with the Adivasi culture, and were determined to change it, either by persuasion or sanction. Much as with nature, they attempted (and succeeded, although perhaps not in the way they had planned) to radically alter Adivasi society. Also, as with nature, they brought about these changes under the guise of *noblesse oblige*.

It is here that Skaria's concept of 'wildness' becomes important. If we look at the dominant Western view of nature at this time, wildness was dangerous. The slaughter of Native Americans by white settlers provides a case in point. Throughout the history of the United States, the genocide of American Indians was legitimized with the use of terms such as 'civilization' and 'progress'. In the American West being 'civilized' meant settled land, law and order, an end to roaming, with all the social attributes that entailed. And most importantly, it meant an end to wilderness. It is not a coincidence that the root word for unsettled land is wild. The industrial West found its self-importance in 'making the desert bloom'. If that meant an end to the non-sedentary ways of the indigenous inhabitants, that was the price of progress.

In Europe, it was the gypsies who took the brunt of this attitude. John Bledsoe, one of the better-known English anthropologists at the turn of the twentieth century, said as much: 'I regret the diminution of the old blond lympho-sanguine stock, which has hitherto served England well in many ways, but is apparently doomed to give way to a darker and *more mobile type*, largely the offspring of the proletariat. . . .'[25] One need only look at the prevailing European attitudes towards gypsies (who, ironically, are believed by some to have originated in India) to see the genesis of this view. Gypsies were perceived as extremely untrustworthy; they were vagabonds, in the very pejorative sense of the word. They were always sneaking off into the night; since they did not settle down, they were assumed to be up to something illegal. British children's books were full of tales of teenage detectives capturing thieving gypsies in the act, or barely missing them as they (the Gypsies) went about their vagabond ways.[26] This attitude was prevalent throughout Europe, so much so that 'of the non-Jews, Gypsies [were treated] most murderously by the Nazis'.[27] Over 200,000 of them were systematically exterminated by the Germans and their cohorts during World War II.[28]

Unsettled land was often described with the same adjectives as wandering tribes. It was wild. It was exotic. It was wasteland, in the literal sense of the word. It conjured up images of dangerous creatures. It needed to be exterminated. By the nineteenth century in colonial India, wilderness had little, if any, intrinsic value. Ironically, the people most willing to put up a fight for it were hunters. They simply confirmed the contextual view of non-commercialized land as dangerous.

Nature thus became the metaphor for both wild and civilized. Wild nature and wild people were uncontrolled. They wandered, feeding off each other, neither one owned or owning. Imperialism could not, by definition, tolerate such a notion. *Pax Britannica* demanded that in order to receive the blessings of British Rule, one must be stationary. Inherently, of course, part of those blessings come from a control over nature. This is why famine took on such an urgency during the Raj. It was not merely the fact that people were dying. Of equal or perhaps more importance was the symbolism involved in the inability of the government to make nature produce. Even in the many cases where famine was caused by man-made circumstances, there was still a desperation to be seen, a sense that colonialism could not justify itself without visible control over all of its subjects, be they human or not. Wildness, then, took on a meaning that extended far beyond the 'uncivilized' peoples of India. It connoted a danger to both suppression and rule.

The final irony in the development of this juxtaposition between 'primitive' and 'progressive' is that it did not end with Indian independence. It tells us something about nature and society that, while the ideology of empire has been discredited, the ideology of the utility of nature has not. It was, after all, India's first Prime Minister, Jawaharlal Nehru, who proclaimed dams to be the temples of modern India. Social groups which refuse to accept this view of ecosystems as commodities are still labeled as either dangerous or uncivilized by the state, whether socialist or neo-liberal.

In her study on Jharkhand, the anthropologist Susana B.C. Devalle makes this contemporary context more clear. Devalle sees three distinctive groups that have used ethnicity as an excuse for subjugation: the colonial rulers, who used tribalism as a process to forcefully incorporate Adivasis into the emerging world economy; the elite in post-colonial India, for whom 'ethnicity can serve as an element of support for the hegemony of the dominant classes and of the state'; and finally, those whom she calls 'Reformist ethnicists', mainly missionaries and educated Adivasis, who perpetuate the stereotype of the primitive savage, doomed by progress.[29]

Sumit Guha also argues that these primitive stereotypes of tribals continue in independent India, particularly in a racial sense. Thus, the old colonial geological metaphor can be used to justify continued governmental control over tribal areas. Guha includes an astonishing quote from a 1968 publication by V. Raghaviah:

> Though cruelly and unjustly driven into these unwholesome, unwelcome mountain fastnesses by ruthless invading hordes *superior in numbers as in their brain power*, and the tribals' fertile and alluvial lands in the Ganjetic (*sic*) valley occupied, yet these millions of militant patriots acted as the sentinels of India's freedom, through ages of unrecorded and perhaps unrecognised history.[30]

Both DeValle and Guha convincingly demonstrate that the colonial attitude toward migratory groups is still holding strong, fifty years after Indian Independence. A final example can be found in the following quote from the popular weekly news magazine, *India Today*. The issue in which this article appeared is dated 30 April 1997.

> Across the length and breadth of the country, marriage may be a time for noisy revelry, but for the 25,000 strong Dafer community spread across Gujarat, it calls for certain degrees of secrecy. Known throughout the state as a criminal tribe, a wedding among them is a police officer's dream—a convenient gathering where several suspects could be rounded up at one go. . . . Why should the police harass them? The answer comes promptly. Says state DGP P.K. Bansal: 'Among the criminal tribes of Gujarat, the Dafers would top for their cunning, shrewdness, and modus operandi.' . . . Before Independence, it is said, many petty rulers would encourage Dafer gangs in the states of their rivals. The fear and hatred have travelled down the ages. . . . Although they are technically OBCs, the government has done little for them. For want of a marketing outlet, the elaborate embroidery work done by the women is usually sold at throwaway prices. . . . Landless, homeless, and unlettered, they are left to rally around themselves.[31]

In one of his essays on deforestation in colonial Burma, Michael Adas mentions a revenue department official who was frustrated with the primitive methods of subsistence that he found among the Burmese peasants. This officer argued that if the people were not willing to voluntarily change their modes of production, they should be forced into implementing more modern methods of rice-cropping: 'We are dealing with a semi-civilized race; we should assist them in advancing themselves; they cannot without our assistance; we should induce them—I go further, we should press them—to accept our system beneficial to advancement; our superiority as a nation warrants us to do this.'[32]

This same attitude evolved into policy throughout colonial-constructed tribal areas, and irrevocably changed the lives of the 'wandering tribes' of Jharkhand.

NOTES

1. Walter Hauser, ed., *Swami Sahajanand and the Peasants of Jharkhand: A View from 1941*, Delhi: Manohar, 1995, p. 107.
2. See Christopher V. Hill, 'Ideology and Public Works: "Managing" the Mahanadi River in Colonial North India', *Capitalism, Nature, Socialism*, vol. 6, no. 4, December 1995, pp. 51-64; and Christopher V. Hill, *River of Sorrow: Environment and Social Control in Riparian North India, 1770-1994*, Ann Arbor: Association for Asian Studies Monograph No. 55, 1997.
3. Sir Arthur Cotton, 'Report on the Cutting of a Canal between the Ganges and the Hooghly', 15 June, 1858. Bengal Public Works Proceeding, Vol. p/16/33, January to February 1859. India Office Library and Records, The British Library, London.
4. Ajay Skaria, 'Shades of Wildness: Tribe, Caste, and Gender in Western India', *Journal of Asian Studies*, vol. 56, no. 3, August 1997, pp. 726-45; Sumit Guha, 'Lower Strata, Older Races, and Aboriginal Peoples: Racial Anthropology and Mythical History Past and Present', *Journal of Asian Studies*, vol. 57, no. 2, May 1998, pp. 423-41.
5. Skaria, op. cit., pp. 726-7.
6. Ibid., p. 727.
7. Guha, op. cit., p. 426.
8. Ibid., p. 438.
9. This early history of the Jungle Mahals is taken from Chandra Prakash N. Sinha, ed., *India Tracts: Major J. Browne's Report on*

the Jungle Terai People of South Bihar during 1774-1779, Darbhanga: Maharaja Dhiraja Kameshwar Singh Kalyani Foundation, 1996. The quotation can be found on p. A-8. Emphasis is mine.

10. Ibid., p. A-29.
11. Ibid., p. B-52.
12. W.W. Hunter, *The Annals of Rural Bengal*, London: Smith, Elder and Co., 1898, pp. 227-30.
13. For more on this rebellion, see Ranajit Guha, *Elementary Aspects of Peasant Insurgency in Colonial India*, Delhi: Oxford University Press, 1983.
14. P. C. Roy Chaudhury, *Bihar District Gazetteers: Santal Parganas*, Patna: Superintendent, Secretariat Press, 1965, p. 73.
15. Hauser, op. cit., p. 82. Sahajanand was referring to the Bihar Tenancy Act, however in this specific case it is identical to the one in Bengal.
16. Ibid., p. 93.
17. Hill, op. cit., 1997, Chap. 2.
18. Anand A. Yang, 'Dangerous Castes and Tribes: The Criminal Tribes Act and the Maghiya Doms of Northeast India', in Anand A. Yang, ed., *Crime and Criminality in British India*, Tucson: The Association for Asian Studies Monograph No. 42, 1985, p. 109.
19. Ibid., pp. 109-10.
20. Ibid., p. 114.
21. Mahesh Rangarajan, *Fencing the Forest: Conservation and Ecological Change in India's Central Provinces, 1890-1914*, New Delhi: Oxford University Press, 1996, Chaps. 1 and 3.
22. M.C. McAlpin, *Report on the Condition of the Sonthals in the Districts of Birbhum, Bankura, Midnapore and North Balasore*, Calcutta: Government Printing Office, 1909, p. 34.
23. Hauser, op. cit., p. 199.
24. Ibid., p. 82.
25. John Bledsoe, as quoted in Sumit Guha, op. cit., pp. 426-7. Italics are mine.
26. See, for instance, the works of Enid Blyton. Blyton was also fond of using traveling circuses as centres for danger and intrigue. For more on the prevalence of this stereotype of vagabonds in British children's literature, see Rashna B. Singh, *Goodly is our Heritage: Children's Literature, Empire, and the Certitude of Character*, Lanham: Scarecrow Press, 2004.
27. Daniel Jonah Goldhagen, *Hitler's Willing Executioners: Ordinary*

Germans and the Holocaust, New York: Alfred A. Knopf, 1996, p. 175.
28. Ibid., p. 565.
29. Susana B.C. Devalle, *Discourses in Ethnicity: Culture and Protest in Jharkhand*, New Delhi: Sage, 1992, p. 16.
30. V. Raghaviah, as quoted in Sumit Guha, op. cit., p. 431. Italics are mine.
31. 'Marked Men', *India Today*, 30 April 1997, p. 10.
32. Michael Adas, 'Colonization, Commercial Agriculture, and the Destruction of the Deltaic Rainforests of British Burma in the Late Nineteenth Century', in Richard P. Tucker and John F. Richards, eds., *Global Deforestation in the Nineteenth Century World Economy*, Durham: Duke University Press, 1983, p. 101.

Swami and Friends: Sahajanand Saraswati and Those Who Refuse to Let the Past of Bihar's Peasant Movements Become History*

Arvind Narayan Das

The Swami

The foremost of the leaders of the peasantry in Bihar was Swami Sahajanand Saraswati. Sahajanand was born in Ghazipur district in eastern UP in 1889 to a family of Jujhautiya Brahmans. He was the youngest of five brothers and had no sisters. His mother died when he was a child and Navrang Rai (as he was known then) was raised by an aunt. His father, Beni Rai, although a Brahman, was primarily a cultivator, and was so divorced from priestly functions that he did not even know the *Gayatri Mantra*. The family held a small zamindari. The income had sufficed in Sahajanand's grandfather's time, but as the family grew and the land was partitioned, prosperity dwindled and (tenant) cultivation became the only option. However, the family was not so poor

* Editor's note: Unfortunately Arvind Das died before he was able to make revisions to this essay. I have taken the liberty of doing some minor editorial tightening, as well as reference checking in cases where key passages and quotations were lacking endnote references. In some cases, I was able to track down the works in question; however, other references proved more difficult.

that its condition would prevent Navrang from going to school, where he did very well both in the primary grades and in the German Mission high school. Even at an early age Navrang showed signs of brilliance and skepticism of conventional religious practices. He questioned the institution of people taking guru-mantras from fake priests and wanted to study religious texts deeply in order to be able to find real spiritual solace. To prevent him from doing this, his family had him married to a child bride but, before the marriage could stabilize, in 1905 or early 1906, his wife died. The last fetter in his way to *samnyas* removed, in 1907 Navrang Rai was initiated into holy orders and took on the name of Swami Sahajanand Saraswati. This decision prevented him from appearing for the matriculation examination, but he spent the rest of his life, especially the first seven years after *samnyas*, studying religion, politics, and social affairs. In all these he became increasingly radicalized so that towards the end of his life, the world was presented the incongruous sight of a saffron-clad swami who denounced organized religion.[1]

However, before Sahajanand came to this stage, he had to traverse a long road. His first involvement in public activity started from the very narrow casteist Bhumihar platform.[2] Only gradually did he become involved in nationalist Congress politics, and then in peasant movements, progressively in Patna district, then Bihar and, finally, all over India.

But in order to get to the peasant question, Sahajanand first went through active political schooling in the Indian National Congress, under Gandhi. In fact, the Swami and the Mahatma had a curious filial relationship. Sahajanand started off in Congress as a devoted Gandhian, admiring Gandhi's fusion of tradition, religion and politics and from 1920 threw himself into the national movement as defined by Gandhi. However, he soon became disgusted with the petty, comfort-seeking hypocrisy of the self-proclaimed 'Gandhians', especially in jail, and within 15 years he was disillusioned with Gandhi's own ambiguity and devious pro-propertied attitudes. The final break came in 1934 after Bihar had been decimated by the great earthquake of that year. During the relief operations in which Sahajanand was deeply involved, he came across many cases where, in spite of the destruction perpetrated by the natural calamity, he found the suffering of the people to be less from the earthquake than the cruelty of the landlords in rent collection. In the circumstances, Sahajanand went to Gandhi, then camping at Patna, to seek advice and support. Gandhi sanguinely told him, 'The zamindars will remove the difficulties of the peasants. Their managers are Congressmen. So they will definitely help the poor.'[3] These platitudes disgusted Sahajanand and he broke off his fourteen-year association with Gandhi. After that, he consistently viewed Gandhi as a wily politician who, in order to defend the propertied classes, took recourse in pseudo-spiritualism, professions of non-violence and religious hocus-pocus.

After this break Sahajanand kept out of party politics (though he continued to be a member of the Congress) and turned his energies into mobilizing the peasants.[4] By the end of the decade, he emerged as the foremost kisan leader in India. In this task of organizing the peasants, his political impetuosity took him close to different individuals, parties, and groups. He first joined hands with the Congress socialists for the formation of the All-India Kisan Sabha; then with Subhas Chandra Bose he organized the Anti-Compromise Conference against the British and the Congress;[5] then he worked with the CPI during the Second World War;[6] and finally broke from them, too, to form an 'independent' Kisan Sabha.[7] In spite of these political forays, Sahajanand remained essentially a non-party man and his loyalty was only to the peasants for whom he was the most articulate spokesman. As a peasant leader, 'by standards of speech and action, he was unsurpassed'.[8] He achieved that status by a remarkable ability to speak to and for the peasants of Bihar; he could communicate with them and articulate their feelings in terms whose meaning neither peasant nor politicians could mistake. Determined to improve the peasants' condition, he relentlessly pursued that objective with such force and energy that he was almost universally loved by the peasants, and almost equally both respected and feared by landlords, Congressmen, and officials. The Swami was a militant agitator; he sought to expose the condition of agrarian society and to organize the peasants en masse to achieve change. He did this through countless meetings and rallies which he organized and which he addressed in his own inimitable forthright manner. Importantly, he spoke the language of the peasants.

Sahajanand was a Dandi Samnyasi and always carried a long bamboo staff (*danda*). In the course of the movement, this staff became the symbol of peasant resistance. The cry of *Danda Mera Zindabad*, was thus taken to mean 'Long live the *danda* (*lathi*) of the Kisans', and it became the watchword of the Bihar peasant movement. The inevitable response by the masses of peasants was *Swamiji ki Jai.*[9] *Kaise Logey Malguzari, Latth Hamara Zindabad* ('How will you collect rent while our lathis are powerful?') became the battle cry of the peasants.

This was the manner in which a common communication was achieved. 'And it was vastly enhanced by the fact that Sahajanand was a Swami, which gave him a tremendous charisma. In 1937, he was reported to have said that as religious robes had long exploited the peasants, now he would exploit those robes on behalf of the peasants.'[10] When landlords raised the question as to how a *samnyasi* (mendicant) was taking part in temporal problems of the poor, Sahajanand quoted the scriptures at them:

Prayen deva munayah swavimukti kama
Maunam charanti vijane na pararthnsihthah
Naitan vihaya kripnan vimumuksha eko
Nanyattwadasya sharanam bhramato nupashye
(Mendicants are selfish, living away from society, they try for their own salvation without caring for others. I cannot do that, I do not want my own salvation apart from those who are destitute. I will stay with them, live with them and die with them).[11]

Such was Swami Sahajanand Saraswati, the charismatic *samnyasi* rebel, who laid the foundations of kisan organization in Bihar, built it up into a massive movement, spread it to other parts of India, and radicalized it to such an extent that what had started off as a move to bring about reform in the zamindari system, ended by destroying it. Sahajanand could not, however, witness the legal death of zamindari in Bihar. He died while this battle was still being fought in the legislature and the courts, on 26 June 1950.[12]

THE ORGANIZATION

Although the Bihar Provincial Kisan Sabha was formed in 1929 and a smaller Kisan Sabha had been formed even earlier in Patna district with a formal organizational structure, it really was institutionalized only in the later 1930s. Actually, it is correct to say that the Kisan Sabha never really became an 'organization', remaining essentially a movement.[13]

But if that is so for the whole of the history of the Sabha, in its first years it was even more nebulous: an idea, a forum, a propaganda platform, a lobby. Almost immediately after the formation of the Sabha, Bihar was plunged, with the rest of India, into the Civil Disobedience Movement, which, although it helped arouse the general consciousness of the masses, did not give the leaders of the Sabha the time to formalize its structure.[14] In fact, the experiences of the Civil Disobedience Movement both outside and inside jails created the beginnings of a rift between the Kisan Sabhaites and some of the Congress leaders,[15] and so disgusted the supreme leader of the Sabha, Swami Sahajanand, that for several years he cut himself off from politics altogether.[16]

It was in 1933 in response to landlord efforts to manipulate tenancy legislation that Sahajanand re-entered the political arena largely through peasant rallies and 'struggles' across the province. This was a reflection of the impatient leadership of Sahajanand, which was not basically concerned with the formal niceties of organization. For Sahajanand, organization was the organization of mass action. He made the point explicitly in one of his many Kisan Sabha rallies:

> You must speak in great numbers. Government officials are here and when you come in tens of thousands they will listen, otherwise they will think you need nothing because you are silent. In Gaya there were 50,000 kisans and it caused a furore. We do not teach you to assault zamindars, only to get what is your right. We do not seek to create trouble between zamindars and tenants. The Government, zamindars and capitalists are strong. I want you to be strong too and the way to do it is to hold meetings. If you do not organise and hold Kisan Sabhas, troubles will not end.[17]

While its agitational character marked the movement as necessarily transitory in nature, it also provided it with an element of spontaneous strength. While the Congress relied on its organizational character for mobilizing the people for its movements, the Kisan Sabha drew its organizational vitality from the different movements and struggles. And, for the time being at least, the Kisan Sabha's mode of working was more effective. Even the officials remarked that the 'Kisan Sabha touches the ryot more directly and its meetings are larger than the [those of] Congress'.[18]

In practice, the formal organization of the movement was confined to the activities of the Provincial Kisan Council and the annual provincial *sammelam*, or rally and meeting. *Sammelans* were also held at local and district levels, though not on a regular basis. In addition, a secretary was active for the period 1935 to 1940 and an office was maintained at the Bihta ashram of Sahajanand. In very large measure, the Swami himself co-ordinated much of the work of the Provincial Kisan Sabha.

The membership of the Bihar Provincial Kisan Sabha was estimated at upwards of 250,000 in 1938. A more accurate measure of involvement and influence, however, may be gained by understanding that at the height of the agitation in the late 1930s, Sahajanand consistently addressed local village meetings of up to 5000 peasants, and the estimates of peasant rallies in Patna were commonly as high as 100,000.

With the formation of the All-India Kisan Sabha at Lucknow in April 1936, the Bihar Kisan Sabha became one of the provincial units of that national body. The Congress Socialist Party pressed for the organization of an all-India peasant association, and N.G. Ranga[19] became a prime mover in the effort. While Sahajanand was named president of the first meeting at Lucknow, he had come to support the idea reluctantly, holding that a national organization could function effectively only on the basis of a network of well-developed provincial bodies, which did not in fact exist.[20] While Sahajanand, once involved, extended total support, and to a large extent created and maintained the organizational framework by his own efforts, the AIKS suffered from the very shortcomings he had indicated: there was insufficient local and regional depth to sustain a national movement.[21]

The Movements

The Kisan Sabha may have faltered in finding its feet in other parts of India, but in Bihar, from its very inception, it was involved in strong movements both based on and in turn generating, mass enthusiasm. Its very foundation in 1929 was marked by the dropping of the proposed tenancy amendment. This was construed by the peasants as a significant victory and proved to be a tremendous morale-booster. On the heels of this came the Civil Disobedience Movement, the Great Depression, Provincial Autonomy, the Second World War, and the Quit India Movement. And finally, Independence. The Kisan Sabha grew from strength to strength on the crest of these waves of stirring political and economic events.

No earlier political campaign in India had fired the imagination of the rural population and become intertwined with agrarian issues, as the Civil Disobedience Movement of the first few years of the 1930s did. The simple and yet deep issues behind the agitation and the innovative methods of struggle—illegal manufacture of salt, boycott of government officials, non-payment of taxes, mass courting of arrests, campaigns against foreign cloth, liquor and various cesses and levies, combined with boycott of courts, schools and colleges—mobilized the vast forces of the agrarian population in unison with the urban masses. The campaign became so intense and widespread that an official view was that: 'The political history of 1930-1 is a tale of constant agitation, and of the measures taken by the government to combat this dangerous movement. In the "war" which resulted, there were frequent and sometimes serious clashes between the forces of law and order and those of unrest.'[22]

There were in fact elements of celebration and agitation in the political climate of the Civil Disobedience movement. Rajendra Prasad described the sense of rivalry prevailing in the countryside: 'Every village wanted to have the honour of getting the largest number of people arrested. None broke the law clandestinely because it was an open Satyagraha. During my tour of the countryside I often saw the villagers gather in open places decorated with buntings and plantain leaves and manufacture salt with great ceremony.'[23]

But the movement did not remain at the level of ceremonies: the peasants translated the movement into their own terms and that greatly disconcerted not only the government and the loyalist zamindars but even a section of the Congress leaders. Jawaharlal Nehru[24] had foreseen this. With the participation of the peasantry, the campaign, he said, 'would again become a mass movement touching the vital interests of the masses, and what was to me very important, would raise social issues'. These social issues were raised by transforming the no-tax campaign into a no-rent movement. The movement in Bihar did not reach the proportions of the extensive campaign in the United Provinces and, in fact, in Bihar it developed in such a manner that in practice the zamindars tried to camouflage its seriousness by paying their revenue in most cases while the tenantry desisted from the payment of rent. In fact, neither the government nor the zamindars took any drastic action, except in isolated cases, to terrorize a recalcitrant tenantry for several months because they were 'not sure of their grounds, as they had the political struggle with civil disobedience on the one side, and the economic slump, resulting in agricultural distress on the other. The two merged into each other, and the Government was always afraid of an agrarian upheaval.'[25]

Despite the example of the no-rent 'victory' of the UP peasantry, however, Congress leaders in Bihar did not press for rent and revenue remissions, nor in fact did they show much enthusiasm for the radical declarations made at the Karachi session of the Congress. By and large, the Congress leaders in Bihar were 'Gandhians' rather than 'Nehru-ites'. Gandhi himself had much earlier made his position clear:

> While we will not hesitate to advise the Kisans, when the movement comes, to suspend payment of taxes of the Government, it is not contemplated that at any stages of non-cooperation we would seek to deprive the zamindars of their rent. The Kisan movement must be confined to the improvement of the status of the Kisans and the betterment of the relations between the zamindars and them.[26]

In spite of the waverings of the Congress leaders in Bihar, the peasants did agitate in their own manner and even the officials were constrained to record that

. . . the lawless spirit born of civil disobedience was always liable to drive dissatisfied tenants to violence when a dispute occurred between them and the landlords.[27]

This also led the tenants to agitate militantly on agrarian issues and organize themselves into Kisan Sabhas which were formed in Patna, Gaya, Monghyr (where three village officials were killed by irate tenants), Champaran (where the Bettiah estate, under the Court of Wards, tried to contain peasant anger by granting concessions) and Palamau where the genuine grievances of the raiyats gave new life to the local Kisan Sabha, but agitators used the opportunity to preach the non-payment of rent and chaukidari tax, the wholesale cutting down of the jungle, and physical resistance to the landlords' agents.[28]

In addition, '. . . orators toured Bihar making violent speeches. Large numbers of volunteers, mainly loafers and unemployed persons were collected in (rural) training camps in the Muzaffarpur, Champaran, Saran and Manbhum districts and gave displays to impress the public.'[29] The 'public' may or may not have been impressed by this display of the force of the lumpen proletariat and peasantry, but the Civil Disobedience movement did affect the kisans themselves in terms of arousing their consciousness. Even Sahajanand, who had remained aloof from the movement in large part,[30] observed, 'The Satyagraha brought unprecedented awakening among the Kisans. The result was that their problems also came to the forefront. They had sacrificed their utmost at the behest of the Congress. How could these (Congress) leaders neglect them when they had to utilize the Kisans in the coming struggle?'[31]

In spite of their largely pro-landlord bias, even the provincial Congress leaders knew that they could not neglect the peasants. Besides, the peasants themselves by their repeated militant actions were drawing attention to their plight and were giving signals that if nothing was done soon to ameliorate their condition, matters would go out of the hands of the Congress leaders. In order to control this peasant anger as well as to give an impression of doing things for the kisans, the Bihar Provincial Congress Committee (BPCC) decided to investigate the conditions of peasants in Gaya district. This was in 1931. No report was prepared nor was any statement issued to the press after the investigation. The BPCC Enquiry Committee, under the chairmanship of Rajendra Prasad, toured extensively and took copious evidence from the villagers but '. . . its findings resulted in no recommendations for change, beyond seeking the reconciliation of landlord-tenant differences'.[32] In fact, some government officials saw in the activities of the Congress Enquiry Committee and the tours of prominent leaders a specific effort to disabuse the peasants of the belief that Gandhi's Civil Disobedience Movement and the economic dislocation of the Great Depression were somehow related.[33]

The very failure of the BPCC's Enquiry Committee to come up with a report, however, resulted in highlighting the plight of the kisans of Gaya. For, in order to do the work the Congress had not done, in 1933 the Bihar Provincial Kisan Council appointed a Committee to inquire into the problems of the peasants and to publish a report. The five-member committee consisted of Sahajanand, Yamuna Karjee, Yadunandan Sharma, Yugal Kishore Singh and Badri Narain Singh. This committee also interviewed peasants extensively and published its findings in the form of a pamphlet prepared by Sahajanand.[34]

Sahajanand's damning indictment of conditions in Gaya drew two sorts of reactions from the government. While one lot of officials felt that 'Kisan Sabhas established in Patna and Gaya districts were never a source of danger'[35] although Sahajanand was '. . . a dangerous individual engaged in a sinister conspiracy to set up the cultivator against the landlord and initiate a "Communist Revolt", on the Russian model',[36] on the other hand there was more sober assessment in the admission by various administrators that Sahajanand's case was strong and based on solid facts. A member of the Bihar Executive Council admitted that the Swami was '. . . clever and (had) justification for a great deal of what he said',[37] while a local official observed that Sahajanand was 'genuine in his work for the ryots' and drew attention to facts that 'really need investigation'.[38] The government launched such an investigation, and concluded that Sahajanand's charges were essentially true. It was admitted that in matters of receipts and rent reduction the law favoured the zamindar and the courts, which in any case were out of reach of the tenant; that kisans were subjected to 'harassment and illegal exactions', the conditions of *bhaoli* (produce rent) tenants were the worst 'as they cannot take a grain of crops without the zamindar's consent'; and that commuted rents were excessive and squeezed the tenant dry when prices fell. Only on the questions of canal rates and the upkeep of irrigation facilities did the investigating officer (the District Collector) differ with the Kisan Sabha report. He concluded significantly that the tenants knew their difficulties, 'only they do not know the remedy'.[39]

Not that the government knew the remedy. It 'felt that nothing could be done about any of these matters and that the legislative council in any event would not agree to strengthening the law to the detriment of the majority of its zamindar members. In apparent good faith the Governor periodically called together deputations of zamindars urging on them the establishment of goodwill with their tenants. This was an oft-repeated and oft-neglected plea.'[40] But one thing that all three enquiries revealed was that the issue was no longer capable of being decided merely by political or administrative policy-decision. Economic forces had taken the stage decisively and they created their own dynamic. The Great Depression was on.

The Economic Context

The effects of the depression were inevitably widespread. For example, the circumstances for moneylenders varied widely, depending on the situation outside the immediate context of the village economy. Fluctuations of prices of agricultural produce caused by such factors as World War I or the general world economic crisis resulted in dramatic changes in the fortunes of money-lenders. Nevertheless, they and the traders made substantial 'hay' in the sunshine of generally rising prices and increased their activities several-fold. This was particularly marked in the economic boom that followed World War I. There was a rush to corner whatever land was available. Peasants were increasingly thrown off the land and moneylenders also turned speculators, going even to the extent of borrowing in order to buy land. When the crash came many of the money-lenders who had speculated in land were ruined as land prices plummeted. The economic crisis of the late 1920s and 1930s also resulted in a steep fall in the prices of staple food crops. This in turn resulted in great hardship for the peasants and in the context of a general political upheaval, created tremendous agrarian torment leading to the emergence of the Kisan Sabha as a powerful political movement.

From the late nineteenth century until 1922, there had been a steady rise in the price of staple food crops. Brief exceptions occurred in 1911, 1913 and 1917–18, but from 1922 again the high level remained steady. Suddenly, with the depression, prices dropped sharply reaching the lowest point in 1933 when prices were equivalent to the 1912 level. Taking the decade 1919–29, the average annual price of rice is shown to have been from 25 to 48 per cent higher than that of 1938. The level of the price of maize in this period was even higher.[41] It was at that level of prices that commutations of rents had generally taken place. In the depressed price situation of the 1930s, therefore, the rent-price discrepancy was enormous. And this discrepancy was reflected in a greatly increased number of rent suits[42] and growing peasant discontent.

There were many other aspects of the Great Depression, causing a 'catastrophic fall in prices of agricultural produce which began in October and was so rapid that grain was selling in December at two-thirds of the price at which it was sold a couple of months before; the fall in price did cause difficulty in the disposal of stocks, and therefore the payment of rent and cess. There was a very distinct shortage of money and credit which got no less acute as time went on.'[43] The low prices were particularly unfortunate for those whose rents had been enhanced in the years of high prices, and still more for those who, holding land on produce rent, had the rents legally commuted to cash rents in the years when prices were high. Because of fairly good crops, there was no major shortage of food, but the general standard of living fell. However, the severity of rent collection did cause hardship. It is remarkable that throughout the depression the land revenue collection was almost always more than 90 per cent of the total demand,[44] the bulk of the deficit being in Government estates '. . . where any default in the payment of rent constitutes *ipso facto* a default in the revenue'.[45] In the private estates, the zamindars showed no remorse in collecting the rents and were fairly regular in paying the revenue. Because of those factors, land prices plummeted: 'in the first quarter of 1931 land prices of raiyati holdings were about two-thirds of what they had been in the first quarter of 1930'.[46] In 1931 'the rural population of the province, which accounts for as much as 96 per cent of the total population of thirty-eight millions, was exposed to the full effects of the slump in commodity prices'.[47] The depression had a chain reaction effect. For instance, jute prices fell along with those of chillies and tobacco. This caused great distress in Purnea where these were the chief cash crops. The cattle-breeders of Muzaffarpur lost their 'export market' because jute growers of Purnea (and Bengal) had no money to replace their cattle.

The problems caused by the Great Depression were compounded by other factors. For one thing, nature itself seemed to have turned against the peasantry. Floods, a perennial problem in Bihar, wiped out crops in 1934–5.[48] In the following year, 1935–6, there was drought.[49] But much more serious than these was the great earthquake of 1934.[50] Although expenditure on relief put some money into circulation, the damage done to land by sand being thrown up caused severe dislocation in cultivation and hence in agricultural employment. As a consequence, agricultural wages were depressed from the already low level and, combined with the fact that demand for Bihari labour in the depression-hit industrial and plantation sector outside the province also became low, tremendous hardship was caused to the lowest strata of the rural population. In 1934–5, the government instituted an enquiry into the indebtedness of the cultivators with the special object of ascertaining whether the situation was deteriorating, and in particular, to what extent transference of land or crops to moneylenders was on the increase. The result indicated that, except among improvident aboriginals of Monghyr and Bhagalpur districts, who had to be protected by special legislation in March 1935, there had been no marked increase in the transfer of land or in the taking over of crops, chiefly because land and crops fetched prices too low to influence or induce shrewd moneylenders to lock up their capital in real estate. This conclusion is supported by the appreciable increase in the deposits during the year in the Post

Office Savings Banks in the province, in spite of the earthquake which must have hit a good many persons of the moneylending middle classes.[51] The peasant was little concerned with rises in Savings Bank deposits, and his condition kept deteriorating. For, while the government's enquiry did not disclose any marked increase in rural indebtedness due to the contraction of new debts, arrears of interest to moneylenders had kept increasing.

While on the one side the economic forces were pushing the peasants, especially the poorer peasants, against the wall, on the other the zamindars continued their depredations. Year after year, officials reported the exaction of illegal cesses,[52] refusal by the landlords to accept rents through money orders,[53] denials of receipts for rents paid,[54] neglect of irrigation systems,[55] oppression practised by the zamindars, or if they were absentee landlords, by their agents charging exorbitant *salaami*, even for distress sale of lands by tenants. These practices even in normal times caused agrarian tension and in the disturbed period of the great depression they proved to be sure breeding grounds for agrarian unrest.

This was particularly so because of the peculiar weight of discrimination in the legal system. One official who had vast experience of the working of tenancy laws reported:

> . . . in Bihar the enforcement of the tenancy laws is left to the tenants' initiative by way of suit in the civil courts and the revenue officers are not given an opportunity to stop illegal acts which are feared to be only too prevalent. The tenancy law permits the landlord to file a suit in the courts for the enhancement of the rent due from a tenant. The enhancement, if allowed, continued in force for fifteen years. The law also lays down that the court shall not decree any enhancement which is unfair or inequitable. During the 1930(s) there was an appreciable increase in the number of these suits filed in Bihar and in spite of the falling prices the courts were inclined to allow enhancements according to a mechanical rule which overlooked the cultivator's lower purchasing power. To ignore the economic changes of the last few years clearly (was) to render the money value of the proportion left to the tenant as low as to involve serious hardship.[56]

This indifference of the courts to economic realities, along with the continuing exploitation and oppression by the zamindars, left the tenants no avenue other than to organize themselves into Kisan Sabhas and launch agrarian movements.

Ideology and Programmes

The experiences of various struggles taught the leaders of the Kisan Sabha much. When the Sabha was started, the approach was admittedly 'class collaborationist'.[57] There was even confusion about the definition of the term 'peasant'. The earliest constitutional document of the Kisan Sabha defined a peasant as anyone whose primary source of livelihood was agriculture and even the more elaborate constitution of the BPKS in 1936 said essentially the same thing.[58] In the introduction of the Hindi edition of the Manifesto of the BPKS, written by Swami Sahajanand, the agricultural labourer for the first time was considered a peasant, with an explicit awareness by the author of the difficulties inherent in this concept. Sahajanand wrote:

> A peasant is known as a *grihastha*, a person who earns his livelihood by cultivation and agriculture, be he a petty landlord, ryot or the labourer working for wages for ploughing fields. The Kisan Sabha does not desire that by creating a separate organization of agricultural labourers, any strife should be let loose between them and the ryots, nor should the latter oppress agricultural labourers. . . a grihastha should not be called a landlord. Only a handful of princes, big feudal chiefs and wealthy individuals are landlords.[59]

The struggles of the Kisan Sabha taught it otherwise and made its leaders rely more and more on agricultural labourers and the poorer peasants. By 1941, Sahajanabad was writing that the agrarian problem could not be solved without solving the problems of agricultural labourers. He stated, 'The Kisan Sabha belongs to those exploited and suffering masses whose lot is connected with cultivation and [who] live by it. The more they are oppressed and distressed the nearer they are to the Kisan Sabha and the nearer it is to them.'[60] Sahajanand argued that through the process of de-peasantization, the poor peasants and agricultural labourers come so close that 'no demarcation line can be drawn. Hence, it is proper to regard agricultural labourers as kisans so that the kisans and agricultural labourers may struggle together.'

In spite of the best of intentions, however, this did not happen, so that in a few years, Sahajanand admitted[61] that the Kisan Sabha was unable to get all peasants together and that 'the middle and big cultivators (were) for the most part with the Kisan Sabha'. With characteristic bluntness, he stated:

> They (middle and big cultivators) are using the Kisan Sabha for their benefit and gain, while we are using or rather trying to use them to strengthen the Sabha, till the lowest strata of the peasantry are awakened to their real economic and political interests and needs and have become class conscious. It is they, the semi-proletariat or the agricultural labourers who have very little land or no land at all, and the petty cultivators, who anyhow squeeze a most meager living out of the land they cultivate and eke out their existence, who are the kisans of our thinking and who make and must constitute the Kisan Sabha ultimately.

This, however, did not happen in Sahajanand's lifetime. Nor was he able to convince his associates fully on this. Even Rahul Sankrityayana, a founder-member of the Communist Party in Bihar, wrote provocatively in the 1940s:

> There is no doubt that ultimately the rights of the peasants and agricultural labourers are two sides of the same problem. It is also undeniable that the conditions of agricultural labourers are piteous and their problems must be solved. However, we should remember that all revolutions cannot be made at the same time. Even if agricultural labourers remain labourers, their wages will go up only if the income of the kisans increases. I feel that it will be a serious mistake on their part if they enter into a quarrel with the kisans just now.[62]

Thus although the Kisan Sabha kept debating this question without taking decisive steps to involve agricultural labourers in the organization, the agricultural labourers slowly organized in two ways. The first was 'bogus' organizations[63] had been set-up by the zamindars and their agents who tried to take advantage of the differences between the kisans and agricultural labourers. Several paper organizations, 'patronized and financed by the zamindars for duping the agricultural labourers and taking advantage of their numbers to win elections were set-up'.[64] The second was a move on the part of some leaders of the scheduled castes like Jagjivan Ram to set-up a Bihar Provincial Khet Mazdoor Sabha in 1937.[65] Rahul exposed the first move by the landlords through a series of blistering attacks (and when the second was set-up) he advised restraint on the part of the 'harijan' leaders. He suggested that instead of taking up the issues of agricultural labourers as a whole these leaders should set-up caste organizations to carry out social reforms among them and to take up constructive educational programmes. To the agricultural labourers he promised a 'pie in the sky': 'Their problems will be solved after the advent of communism and the revolution which has started today and will definitely go on to communism, not stopping at merely abolition of zamindari but going on to abolish private property in land. Till then, the agricultural labourers should aim at furthering the cause of the coming revolution.'[66]

When it was first set up, however, the Kisan Sabha, far from taking up the issue of the abolition of the right to private property in land, was not even concerned with the abolition of zamindari. At first, all its leaders including Sahajanand merely wanted that the zamindars should give 'more concessions to the kisans'. It was with great difficulty and after serious debate that the Sabha adopted the demand of zamindari abolition.[67]

It was only after the great earthquake in 1934 that, when the younger Congress elements were released from jail, they formed the Congress Socialist Party. Many members of that party (some of who had earlier opposed the very formation of the Kisan Sabha) decided to work with Swami Sahajanand in the Kisan Sabha. These radical elements quickly pressed for the adoption of zamindari abolition as a policy of the Sabha. Sahajanand was moving in that direction, but was not yet prepared to accept so drastic a step. Socialist Kisan Sabha members introduced an abolition resolution at the first meeting of the Kisan Council after they became members, and, with an 8-member group in a council of 15, got the resolution passed. Sahajanand resigned but was persuaded to continue and the resolution was withdrawn at the intervention of a leading socialist member. Another reason why the resolution was withdrawn was because there was no agreement about the question of compensation. Many socialists who, at that stage, were close to Purushottam Das Tandon (whom they had elected president of the BPKS in 1934) were in favour of compensation being paid after the abolition of zamindari. Sahajanand and a few others insisted that if zamindari abolition was demanded, there was no question of agreeing to payment of compensation. In any case, the resolution could not be passed in 1934.[68]

Through 1935, the socialists introduced resolutions in village and district level meetings demanding zamindari abolition whenever a 'suitable opportunity' arose. Gradually, Sahajanand too came round to the view that the zamindari system was 'an obstacle in the way of economic and social advancement of society' and that 'zamindars were parasitical elements fattening on the blood of the toiling peasantry'. Thus at the third session of BPKS at Hajipur in Muzaffarpur district in November 1935, the policy of zamindari abolition without compensation was adopted. This shift from compromise to class struggle had been achieved and a new ideological framework had been built for the peasant struggle in Bihar. The Council of Action of the Bihar Socialist Party described these developments in the following terms:

> The peasant leaders were provided the organic connection between the social and economic structure and the poverty of the masses. They could (now) see that the problem had its roots in the social structure based on exploitation of one class by another. They could (now) see that the peasant problem was a part of the wider problem affecting and embracing the whole society in all its aspects and could not be solved in isolation.[69]

In spite of these glowing tributes paid by the socialists to themselves, Sahajanand remained the most radical peasant leader in Bihar. When, after Independence, the socialists were getting lost in the morass of ideological pretension and incompetent actions through the setting up of such splinter organizations as the Hind Kisan Panchayat,[70] Sahajanand, just before his death, pointed the direction of the future peasant movement by forming an All-India United Kisan Sabha (AIUKS) whose fundamental demand was 'the nationalization of land and waterways and all sources of energy and wealth. Such nationalization must also result in a planned system embracing not only agriculture and the land but also industries and social services'. As its immediate demand, Sahajanand's AIUKS stood for the 'acquisition of land from those who possess vast domains (and) distributing them on reasonable basis among landless labourers or holders of very small plots'.[71] In the 1970s, a leading ex-socialist of Bihar, Jayaprakash Narayan, when defending the landowners in Musahari from the onslaught of the laborers through futile Sarvodaya attempts,[72] would have done well to remember Sahajanand's experiences and recall his prophetic statement made in 1949 that 'the rural proletariat is becoming aware of its rights, duties and responsibilities. When it becomes fully aware, there will be the final dance of destruction and then the present iniquitous agrarian system will start crumbling.'[73]

Today, when agricultural laborers, mostly harijans and adivasis, have started agitating for their rights in different parts of Bihar, the peasant movement of the 1930s seems finally to have reached its culmination. For many former peasant leaders, representatives of the then 'substantial tenantry' and today's rich peasantry, the chickens then hatched have now come home to roost.

The Process

For many years, in spite of Engels' reflections on the Peasant Wars in Germany and his consequent views on the materialist conception of history, scholarship on the peasant question got embedded on the shoals of mystification and demystification of concepts and categories. The increasing sophistication of academics did not take into account that, in the final resort, learning is not a 'question of dialectical reconciliation of concepts' but 'of the understanding of the real relations' whose conceptual format would give help in the commitment to define dimensions of oppression of men by men and of the ways to struggle against them. Thus, in the quagmire of 'scientificism' (which, for instance, considered Marx's Capital more 'scientific' than his Eighteenth Brumaire), the peasantry, as a living organic entity, was forgotten in the interest of studying capitalist transformation. In any case, capitalism was taken to mean 'de-peasantization'; industry would, according to this approach, inevitably outstrip, subordinate, and finally destroy peasant agriculture. So what was the need to waste time over the genus potato in the sack of potatoes?

Hence, in the hands of 'the brilliant theorist and indifferent politician Plekhanov' the peasants conceptually disappeared: 'Peasantry is not a class but a notion'. Other scholars, who did not go so far, concerned themselves with studying ways in which capital penetrates agriculture and finally conquers it through a conflict of disembodied, inhuman 'forces'. Yet others, nearer to the ground, were absorbed in the economic phenomena: they study 'production relations', 'market relations' and the gradual disappearance of the peasantry through the process of 'differentiation'. The logic of commodity relations, and the exploitative capacity of the richer peasants, indicated a necessary polarization of the peasants into rich and poor, and eventually into 'rural' capitalists and 'rural' proletarians. And, as for production, it would inexorably move through the stages of serfdom: peasant farming, agriculture, and finally, agribusiness. Marxists indulging in the Indian 'Mode of Production' debate followed the process of differentiation as a law of nature and received nods of approval from neo-classical economists. Once in while, political activists like Lenin and Mao Tse-tung have suddenly conjured up the differentiating, disappearing peasantry as a major political force: in their hands, peasants seemed to be transformed from derivations and deductions to armies and actors. But every time the dust settled, the scholars got back once again to work out the dates for the disintegration of the peasantry in the face of the onward march of industry, capital, and the nation-state. Only disintegration was not necessarily inevitable.

Without doubt capitalism transformed agriculture and differentiation played an important part in the capitalist transformation, which often represented very significant structural change. The theoretical and factual claims in support of this argument are valid. It is the interpretation of it as the axiomatically necessary and exclusive pattern that is not. The model should lead to increasing capital accumulation at the top. Such a process would de-peasantize, create a reserve army of labour, procure jobs for many of the newly pauperized, turning them into proletarians and extending capitalism in the classical sense.

This did not happen. Agrarian surplus accumulated neither in the village nor in the towns nor even in the country, but in a metropolis thousands of miles away. What followed was indeed polarization, but a twisted one in which the downward trend was not matched by an upward one. What occurred was not differentiation and proletarinaization of the majority, but a process of pauperization expressed in the phenomena of 'surplus population', 'rural underemployment', and 'culture of poverty'. It was not a 'reserve army of labour' which was produced, for there was nobody to call on those reserves.

The peasants did not dissolve and differentiate into capitalist entrepreneurs and wage labourers, nor were they simply pauperized. They persisted, while gradually transforming and linking into the encapsulating capitalist economy, which pierces through their lives. Peasants continued to exist, though in the economy as a whole, many of them were marginalized, being both within capitalism and outside it. They serve capitalist development (or lumpen bourgeois development of under-development), though in an indirect manner, a type of permanent 'primitive accumulation' offering cheap labor, cheap food, cheaply captured markets for profit-making goods. 'They produce also healthy and stupid soldiers, policemen, servants, cooks and prostitutes; the system can always do with more of each of these. And, of course, peasants produce tasks and troubles for those scholars and officials who puzzle over 'the problem of their non-disappearance.'

Scholars in their optimistic, classical view of capitalism have been proved wrong. They had seen it as aggressive, constructive, overwhelming and supra-energetic in its capacity to spread. Like the finger of Midas, which turned everything it touched into gold, capitalism was expected to turn everything it touched into capitalism. This did not happen. 'The capacity of capitalism to milk everything and everybody around it is undoubted; it is capitalism's capacity or need (in terms of optimization of profits and accumulation of surplus) to transform everything around it into the likes of itself, which is not.' The peasants are a case in point. The alchemy of capitalism did turn them from baser metals into higher ones but at best they became merely 44 carat and not genuine 22 carat gold. But most scholars missed this process. They missed it not because their scholarship was wrong or not 'scientific' or 'rigorous' enough, but because while they were busy searching for the 'peasantry as a theoretical economic category', real flesh and bones peasants were living their day-to-day existence, encountering flesh and bones landlords, merchants, moneylenders and, last but not the least, functionaries of the state; in this actual historical confrontation, they were, if not stopping, at least diverting the onward march of capitalism, and upsetting the neat of industrialization and modernization theories and prescriptions.

In our study of the peasantry in Bihar we have tried to deal with just such flesh and bones beings and their actual, lived experiences. While the advent of the Raj of the capitalist, colonialist British brought trade, some industry, and even a middle class in the towns, it plunged Bihar into continuing backwardness. For long Bihar suffered from the exploitation and oppression which went along with the Raj and its Permanent Settlement with intermediaries who supplied the Raj with considerable revenue. Bihar got very little of the mitigating benefits that were available to the nodal points of contact with imperialism. For instance, even the cultivation of cash crops—opium and indigo—did not provide any healthy aspects of growth, being cancerous developments fostered and cut-off according to the interests of external agencies. At the same time, the Permanent Settlement created a class of parasitic landlords who, by and large, were interested neither in the improvement of agriculture nor in the contemporary cultural awakening. Bihar had neither the development of patni-holding, jotedar-type of prosperous raiyats as a general feature, nor anything equivalent to the 'renaissance' in Bengal as a movement.

However, without plan or conscious effort, but as sporadic, spontaneous features, some of the peasants of Bihar slowly started adopting new methods of agriculture and cultivating new crops like potato, jute, sugar cane and wheat. Money came into the village with these crops. There gradually developed a class of 'substantial tenants'. Their prosperity was increased by markets for the goods they produced, in the towns which emerged around British administrative outposts and around irrigation schemes like the Sone, and later the Tribeni Canal systems, created by the Raj for its own reasons of countering zamindari turbulence. As the prosperity of the 'substantial tenants' increased, so did their hostility towards the zamindars who were skimming off a large share of the agricultural surplus. In areas where the rate of evolution of agriculture was a little faster, where cash-crop cultivation became somewhat widespread, which were linked with the urban consumers, landlord-capitalists, junkers, developed on the one side and peasant-capitalists, kulaks, developed on the other.

It was in these areas, like Patna, Gaya, Shahabad, Monghyr and Champaran, that landlords unleashed particularly severe oppression to stall the process of change. Simultaneously, resistance developed among the tenants. First they tried processes of social reform amongst themselves, through caste associations. But soon they were in confrontation with the zamindars. The latter were standing in their way of dealing with the increasing pauperization, immiserization and marginalization by extorting rent in addition to the revenue that the state demanded. Thus, right from the beginning the movement had a combined anti-government, anti-landlord character. The movement articulated itself through the Kisan Sabha. However, the Sabha, though powerful and fairly widespread, was spontaneous, effervescent and largely outside the control of political parties. The Congress, Socialists, and Communists repeatedly tried to fit the movement into their respective ideological straightjackets, but in vain. The movement remained what it was—an expression of the urge of the relatively better-off tenantry to find ways of avoiding the depredations of the zamindars, and of the poor peasantry to prevent its own obliteration.

In this whole process, the state was not a silent spectator. In the first phase of British rule, the government was merely interested in the security of its revenue. Later, the need to expand a market for its produce as well as avenues of investment, made it enact greater security for substantial tenantry. Still later, successive peasant movements brought state power face to face not only with evidence of zamindari oppression but also with the fact that a substantial portion of the agricultural surplus which could be used as capital was being frittered away in conspicuous consumption. Emergent capitalists, Birla *et hoc genus omne*, particularly resented this and their organs—political and media—increasingly turned against the institution of zamindari. At the same time, the State was promoting agricultural growth and in this it was assisted by the organizations of the substantial tenantry which, at times, even gave up agitation against landlordism and took up campaigns like 'Grow More Food'.

The zamindari system could not withstand the assault from three sides, the substantial tenants, the Indian capitalists and the state. After the dissolution of the British Raj in 1947, the Permanent Settlement was soon unsettled. The substantial tenants and the Indian capitalists had won their battle for accumulation and investment. And the state, through zamindari abolition, had succeeded in maintaining law and order.

But what of the poor peasantry which was getting increasingly pauperized without getting proletarianized? Soon it was on its feet striving for a process of 're-peasantization'. It wanted land and started agitating for it. The challenge posed by the poor peasants was sought to be met through ameliorative action such as Bhoodan on the one side, and promoting faster agricultural development on the other. The idea was to do away with conflict, promote harmony, and at the same time expand the restricted home market that was proving to be a bottleneck in the economy. In this attempt, the state tried the 'trickle down' approach, developing the already better off in the process. The approach was called 'betting on the strong' and seemed logical enough, given the presumption of a harmonious countryside after the abolition of zamindari. But the presumption was wrong. The gamble failed. And the Green Revolution started slowly staining itself red at the edges.

Not only did the depeasantized poor peasantry want land, but the pauperized landless laborers wanted higher wages and dignity—*izzat*. The strategy of countering the upsurge this time was repression. Thus, agrarian unrest in Bihar in the twentieth century has had two rounds: the first at its height in the 1930s and 1940s and the second beginning from the 1960s and 1970s. Both rounds have actually consisted of two fights each. The first one was of (1) the capitalists and middle class utilizing peasants as cannon-fodder against British imperialism and, (2) of the substantial tenants against the zamindars. The second round too has two fights within it. While on the one side the poor peasantry is struggling for its survival, on the other, the emergent kulaks, not finding further sources of accumulation and avenues of investment in agriculture, are turning their energies to getting hold of the eternal milking cow—the government. This is the content of the current 'Backward Caste' phenomenon in Bihar.

YESTERDAY, TODAY, AND TOMORROW

Enough has been written on the appalling agrarian conditions in eastern India, particularly Bihar, for people at large to recognize that something is rotten in that benighted region. With economists writing on the consequences of semi-feudalism, sociologists bemoaning the brutalization of society, political analysts predicting the erosion of political morality, social ecology developing a new and appropriate discipline of disaster studies, and journalists reporting horror stories *ad nauseum*, it has been clear for some time that something had to give and something new had to come out. And so it has.

In response to the near total breakdown not only of the democratic polity but also of established norms of law and order, reflected in Bihar in the phenomena of booth-capturing, mafia maraudings and macabre harijan hunting, all springing from the tension between an antiquated agrarian base and a lumpenized cultural and political superstructure, the subaltern people in the region have always struggled to create a space for themselves to survive in dignity, if not in peace. Much of the struggle has been unassuming, unspectacular, and even mundane. Occasionally it has burst out into great upheavals such as those led by Birsa Munda or Sahajanand Saraswati. The present episode of this continuing struggle is qualitatively different from the earlier ones inasmuch as it combines both the elements of long drawn day-to-day resistance to oppression at the village level and spontaneous combustion of the overall polity exemplified in the creation of a new democratic consciousness. Demonstrations in Patna intervening in the process of changing the grand structure of prevailing politics have as their point of departure the flaming fields where the fire now has spread far and wide.

The emergent counter-force in Bihar is no flash in the pan. As early as May 1982, the Bihar Government in its *Notes on*

Extremist Activities-affected Areas reported that as many as 47 out of a total of 587 blocks, spread over 14 districts, were affected by the 'Communist extremist' movement. In a research paper in the *Economic and Political Weekly*, Pradhan H. Prasad reproduces a table from the *Notes* which shows that 10.28 per cent of the villages, 8.23 of the population, 7.24 of the area, 9.46 of the net sown area and 11.98 of the gross sown area had been affected. Subsequently, if anything, the movement has grown in the face of the corrupt, casteist, and incompetent administration of Bihar.[74]

Let us examine the nature of this 'communist extremism'. What has it actually done which would put it outside the pale of 'mainstream' politics? The most common charge is that the 'extremists' have rejected the idea of change by peaceful means in favour of violence. The charge carries some truth given the experience of the first phase of the Naxalite movement, which was characterized at times by mindless violence. But the situation in Bihar today is very different.

In a state where violence has become the mode of social intercourse, according even to government figures more murders are committed every day than in Punjab. Or as Arun Sinha has pointed out, 'The major feature of social as well as political life (in Bihar) is the prevalence of the language of force, arms in particular'; 'landlords of every village are armed to the teeth and control some private gang of lumpens or other'; and 'the focal point of armed violence is the institution of landlordism which, on account of its dispersed existence, presents a brilliant demonstration of the Gandhian mode of decentralization of power.'[75] In the circumstances the approach of the 'new Naxalites' towards social violence is indeed a marked contrast to prevalent mores.

The prime organization representing the 'new Naxalites', the CPI (ML) Liberation group, states unequivocally, 'First of all, we do not subscribe to any theory of "excitative violence" and still less to "individual assassination".' On the issue of violence, its position is conditioned by the prevailing situation:

Everywhere in Bihar, it is the landlords who are armed, they derive a sadistic pleasure by beating and killing poor peasants, burning their houses and raping their women. Secondly, by any human logic whatsoever, the rural poor cannot be denied their right to organize their own resistance forces to counter the attacks of landlord armies. Thirdly, if peasant struggle takes violent forms in Bihar, the root must be sought in the forms of oppression.[76]

In fact, reports from Bihar indicate that wherever these 'new Naxalites' have managed to acquire significant strength the incidence of day-to-day rural violence has gone down considerably. It is they rather than the established police machinery who are the best guarantors of law and order in the complete sense of the term.

Another feature attributed to 'extremists' is their lack of participation in the processes of electoral democracy. Again, this was true of the first phase of the movement, which was characterized by infantile adventurism. Emerging out of a long and sustained struggle among peasants in the Gangetic plains of Bihar, the 'new Naxalites' appreciate the potential of the electoral processes, though the stars of parliamentary practice have not blinded them. It is clear to them, as to any observer of the electoral scene in Bihar, that a massive charade has been going on in the name of elections. For example, the practice of 'booth capturing' has been institutionalized and has, in effect, disenfranchized large numbers of voters, in particular those among the scheduled castes, tribes, landless laborers, and women.

Thus, the first task of deepening and extending social democracy in Bihar involves not simply aiming for electoral victory but rather achieving full participation in the process of universal adult suffrage. The unobstrusive but significant engagement of the 'new Naxalites' in Bihar with electoral democracy found expression in their participation in the 1985 assembly elections under the banner of the mass organization known as the Indian People's Front. Although their candidates did not win, the signal achievement was that in every constituency that they contested, booth capturing was prevented and democratic norms, tomtomed by others but seldom put into practice, were actualized by those who are most criticised for lack of faith in elections. In this context, the organization noted, 'Defying severe police repression and attacks by the armed gangs of the landlords, the peasants cast their first ever vote in their life. While all the champions of parliamentary democracy—Congress, Lok Dal and CPI alike—were busy capturing booths, the fighting peasants of Bihar, through their conduct in the elections, proved that they are the real representatives of democracy.' The recent setting up by the IPF of *matdata suraksha samitis* (voters' protection committees) is part of the process of actualizing democracy at the grassroots.

Given this kind of non-dogmatic approach and their record of not only ensuring economic gains for the rural poor by enforcing the payment of minimum wages (prescribed by law but seldom actually paid by landowners), and an even distribution of some ceiling-surplus lands in accordance with long-enacted but hardly ever implemented legislation, but also taking up 'constructive activities' like the upgrading of community irrigation works, wells, pastures, etc., the 'new Naxalites' in south-central Bihar have been engaging in both regulatory and promotional activities. In short, their struggle has come to represent the process of state formation in an otherwise anarchic situation.

The qualitatively new aspect of the 'new Naxalite' movement as an important force in Left politics that has been widely ignored by most observers, is the broad correspondence of the caste and class structure it has recognized. A refreshing aspect of the movement has been that, unlike vulgar Marxists, it has neither ignored the caste question nor has it gone overboard on non-class understanding of caste, culture, and ethnicity. Its creative encounter with caste in Bihar is evidenced by the appeal to Kurmi and Yadava peasants as well as to Dalit laborers, but at the same time it recognizes that caste is not an invariant absolute. The non-dogmatic and non-sectarian approach is also reflected in discussions of other extra-economic matters such as the position of women and cultural heterogeneity.

The new politics of the Left in Bihar has been spreading not only in the areas of original Naxalite activity like Bhojpur but also into tribal Jharkhand and eastern UP. Organizationally, there are a variety of groups involved in the movement. They range from various factions of the CPI (ML), the most prominent being the Liberation and Party Unity groups, guerilla groups, like the MCC, mass organizations like the IPF and Mazdoor Kisan Sangram Samiti, and agrarian trade unions like the Kisan Sabha. Although many of these groups have distinct organizational forms and there is even some rivalry between them concerning 'spheres of influence', there is similarity in their intent if not in their aims.

In spite of the existence of several such organizations, fratricidal conflict, which was a marked feature of the earlier Naxalites, is much less today. There are occasions when these organizations criticize one other even severely, as for instance in the Liberation group's denunciation of the tactics of the MCC in utilizing caste conflict—which led to the Dalelchak-Baghaura and other massacres. Yet there have been instances of cooperation between these groups and indeed between them and other democratic elements even in parties like the Samajwadi Party and CPI. The re-enactment of Jallianwalla Bagh at Arwal in April 1986 saw a broad movement arising with the participation of all who were horrified by the extent and nature of police atrocities. The fodder scam once again provided the opportunity for the Left and democratic groups to unite. For example, the emergence of the radical and militant agrarian movement in recent years outside the CPI has put pressure on its cadre to reactivate and again start intervening in the anti-feudal and broadly democratic movement. And the involvement of the 'New Left' with the re-emergent Jharkhand movement in terms of highlighting the genuine grievances of the tribal people is also not insignificant At the same time, the role of organizations like the Jan Sanskriti Manch, All India Student Association, Revolutionary Youth Organisation, Inquilabi Minorities Manch, and Janwadi Mahila Morcha, in the struggle against religious fundamentalism, obscurantist ideology, rank casteism, and the feudal oppression of women, in short in a democratic awakening in semi-feudal Bihar, is increasing.

In the 1970s, the Naxalite movement in Bihar weakened on account of three major factors: its own adventurist stupidity, the developmentalist and co-optational intervention of Jayaprakash Narayan, and repression by the state. But the movement did not collapse. Indeed, the grim agrarian situation and overall deterioration of the political scenario of the state created a new and more robust Left. Its challenge cannot be met by old prescriptions. It embodies the emergence of a specific social democracy in the peculiar situation of Bihar.

It is difficult to delineate the formal organizations that are involved in the peasant upsurge and related political, social, and cultural movements that are taking place in central Bihar. At most a general picture of the organizational networks can be drawn with only an approximation of the complexities that hold the network together.

In fact, the conglomeration of organizations can trace its beginnings to the organized peasant movement in the area begun in 1928 with the formation of the Patna District Kisan Sabha under the leadership of Swami Sahajanand Saraswati. Later it developed into the Bihar Provincial Kisan Sabha and became the core of the All India Kisan Sabha which struggled against zamindari. After zamindari abolition in the 1950s, although the formal organization remained in fact and under the control of the Communist Party of India (CPI), it lost its teeth. In the 1970s when the peasant movement arose again in the region, albeit on different premises and demands, several rudimentary mass organizations of peasants came up here and there. In the early 1980s, the need was felt to consolidate them into one formation and the Bihar Pradesh Kisan Sabha was launched once again. It claimed continuity with the original Kisan Sabha of Sahajanand, even as it took up new issues related primarily to the demands of the small peasants and agricultural labourers.[77]

The peasant militancy in the region proceeded from the late 1960s under the direction of and impetus provided by the Communist Party of India (Marxist-Leninist) (CPI-ML). Lack of proper ideological orientation, internal dissension and repression by the state and local vested interests brought about the effective collapse of this once formidable organization so that by the mid-1970s, it had for all practical purposes fragmented beyond recognition. The largest surviving faction was known as the CPI (ML)—Liberation Group, so called on account of its party organ, *Liberation*. Over a period of time, this group re-organized and has today grown into a formidable force. Another faction which had a small presence in the area in the 1970s but which has grown subsequently goes by the name of the Central Organizing Committee of the CPI (ML)—Party Unity. These two have minor ideological differences and retain their separate identities. They also have separate mass organizations.

Many of these organizations combined in the 1980s into a large umbrella organization known as the Indian Peoples' Front (IPF). It is difficult to today delineate the various elements of the IPF one from the other or from the whole, and in any case, when the CPI (ML) itself emerged from the underground a few years ago, the IPF virtually became defunct. Hence in this account the names of different organizations like the BPKS, CPI (ML), and IPF have been used interchangeably. The movement in central Bihar covers several districts: Bhojpur, Rohtas, Patna, Gaya, Jehanabad, Aurangabad, and Nalanda. In north Bihar, it is growing in Siwan and other areas. The CPI (ML)—Liberation is the leading force behind it. This phase of peasant struggle had its genesis in the heroic struggles of Bhojpur and Patna between 1972 and 1979.[78]

Then in the 1980s peasant struggle began in the rural areas of Patna and soon spread to Nalanda and Jehanabad. A new awakening took place in Bhojpur, Aurangabad, Rohtas and parts of Gaya. The government replied with massive police action. Assisting the armed gangs of landlords (better known as private armies), undertaking certain administrative and economic reforms, mobilizing the support of different political parties, particularly the CPI and Sarvodaya groups, as well as of the news media, the government made multi-pronged attempts to suppress the movement. The organization records:

In the face of these governmental measures and due to our own tactical mistakes, we suffered setbacks and losses in certain areas and had to make retreats and readjustments in many other areas of operation. On the whole, however, we successfully countered these measures and succeeded in disintegrating the private armies, restricting our losses to a minimum and retaining the initiative in our hands.

In essence, the entire struggle revolves around three issues:

(i) For an increase in the wages of agrarian labourers, who account for 30–40 per cent of the rural population in these areas;

(ii) For the seizure of surplus, vested and homestead land in occupation of landlords, mahants, and rich peasants; and distribution of the same among landless and poor peasants;

(iii) For the social dignity of dalits and backward castes. As it strikes at the root of feudal authority, this struggle tends to become intense and the entire range of upper castes of babusahebs, babhans and babajis becomes the target. On the other hand, such struggles draw support from almost all classes of backward castes. There are always some exceptions though, on both the sides. Generally, in all the villages a small section of progressive people from upper castes cooperate with this struggle, while sections of backward castes join hands with reactionaries from upper castes. Under the impact of struggle over all these years, certain sections of upper castes in several areas have begun to change their traditional attitudes.

To effect a greater polarization among people on class lines and to unite broad sections of rural population, we are trying to take up many other related issues as well, say, recording of tenancy rights, mobilizing people against the corruption of block officials, etc. The question of corruption is linked with agrarian development, as the lion's share of benefits is usurped by these officials in collusion with local reactionaries. Besides, action against dacoit gangs, certain village development works, relief measures etc. are also taken up to unite the broad masses of rural population.

We hold that only an integrated programme of struggles and activities on all such issues can ensure broad peasant unity under the leadership of agrarian labourers and poor peasants. We are often accused by opportunists of all hues of disrupting the broad peasant unity and of pitting agrarian labourers against peasants. By sacrificing the interests of agrarian labourers and poor peasants and by refusing to mobilize them in mass struggles, their class consciousness and class solidarity cannot be developed, nor can their leadership be established over the peasant movement. Naturally, the so-called broad peasant unity simply boils down to unity under the leadership of rich peasants. There is no middle way.

We still cannot claim to have altered the class and caste balance in our favour, but gradually we are heading towards building this unity on a new basis. In certain areas, middle peasants and middle sections of upper castes are also being mobilized under the banner of Kisan Sabha.[79]

WHODUNIT

There remains the task of identifying the *dramatis personae*. Just as the acts and scenes themselves have not followed a neat sequence, the cast of characters has also changed. The initial lead was taken by 'outsiders', in particular Sahajanand who stood outside the production process as a *samnyasi*, and as such may fall in the category of the lumpen intellectual. The other important characters too, like Gandhi, Jayaprakash Narayan, Rahul Sankrityayana, and K.B. Sahay, though having more interest in land and its ownership than Sahajananad, were also essentially 'outsiders'. They were not directly affected by the process of the agrarian economy. Their action was not a result of experience but of consciousness acquired extraneously. Their process of action, in fact, followed the sequential course: consciousness—action—experience. These 'outsider' leaders did not directly go to the peasants but operated through local level leaders like Yadunandan Sharma, Ramnandan Mishra, Raj Kumar Shukla and others who were conscious of deprivation because of their own, actual experience, and wanted action to remedy the situation. For them the process was experience—consciousness—action. Finally, there were (and are) the peasants themselves who, having neither sophisticated theory nor wide experience, acquire both experience and consciousness through action. Hence for them the sequence was action—experience—consciousness.

The interaction of these three sequential elements was not confined to one stage either. In the first stage, in the period before the Second World War, initiative was with outsiders and reached the peasants through local leaders, thereby generating the development of consciousness. In the period of the Second World War, the Quit India Movement and the advent of Independence, the 'outsiders' were either busy with high political affairs, or in jail, or in government. Hence the initiative came to the hands of the local leaders who launched struggles through which a great deal of experience was gained. In this process zamindari was abolished and many local leaders benefitted either personally or as members of a class of substantial tenants. They acquired vested interests in the changed situation as a consequence of which agrarian movements took a back seat. For several years, there were indeed no significant movements. With time, however (in the 1960s), a new set of ideologically oriented 'outsiders' emerged and reached the countryside to join the peasant masses in their struggles. By then, in many areas like Champaran, Purnea, Bhojpur, and Dhanbad, the peasants themselves had already grasped the initiative. Hence there followed a process of action. It is this action that is taking place in many parts of Bihar today. The action is sporadic and spontaneous. It is countered by brutal repression by the landlords, rich peasants and the state. In many instances it takes the form of caste, rather than class, conflict. In some cases the former allies and even leaders of the poor peasantry have become its oppressors and it is not uncommon that yesterday's substantial tenants are today killing poor peasants, burning their miserable huts and raping their women. On the face of it, the situation of the poor peasants, agricultural labourers, and other toiling people in Bihar is desperate; it seems it will never change. But propelled by the very desperation of the struggling, toiling people, Bihar is changing. 'And yet it moves.'

. . . And Friends

Swami Sahajanand Saraswati died not three years after Independence and before the legislation abolishing zamindari could be enacted. However, he had led a strong enough movement to make that phase of 'land reforms from above' inevitable. However, as the agrarian change process got bogged down in legalisms on the one side and resistance by vested interests on the other, the focus of politics changed. Class issues were relegated to the background as wheeling and dealing for the loaves and fishes of office took precedence.

Scholarship in the social sciences has a habit of following political trends. Thus it is not surprising that in the years following Independence, the attention of most academics was focused on the 'mainstream' political parties, in particular the Congress. It required academic imagination in that context to research peasants, peasant organizations, and their leaders. Walter Hauser was among the first to do so. When the smouldering embers of peasant activism appeared to be lost under the ashes of realpolitik, it required moral and intellectual courage to look at peasant activists as the subjects—rather than the objects—of research. Mind you, this was before the period when environmental studies or gender studies became 'valuable' because not only were they politically correct but also academically pragmatic. Besides, this was also the period before the *Journal of Peasant Studies* and other such publications lifted the peasant from the footnote to the text of history.

Swami Sahajanand was re-discovered by Walter Hauser well before Subaltern Studies turned history into literature and social science into mere literary criticism. Hauser's tools were imperfect perhaps, being conventionally accepted and tried and tested. He did not, and perhaps could not too, indulge in looking at the various meanings of discourse and the subtext of records. And yet, somehow, anyhow, the moral imperative mattered. Just as it did in the case of the saffron-robed 'red Swami'.

It could not have been easy for Walter Hauser to carry out his research when he did. Those were still the years of the 'Ugly American', when *Time* was denouncing Jawaharlal Nehru as a dangerous crypto-communist and Non-Alignment was seen as a vile plot against the 'Free World'. In India too, not only had the strength of the Kisan Sabha ebbed after the Telengana Uprising but probing into its past—particularly by an American—must have seemed distinctly odd. The fact that Hauser's thesis remained unpublished only added to the mystery.

And yet, Walter Hauser did not let the past of the Kisan Sabha become mere history. Not only did he make copies of his thesis available to libraries like that at the A.N. Sinha Institute of Social Studies in Patna and the Nehru Memorial Museum and Library in New Delhi, he continued to research the discourse of Sahajanand as well as the Phoenix-like quality of the Kisan Sabha which rose from its own ashes in the 1970s.[80] Of course, in the latter case, it was the fact that the peasants of Bihar reinvigorated a comatose organization that added to the effort of the scholar.

Swami Sahajanand Saraswati has still not got his due from history. Despite the efforts of Walter Hauser and others who have studied the life and times of this absolutely fascinating personality, Sahajanand has been largely forgotten—and when he is remembered, it is as a leader of the Bhumihars. Recently, peasant assertiveness has made some dent in this image-creation and historical misappropriation, but in a time when the agrarian conflict paradigm has shifted from the tenant-zamindar tussle to the laborer/poor peasant–junker/kulak antagonism, when the Ranbir Sena of the Bhumihars is aggressively ranged against today's Kisan Sabha, it is necessary perhaps to review the evolution of Sahajanand. Walter Hauser is doing that. More strength to his elbow.

Acknowledgements

A more detailed account of peasant movements in Bihar is contained in my book, *Agrarian Unrest and Socio-Economic Change in Bihar.* I am grateful to all those who helped me in many ways in completing that study. It is not possible here to name all of them, but in particular I wish to record my debt to Laksmi Mandal and Jahoor Ali, poor peasants in Bihar, who not only aroused my interest in the subject but also bore with me in many ways, and to Professor B.B. Chaudhury and Dr. Walter Hauser, from whose pioneering works I have drawn heavily. I also specially thank Vinay Kumar Sharma who cheerfully typed the present work, square brackets and all.

Much of the description of the Kisan Sabha is taken from the unpublished work of Dr. Walter Hauser who had the opportunity to look at organizational documents of the Kisan Sabha in the 1950s and 1960s before many of them disappeared from Bihta. The references to Hauser's work cited here may not match the original pagination as it is taken from a typescript prepared from Dr. Hauser's thesis, a copy of which he has kindly made available to the A.N.S. Institute of Social Studies, Patna.

NOTES

1. Swami Sahajanand, *Gita Hridaya (Heart of the Gita)*, Allahabad: Kitab Mahal, 1948, pp. 96-123.
2. Walter Hauser, 'Swami Sahajanand and the Politics of Social Reform, 1907-1950', *Indian Historical Review*, vol. 18, nos. 1-2, 1991-1992, pp. 64-71.

3. Swami Sahajanand, *Mera Jivan Sangharsha (My Life Struggle)*, Bihta: Sitaramashram, p. 426.
4. Walter Hauser, 'The Bihar Provincial Kisan Sabha, 1929-1942: A Study of an Indian Peasant Movement', PhD Thesis, University of Chicago, 1961, pp. 109-33.
5. Swami Sahajanand, 'Address of the Chairman, Reception Committee, The All India Anti-Compromise Conference, First Session, Kisan Nagar, Ramgarh, Hazaribagh', nos. 19 & 20, March 1940, Ramgarh.
6. Arvind N. Das, *Agrarian Unrest and Socio-economic Change in Bihar, 1900-1980*, Delhi: Manohar, 1983.
7. Algu Rai, *A Move for the Formation of an All-Indian Organisation for the Kisans*, Azamgarh, 1946.
8. Hauser, 'The Bihar Provincial Kisan Sabha', p. 85.
9. Ibid.
10. Ibid.
11. Sahajanand, *Mera Jivan*, p. 171.
12. T.S. Sudhakar, *Lok Nayak Swami Sahajanand Saraswati*, Gaya, 1973, p. 14.
13. Hauser, 'The Bihar Provincial Kisan Sabha', p. 87.
14. R.A.E. Williams, *Bihar and Orissa in 1931-32*, Patna: Superintendent, Government Printing, 1933, pp. 1-30.
15. BSCRO (Bihar State Central Records Office), File 21/1933, Agrarian Affairs, Kisan Sabhas.
16. Sahajanand, *Mera Jivan*, pp. 373-81.
17. BSCRO: 16/1935/I.
18. BSCRO: 16/1935.
19. N.G. Ranga, *Revolutionary Peasants*, New Delhi: Amrit Book Co., 1949 p. 69; N.G. Ranga, *Fight For Freedom*, Delhi: S. Chand, 1968, p. 216.
20. Sahajanand, *Mera Jivan*, pp. 449-53.
21. N. Mitra, ed., *Indian Annual Register*, vol. 2, July–December 1937, Calcutta, 1938, pp. 387-9.
22. P.T. Mansfield, *Bihar and Orissa in 1930-31*, Patna: Superintendent, Government Printing, 1932, p. 1.
23. R. Prasad, *Autobiography*, Bombay: Asia Publishing House, 1957, p. 312; Arvind N. Das, *Changel: The Biography of a Village*, Delhi: Penguin Books, 1996.
24. Jawaharlal Nehru, *An Autobiography*, London: John Lane, 1936.
25. Ibid., p. 237.
26. M.K. Gandhi, 'The Zamindar and the Ryots', *Young India*, vol. III (New Series), no. 153, 18 May, 1921.

27. Williams, *Bihar and Orissa*, p. 32.
28. Ibid., pp. 9-16.
29. Ibid., p. 10.
30. Hauser, 'The Bihar Provincial Kisan Sabha' p. 61.
31. Sahajanand, *Mera Jivan*, pp. 327-77.
32. Hauser, 'The Bihar Provincial Kisan Sabha', p. 51.
33. BSCRO: 34/1931
34. Swami Sahajanand, 'Gaya ke Kisanon ki Karun Kahani' (Pathetic Plight of the Peasants of Gaya), Patna.
35. Williams, *Bihar and Orissa in 1931-32*, p. 9.
36. Hauser, 'The Bihar Provincial Kisan Sabha', p. 97.
37. BSCRO: 163/1934.
38. BSCRO: 163/1935.
39. BSCRO: 163/1934.
40. Hauser, 'The Bihar Provincial Kisan Sabha', p. 98.
41. Bihar, Board of Revenue, *Average Prices of Staple Food Crops from 1888*, Patna, 1938.
42. Bihar & Orissa, *Report on the Administration of Civil Justice in the Province of Bihar and Orissa, 1933*, Patna: Superintendent, Government Printing, 1934.
43. Mansfield, *Bihar and Orissa in 1930-31*, p. 14.
44. Mansfield, *Bihar and Orissa in 1930-31*; Williams, *Bihar and Orissa in 1931-32*; Wilcock, *Bihar and Orissa in 1932-1933*, Patna: Superintendent, Government Printing, 1935; S. Solomon, *Bihar and Orissa in 1934-35*, Patna: Superintendent, Government Printing, 1937; K. Narayan, *Bihar and Orissa in 1935-36*, Patna: Superintendent, Government Printing, 1938; S.M. Wasi, *Bihar in 1936-37*, Patna: Superintendent, Government Printing, 1938.
45. Mansfield, *Bihar and Orissa in 1930-31*, p. 80.
46. Ibid., p. 81.
47. Williams, *Bihar and Orissa in 1931-32*, p. 20.
48. Solomon, *Bihar and Orissa in 1934-35*, p. 17.
49. Narayan, *Bihar and Orissa in 1935-36*, p. 21.
50. Sahajanand, *Mera Jivan* pp. 421-7.
51. Solomon, *Bihar and Orissa in 1934-35*, pp. 18-19.
52. Ibid., p. 116.
53. R. Jagmohan, *Bihar and Orissa in 1929-30*, Patna: Superintendent, Government Printing, 1931, p. 89.
54. Mansfield, *Bihar and Orissa in 1930-31*, p. 82.
55. R.L. Gupta, *Bihar and Orissa in 1932-33*, Patna: Superintendent, Government Printing, 1934, p. 81.

56. Williams, *Bihar and Orissa in 1931-32*, pp. 29-30.
57. Swami Sahajanand, 'The Origin and Growth of the Kisan Movement in India', Bihta: Unpublished ms., n.d.
58. BPKS (Bihar Provincial Kisan Sabha), *Bihar Prantiya Kisan Sabha ka Vidhan* (Constitution of the Bihar Provincial Kisan Sabha), Patna: 1936; BPKS, *Bihar Prantiya Kisan Sabha ka Ghoshna Patra aur Kisanon ki Maangen* (Manifesto of the BPKS and Peasants' Demands), Bihta.
59. Walter Hauser, ed., *Sahajanand on Agricultural Labour and the Rural Poor*, New Delhi: Manohar, 1994; Walter Hauser, ed., *Swami Sahajanand and the Peasants of Jharkhand*, New Delhi: Manohar, 1995.
60. Swami Sahajanand, 'Khet Mazdoor' (Agricultural Labourer), written in Hazaribagh Central Jail. See Hauser, op cit., 1994, pp. 59-60.
61. Swami Sahajanand, 'Presidential Address', 8th Annual Session of the Kisan Sabha, Bezwada 1944.
62. Rahul Sankrityayana, *Dimagi Gulami* (Mental Slavery), Allahabad: Kitab Mahal, 1957, pp. 70-3.
63. Swami Sahajanand, *Kisan Sabha ke Sansmaran* (Recollections of the Kisan Sabha), Allahabad: New Literature, 1947.
64. Sankrityayana, *Dimagi Gulami*, p. 72.
65. Hauser, 'The Bihar Provincial Kisan Sabha', p. 20; *The Searchlight*, Patna: 8 January 1948.
66. Sankrityayana, *Dimagi Gulami*, pp. 70-3.
67. Sahajanand, 'The Origin and Growth of the Kisan Movement', pp. 442-3.
68. BSCRO:16/1935.
69. *The Searchlight*, Patna: 3 April 1941.
70. *The Searchlight*, Patna: 13 March 1949.
71. AIUKS (All-India United Kisan Sabha), *The Programme and Charter of Kisan Demands*, Patna 1949.
72. 'Sarvodaya and Development', *Journal of Social and Economics Studies*, vol. IV, no.1, (Patna), 1976.
73. Swami Sahajanand, *Maharudra ka Mahatandav*, Bihta, n.d.
74. Pradhan H. Prasad, 'Agrarian Violence in Bihar,' *Economic and Political Weekly*, vol. 22, no. 22, 30 May 1987, p. 851.
75. Arun Sinha, *Against the Few: Struggles of India's Rural Poor*, London: Zed Books, 1991.
76. CPI (ML), *Report from the Flaming Fields of Bihar*, Calcutta: Prabodh Bhattacharya, 1986, pp. 68-9.
77. CPI (ML), 1986; Walter Hauser, 'Violence, Agrarian Radicalism

and Electoral Politics: Reflections on the Indian People's Front', *Journal of Peasant Studies*, vol. 21, no. 1 (Oct. 1993), pp. 85-126.

78. Kalyan Mukherjee and Rajendra Singh Yadav, *Bhojpur: Naxalism in the Plains of Bihar*, New Delhi: Radha Krishna, 1980; CPI (ML), 1986; Hauser, 1993.
79. CPI (ML), 1986.
80. Hauser, 'Violence, Agrarian Radicalism and Electoral Politics'.

The Reora Satyagraha (1939): Its Contemporary Relevance

Sho Kuwajima

Jadunandan (Yadunandan) Sharma was one of the most trusted comrades of Swami Sahajanand Saraswati in the kisan movement in Bihar. The village survey in Gaya district that the Kisan Sabha made in 1933 was elaborately prepared by Jadunandan Sharma. It was after the survey that Sahajanand came to his conclusion that the zamindari system was an incurable disease.[1]

The simplicity of Jadunandan Sharma's clothes and manners is widely known. Rahul Sankrityayan, who led the peasant Satyagraha in Amwari, 1939, recollects in his autobiography that in his speech Jadunandan Sharma did not use the words that kisans could not understand.[2] Rahul devoted one chapter of his book, *New Leaders in New India*, written in Hindi, to the life of Jadunandan Sharma, and said that the peasant Satyagraha of Reora, which Jadunandan Sharma led, held a prominent place in the history of the kisan struggle not only in Bihar, but also in India.[3]

Here, I try to seek the historical meaning and contemporary relevance of the Reora Satyagraha, while presenting the English translation of the related part of my interview with Jadunandan Sharma in Gaya in April 1966.

I

Jadunandan Sharma was the chairman of the Reception Committee of the fourth session of the All India Kisan Sabha which was held at Gaya on 9 and 10 April 1939. M.A. Rasul, who attended this session, writes:

The session was held at a time when a mighty struggle of the kisans of

Bakasht land was still going on in a number of districts of Bihar and when it had already been victorious at Reora (Gaya).

The Reora kisans (Gaya district) resorted to satyagraha for 1,000 bighas dispossession from which was threatened. Yadunandan Sharma initiated the campaign, was thrown into jail where later the district magistrate of Gaya negotiated with him and reached an agreement for leaving 850 bighas to kisans. Sharma and his colleagues in jail were released. The kisans of Reora decided to take to collective farming of the land.[4]

However, the welcome speech of Jadunandan Sharma at the Gaya session claimed that the Kisans of Reora won the satyagraha and were proud of its victory, but did not mention anything about the collective farming.[5]

The *Congress Socialist,* a weekly organ of the Congress Socialist Party, traced the development of the Reora Satyagraha from its start. Before his arrest, Jadunandan Sharma described how the movement began and how its early stage went. Besides the work of cutting and threshing of the crops, women workers were specially assigned to shower 'sacred rice' on constables and soldiers, and to make them understand that they were sons of kisans too.[6] As his recollection showed, Jadunandan Sharma led the satyagraha, but at the same time the kisans, and particularly women, led Sharma and other leaders to the satyagraha. At this stage of the movement there was no reference to collective farming. In the same weekly, dated 29 January 1939, the slogan of the movement, which the Congress Socialists carried, was still 'Land to the Tillers'.[7] After a month, they appealed to the Kisans to respond to their special message on the basis of their victory:

The Reora kisans deserve our warmest congratulation on their magnificent victory. May we hope that they will further their strength and solidarity by refusing to fragment the 500 acres into individual holdings and decide to cultivate them collectively and thus teach yet another lesson to the rest of India and assure their place permanently in the vanguard of India's kisan movement.[8]

In May 1939, after the Gaya session of the All India Kisan Sabha, Awadeshwar Prasad Sinha wrote in the same journal about the historical mission of Reora Kisans:

The kisans of Reora decided to resort to collective farming which is going to be a landmark in the history of agrarian movement in India. Though the problems connected with collective farming have still to be grappled with at Reora the very fact that the land owning kisans have agreed to pull their resources with landless kisans points out unmistakably to the fact that our own land-owning kisans are not so keen about their private property in land as they are depicted to be.[9]

After Jadunandan Sharma was arrested, it seems that, in deciding the direction of the Satyagraha after the 'victory', the role of the Congress Socialists (particularly of Jayaprakash Narayan, the President of Gaya District Congress Committee) became larger. Yet the Kisans placed their firm trust in Jadunandan Sharma, and the final settlement was reached between Sharma and the Magistrate. The last part of the recollection of Jadunandan Sharma, which he talked about with a smile, seems to express his complex feeling about the unexpected development of the discussion after the 'victory' of the satyagraha. At the very least, the idea of 'collective farming' does not seem to have originated from the words of Jadunandan Sharma, though he led the 'collective cutting' of crops in the satyagraha.

Jayaprakash Narayan has some writings on co-operative and collective farming. It was one of his socialist projects of the 1930s. Yet he was cautious about it: 'Common ownership being our goal, it would appear rather strange that we should think of redistributing land to peasants. This necessity arises from the fact that common ownership and cultivation of land would be slow to develop and therefore we will have to begin with peasant proprietorship.' Narayan found in Russia, 'where alone socialism was being built up', the growth of three types of socialized agriculture. The first form is simply co-operative farming, while individual holdings remained. For the purposes of cultivation, the holdings are pooled together and the crop is raised and harvested with joint labour. The next step is the collective farm, without individual holding, though individual ownership of tools and cattle may remain. The third stage is the 'commune', the highest stage of common living. But Narayan warned against hasty steps:

Let us be slow instead of hasty as the Russians. Let us use no coercion. Nor does the Party advocate forcible socialization of agriculture, as it does with industry. *Encouragement and promotion* of co-operative and collective farming is the phrase used—encouragement and promotion through education, propaganda, demonstration, subsidy, preferential taxation.[10]

At Reora, Jayaprakash Narayan seems to have been 'hasty as the Russians', or even hastier than the Russians in 1929–32. The initiative of the kisans and the unprecedented strength of their collective action in defending their land rights may have led him to the conclusion that this was a golden chance for collective farming.

Anugraha Narayan Sinha, who was Minister of Finance, Self-Government and Public Works under the Congress Ministry of 1937–9, later recalled this episode:

In my view the agreement certainly yielded some benefits to the Kisans of Reora. Jayaprakash Narayan's assertion that the Congress Socialists won the struggle has some truth. However, his plan that by force of the agreement they can start co-operative farming at Reora according to their socialist theory and establish an ideal society was baseless. Even then, when he had a talk with me, I said that we would support a co-operative farm. I even made my promise that our Government would finance 5,000 Rupees, and bear all expenses for irrigation. I also promised to go to preside over its opening ceremony. Afterwards, the Kisans refused to divide their lands on the basis of socialist theory, and insisted that they should be allotted their land according to the proportion of the land they had so far. As a result nothing was realized.[11]

As for the official view of this drama, the Patna Commissioner's Fortnightly Reports traced the movement of Jadunandan Sharma. The fortnightly report up to 27 April 1939 stated, 'Pandit Jadunandan Sharma has still to visit to Reora to fulfil the undertakings which he has given at the time of recent settlement and about which he expressed so much confidence.'[12] Again the report up to 13 May 1939 stated conclusively, 'It appears that a sort of stalemate has been reached in the Reora affair. The tenants will not accept the socialistic distribution of land by Jadunandan Sharma. They are unwilling to divide equally among themselves the land allotted to the tenants, and, when appealed, Jadunandan Sharma is keeping quiet.'[13]

The report up to 27 May maintained, 'Pandit Jadunandan Sharma has not yet been able to visit Reora to make the distribution of lands undertaken by him', but after this last reference, Reora disappeared from the official observation. The drama seems to have ended around this time on the official side.

As an interview with Jadunandan Sharma shows, a way to the settlement at Reora was prepared by Jayaprakash Narayan and his socialist colleagues. Although Sharma opposed the compromise, he finally agreed to it, knowing the response of the peasants. The recollection of Sharma gives an impression that he was not so optimistic about the settlement at that stage. After the 'victory' of the Satyagraha the socialist experiment at Reora did not reach even the first stage of co-operative farming that Jayaprakash Narayan had described.[14] Shriramvriksh Benipuri, a writer and one of the socialist colleagues, said in a biography of Jayaprakash Narayan that the *Bakasht* movement of Reora had become widely known all over India because of JP's competent leadership.[15] Yet in this work there was no reference to the socialist experiment at Reora. Later, when Benipuri wrote his autobiography, he devoted many pages to the kisan movement and Jayaprakash Narayan, but no reference was given to Reora.[16]

While he was in jail during the Second World War, Swami Sahajanand looked back on the kisan movement in the 1930s, and learned his lessons from it. He was careful in his appreciation of the 'victory' of Reora:

> The most remarkable point is that we now like the talk of the truce after the struggle. Almost everywhere it was just like that. We never refused the truce. But our experience taught that this was not right. Zamindars and bureaucrats involved us in a great deal of trouble. In Darbhanga our comrades had very painful experiences. More or less it was the same in other areas too. In Gaya similar matters occurred. Even at Reora we had to face many difficulties later. There till now imbroglio more or less continues. Therefore I came to this conclusion that, generally speaking, after starting our struggle, we should not be involved into the imbroglio around the truce, even if we suffered defeat. On that occasion we get benefit from our defeat, because we know our own weakness.[17]

Though Sahajanand did not refuse the 'necessity of manoeuvring and retreating' in the complex stage of imperialism, he did not have a static and unchangeable image of the Kisan Sabha.[18] The lesson from Reora also lies here in the undercurrent.

By the eve of Independence, Jayaprakash Narayan became very critical of the Russian internal and foreign policy, but still believed that the next stage in the evolution of human society was socialism.[19] He also visualized the abolition of landlordism and a fairer redistribution of land leading to co-operative farming and collectivization.[20] Though he did not like the Russian type of collectivization 'pushed through at great human cost and under a ruthless dictatorship', Jayaprakash Narayan had to admit that co-operative farming itself would require a good deal of coercion. Even after his failed experiment at Reora, there was no basic change in his idea of co-operative farming and collectivization.

In 1969 and 1970, Mushahari Block of Muzzaffarpur District in Bihar became one of the focal points of Naxalite activities. Jayaprakash Narayan tried to strengthen the Gandhian *sarvodaya* movement under the name of *gramdan* from 1970 to 'generate a voluntary process of individual and social change, and of village reconstruction and community self-government or Gram Swaraj'.[21] In this experiment he noticed the different response to the movement from the different classes:

> As a rule the landless labourers are the first to respond, then the small farmers. Gradually the middle farmers come over, and a time comes when the resistence of the bigger farmers too begins to break. What seems to stick in their throats are: (a) renouncing their proprietary title to their land; and (b) joining the direct democracy of the Gram Sabha (Village Assembly). Their feudal and upper-caste mentality inhibits them from reconciling themselves to the political equality of the Sabha. They fear the overwhelming majority of the poor, even though they are assured that decisions can be taken only by unanimity or concensus. The moneylenders are the last to change. There are, of course, exceptions to this general pattern.[22]

Here 'a voluntary process of individual and social change' is proposed instead of 'coercion' in the co-operative farming. However, the survey conducted by the A.N. Sinha Institute of Social Studies, Patna concluded that the development effort in

Mushahari on behalf of the Gram Swaraj movement could not produce any substantial results for the rural poor:

> The semi-feudal social formation had got a rude shake up in the wake of the poor peasant movement in Mushahari but did not last long. There was some evidence to suggest that the *sarvodaya* movement strengthened rather than weakened the semi-feudal bondage. One of the authors does not see the *sarvodaya* movement even remotely leading anywhere near social and economic justice. In some cases, the rural rich have continued to grow economically and politically by cornering the bulk of the benefits flowing out of the development work in the villages of the region under the auspices of *sarvodaya*. In his opinion ruthless exploitation continues as before.[23]

Needless to say, the activities of Jayaprakash Narayan in the 'Quit India' movement became an indispensable chapter of the history of the freedom movement in India. His leadership in the movement against authoritarianism, which was started some years after the Mushahari experiment, was likewise crucial in removing Indira Gandhi from the seat of the Prime Minister. However, the main purpose of his work in Reora and Mushahari was only partially and unsatisfactorily realized. Jayaprakash Narayan himself wrote in his report on Mushahari as follows:

> My first reaction on coming face to face with the reality was to realize how remote and unreal were the brave pronouncements of Delhi or Patna from the actuality at the ground level. Hiss-sounding words, grandiose plans, reforms galore. But somehow they all, or most of them, remain suspended somewhere in mid-air. They hardly touch the ground—at least not here. Or touch it very lightly. In the event, what meets the eye is utter poverty, misery, inequality, exploitation, backwardness, stagnation, frustration, and loss of hope.[24]

Narayan may have had the same feeling of distance between his idea and the reality at the ground level in Mushahari as he experienced at Reora. The poor results in Reora and Mushahari may be partly explained by his idea of 'utopian socialism' in the 1930s and 'utopian Gandhism' in the 1970s. But there was continuity in his basic approach. Of course, the class character of the problem was an important factor that prevented his idea from its fruition.

Apart from the position of agricultural laborers and rural

poor, what relevance does the Reora Satyagraha have to the contemporary history of India and the world? As for the historical role of the work of Jadunandan Sharma after the abolition of the zamindari system in Bihar, the view of Arvind N. Das is very clear:

He survived his leader Swami Sahajanand Saraswati and tried to keep the light of the non-party Kisan Sabha burning in Bihar. However, Zamindari Abolition marked the end of the one phase in the kisan movement and after that, almost automatically, the leaders of that phase suffered 'obsolescence'. Yadunandan Sharma was no exception to this, although for the next twenty years he remained a very popular and respected person among the peasants. He died in 1975, a lonely man who after achieving one mission had not been able to move on to the next.[25]

However, it is also to be noted that, despite his 'historical limitation' as a kisan leader, the movement led by him has some remarkable contemporary relevance.

First, as Swami Sahajanand pointed out, the movement at Reora showed that, while Jadunandan Sharma led the kisan movement, the kisans led their leader to action. The relations between the kisans and their leader were not one way, but a reversible process, and this gave the strength to the kisan movement:

Then Sharmaji said, 'Plough the field, and, those who even a little planted rice, cut crops'. Kisans replied, 'We don't want your advice. We had thought that you would walk on some right road. But, if you also give us a lecture, leave this place. Let us die. And, if not so, you should first plough the field and reap paddy crops. We will follow you, and die with you.' These words pricked him, and at that very moment he put his foot down. He sent me a message, 'Now I am going to jail.'[26]

This scene reflected one of the distinctive features of the kisan movement in Bihar led by Sahajanand in the 1930s. This was a great contribution to the discussion on the method of the people's movement.

Second, the history of the kisan movement in Bihar in the 1930s is not complete without the reference to the part played by women. As the memoir of Jadunandan Sharma shows, the women of Reora led the Satyagraha to 'victory'. But this was not an isolated case, and this kind of scene was observed in other areas too. From where did this strength come? It seems that this aspect of the kisan movement has not been adequately explored so far.

Despite his conviction as a socialist, Jayaprakash Narayan vacillated between 'coercion' and 'encouragement' at Reora. On the other hand, the 'indecision' of Jadunandan Sharma after the 'victory' at Reora seems to have come from the fact that he knew well the true position of the kisans. At one time, co-operative or collective farming was expected to be an effective solution of Indian land problems in various quarters, including the platforms of the Indian National Congress from the 1930s to the 1950s. Though he was critical of the Russian foreign policy and the Stalinist regime of centralization in the 1930s, the attachment of Jayaprakash Narayan to co-operative farming seems to have survived even after he adopted the Gandhian approach in the 1950s.

In the survey of the land reform in a Japanese village after the Second World War, one Indian scholar, who visited there in 1961–2, found that the villagers with their traditional outlook saw the smooth and effective implementation of land reform as a 'victory for the family system of the country'.[27] In fifty years after the land reform, and under the critical condition of agricultural management in Japan where there is a dearth of the young labour, even the proposal of 'corporate' farming is made as one of the ways out of this painful circumstance.

The struggle at Reora has contemporary relevance in this respect too.

Appendix: Peasant Satyagraha of Reora told by its leader Jadunandan Sharma[28]

....The Reora movement was a very mighty movement. The Zamindar of Reora was a very rich and very cruel person. He was the Chairman of the Gaya District Board. His name is Rameshwar Prasad Singh.

He came to our village on his tour from Jehanabad. He was passing through near our Ashram. In his car was his brother-in-law who was a friend of mine. Rameshwar Prasad Singh stopped his car, and came to our Ashram.

I asked, 'Why, Rameshwar Babu?'

He answered, 'I came to drink water.'

I helped him to drink. After that Rameshwar Babu sat in the seat of the car. I went to his side and, folding my hands, said, 'Kisans of Reora came to my place, and told their sad story. Make compromise with him. Take some money and let them cultivate their land.'

Rameshwar Babu was agitated, and said, 'I can't do so.'

I said, 'I am going to Reora tomorrow.'

He retorted, 'You can't reach Reora.'

I said, 'Alright, I am going tomorrow.'

This is an introduction to the Reora Satyagraha.

I reached Reora. At that time there were some standing crops in the field, and there we held a meeting. Both women and men joined the meeting. The largest number of kisans of Reora are Bhumihars. Rameshwar Prasad Singh is a Bhumihar. But he did not allow the kisans to live [a life] worthy of Bhumihars. Kisans were really like *fakirs*. For want of food, their little children went nearer to trees early in the morning, and ate *gular, pipar,* and *pankar* which animals can eat, but not men. Kisans sold their daughters, and managed their livelihood with that money. On the one hand, a six-year old girl, and on the other, thirty or thirty-five year old man. Her father made her get married, and got some money. The situation reached this miserable condition.

In the morning it was decided that we would cut standing crops tomorrow, even if we were arrested. At that time Swamiji (Swami Sahajanand Saraswati) was holding a meeting at Masaura. Jayaprakash Narayan, Dr Lohia and others were present. Though it was my duty to proceed there, I could not go due to my work at Reora.

After the meeting at Reora, I was going back to my ashram. Then women came, touched my feet, and said that there will be no cutting if you were not here. No men will go to cut crops. Please come back, and stay with us. We will cut together. I went back. The next morning were assembled a hundred women carrying in their hands sickles for cutting and threads for binding. I started cutting, so did the women. The police got to know of this, but by the time they arrived the crops had been cut, and put away in the kisans' houses. We went back to my ashram.

After this, a case was registered. I sent a telegram to Swamiji, stating that the satyagraha was started at Reora and I could not go to the meeting. At that time the District Magistrate was one Whittaker, an Englishman. He was a first-class rascal, and even fired on the people. I came back to Reora again, and after the meeting we began to cultivate the land with ploughs, and to dig wells in some places. Thus our work was started. The police reached the spot, and so did Whittaker Sahib. They were armed with guns and said that these acts of the kisans were illegal. We said, 'People are starving to death. Which do you care about, law or starvation? We are cultivating to fill our stomachs. We will not leave this work.' They did not say anything at that moment, and returned after having seen things for themselves.

After this incident I came back to my ashram, and from the ashram I was on the way to Gaya. A Magistrate came from there to arrest me. At Chakand Station this Magistrate called me, and said, 'Take a seat in our car. I have come to arrest you.' I took a seat in the car, and was moved to a jail. Afterwards I got information that Swami Sahajanand Saraswati, Jayaprakash Narayan, and almost all out leaders had reached Reora. Many activists came to Reora, and their camp was set-up. A police camp was also opened. Whenever someone tried to work, the police 'interfered'. When a worker entered the field with a hoe, they grabbed it. When someone went with a *lathi,* they grabbed it. When someone went with a sickle, they grabbed it.

I was then in the jail. It was a very mighty Satyagraha, a big stir. Many people began to come to Reora. On the last day, after all the happenings, the police was ready to bury the wells which had been dug earlier. Women were there to obstruct it. Six women were standing near each well. There were ten wells. Sixty women were standing. Police said, 'You must fill in the wells.' Women answered, 'Alright.' Five women jumped into each well, and said, 'Alright, go ahead.' Five women were inside each well. Police could not take any action. They ran away from the scene, and later the Magistrate's order was announced that they should close their camp and return.

Now a way to the settlement was opened. Whittaker wrote to Rameshwar Prasad Singh, a zamindar, that he should make a compromise with his kisans. Some kisans had been arrested, and were in jail. I was also in jail. Whittaker wrote that he should make a compromise with Jadunandan Sharma. Negotiations started. In this respect, the will of Jayaprakash Narayan was that there should be a compromise. I was not ready to do so. But, the kisans said, 'No, we should make a compromise.' Negotiations centered a round the proposal that three-fourths of the land should be allotted to the Kisans, and one-fourth to the zamindar. We reached the settlement. Later the details were discussed. The settlement is known as 'Whittaker Award'. According to this award three acres should be allotted to every family. All should be allotted the same size of land.

I asked Whittaker, 'Are you a socialist or an imperialist?'

He replied, 'No, I am an imperialist.'

'Then, why are you adopting socialism? Three acres to every kisan is nothing but socialism.'

'Sharmaji, now accept the situation as it is. Then, if you have to fight again, do so.'

That's how our discussion went.

And thus ended the Reora Satyagraha. Those kisans who had no land got their land. The characteristic of the kisan movement in Gaya district was that the landless labourers also co-operated with the kisan movement. I provided land that we got to the landless labourers too.

Notes

1. Swami Sahajanand Saraswati, *Kisan Sabha ke Sansmaran,* Allahabad: New Literature, 1947, p. 94.

2. Rahul Sankrityayan, *Meri Jivan-Yatra,* Allahabad: Kitab Mahal, 1950, p. 525.
3. Rahul Sankrityayan, *Naye Bharat ke Naye Neta,* Allahabad: New Book Syndicate, 1943, pp. 130.
4. M.A. Rasul, *A History of the All India Kisan Sabha,* Calcutta: National Book Agency, 1974, pp. 49-50.
5. Yadunandan Sharma, 'Akhir Bharatvarshiya Kisan Sabha-Chaturth Adhiveshan', *Gaya,* 9-10 April 1939, *Swagatadhyaksh ka Bhashan.*
6. Yadunandan Sharma, 'Bihar kisans launch Satyagraha', *Congress Socialist,* 8 January 1939.
7. Farid Ansari, 'Land to Tillers—Reora Lights the Torch of Agrarian Revolution', *Congress Socialist* 29 January 1939.
8. 'Reora Kisans Win', *Congress Socialist,* 26 February 1939.
9. Awadeshwar Prasad Sinha, 'Behar's Bakasht Struggle', *Congress Socialist,* 7 May 1939.
10. Jayaprakash Narayan, *Towards Struggle—Selected Manifestoes, Speeches and Writings,* ed. Yusuf Meherally, Bombay: Padma Publications, 1946, p. 94.
11. Anugraha Narayan Sinha, *Mere Sansmaran,* Patna: Kusum Prakashan, n.d., p. 274.
12. 'Fortnightly report for the period ending April 27, 1939', *Patna Commissioner's Fortnightly Report, 1939,* Bihar State Archives.
13. 'Fortnightly report for the period ending May 13, 1939', ibid.
14. On 8 January 1966, in Gaya, Jayaprakash Narayan told me that Reora was not so responsive to his call for Bhoodan either.
15. Shriramvriksh Benipuri, *Jayaprakash* (in Hindi), Patna: Sahityalay, 1947, p. 116.
16. Shriramvriksh Benipuri, *Mujhe Yad Hai-Sansmaran,* 2nd edn., Allahabad: Lokbharati: Prakashan, 1985, pp. 143-56.
17. Swami Sahajanand Saraswati, *Mera Jivan Sangarsh,* Bihta: Sri Sitaramashram, 1952, pp. 526-7.
18. Khet Mazdoor, *Sahajanand on Agricultural Labour and the Rural Poor: An Edited Translation with the original Hindi text and an Introduction, Notes and Glossary,* ed. Walter Hauser, New Delhi: Manohar, 2005, pp. 118-19 and pp. 206-8.
19. Jayaprakash Narayan, *Towards Total Revolution: Search for an Ideology,* vol. 1, ed. Brahamanand, Bombay: Popular Prakashan, 1978, p. 55.
20. Ibid., pp. 59-60.
21. Ibid., p. 246.
22. Ibid., pp. 248-9.
23. Sachchidananda et al., *Sarvodaya and Development: Multi-*

Disciplinary Perspective from Mushahari, Patna: A.N. Sinha Institute for Social Studies, 1976, p. 109.

24. Narayan, *Towards Total Revolution,* Vol. 1, p. 236.
25. Arvind N. Das, *Agrarian Unrest and Socio-economic Change in Bihar, 1900-1980,* New Delhi: Manohar, 1983, p. 103.
26. Sahajanand, *Mera Jivan Sangarsh,* pp. 518-19. Also, see Sho Kuwajima, 'Swami Sahajanand Saraswati (1889-1950)—Thought of a Peasant Leader in India' (in Japanese), *Journal of Osaka University of Foreign Studies,* No. 21, 1969. This article is attached to my Japanese translation of Swami Sahajanand Saraswati, *Kisan Sabha ke Sansmaran,* Kyoto: Sagano Shoin, 2002.
27. S. Seshaiah, *Land Reform and Social Change in a Japanese Village,* Bangalore: Shiny Publications, 1980, p. 189.
28. This is an English translation of a part of my interview with Jadunandan Sharma recorded in Hindi at Gaya on 10 and 11 April 1966. For the original, see Sho Kuwajima, *Sakshatkar-Bihar ke Kisan Neta Pandit Jadunandan Sharma se Batcheet*, Patna: Pratyaksh Prakashan, 1996, pp. 29-34.

PART III

Beyond Bihar

A Stranger's View of Bihar: Rethinking 'Religion' and 'Production'

Frederick H. Damon

Connections and the Properties of Things

This paper flows directly from the enthusiasm and support Walter Hauser gives to everyone and anyone interested in India, and especially those whom he can convince to travel to and learn something of his Patna and Bihar. To Hauser's intellectual excitement about India I add experience and expertise from my own region, Melanesia, and using both, take the liberty of a complete novice in Buddhist studies to make a suggestion as to what Buddhism really was some 2500 years ago. This was when it and transplanted irrigated rice agriculture first developed near Patna and then spread throughout the world. I do this by addressing a problem I think we have in understanding ways of apprehending the material and social world, a problem which begins with changes in ways of thinking and representing thought that become fixed by, roughly, the mid-nineteenth century. I proceed through a comparative analysis of production and ideological systems ranging across places and peoples from the Ganga to the outer islands of Melanesia.[1]

Several coincidences generate this attempt to honour Walter Hauser's unique role in Indian studies. Long interested in South Asia because of comparative questions concerning kinship and caste, I was privileged to participate in the 1997 Hauser symposium as a last 'minute commentator filling in for Hauser's friend and close associate, Barney Cohn. If nothing else, this paper is a small testimony to Hauser's long-term engagement with anthropology and anthropologists.

As an anthropologist I had just finished ten months of ethnobotanical research in the area of my expertise, the Kula Ring of south-eastern Papua New Guinea. Still finding my way in a burgeoning ethnobotanical literature, I was searching other parts of the world where I could see knowledge about and imagery of flora playing as important imaginative and productive role as in the culture I was beginning to understand. So hearing Hagen's description of how forests were integrated with irrigated rice agriculture in India (see above, pp. 155-73) and then discussing his thesis with him and other members of the symposium was just what I needed. In my experience as a researcher and writer on things Melanesian,[2] I had found few there who had focused on the critical place of botanical forms in these cultures. I was, therefore, unprepared for the quantity and quality of the information I collected as fast as my understanding allowed. As I shall be arguing here, partly because of the forms of knowledge upon which the contemporary world is organized, this was not very fast at all.

The second coincidence followed immediately upon the first. Attending the symposium were scholars from Bihar, Arvind N. Das the foremost of them. These people were planning a conference on Bihar and its place in Indian and world history. Ever the proselytizer, Hauser convinced Das that in addition to experts on Bihar they needed an outsider who, however well established elsewhere, knew nothing whatever about Bihar. I was that person. Discussion during the symposium convinced me that going to the Bihar conference would give me a chance to further an incipient understanding of Indian flora and learn about the concurrent origins of Buddhism and transplanted irrigated rice agriculture. And so this comparative paper.[3] A comparative or contrastive view of Melanesia and India may help us learn more about both.[4]

At the same time I do not wish to rule out the possibility of historical connections, of transfers of technological as well as ideological systems throughout the water-way systems connecting the Asias to island Southeast Asia, Melanesia, and beyond.[5] As our own world is becoming interrelated in new ways, we are beginning to appreciate the interconnections established in earlier epochs. In his stimulating essay, *The East in the West,* Jack Goody makes the case that for long ideas and people have flowed back and forth across the Europe-Asia landmass, including a third-century BC trade route that connected Patna to the Ionian seaports.[6] If this is indeed the case then it is perhaps wise to suggest that the extremely diverse island environments extending south from the Asias may have been a great 'testing ground' for cosmological, political, and technological regimes over the course of several millennia at least.[7]

The region I know best is dominated by those peoples anthropologists refer to as Austronesian, a group of related languages and peoples that beginning about 6000 years ago, spread from near Taiwan eventually to New Zealand in the south, and between Madagascar to Easter Island across the Indo-Pacific region. People speaking languages of this family dominate mainland and island South-East Asia. Austronesians were sailors and traders, and (as Wheatley shows) for as long as records indicate, situated in regional social systems connecting hinterlands to other polities, either by river systems or inter-island communication links.[8] Swadling charts a history of relations between Melanesia and the Asias extending backwards nearly 2000 years.[9] Interaction between Austronesians and South Asia was well developed into the seventeenth century,[10] and features of one region are readily found amidst the social forms of the other. Indic rituals and state forms of course once dominated Javanese kingdoms, Hindu forms remain central to Bali, and eastern Indonesia shows many influences from South Asia. Sanskrit-derived words play important roles in island cultures as far south and east as Tanimbar,[11] and articles from 'mainland Asia' find a presence in the exchange dynamics of even small groups of people in Seram.[12] Timor, an Austronesian locale, has been a major source of sandalwood for the Asias for long. Betel nut (*Areca catechu*), which probably originated in the Philippines or Malyasia, flowed throughout this region and well into India as *pan.* Exactly how its cultural significance moved with the nut is unclear. But is it remarkable that I could produce a description of its physical, aesthetic and erotic significance for the region I know in Papua New Guinea that is quite similar to that which

White produces for 'Tantric sex' in South Asia?[13] Following my presentation of this paper in Patna, and though skeptical about some of its thrusts, Arvind Das pointed out that the place of coconuts in Hindu ritual probably derives from Indian interactions with South-East Asia. My inexpert eyes imagined they saw evidence of South-East Asian artistic influences beginning about the ninth century AD in the Patna Museum; South Asian art historian Dan Ehnbom confirmed this as likely since Patna was a centre of Buddhist studies for the Buddhist diasporas into South-East Asia to the fourteenth century. Colin Groves finds it 'surprising' that the apparent 'wild ancestor' of the Asian water buffalo (*Bubalus arnee*) found in the South-East Asian areas of irrigated rice agriculture share the most in common with wild ancestors located around 'Bihar/Orissa. . . (centering on the Mahanadi delta)'.[14] However, Groves' 'surprise' may derive from a view of society that presumes autonomous states or regions connected, if at all, only by the accidents of trade. If, however, in other times and places trade was, and/or is, part of the social fabric—which is the case in my much smaller region—then ties between the rice technologies of South-East Asia and Bihar and the Buddhist monastery, might not seem so 'surprising'. It should be noted that the *naga* tree, *Mesua ferrea,* has roughly the same distribution as the water-buffalo, and perhaps for similar reasons.[15] There may also be historical reasons for why the woods used in boats made in Kerala and my area in south-east Papua New Guinea, come from identical or analogous species of the genus Calophyllum.

Confusing similarity for contiguity, and vice versa, have for decades been the bane of historical and anthropological research. So one plays with these relations with care. Yet for my purposes it is worth pursuing the matter of these Calophyllum trees for a moment. The logical reasons for why there is a commonality between these apparently distant places seem to be clear. One species of a tree (*Calophyllum inophyllum*) found throughout the Indo–Pacific region has extremely interlocked grains and grows out over the water's edge forming naturally arcing trunks and large branches. Both the interlocked grains and curves are properties boat-builders find attractive for boat parts that have to bear complex stresses coming from different angles. By contrast, other species of the same genus that grow inland, and straight up, were often used for spars and masts. In Kerala and to the north these trees have been identified as *C. tomentosum.* Sailing was a significant dimension to the social systems of Kerala so it is of interest that before its territoriality was reorganized by colonial relations at least some Kerala kingdoms were spatially organized to run from the coast inland to the highlands, thus presumably containing the critical resources for constructing the necessary water craft.[16] In my region the analogues seem to be *C. goniocarpum* or *C. Soulattri.*[17] These are straight, rather than interlocked, grained trees, a property that my informants told me allowed the masts to be fixed at the bottom but bend slightly at the top so that the wind may spill out of the sail in the appropriate fashion.

I must note here that I could write down my informants' words correlating interlocked grains with resistance to stress and straight-grained with principled bending facilitating sail aerodynamics. However, I did not understand at all why this should be so until I spoke with a materials scientist. My education was for manipulating and circumventing difficulties associated with managing the properties of words. But, as an anthropologist trained in the historical and social sciences of the last 100 years, I was not trained to deal with *the properties of things*, nor particularly well trained to interact with people—my informants as well as the materials scientists—who are trained to interact with the properties of this world.

The parallels or continuities I note may suggest real historical connections between the Bihar of about 500 BC and the specific area I know best in the Indo–Pacific region. I suspect the islands of Melanesia are not as far from the Gangetic plain as we have been led to believe. What leads me to this suggestion are common uses of the flora in my area today and Bihar some 2500 years ago. Yet the issue may also be different peoples recognizing and manipulating similar or identical properties in their necessarily differently constructed environments. This essay is intended neither as an attempt at historical reconstruction nor an argument for the historical continuity of the poles of my comparison—though there may be more of these than the received wisdom of contemporary scholarship would allow. It is, rather, intended as a critique of our understanding of society, perhaps of our analysis of non-Western systems we call 'religious', and, in keeping with much new work, a suggestion that the understanding of complex systems achieved by societies prior to the advent of 'science' has much to offer us.

Two Contexts for Viewing Buddhism

Tree Worship?

There are enormous gaps in the analytical story I wish to tell. So let me begin with a view that perhaps connects some of the holes in my argument, abbreviated accounts of Buddhism on the one hand and a kind of intellectual current in late twentieth-century social anthropology on the other.

First, while Buddhism starts in the Gangetic plain, in the received scholarly view social forces lead to a transformation into two forms, Mahayana (a reference to movement in space), and Theravada, the Way of the Elders (a reference to time). These forms sandwich India and the very origin spot of the movement. The Mahayana division arced into central Asia and extended east to Japan while Theravada bottoms out into South-East Asia. Although the Mahayana version is undoubtedly associated with different labouring processes, it is clearly linked to the trading systems that once connected the Mediterranean empires to the reaches of East Asia.[18] By contrast, it seems to me that Theravada Buddhism became specifically associated with the systems of rice production in Sri Lanka, and mainland and to some extent island South-East Asia. In those regions trading *per se* seems to have been more closely tied to Austronesian peoples and their cultural accoutrements—and later Islamic forces coming across the Indian Ocean and down through China.

For me it is this tie between Buddhism and production, and especially rice production, that is interesting.

For the second let me go back to a significant moment in anthropological history, and its bearing on our topic. This is to 1968 and Edmund Leach's introduction to the essays in *Dialectic in Practical Religion*.[19] I might note that Leach's Introduction was also his introduction to the anthropological world of Gananath Obeyesekere and S.J. Tambiah, and so began their legacy of South Asian studies in the anthropological world. Their works remain major vehicles for emulation and productive criticism to the present.

Leach was then much influenced by Lévi-Strauss, whose books *Totemism* (1962 [1964]) and *The Savage Mind* (1962 [1966]) had just been translated. Lévi-Strauss's relevant thesis for us here is that non-Western societies used their understanding of nature to communicate with themselves, and this idea unleashed a whole line of brilliant descriptions of aspects of non-Western societies, in so far as their social relations were concerned.

A major tenet of Leach's essay, and what he thought Obeyesekere and Tambiah's work illustrated, was that 'Buddhist virtue is an exaggerated ascetic ideal which serves as an unattainable model for the common man; the practical significance of the monk is that he should actually exist, a living reminder of the impossible, and exemplar for the layman not of what he should be but of what he cannot hope to be.'[20] This done, anthropologists could get on with the business of analysing what they call religion, what it means for real people, and leave theological issues aside as irrelevant, or for those involved in matters of comparative religion.

So in his Introduction to *The World of Buddhism: Buddhist Monks, and Nuns in Society and Culture*, Gombrich can write, 'Buddhism . . . is not about this world. Such spheres of human activity as the arts and sciences are not part of its concerns . . . Buddhism is a way of salvation which is open to all and depends for its attainment neither on faith nor on divine grace. . . . This goal (salvation) is something for individuals to aim at and reach, and is essentially independent of culture.' However, in carrying out this goal it has acquired what Gombrich calls 'a certain amount of cultural baggage from its Indian origin. The most important item in this baggage is Buddhism's central institution, its monastic order.'[21] But in Gombrich's account these items are accretions around the essential core of individual salvation, not particularly significant in themselves.

However, when I turn to a different source on things Buddhist I begin to receive a different message. The Randhawas tell me that:

Gautma was born under an *asoka* tree, received enlightenment under a *pipal* tree, preached his new gospel in mango groves, and under shady banyans, and died in a *sal* grove. Never before or after has a religion been so closely associated with vegetation. Buddhism adopted the cult of tree worship from the older religions which prevailed in the country. The trees which are associated with the birth of the Buddha are *sal, asoka*, and *plaksha*, and hence they were regarded as sacred by the Buddhists.[22]

Why these trees? I think this account suggests something fundamental about the critical properties being conveyed by and to the participants of this order. We had better look more carefully at the contexts of this situated living, contexts quite different than today's sense of 'religion' provides us.

WHAT IS 'RELIGION'?

The two traditions . . . on ungarbling an incomplete translation of the visual image.

To put quotes around this word 'religion' is to mark the idea about which we have had a peculiar understanding since the middle of the nineteenth century. While I am passing over uncritically an enormous scholarship which I do not mean to ignore or belittle, I think it is important to note that virtually all scholars of religion, foremost of whom is Durkheim, wrote after the great religious revivals of the late eighteenth and nineteenth centuries, a time when much of western Europe and the United States was coming to terms with what we now call industrial capitalism, its contradictions, its re-organization of the labour process and the pressing social problems that reorganization of the world created. This cosmological transformation was not only accompanied by theories of evolution that relegated our pasts to the dustbin of ignorance. It re-organized some of the most important ideas about what thinking and acting in fact were. And it created a divide between the tactile and sensual on the one hand, and the conceptual and the abstract on the other.

I suggest, for example, that Gombrich's view of Buddhism derives from a post-mid-nineteenth-century orientation to the world. He is on the writer's side of the divide.[23]

I wish to call this problem to our attention by virtue of a discussion of machinery provided by the American anthropologist and ethnohistorian Anthony Wallace. In his book *Rockdale*, Wallace describes the total re-organization of a community between about 1820 and 1870 in the emerging industrial centre of the eastern US seaboard. This is, I take it, a specific instance of the transformation many Western societies went through, the US perhaps a bit later than some in western Europe. Since machines played a large role in this transformation, Wallace locates the pivotal transformation with respect to them. One is, in my terms, 'where do people think?' He discusses this with respect to a class of persons he refers to as mechanicians, men who became engaged with making the mostly water-powered machines of the new industrial age. I bring this up because I think the problem we have of recognizing the 'thought of the mechanician', as Wallace puts it, is the same problem we have in viewing the organization of thought in some non-Western or pre-modern mentalities.

> The work of the mechanician was, in large part, intellectual work. This was true in spite of the fact that he dealt with tangible objects and physical processes, not with symbols, and that some of what he did was done with dirty hands. The thinking of the mechanician in designing, building, and repairing tools and machinery had to be primarily visual and tactile, however, and this set it apart from those intellectual traditions that depended upon language, whether spoken or written. The product of the mechanician's thinking was a physical object, which virtually had to be seen to be understood; descriptions of machines, even in technical language, are notoriously ambiguous and extremely difficult to write, even with the aid of drawings and models.[24]

Wallace then goes on to write that schools were created—the Franklin Institute being one example—to bridge this gap between the kind of experiential, almost fluid-dynamic, thought of the mechanician and the text-based, linguistic-symbol orientation that was increasingly coming to dominate what it meant to be educated in the newly emerging or newly conceived social hierarchies. What is critical in the linguistic-symbol orientation is classing an item in the correct place, most emphatically after the eighteenth century in one or another Linnaean-like order. In any case, these schools tended to fail because the very nature of the machines being created was that they were incomplete, and could only be completed, and then transformed, in the social experiences of production.[25] Words never sufficed to convey their realities.

Wallace attempts to state what the difficulty was in this gap of knowing:

The kind of thinking involved in designing machine systems was unlike that of linguistic or mathematical thinking in its emphasis on sequence as opposed to classification. . . . To the mechanical thinker, the grammar of the machine or mechanical system is the successive transformations of power—in quantity, kind and directions—as it is transmitted from the power source (such as falling water or expanding steam), through the revolutions of the wheel, along shafts, through gears and belts into the intricate little moving parts, the rollers and spindles and whirling threads, of the machine itself. The shapes and movements of all these hundreds of parts, sequentially understood, are a long yet elegantly simple moving image in three-dimensional space. In this mode of cognition, language is auxiliary—often so lagging an auxiliary that the parts and positions of a machine have no specific name, only a generic one, and if referred to in words, have to be described by . . . circumlocution. . . .

Wallace goes on to the increasing separation between those technically oriented and those—'theologians, humanists, even scientists'—who began to understand that all thought was a kind of speech, relegating other forms of communication to more primitive existences. He concludes his powerful descriptions with a return to one of the characters in his specific account, and the passage is worth quoting: 'Daniel Lamont could and did write fluent pages on the problem of determining the relations between the truth of good and the good of truth in Swedenborgian theology; but he had difficulty finding out how cotton machinery worked. . . .'[26] Swedenborgian theology was based on the massive writings, Biblical commentaries mostly in Latin, generated by the religious crisis of Emanuel Swedenborg (1688-1772). The first societies and churches that formed under his writings started in London in the 1780s. Among the people influenced by his work were Balzac, Charles Baudelaire, Ralph Waldo Emerson, William Butler Yeats, and August Strindberg, all people who throughout the nineteenth century enshrined the place of a verbal understanding in the cosmologies of the West.

I have entered into this apparent digression because I think that what we are dealing with in Buddhist imagery was something akin to what Wallace is intending by the 'mechanician's thought'. Buddhism was concerned with monasteries devoted in part to creating systems of irrigated rice agriculture. All this entailed complex attention to watercourses, relations *among* many different life forms (including human labour as well as the aquaculture that accompanied the irrigation systems), and the endless details of micro-environments, including the proliferation of seed varieties that went along with them. Earlier when discussing Edmund Leach's attempt to redefine how anthropologists should analyse Buddhist religious forms I noted that he was then much influenced by Lévi-Strauss. Lévi-Strauss's ideas—though not necessarily Leach's—are strongly marked by Plato's theory of knowledge. In this perspective, different levels of awareness build on one another, a sensuous experience of physical properties is turned into systems of differences *based on those empirical properties*, which in turn are transformed into models for social and other relations.[27] This is not a consciousness that ignores the properties of the world for its own self-transcendance; this is a kind of consciousness that organizes the world in terms of its manifold complexities.[28]

This brings us to the trees.

THE EVIDENCE

More Than a 'Poetry of Properties'

In Chapter 5 James R. Hagen describes the recent transformations of productive systems that have led to contemporary social and environmental problems in Bihar. But in so doing we learn much about what the area was beforehand, and I shall stress the positive image that can be created from his account.[29] The paper contrasts Chinese—raw—and Indian—simmered—cooking methods. According to Hagen the two forms resulted from the respective environments each region created and, consequently, the different amounts of fuel they could regularly harness—China a little, and India a lot. The prime points are that India has 'agricultural systems within an abundant forest and biomass context of adjacent agriculture'. We learn that over the centuries there was 'a relatively large area of forest, woods, and natural vegetation that was inter-patterned with natural topography and human settlements', so that until at least 1600 as much as 'two-thirds of the Gangetic plain remained under natural vegetation'—or what we currently view as natural vegetation. This is the context, I suggest, for viewing the 'symbolism' apparently so evident in various Indic ideological systems.

I shall attempt to concretize the model I am proposing by a brief description of pivotal relations in my own area of research,[30] and some of the images I had to fathom before I could understand what my Melanesian instructors were doing. I may begin by noting an extraordinary scene of several trees overhanging Boagis village. Blue sky is in the background, sand and coral colored waters in the foreground. I thought the image was beautiful; I learned that local people appreciate it as well. When I went up to the trees I was told to be careful because ancestors were buried near them—a first implication of magical-religious connotations. But while trees in that location are known throughout the whole region in which the village exists, I discovered the point was not 'magic'. The trees are known for two purposes. For the village itself, the wood is special ritual firewood that in-laws must give to one another. As it turns out, practically every village and island in this part of this regional system has some tree it uses for this purpose. Which tree used varies, and the variation conveys important information about the particular location to other people. The one at issue here is important to these people because the members of this village are sailors whose job it is to maintain and sail the largest class of outrigger canoes in this social system. The tree is important to those boats because its wood is the prime material for what is considered the most important part of the boat, its 'heart' or 'lungs'. The part is a kind of spring consisting of two tapered pieces about 60 cm long. The two ends are relatively small in circumference whereas the middle is larger (about 9 cm). They are tied down from their ends so that the contraption is put under considerable tension. Upon the construction sits a ladle-like looking piece of wood cut from the cross-grained Calophyllum mentioned above and found also in Kerala. The long handle part of this piece arcs up and extends out over the outrigger platform. It is then attached to the craft's outrigger. The spoon-shaped portion holds the boat's mast, preferably constructed from one of the two straight-grained Calophyllum trees. In effect the 'heart', the two tapered pieces, functions as a shock-absorber modulating the intersection of the two most violent sets of forces to which the boat is subjected, the forces generated on the outrigger as it moves through the water and absorbs the first shock of oncoming waves and the effect of the wind in the sail. In order to fulfil this modulating function the 'heart' is very carefully shaped out of this tree—one other may be used as a substitute—and it is the last piece of the canoe that is fit, carefully, for a boatbuilder should not release the craft to those who will actually use it until under a good wind everything feels right. Usually pieces of pumice are used like sandpaper to mould the form so that it feels just right. In short, the beautiful scene encompasses the ways in which mastered technical knowledge—of trees and their material properties, of boat design, which includes sailing dynamics—fits into a social order.

This tree is for a sailing village. Ritual firewood for other villages depends on their locations and stereotypical functions. Three sets of villages—among others with different trees—on the island where I did my research are distinguished by the age of the forests from which they stereotypically cut their gardens—early, middle, and late aged forests. And the ritual firewood these places use derives from the different trees that characterize these relations. So, when these people see certain bundles of firewood, they do not just think of flames. The various trees model sets of activities, activities that relate villages in complementary fashions, and orient all of them in time phases that govern their chief products, persons (a combination of kinship and inter-island exchange activities).

All this information is, not surprisingly, a mere snapshot of what I learned. My project started when I sought to figure out what people meant when they told me they used a certain tree to reproduce their soil fertility. I quickly learned that the use of this tree varies among the islands but everyone understands it to be a 'sweet' tree, and therefore good for crops (as opposed to a 'salty' tree, which is bad). In the universally known model about these trees, the sweet one puts good things into the soil and so crops should be crowded around its trunk after it is killed. By contrast the salty tree puts bad things into the soil, and so should be avoided. Although this is not the place to explicate what these beliefs entail, two points are relevant. First, these trees, generated by repeated burning of early fallows for a specific regime of slash-and-burn horticultural practices, are one side of a complicated set of forest/garden relations that knowledge and practice produce on these islands. An inverted practice creates the other side, as meadows are preserved in upland forests far removed from the areas regularly cut for horticulture but situated amidst sago orchards. Both these regimes entail forest, fire, and productive relations that produce vegetable carbohydrates, protein, and forest products, not unlike the situation Hagen describes for the pre-colonial Ganga plain.[31] Second, the local expert understanding of the actual operation of these trees was different, and in a way more complicated, than the well-known model. The best gardeners espoused the model, and especially its implications—seek out one tree and avoid another—but they denied the model was literally true. They claimed they did not understand how the 'sweet' tree worked, only that it did, on extensive experience.[32] And they asserted that the 'bitter' tree was bad because its dense root structure, extremely thick bark, and very tough wood made it very difficult to kill, even with steel axes. This shows how detailed knowledge about relations among different life forms is turned into intelligent and evocative patterns for repeatable social action, yet there is not necessarily a straight line between the literal model and the facts of the matter.

Not that anthropologists confused these trees with religious practice: they did not. And for two reasons. First, although throughout the twentieth century Melanesia has been used to break various Western stereotypes about non-Western peoples, in the received evolutionary schemes these societies were still at the stage of magic, hadn't yet got to religion, and of course were a long way from science. Second, *all* the anthropologists who have studied this region, including myself, were out of that division of intellectual labour that puts 'writers' on one side and 'mechanicians' on another. Nobody suggested to us that we ought to know about the concrete properties of the world our subjects inhabited.

When I told the art historian Dan Ehnbom what I was trying to do for the Bihar conference he told me, wisely, that I needed to examine Coomaraswamy's work.[33] I've subsequently come to realize how this work was a standard reference for decades of research, perhaps foremost of which is Randhawa's. However, as near as I can tell Coomaraswamy writes from the 'writers' side of the divide'. The main difference I see in his work and the area of my own research is that, obviously, the India he writes about had 'religion'. Again, this is not to belittle the magnificent labors of others, but it is to repeat my point that I do not think the world's Western-trained intellectuals for the last one hundred years or so have been equipped to appreciate the complexity of other modes of organization. Having an at least abstract idea of what Hagen means by the 'abundant forest and biomass context of adjacent agriculture' of the Gangetic plain, by which he means a complex interweaving of river and irrigation systems, aquacultures, and rice paddies and their associated and diversely aged forests, I do not have to read much of Coomaraswamy's discussion of, for example, 'The Lotus'[34]—before I realize that this 'symbolism', whatever else it may be, is an extremely condensed model of exceedingly complex, and probably non-linear, relationships among various manner of life forms.

In Coomaraswamy's interpretation the lotus represents how the earth and its activities are founded around water. It is no accident that water was the great theme from at least Bihar to Melanesia and beyond. My informants in Melanesia told me they planted their crops when tides force underground fresh water up as high as possible toward the top of the ground during the day, as it turns out in the warmest part of their year. An informed aerodynamic understanding governs the selection of trees for boat-building; a hydrological model informs their planting schemes.

Between Bihar and Melanesia there are, of course, many

other areas where aspects of these dynamics are now visible, or nearly so. One might review some recent literature from Borneo,[35] and a recent discussion of Angkor Wat[36] provides a suggestive overview of how astronomical principles were built into the complex palaces and irrigation pools of that productive and cosmological centre—again the issue is the representation of complex ideas about time in-built environments. I cannot, however, refrain from a simple note concerning Bali.

As many people now know, in a number of publications and presentations J. Stephen Lansing has made a major contribution to the understanding of non-Western productive systems through his analysis of Balinese temples and their relationships to the complicated irrigation system of Bali. Lansing has proved that there is some 'science' in the 'religion', and in fact perhaps more than his computer programme has been able to reveal.[37] While Lansing has convinced us that Bali's temple/religious system funds a balance between the contradictory requirements of water demands and pest dynamics, he has done less to explain the positive knowledge of the world that seems contained in the temples and priests. He narrates an encounter with the High Priest (*Jero Gde*) in which the man says of a forest watershed area: 'Now apparently this forest area is only producing about a hundred litres of water'.[38] Unlike Wallace's Lamont, who 'had difficulty finding out how cotton machinery worked', this man knows how his system works.

The forests of Indonesia are disappearing now as forest disappeared over the last two centuries in the Ganga plain. But from Hagen's description there is every reason to assume there were similarities between what that Gangetic plain was, what some of Indonesia partly remains, and large portions of Melanesia are today—well-formed, if not linearly formed, patterns of forests, various vegetable crops, and human occupations.[39] Landscapes where I do my research are intentionally formed by keeping high forest clumps interspersed among gardens. These clumps are called *tasim,* best translated here as 'island'. Gardens in fact are considered boats, and one of the models for the productive process is that the 'boats' should weave around the islands. The 'islands' are thought to facilitate both crop and fallow regrowth as they partially block out the sun; similar ideas concerning what people call sacred groves and perhaps more often concerned with water rather than the sun, are found throughout South-East Asia. But these islands produce more than sun and a necessary biomass. They produce the trees of primary significance for these peoples' large outrigger canoes. These are another species of the genus Calophyllum with which I ended my introduction. This tree is personified, it is considered a human, and a woman. Concerning this personification process[40] two basic points are simple. The first is that the properties of the tree are part of the representation: my informants knew these properties in greater depth than the systematist, P.F. Stevens, who is *the* expert on this genus. The second is that to understand the other side of the equation, you have to know what the Melanesian consider 'people' to be. People here are first and foremost products, for my informants think their major work is producing people. These facts explain the 'symbolism' of this tree because the tree can only grow to maturity if humans create gardens interspersed among those 'islands' of high growth. The tree cannot survive beyond the sprouting stage unless it has a partially opened canopy. The opening gives an arc to the growing tree that is used for making an outrigger canoe's bend. Behind the animism, the attribution of humanity to nature, is a detailed, virtually ecological, understanding of the fact that the two orders reproduce one another.

Conclusion

The Buddha's Trees

I conclude with the bearing this may have on our investigation of Bihar and Buddhist monastery. Gombrich wrote 'Buddhism . . . is not about this world. Such spheres of human activity as the arts and sciences are not part of its concerns.' Yet when I read Randhawa I think he (Gombrich) may be wrong, if not for what Buddhism is now, then certainly when it was put together. What are these trees associated with the Buddha?

The accounts vary, but the primary trees seem to be the two or three he was born under or by, *asoka* or *plaksha*, and near if not under *sal,* under which he also died. And of course he received enlightenment under a *pipal* tree. From the properties and probable places of these trees I could find in various books, it seems to me there is little doubt that all of these trees convey important messages about an environment that, I suggest, the stories and imagery of Buddha models. Most obvious of course is the model of vitality that, throughout much of South, East, and South-East Asia, pipal (*Ficus religiosa*) and banyan (*Ficus benghalensis*) trees present. For societies founded on the interweaving of differences, these trees are tangible forms of what often is a reality too complex to disentangle.

Asoka (*Saraca asoca*) and *plaksha* (*Butea monosperma*) are both Leguminosae. Legumes are often nitrogen enhancers, and most close observers of environmental interrelations pick up on these qualities whether or not they know anything about nitrogen. Accounts tend to stress the flowers of many of these trees, but they also had medicinal uses, and one source notes that the genus in which the *asoka* is located is 'characteristic of particular streams'.[41] The *plaksha*, also a legume, has, among its other properties, an ability to reclaim saline soils.[42] Especially this one, but perhaps also the *asoka*, may be pioneer trees, that is, trees that can reproduce conditions of fertility after soil has been depleted of its nutrients in part or whole.[43]

If these two suggest early stages of a reproductive process, the *sal* tree brings us to the other end of an image of a complex biomass. The *sal* (*Shorea robusta, Dipterocarpaceae*) is the most important timber tree in Asia, notably used for construction as well as dyes. An 'emergent tree', it has the property of being able to sprout under a canopy and grow up through it. Among other uses, it has been appropriated as a sign of successional relations, and therefore an encompassing image of time in Indian mythology. The stories in Shakti Gupta's *Plant Myths and Traditions in India* give a useful account. We read of a 60,000 years old *sal* tree that was going to be used as a single column for a palace.[44] One does not have to take that literally to get the point. In fact, I would presume that taking it literally, realizing that it cannot be true, but then calling it 'religion', is a more or less accurate summary of the Western interpretation of such ideas. Randhawa describes the Buddha's birth scene as on the border of Nepal with 'rice fields surrounded by a *sal* forest' which calls to mind Hagen's 'abundant forest and biomass context of adjacent agriculture'.[45] And I suggest that that is what the Buddha, and his splendid representations, were modelling.

In short, I think it would be incorrect to think that what Buddhism and Bihar offered the world was analogous to a disquisition 'on the problem of determining the relations between the truth of good and the good of truth in Swedenborgian theology'. I suspect, instead, the issue was knowing about the terms of creation.

NOTES

1. Lisa Gottschalk helped prepare the website that accompanies this paper, http://www.people.virginia.edu/~fhd/Stranger. The Deans of the University of Virginia are also to be thanked for facilitating much of the experience I report on here as well as the Asian Development Research Institute, Patna, and the European Science Foundation, France which reimbursed travel expenses that facilitated this paper. More formal acknowledgments of my Papua New Guinea research can be found in other publications.
2. Frederick H. Damon, 'The Kula and Generalised Exchange: Considering some Unconsidered Aspects of the Elementary Structures of Kinship', *Man* (n.s.) vol. 15, no. 2, 1980, pp. 267-93; F.H. Damon and Roy Wagner, eds., *Death Rituals and Life in the Societies of the Kula*, DeKalb: Northern Illinois University Press, 1989; F.H. Damon, *From Muyuw to the Trobriands: Transformations Along the Northern Side of the Kula Ring*, Tucson: University of Arizona Press, 1990.
3. This paper was first prepared for the conference, 'Bihar in the World and the World in Bihar' 15 to 21 December 1997, in Patna, Bihar. Daniel Ehnbom and Ruhi Grover provided needed knowledge about Indian imagery and mythology for the initial stages of this effort. I would not have considered this paper worth preparing for publication had not the conference organizer, Arvind Das, his assistant, Kathinka Sinha, and several participants greeted it with useful criticism and support. I thank especially Nirmal Sengupta; our conversations during and since the conference have enriched me immensely. Shortly after I returned from Bihar I reviewed a central thesis of this paper with Wimal Dissanayake concerning a fundamental misunderstanding of Asian thought on the part of some Western intellectuals. I also thank Lauren Leve for reading

and comments in early 1999. Jean-Claude Galey, mindful of the author's limitations, provided a useful interest. Walter Hauser has read and creatively commented on several drafts of this endeavour and so deserves much more than thanks.

4. Almost out of sight of English reading scholars there is, in fact, a productive comparison contrasting India with Melanesia, largely due to Louis Dumont's equip ERASME. Exemplifying how some India-inspired work enables new insights in contemporary Melanesia is Joel Robbins' book, *Becoming Sinners: Christianity and Moral Torment in a Papua New Guinea Society*, Berkeley: University of California Press, 2004.
5. Archaeological research highlights major changes in south-east Papua New Guinea beginning about 1200-1500 years ago with the building of megalithic structures, activities that perhaps ended about 600 years ago. See Simon Hillel Bickler, 'Prehistoric Stone Monuments in the Northern Region of the Kula Ring', *Antiquity*, vol. 80, no. 307, 2006, pp. 38-51; Simon Hillel Bickler, 'Eating Stone and Dying: Archaeological Survey on Woodlark Island, Milne Bay Province, Papua New Guinea', PhD Dissertation, University of Virginia, 1998; and Simon H Bickler and B. Ivuyo 'Megaliths of Muyuw (Woodlark Island), Milne Bay Province, Papua New Guinea', *Archaeology in Oceania*, vol. 37, 2002, pp. 22-36. This work suggests significant changes in this part of Melanesia roughly paralleling the spread of irrigated rice agriculture to places like Bali, though evidence of interaction between Bali and India begins some 500 years earlier (see S.J. Lansing, *The Balinese*, Ft. Worth: Harcourt Brace College Publishers, 1995, pp. 13-15). A kind of episodic flow of cultural systems, undoubtedly following extensive trade routes, roughly correlates with minor changes in climates. I am much indebted to Joel Gunn for discussing these climatological shifts and for attempts at thinking out how humans may have reacted to them. See Gunn, 'Global Climate and Regional Biocultural Diversity', Chap. 3 in Carole L. Crumley, ed., *Historical Ecology: Cultural Knowledge and Changing Landscapes*, Sante Fe: School of American Research Press, 1994, pp. 67-97.
6. Jack Goody, *The East in the West*, Cambridge: Cambridge University Press, 1996, p. 255, and appendix ('Early Links').
7. This idea derives from Geoffrey Irwin's *The Prehistorical Exploration and Colonisation of the Pacific*, Cambridge: Cambridge University Press, 1992. For Irwin the area between New Britain and Fiji, island arcs which provided virtually inter-visible sailing conditions, became a testing ground for perfecting the sailing and navigational

technologies that eventually, after the time of Christ, led to the settlement of Polynesia. In the received European view Austronesian societies are backward compared to the great traditions of the Asias. However, these regions were never isolated, and given the Islands' fantastic biological and geological diversity they may have served as a laboratory for human invention over the millennia. I am indebted to James J. Fox of the Australian National University for the germ of this suggestion. Although the central thesis governing this point of view remains speculative, it is in fact considerably less ambitious in scope than that put forth in Tim Flannery's highly regarded *The Future Eaters: An Ecological History of the Australasian Lands and Peoples*, New York: Grove Press, 1994.

8. See Paul Wheatley, *Nagara and Commandery: Origins of the Southeast Asian Urban Traditions*, Chicago: University of Chicago, Department of Geography, 1983.
9. Pamela Swadling *Plumes from Paradise: Trade Cycles in outer Southeast Asia and their Impact on New Guinea and Nearby Islands until 1920*, Boroko: Papua New Guinea National Museum, 1996.
10. Aceh was a central place for South Asian, East Asian, and Mainland and Island South-East Asian peoples. In June 1601 a British ship reports upon its anchorage off Aceh: 'Here we found sixteen or eighteen sail of shippes of diverse nations—Gujeratis, some Bengal, some of Calicut (south India) called Malibaris, some of Pegu (Burma) and some of Patani (Thailand) which came to trade here.' Quoted in John Keay, *The Honourable Company: A History of the English East India Company*, New York: Macmillan, 1991, p. 16.
11. Susan McKinnon, *From a Shattered Sun*, Madison: University of Wisconsin Press, 1991, p. 7.
12. Valeri Valerio, 'Buying women but not selling them: gift and commodity exchange in Huaulu alliance', *Man*, vol. 29, no. 1, 1994, p. 3.
13. David White, *Kiss of the Yogini: 'Tantric Sex' in its South Asian Contexts*, Chicago: University of Chicago Press, 2003, pp. 85-90.
14. Colin Groves, 'Domesticated and Commensal Mammals of Austronesia and their Histories' in Peter Bellwood, James J. Fox, and Darrell Tryon, eds., *The Austronesians: Historical and Comparative Perspectives*, Canberra: Australian National University, Department of Anthropology, RSPAS, 1995, p. 155.
15. Most Indian, Javanese, and Malay names for this tree derive from some aspect of the Sanskrit *nagakesara*. Although Ruhi Grover confirms its associations with cobras, the (*nagas*), I have been able

learn no more than restate its association with Buddhist monasteries (see M. S. Randhawa, *Flowering Trees*, New Delhi: National Book Trust, 1969, p. 106), probably irrigation systems, and mythology. I.H. Burkill's 'The Early Economic History of the Tree Mesua Ferrea (Guittiferae)', *Proceedings of the Linnean Society of London*, vol. 156, no. 2, 1944, pp. 85-91, is the most complete description I have found to date. The tree's association with water is similar to that of the *sal* tree. Burkill implies the tree is cultivated, and this and other aspects recall characteristics of the Calophyllum discussed in this paper in my own region. Mesua and Calophyllum are closely related trees, classed in the same family (Guttiferae or Clusiaceae), according to current Western classificatory principles. For the present, it is of some comparative interest to note that (for the west) the *sal* tree is to mainland Asia as several species of Calophyllum are to South-East Asia and Melanesia. Both are high quality construction timbers exploited by the international market.

16. For the organization of Kerala until the end of the eighteenth century, see J.R. Freeman's 'Gods, Groves and the Culture of Nature in Kerala', *Modern Asian Studies*, vol. 33, no. 2, 1999, p. 258. See Jacques Pouchepadass and J.-Ph. Puyravaud, eds. *L'homme et la forêt en Inde du Sud*, Pondichéry: Institute Français de Pondichéry, 2002. I thank Jacques Pouchepadass for alerting me to this collection and to Freeman's work. Freeman contests the idea that there was a modern ecological wisdom embedded in traditional Indian thought, especially as it can be ascertained from colonial records and his own anthropological research. My paper was conceived long before I was aware of Freeman's work. After thorough examination of his important debate about sacred groves, discussion of it with James Hagen, and consideration of Uchiyamada's suggestive discussion of Kerala *kaavu* (see Yasushi Uchiyamaḍa, '"The Grove is Our Temple": Contested Representations of Kaavu in Kerala, South India', Chap. 8 in Laura Rival, ed., *Social Life of Trees*, Oxford and New York: Berg, 1998, pp. 177-96), I have decided to maintain the thrust of my original presentation. Modern ecological ideology is not the issue, but understanding the ways in which other societies and times understood, built, and rebuilt their social systems.

17. Peter F. Stevens identified of my voucher specimens (Damon 148, 164 and 290) for which thanks. The information on Kerala Calophyllum comes from P. S. Person, R.S. and H.P. Brown, *Commercial Timbers of India*, Calcutta: Central Publication Branch, 1931, p. 47 (*C. inophyllum*), and p. 49 (*C. tomentosum*). Stevens,

the authority on the genus, considers *C. tomentosum* of south-western India to be what he calls *C. polyanthum* (see P.F. Stevens, 'A Revision of the Old World Species of Calophyllum (Guttiferae)', *Journal of the Arnold Arboretum*, vol. 61, no. 3, 1980, pp. 220-26, 235-38.

18. Buddhism's 'supremely civilized ethos of benevolence, honesty and self-control appealed to merchants and rapidly spread along trade routes.' Richard F. Gombrich, *The World of Buddhism: Buddhist Monks, and Nuns in Society and Culture*, H. Beckert, ed., London: Thames and Hudson, 1984, p. 9.
19. E.R. Leach ed., 'Dialectic in Practical Religion', *Cambridge Papers in Social Anthropology*, No. 5, Cambridge, 1968.
20. Leach, *Dialetic*, p. 3: 'In studies of comparative religion a failure to take into account this distinction between philosophical religion and practical religion has often led to grave misunderstanding. Thus Western interpretation of Buddhism has, until very recently, been derived almost exclusively from a scholarly study of the ancient Pali texts glossed by the modern commentaries of professional Buddhist theologians. . . .' (ibid., p. 1).
21. Richard Gombrich 'Introduction: The Buddhist Way', in Gombrich, *The World of Buddhism*, pp. 10-11.
22. M.S. Randhawa and Doris Schreier Randhawa, *Indian Sculpture: The Scene, Themes and Legends*, Bombay: Vakils, Feffer & Simons, 1985, p. 23.
23. It was this idea, and that Western scholarship has looked at the Asias through this divide, that I discussed in 1998 with Wimal Dissanayake. Although it is an analysis based on Hindu texts rather than South Asian imagery, Zimmermann's remarkable study strikes me as a fairly successful attempt to bridge this divide by focusing on the representation of humoral and trophic—who eats whom—relations in several texts. See Francis Zimmermann, *The Jungle and the Aroma of Meats: An Ecological Theme in Hindu Medicine*, Berkeley: University of California Press, 1982.
24. Anthony F.C. Wallace, *Rockdale: The Growth of an American Village in the Early Industrial Revolution*, New York: Alfred A. Knopf, 1978, p. 237.
25. Wallace writes: 'When a basic innovation was introduced, it was embodied in an actual machine; the machine, and copies of it, rather than verbal descriptions, communicated the paradigm. But with each machine came problems to eliminate and improvements to add, all within the ambit of the original conception. . . . Machines were not 'invented' in complete and finished form; rather they

were the product of generations of collective effort' (ibid. 237). This indicates how we can imagine productive processes moving across the island world, each move bringing solutions to previous encounters, and new solutions to new problems having to be invented in each new context, social and environmental. From an environmental point of view, perhaps the critical issues moving from the Asias towards Australia and back would be dealing with water, the issue being both climatic and geological/hydrological. 'Inventions' would have to be modified as they moved across spaces. Flannery (op. cit.) convincingly outlines some of the necessary transformations humans effected as they moved into the South Pacific. It would thus probably be productive to view the public buildings such as those at Angkor Wat as models of fluid dynamics—miniaturizations of a universe of essential relations. On the idea of models, miniaturization, and understanding see Claude Lévi-Strauss, *The Savage Mind*, Chicago: University of Chicago Press, 1966, pp. 22-30.

26. Wallace, op. cit., p. 239.
27. Zimmermann's discussion of Vedic ritual and antelope suggests the kind of analysis appropriate to this discussion (op. cit., pp. 59-60).
28. Although undeveloped here, the original stimulation for thinking that tiered levels of knowledge was a relevant problem for the case of Bihar came to me when listening to and then reading Arvind N. Das's paper in this volume.
29. Positive descriptions of these systems are beginning to develop. See Winin Pereira, 'Traditional Rice Growing in India', *The Ecologist*, vol. 21, no. 2, 1991, pp. 97-100, and Winin Pereira and Jeremy Seabrook, *Asking the Earth*, London: Earthscan/WWF, 1990.
30. Images I note may be found at http://www.people.virginia.edu/~fhd/Stranger. I conduct research in one of the classic areas of anthropology, the Kula Ring of south-eastern Papua New Guinea. First made famous by Bronislaw Malinowski, scholars have returned to the area in the last thirty years. See J.W. Leach and E.R. Leach, eds., *The Kula: New Perspectives on Massim Exchange*, Cambridge: Cambridge University Press, 1983; for a recent summary that contains an historical positioning consistent with this paper, F.H. Damon, 'Kula Valuables, the Problem of Value and the Production of Names', *L'Homme*, vol. 162, April-June 2002, pp. 107-36. The pattern of forests and agriculture of which Hagen speaks extended into South-East Asia and beyond at the time of European contract. Since humans had occupied these parts of this region for up to

50,000 years one must presume that the regime of forests, developed horticultural regimes, and relatively modest populations, much lower than those of South or East Asia, was an intentional outcome of human imagination and organization.

31. Fire in these productive regimes takes the place of water in the irrigation systems of the Asias. Both work as purifiers and fertilizing agents.
32. The tree is an *Anacardiaceae*, genus Rhus. In 1998 root crops planted near two dead trunks had approximately twice the number of tubers as those planted some 10-12 metres distant. There is nothing in the literature on this tree to suggest what it might be doing biochemically, but my results suggest the tree is associated with nitrogen fixation and that it significantly increases the amount of phosphorus and potassium in the area immediately around its roots. Other trees are also supposed to be good for plants and readily appear to do what the locals say, i.e. enhance growth. One of these is in the same family as the Neem tree.
33. Ananda K. Coomaraswamy, *Yaksas: Essays in the Water Cosmology*, Washington, D.C.: Smithsonian, 1928-31.
34. Ibid., Part II, pp. 56-60. For example 'text . . . cited in the Satapatha Brahmana show that the lotus was primarily understood to represent the Waters; secondarily also, inasmuch as the flower and still more obviously the leaf rest on the waters, the earth—for the earth is conceived of as resting on the back of waters, and supported by the waters, which extend on either side of it. These . . . interpretations sufficiently account for the use of the expanded lotus flower in iconography and architecture as the typical basis or support of a figure or building . . . the whole building is supported by a widely extended lotus flower, that is to say, by the earth, and in the last analysis by the Waters'(ibid., pp. 56-7).
35. See Christine Helliwell, 'Evolution and Ethnicity: A Note on Rice Cultivation Practices in Borneo', in J. Fox, ed., *The Heritage of Traditional Agriculture Among the Western Austronesians*, Canberra: Department of Anthropology, Australian National University, 1992, pp.7-21; and Clifford Sather, 'Post, Hearths and Thresholds: The Iban Longhouse as a Ritual Structure', in James J. Fox, ed., *Inside Austronesian Houses: Perspectives on Domestic Designs for Living*, Canberra: Australian National University, Department of Anthropology, 1991, pp. 65-115.
36. Eleanor Mannikka, *Angkor Wat: Time Space and Kingship*, Honolulu: University of Hawaii Press, 1996.
37. Much of the significance of Lansing's work is political/educational,

conveying recent scholarly discoveries to policy makers, natural scientists, and others—whose primary realities now are governed by computer screens.

38. Op. cit., p. 84. See also note 60, p. 102.
39. Note Waterson's discussion of South-East Asian forms at the time of contact: '(T)he style and layout of these urban centres was very unfamiliar to Europeans. Reid notes that a "rural" pattern of life was continued in the city, with airy, pile-built wooden houses half-concealed within their own yards of coconut, banana, and other fruit trees. . . . Early travelers were delighted by the rural appearance of the city of Aceh, which one described as 'very spacious, built in Wood, so that we could not see a house till we were upon it. . . .' (Roxana Waterson, *The Living House: Anthropology and Architecture in South-East Asia*, New York: Whitney Library of Design, 1998, p. 27). In a recent study we read that the term 'nagara is described in the *Mayamata* as a town situated in a forested country with houses for all classes of people and with shops as well' (Anita Raina Thapan, *Understanding Ganapati: Insights into the Dynamics of a Cult*, New Delhi: Manohar, 1997, p.162). Examination of Dagens's translation of the *Mayamata* makes the association a bit more interesting. The reference is found in Chapter Ten, 'Towns', section 10.21b-26a: 'A town called "royal capital" is impregnable at the north and at the east; it is encircled by a wall beyond. . . . It is frequented by all sorts of courtesans and has a number of gardens. . . . It is called pura or nagara when it is situated in forested country and when it contains houses for all classes, and shops' (*Mayamata: An Indian Treatise on Housing, Architecture and Iconography*, trans. Bruno Dagens, New Delhi: Sitaram Bhartia Institute of Scientific Research, 1985, p. 40). I take this as a suggestion that we understand the term *negara/nagara* as a word designating an epitomizing social position whose syntagmatic context includes forested areas, consistent with Hagen's sense of 'inter-patterned'.
40. See F.H. Damon, 'Selective Anthropomorphization: Trees in the Northeast Kula Ring', *Social Analysis*, vol. 42, no. 3, 1998, pp. 67-99.
41. David Mabberly, *The Plant-book*, Cambridge: Cambridge University Press, 1987 p. 520.
42. Ibid., p. 86. Mabberly implies the following for this tree: 'seed-oil (muduga oil), vermifuge, flowers give red dye, leaves stitched together as plates in restaurants in India, bark for cordage and sails, timber good under water [and] also for charcoal; lac insects

feed on it; it can be used to reclaim saline land and is one of the most beautiful of all flowering trees (fls bright orange-red).'

43. Shortly after the Patna conference Nirmal Sengupta presented a paper describing how the peasants of northern Bihar opposed mid-century giant irrigation projects, because they feared they would interfere with the complex soil conditions which prevailed there.

    North Bihar is prone to salinity. In northern India, in particular, salts are transported in solution by the Himalayan rivers which later percolate in the sub-soils of the plains and goes on accumulating in the area of inefficient surface drainage. . . . Yet however pure irrigation water is, it always contains some salt. Salts are added to the soil with each irrigation. Crops remove much of the applied water . . . but leave most of the salt behind. At each irrigation more salt is added. This requires more irrigation; a portion of the added salt must be leached from the root zone before the concentration affects crop yield. This was essentially what the peasant of proposed Kamla canal were objecting to. . . . The soils of Indo-Gangetic plain are very fertile and well supplied with potassium, phosphorous, calcium, iron and manganese. But under waterlogged condition the alkali soils have zero water infiltration and diffusion rate. Thus productivity decreases. . . . Probably, heeding to local wisdom is the only way out.

44. Shakti Gupta, *Plant Myths and Traditions in India*, New Delhi: Munshiram Manoharlal, 1991, pp. 87-90.
45. J. B. Lal writes that a 'drop in the level of soil moisture beyond the minimum level in the forests of eastern Madhya Pradesh . . . has caused a mass mortality of sal (*Shorea robusta*) trees of all age classes in the last few years.' J.B. Lal, *India's Forests: Myth and Reality*, Dehra Dun: Natraj, 1989, p. 62. I would suspect the tie between moisture and *Shorea robusta* was known and represented by the narrators of the Buddhist legends.

From 'Fanaticism' to Power: The Deep Roots of Kerala's Agrarian Exceptionalism

Ronald J. Herring

> Fanaticism of this violent type flourishes only upon sterile soil. When the people are poor and discontented, it flourishes apace like other crimes of violence. The grievous insecurity to which the working ryots are exposed by the existing system of landed tenures is undoubtedly largely to blame for the impoverished and discontented state of the peasantry, and a measure to protect the ryot, of whatever class, is the means which seems to commend itself the most for amelioration of their condition. With settled homesteads and an assured income to all who are thrifty and industrious . . . it is certain that fanaticism would die a natural death.[1]
>
> —William Logan (1887)
> Collector and Magistrate of Malabar District

The Political Dilemma of the Agrarian Left

Wolf Ladejinsky wrote in 1951 that the American-induced land reforms in Japan (in which he played a major role) 'stole communist thunder' and produced conditions of rural social stability and political conservatism.[2] Like Barrington Moore, Jr., Doreen Warriner, Gunnar Myrdal, and Samuel Huntington, Ladejinsky concluded that the possibilities for radical land reform in India had passed; such policies were structurally impossible given the distribution of political power in rural India. Official proclamations from Delhi have documented the failure of land reforms meant to transform rural India's society and economy.[3] An obvious puzzle is why radical reforms in the south Indian state of Kerala not only remained on the agenda for generations, but were effectively implemented in the 1970s. The answer to that puzzle—anomalous peasant mobilization and political power—poses another: what explains Kerala's agrarian exceptionalism?

William Logan's views, quoted at the head of this essay, represent one of the antinomies of the colonial understanding: 'thrifty and industrious' peasants with security have no inclination to organized violence. Ladejinsky's cold-war perspective on 'stealing thunder' from the left via land reform explains the seemingly paradoxical support for land reform from conservative positions—during the Cold War, both the United States and the Soviet Union supported land reform in their foreign policies. Ladejinsky's position coincides with William Logan's world-view as a colonial official beset by organized violence and crime in the nineteenth century.

Both explanation and prescription proposed by William Logan lost out politically within the colonial state, defeated by an alternative model of causation—'religious fanaticism'. Organized violence erupted on a larger scale in Malabar decades later; eventually the colonial state began a dialogue of reform which was carried by the communists to mobilizational strength and electoral power as the first freely elected communist government of any size in the world.[4]

If the conservative logic of land reform (which dates from antiquity) is well understood, reformism from radical political forces poses a puzzle. Since Lenin, there has been explicit recognition in leftist agrarian theory of a contradiction between the tactical imperative of promising land to the agrarian underclasses and the strategic threat that successful land reform will 'conservatize' precisely those classes which form the tactical roots of mobilizational success. In landlord-tenant systems in the areas of greatest communist electoral success in India (Kerala and West Bengal), the issue presents this classic dilemma for a radical party: the tactical means of organizing political power carry the strategic potential of 'conservatizing', via 'embourgeoisement', radical social forces.[5] Samuel Huntington summarized a distinguished lineage of social science lore in explicating the logic underpinning conservative use of land: 'No social group is more conservative than a land-owning peasantry, and none is more revolutionary than a peasantry which owns too little land or pays too high a rental'.[6] This Janus-faced character of the peasantry is widely recognized in social theory and *realpolitik*. Land reform as a 'conservatizing' force was explicitly promoted not only by an isolated colonial official facing insurrection, but also by that strand of United States foreign policy that sought to apply lessons from the 'loss of China' to the eradication of 'breeding grounds' of communism in poor societies from Vietnam to El Salvador.[7]

Land reform thus presents the agrarian left with a double-edged sword: a mobilizing platform but simultaneously a threat to destroy the social-structural niche which presents mobilizational potential. Agrarian communism in India has diverged along exactly these lines of analysis and opportunity. In Kerala, the Left recognized the potential threat of *embourgeoisement* but nevertheless abolished the landlord–tenant system with a land-to-the-tiller reform. Rejecting land to the tiller, Bengal's communist movement has settled for the land policy of conservative regimes: tenancy reform.[8] The crucial difference is that tenants in West Bengal remain dependent on political-administrative means to retain quasi-proprietary claims (security of tenure) and administratively rigged rents, whereas former tenants in Kerala now hold titles to their land.

Communist leaders in Kerala attribute a great deal of their electoral success to the mobilization of a radical peasant movement, but there are other issues on which the Communist Party may be said to have stolen Congress thunder, including what is frequently called 'nationalism'.[9] As on agrarian-reform issues, the communists took a consistently more militant and uncompromising stance on the ending of colonial occupation. They proved more militant and effective in carrying out the Congress pledge to improve the condition of 'untouchable' groups, to implement policies providing local-level input into the administrative system, to decentralize political power, and even to uphold high standards of personal integrity and austerity in public life. On all these issues, as in agrarian reform, the willingness of

Congress politicians to compromise with powerful interests generated by the existing social structure contrasted markedly with communist efforts to transform that structure.

Communists could credibly make and eventually deliver on those promises precisely because they lacked the ideological and class-based constraints that rendered the Congress—in Kerala and elsewhere in India—incapable of overturning the rural social structure as so often promised in official discourse. The theoretical implication is that not all is choice, even for political entrepreneurs.[10] Simultaneously, the mode of mobilization in Kerala put significant constraints on the forms of public law that could result from mobilization; the 'middle-peasant' tenants, who earned the condemnation of agricultural labourers in the post-reform era, were the leaders and objects of leftist organization in the 1920s and 1930s, in which the shock troops were the landless labourers and sharecroppers. Tactical choices create path dependencies.[11]

The departure of this essay from classical peasant theory[12] is its insistence that the political theory of activists matters. The political theory of the agrarian left was learned from agrarian struggles, but is consistent with strands of its academic shadow. The account demonstrates that the structure-agency dichotomy is infructuous: there can be no account of choice without systematic attention to structure, nor do structures have causal power absent the choices of individuals. These choices in turn cannot be understood absent attention to ideational structures, both normative and empirical, through which interests are defined, weighted, given meaning and priority.[13]

Agrarian Structural Changes: The Colonial Transformation of Malabar

The idea of a great transformation as a cause of peasant radicalism derives from Karl Polanyi's notion[14] of the disruptive effects of the emergence of the market from social relations in which the market was previously 'embedded'.[15] Though unequal and often degrading, pre-market society was characterized by understandings of the normative basis of allocative mechanisms. The fundamental insight of Polanyi should not be to romanticize pre-market society, but to underline the enormity of the normative transformation necessary to accommodate the market as a disembedded allocative device. The 'moral economy' model of peasant radicalism took off from this insight.[16] Yet obviously not all instances of market transformation give rise to peasant radicalism; exceptions generate puzzles.

The present state of Kerala was formed in 1956 from three distinct regions; differences in regional social structure and history are important in explaining the uneven development of a radical agrarian movement. The communist party struck its deepest organizational roots in Malabar, the northern third of contemporary Kerala, and the more radical factions of the undivided (pre-1964) Communist Party originated there. Malabar was under direct colonial rule as part of the Madras Presidency; Travancore and Cochin were under indirect rule through maharajahs until Independence. Malabar thus evidenced long direct competition within the anti-colonial movement between those who became leaders of the Indian National Congress and those who eventually split from the Congress to found the Communist Party in the state.

The conventional wisdom is that Malabar's archetypal disintegrating agrarian system was a direct consequence of two processes, colonial state-making and the imposition of market society. With the introduction of a legal system based on the absolute notion of land as private property, traditional overlords were able to evict tenants and raise rents according to the familiar rule of 'what the market would bear', enforced by the police powers of a colonial state. The great transformation from above was one in which property claims were disentangled from their broader social moorings and functions. As courts and administrative law protected the property claims of landlords, the necessity of good patron–client relations diminished; control of economic assets was guaranteed by the higher authority.[17] Though there is considerable dispute on the issue of whether or not private property in land existed in pre-colonial Malabar, there is no dispute that land control was hedged by social institutions to a marked degree—'embedded in social relations', in Polanyi's formulation.[18] Prior to the ninth century, one-third of the gross produce of landholders was due the king, in what may be conceptualized as either a rent or a tax. Central authority dissolved in the ninth century, giving way to a decentralized prebendial feudalism.[19] From AD 825 until the Mysore invasions (1766–92), the king's share (*rajabhogam*, more generally conceptualized as *pattam*)[20] came to be shared equally by a hereditary superior landholder or *janmakkaran* (*janmi*), and a subordinate known as *kanakkaran*, in whose control of the land elements of usufructuary mortgage and tenancy were intertwined. These titles came to connote 'landlord' and 'tenant' in colonial simplification; their pre-colonial operational meanings connoted 'embeddedness' in Polanyi's sense. The hierarchy of rights in land replicated the hierarchy of social standing.[21] *Janmakkaran* is usually held to have derived from *janmam* (birth right), *kanakkaran* from *kan* ('the eye', related to the Dravidian root *kanuku* 'to see') connoting supervisory functions. Holders of *kanam* rights were so clearly associated with specific caste status in some parts of Kerala that the *Keralolpatti* explicitly identifies the Nair caste as people of 'the eye', the 'hand' and 'the order', whose duty it was to 'prevent the rights from being curtailed or suffered to fall into disuse'.[22] So clearly were the Nairs identified with supervisory functions in the feudal system, that Logan observes, 'they had as a guild higher functions in the body politic than merely ploughing the rice-fields and controlling the irrigated lands'.

Since the Nair guild had 'higher functions' than cultivation, other social strata were necessarily defined by the lower-level functions of labour on the land. In the pre-colonial system, net produce was shared out in thirds: a third to the *janmi* (a share the British perceived as rent proper), a third to the *kanakkaran* (the supervising intermediary, often a mortgagee, whom the British interpreted as the 'tenant'), and a third to those who actually worked the land—sharecroppers (*verumpattakar*) and labourers (*koolikar*) known as *tiyyas* or *cherumar* after their caste identification. Much of this labour was performed by individuals understood to be slaves by colonial authorities, but it was a form of slavery unlike that of the transatlantic chattel business. Baden-Powell described south Indian slaves as *glebae adscripti*, whose position was both circumscribed and secure. 'Brahmans and moneylenders' may be 'swept away before the fury of a Muhammadan invasion . . .' but 'no one molests or moves the slave: whoever may be the nominal owner, or whatever the circumstances of the time, they are safe in their insignificance, and continue, and will ever continue, to till the ground their ancestors have tilled before them'.[23]

The radical simplification of embedded tenurial complexity by application of colonial categories rearranged security, power, and opportunity on the land. With property comes taxes. This combination was held in the materialist theory within colonial administration—*vide* William Logan—to be responsible for sporadic serious agrarian uprisings, named communally as an Islamic phenomenon (hence the 'Moplah [Mappila][24] uprisings', beginning in Malabar in 1836, initially peaking in 1841, and continuing sporadically throughout the nineteenth century). Simmering agrarian tensions exploded in 1921 in a series of encounters known as the Moplah Rebellion, one of the most intense uprisings in Indian colonial history. Scholarship revolves around three causal approaches: a revolt with 'communal' overtones—Muslims (moplahs) rising against Hindu overlords; a class revolt by egregiously exploited tenants against landlords; and a political revolt by an excluded populace against colonial oppression.[25] Colonial discourse for its part was acrimoniously divided on causation; a focus on 'religious fanaticism', associated with T.L. Strange, was contested by a countervailing theme of tenure-induced immiserization associated with William Logan. The latter advocated agrarian reform; fear of rural instability preceded concerns for production and social equity in discussions of land reform.

The Mappila uprisings did not spawn a sustained organization or lasting political projects, but were more in the character of *jacqueries*.[26] Defeat of the final uprising in 1921 led to conservatism and political withdrawal among Muslim peasants.[27] The legacy of the uprisings however was an opening for tenure reform in elite discourse, conditioned by fear of agrarian rebellion. That opening provided the focal point for continually escalating peasant demands in dialectical relation to state intransigence, resulting in an overturning of the agrarian system through public law in the 1970s.

INCHOATE RADICALISM: THE 'MOPLAH UPRISINGS'

Invasions from Mysore in the eighteenth century caused a mass exodus of the Hindu superordinates from Malabar. Muslim tenants (primarily *verumpattakar*)[28] then ceased paying rent and there was general upward mobility of Muslims. The British control of Malabar was established in 1792 following a costly war with Mysore. The immediate problem for the state was to establish a social base for its authority and to recover the war costs. Land taxation requires identifiable property rights; in recognizing the Nair and Namboodiri claimants as 'lords of the soil', the British effectively restored 'the landed aristocracy of Nambudiri *jenmis* and Nayars'.[29] Because of the preceding centuries of decentralized political structure, it was widely held that the actual cultivators in Kerala bore no land revenue claim from the state.[30] As a consequence of the settlement, holdings in Malabar were far more concentrated than in the rest of Madras Presidency and the extent of landlessness was much greater.[31]

The land taxes were over the course of the century recognized by subordinate colonial officials as excessive. Not only was the tax burden heavy, but its incidence was unequal; less well-connected villagers were over-assessed, the well-connected lightly assessed.[32] Within the landlord–tenant dyad, land revenue ultimately became the tenant's burden, concentrated on both weaker owners and tenants.[33] Revenue imperatives were not limited to land taxation, but targeted as well items of importance to the poor; official monopolies and fixed-price procurement of commodities were established to bolster revenue as well. Monopolies on salt, timber and tobacco increased unemployment in those sectors, thus increasing agrarian pressure.[34] By 1849, salt and tobacco monopolies yielded half the value of land revenue, compared to less than 10 per cent in the period 1809-13.[35] Among the fifty or so specific taxes collected, particularly abhorrent were those on items necessary for livelihoods: shops, cattle, looms, tapping knives, fishing nets, ferries, etc. K.N. Panikkar notes that 'nothing' fell outside the colonial state's taxation net.[36] Colonial officials recognized that these taxes, though essential for fiscal reasons, were particularly 'obnoxious'. Sullivan reported as a colonial official in 1843, 'The ferry tax is more obnoxious than the tobacco tax. The poor woman whose livelihood depends upon the bundle of sticks which she is carrying cannot pass until she has paid. So hard does this tax press upon the lower orders that lives have been lost in attempting to swim the river for the purpose of avoiding it.'[37]

Taxes and administered price monopolies combined with land revenue assessments to create considerable misery. H.S. Graeme observed in 1822 that, in contrast to earlier reports on the relative absence of poverty in Malabar, '. . . the province swarms with beggars, and it may not unreasonably be ascribed to their comforts having been seriously encroached upon by the salt and tobacco monopolies, and to the trade of the weavers having been nearly exterminated . . . and to the trade in timber also abolished by the monopoly of that article.'[38]

Resulting agrarian violence was expressed in the idiom of Islamic community and identity; the uprisings were couched by participants and state in oppositional terms: a Muslim community against a European state and Hindu landlords.[39] The colonial diagnosis of 'religious fanaticism'[40] resonated with the modes of organization, symbolism, and ethnicity of participants and victims. Mappilas believed that to kill a landlord was not only no sin, but a source of religious merit; to die fighting the colonial state in *jihad* ensured the benefits of martyrdom. Conrad Wood goes so far as to argue that 'the defining characteristic of the Moplah outbreak was devotion to death'. [41]

The countervailing line within the colonial state was that of District Collector and Magistrate William Logan:

> The real fact seems to have been that the *janmis*, influenced partly by the rise in prices of produce and partly by the novel views of the courts as their real position, had at last begun to feel their power as 'Lords of the Soil' and to exercise it through the courts. The *Mappillas*, who had been peacefully in possession of the lands since the time of Hyder Ali's conquest, felt it no doubt as a bitter grievance that the *janmis* should have obtained the power to evict them—a power which did not intrinsically belong to them—and the influential men among them, looking about for means to protect themselves, set fanaticism in motion. . . .[42]

This causative controversy, begun by T.L. Strange and William

Logan, persisted beyond their active involvement. The Malabar District Superintendent of Police reaffirmed the religious-fanaticism view in his confidential report on the 1921 rebellion: 'These outbreaks, being in the name of religion, proved infectious and had an unsettling effect on the neighborhood, requiring little to induce any poverty-stricken Mappilla to seek a glorious death as an entrance to such a paradise as his ignorant religious teachers pictured for him. . . .'[43]

Scholarly debate has reproduced the colonial discourse opposing religious fanaticism to tenurial grievances.[44] Yet the theoretical extraction is not helpful. Proponents of an Islamic interpretation critique the materialist position of Logan et al.: not all tenants were Muslims in Malabar, nor were all martyrs tenants. This critique fails to consider the effect of tenancy disasters on both extended families[45] and on communities in general. Tenant evictions, whether or not directly experienced, symbolized new power relations; generalized destitution resulted from the new powers of taxation, punitive fines, and the restriction of economic opportunity by an alien state. Likewise, not all the aggrieved would participate in localized uprisings; alternative modes (individualized 'weapons of the weak' and banditry) were available where collective action was not feasible. Nor were Muslims generally engaged in suicidal attacks on the state in areas not characterized by rack-renting and agrarian distress.

Yet Islam does provide an explanation for the disproportionate participation by Muslims: the advantage in collective action. David Arnold argues, following Logan in part, that the mosque provided 'a focus of loyalty and a centre for collective action'. Perhaps as importantly, the specifically Islamic expression of outrage manifested 'a new collective, almost familial, solidarity and mutual supportiveness. . . . Islam offered a language of redemption, a crude egalitarianism, an antipathy to landlords and foreigners, a kind of institutionalized "inversion" of the everyday world of the peasants.'[46] That the great transformation occurred under British rule following the restoration of a landed aristocracy previously defeated at the hands of co-religionists reinforced these messianic tendencies. Even religious practice was affected by oligopsonistic land markets and novel powers to impoverish or evict. A spokesman for the gang involved in the 1851 outbreak commented on the difficulty experienced by local Muslims in purchasing a piece of land for a mosque: '. . . what is the loss to the Nairs and Namboodris if a piece of ground capable of sowing five Parrahs of seed be allotted for construction of a Mosque? Let those hogs (British soldiers) come here, we are resolved to die.'[47]

The tenurial decay noted by Logan and the Mappilas was not an isolated event, but signified multiplex and gradual changes in power relations. Evictions were symptomatic of these new power relations and of the state's support of some rights over others. Eviction is an *economic* problem only in those situations in which superior or equal alternatives are not available. Given the economic changes of Malabar in the nineteenth century, mobilization on tenurial issues was certainly symbolic of economic desperation, and, more importantly, of broader power relations involving the state. That landlords were the targets of looting, violence, and coerced 'gifts' or protection money indicates not only that they alone had the resources to loot in a declining agrarian system, but also stood symbolically for unacceptable market powers and the state that guaranteed them.

As the 'religious' interpretation correctly stresses, Islam provided a mode of organization and a sense of community buttressed by historical relative deprivation. Itinerate preachers were central to mobilization and the mosque as a regular gathering place of a community facilitated communication and organization. Lacking such means of collective action, the Hindu population in the nineteenth century largely turned to more individualistic 'weapons of the weak',[48] largely theft. That Muslims were prominent in organized violence indicates that their solidarity and ideology of martyrdom provided a means of responding to social distress that was different from those of other communities. Moreover, the ritual and social differentiation within the Hindu community created additional obstacles to collective protest, obstacles which were overcome only through the strategic innovations of the leftists in the 1920s and 1930s.[49]

Martyrdom as motivation may have facilitated collective confrontation,[50] but simultaneously undermined its effectiveness. As a leader of a Mapilla unit in 1849 awaited the arrival of more troops, he stated that he was ready to die in '. . . fair fight with the Cirkar (state)'.[51] This was a common theme of the rebels. Meeting soldiers of the *raj* as equals in combat symbolically inverted the subordination and humiliation felt by destitute Muslims. In the 1921 Mapilla rebellion, however, conditions were considerably different. Support from the Congress for the Khilafat agitation and for self-rule provided both external allies (putatively) and new leadership. That rising lasted six months and extended over two thousand square miles until the state's superior military resources effected a brutal suppression. The 1921 uprising was denounced by Gandhi as a perversion of the nationalist Khilafat cause he championed, but was nevertheless characterized in the District Gazetteer as '. . . a gigantic popular upheaval the like of which has not been seen in Kerala before or since'.[52]

A commentary on that struggle by the Malabar Superintendent of Police captured the nuances of this synthesis of nominally competing material and ideational interpretations of the Mapilla *jacqueries*. In his report on the 1921 rebellion, R.H. Hitchcock noted:

> '. . . many of them [Mapilla activists] neither were nor ever would be tenants but were quite ready to fall in with any suggestions which promised a chance of looting the rich and for the same reason to support the *Khilafat* agitation as meaning Mappilla Raj in Ernad. . . .[53]

Hitchcock understood the rebellion primarily in religious terms, and yet understood the significance of its anti-state ('Mappilla Raj' means Muslim rule) and anti-elite character. 'Looting the rich' captures the social banditry strand of the Mappila uprisings.[54] His account stresses the transmission of radicalism by local intellectuals (though he rails against their 'ignorance') and the activities of the Congress through its *Khilafat* mobilization and national conferences—linking poor Muslims in a backward district to an international movement of historic significance. He also recognized the role of the official repression of widespread banditry (which had accompanied all Mappila outbursts) in triggering rebellion.[55]

The Superintendent of Police also understood the role of martyrdom and general destitution in generating radicalism. 'It was the poorest who kept moving inland in search of a livelihood and their mosques could not afford to pay for proper instructors and they had to rely for instruction on self-styled Thangals and Mussaliars, often as ignorant as themselves, who preached and taught fanaticism and sometimes even practised it.'[56]

Hitchcock emphasized that rebels tended to be poor and young and often without a livelihood; periods of 'fanaticism' were preceded and accompanied by a 'general spirit of lawlessness' and increased crime, from 'petty house-breakings' to dacoity.[57] From the earliest injunctions that to kill a landlord was not only free from sin but a religious obligation, the Mappilas had made clear that they perceived tenurial oppression to be a legitimate trigger for violence, having repeatedly attempted remedy through the state and failed.

Conrad Wood concludes that '... as a challenge to British rule the Moplah outbreak was mere ritual'.[58] Both Mappilas and colonial officials knew that the insurgents would die. Yet deadly confrontations against long odds continued in Kerala throughout the struggle for independence and land. Radicalism in Kerala changed form in the twentieth century, but the commemoration of martyrs[59] and struggle against immediately overwhelming odds continued to constitute a distinctive mode of social challenge. Moral outrage congruent with the Mappila charges sustained the movement even as tactical wisdom and organization replaced suicide with mere danger.

The nineteenth-century uprisings were far more extensive than the more familiar Deccan Riots. They were, as suggested by the title of K.N. Panikkar's superb book, *Against Lord and State*, against lords whose novel powers of eviction and wrack-renting were a product of the state just as agrarian distress resulting from the state's policies undermined the bargaining power of the landless and made violence a last resort. They were, as Logan perceived, defensive in character, resonating with Polanyi's view of reaction to novel property forms of market society. Whatever the ethnic composition of the tenantry, the notion that land rights should be subject to market dynamics—and the subsequent dislocations of evictions and enhanced rents and renewal fees (*michivaram*)—was clearly at variance with the prior moral economy of Malabar.[60]

The Mappila risings underline the complexity of agrarian movements, structural and ideational. First, in line with social theory on the causes of agrarian protest, an agrarian structure characterized by high levels of insecure tenancy, extreme inequalities in land ownership, and consequently miserable terms of exchange between landed and landless generated the structural potential for agrarian radicalism.[61] Secondly, 'defensive reactions' of elements of society to dislocations engendered by market forces acting on new property rights drove extreme attempts to re-establish traditional security. But as importantly, the Mappilla revolts illustrate the importance of overlays of social oppression which may accompany economic exploitation. The self-definition of Muslims as Muslims provided the symbols and forms of organization without which collective action is extremely difficult. Similar issues of ethnic identification and mobilization—around caste in particular—were later to play an important role in the growth of a radical and redistributive coalition centered around the communists.[62] As importantly, the futile jacqueries of the Muslim population, and the proto-political rebellion of 1921, sensitized the state to the necessity of responding to agrarian distress. To ignore that threat was to risk its authority and its rural revenues, as was explicitly recognized in the 1940s.

From Jacquerie to Sustained Militance

The Moplah Rebellion illuminated and attacked the structural unity of landlordism and colonial rule. The colonial government clearly recognized its dependence on the landlords for continued hegemony and the landlords reciprocally depended on the colonial state's machinery to quash challenges to their local power. An appreciation of this is crucial for understanding the divergence in support bases for Congress and communist programmes: conservative groups within the Congress came to oppose, with varying resolve and militancy, colonial rule, but were unwilling to attack landlordism as a social institution. Radicals within the Congress movement, on the other hand, came to oppose with increasing militancy both landlordism and the colonial state; they believed this understanding to be crucial for success in the independence struggle. A member of the Congress Left, later a communist leader, noted:

> Not only was the peasantry the most numerous section of the Indian people, but it was in the villages that imperialism had its most reliable ally—the feudal landlords. The police thana functioning in close collaboration with the big landlords was the centre of imperialism's oppressive machinery.[63]

The Moplah Rebellion, and later outbursts of peasant militancy, were denounced and abandoned by Gandhi and Congress conservatives; the radicals supported, nurtured and organized around these social impulses, with incrementally increasing (though uneven) organizational development and tactical success. The basis of organization was both caste and class. Though caste and class largely coincided in this period, specific caste indignities and privileges constituted grounds for collective action. Importantly, whereas a class identity lacks any primordial organic reality or organizational expression, castes existed as functioning social organizations, and thus provided the nuclei of the mobilization of the poor.

Organized peasant movements in Malabar began with the interests of superior tenants. Agitations for the rights of *kanam* tenants were clearly intertwined with the struggles of Nairs as a caste (though the extreme form of this argument overstates the case[64]). Unlike the Namboodiri Brahmins, the Nairs took to English education and government service early, and formed a caste association to knit together various ritually distinct sub-castes to form a political force demanding privileged treatment. As Nairs occupied the lower levels of the imperial machinery, they experienced acute status inconsistency. Describing the conflict within the 'new class of educated young men and officers' (*tehsildars*, police inspectors, 'sub-judges') E.M.S. Namboodiripad wrote deprecatingly about his own caste (and indeed his own family):

> The very same state which made them politically independent of the *Jenmis* [landlords—connoting Brahmans here] made them much more dependent economically on those same *Jenmis* . . . The educated and professional man with a wide outlook and sturdy sense of self-respect

has to humiliate himself before the narrow-minded and conceited ignoramus who is his landlord.[65]

Similar issues of social humiliation—of outcaste communities—were employed in a movement which, in economic terms, served the interests almost exclusively of the superior tenants. Though recognizing the necessity of eventual abolition of the 'feudal' landlord-dominated agrarian system, leftists to the Congress were careful to mobilize to attack the injustices explicitly felt by the peasantry, while linking these to social indignities on which the people's consciousness was well developed. For example, in many villages, the legitimacy of rent was too deeply embedded to be attacked frontally; landlords were instead attacked for the social humiliation or abuse of 'their' tenants or for the illegal exactions that denoted traditional obeisance. One *jatha* (protest march) against a single landlord for such illegal exactions attracted 7,000 peasants in Malabar in the mid-1930s.[66] There were hundreds of similar protests on a smaller scale.[67] These protests, held against almost all important *jenmis* of Malabar, simultaneously raised the consciousness of a similar objective class position, generated popular self-confidence, and helped overcome traditional religious, class, and caste cleavages among peasants, in the same manner that Jeffrey[68] observes among the working class in Kerala.

The Malabar Kudiyan Sangham (tenants' association) was formed at Pattambi in 1920; the leadership was predominantly of the Nair caste (and *kanakkar* class). Clandestine activities predominated in the early years, but over eight years of operation, the MKS formed about one-hundred local units throughout Malabar.[69] Organization of landlords, originally prompted by consideration of land reforms by the colonial administration in the 1880s, was furthered by the activities of the MKS and elections to the Madras Legislative Council in 1923.[70] Public debates and memorials, letter campaigns, and agitations were organized around the formulation of the Malabar Tenancy Bill. One representative of the Mappila tenants explicitly threatened another uprising if the government continued its anti-tenant policy.[71] Radhakrishnan argues that 'the attitude of the government had undergone a favorable change because . . . the agitation was championed by the educated middle class consisting of lawyers and government servants . . . ,'[72] but reverberations of the Mappila uprisings clearly influenced policy as well.

The Malabar Tenancy Act (XIV of 1930) was a victory for the MKS, but mainly for the superior tenants who spearheaded it. Radhakrishnan gives the best summary of colonial politics surrounding the law:

> Malabar is one of the few places in India where land relations were intensively and effectively articulated by an educated middle class as early as in the first quarter of this century. Though the British administration stood stolidly by the *Janmis* throughout nearly a century of agitations by the illiterate, impoverished, and inarticulate Mappilas, when the educated, affluent, and articulate Nayars appeared on the scene, in less than a decade it conceded to their demands as a matter of political expediency.[73]

Yet tenure reform first emerged within the colonial state as political management, to alleviate social tensions that in the view of some generated the 'Mappila outrages'. Discussion of tenure reform in turn prompted the organization of landlords where none had existed before and joined contesting classes in competition before the colonial state through such forums as the colonial state allowed (both political, as in the Madras Legislative Council, and public, through memorials, newspaper debates, and public meetings). Finally, the articulateness of Nairs is perhaps less important than success in capturing the Congress organizational wing[74] and their instantiation in crucial rungs of the state's machinery. The colonial state really rested on two pillars, the *janmis* whose control through landlordism made them a necessary political ally, and the educated middle class, largely overlapping with the Nair community and *kanakkar* class, who carried administrative control to the villages.

Victory for the superior tenants in 1930 created new marketable property rights—'almost liquid gold' in Namboodiripad's assessment.[75] Rent and renewal fees became predictable; security of tenure was largely assured, at least for the stronger of the class. Nevertheless, those below the *kanakkar* (about half the tenantry as well as the 'serf/slave' classes) would have to fight new struggles to receive comparable benefits. The politics of ratchets gave these classes both a model and a political niche to pursue those struggles.

The culmination of well-organized local protests was the formation of the Kerala Karshaka Sangham (peasant association), in Malabar at the sub-district level in 1935. The district-level Malabar Sangham was formed the following year.[76] Left activists of the Congress patiently organized, village by village, building in each one a volunteer defence committee, and establishing study groups and reading rooms. Leading Congress socialists wrote plays with radical content; dramatic presentations were important in mobilization.[77]

These organizational efforts were aided by the enormous respect for learning, and relatively high literacy rate, of Kerala. School teachers and students were important as local leaders and activists. The great peasant leader, A.K. Gopalan, began his professional life as a village teacher.[78] Communist Party elder E.M.S. Namboodiripad gives perhaps the best summary of the fusion of mobilizing agents and issues: 'It is the combination in one person of the office-bearer of the Village Congress Committee, the leader of the Teachers' Union, and the organizer of the Kisan Sangham [peasant association] that made the anti-imperialist movement strike deep roots in the countryside.'[79]

Mobilization of the peasantry was, however, a major source of cleavage within the Congress. Radhakrishnan dates the first organized efforts to protect kanam tenants to 1912; competition within the Malabar Congress shifted the balance of power from *janmis* to tenant leaders between 1916 and 1920.[80] The open split occurred in 1920 when a group of landlords and professionals led by Annie Besant, representing conservatives in the Malabar Congress, walked out when outvoted on both tenancy reform and militancy.[81] Conservative Congress leadership, locally and nationally, had deep reservations about peasant militancy. Leftists had no such reservations, and built a powerful movement around issues of economic exploitation and social indignities, linked organizationally to the nationalist movement and to the burgeoning trade union movement.[82] Their success contrasts sharply with efforts in many other parts of the subcontinent and provided a solid political base for the eventual emergence of the Communist Party.

Beyond Tenure: Expansion of Peasant Struggles

Leadership on the Left has attributed organizational success to intertwined factors of generalized rural misery (exacerbated in the 1930s by the great Depression, magnified by Kerala's extensive integration into international markets) and imperialism, which were structurally linked. Ramifications of the Depression illustrated concretely the linkages; revenue assessments rose in 1929 just as the effects of the depression were hitting rural Kerala.[83] Tax protests joined demonstrations against general economic conditions. Massive hunger marches (*pattinijatha*) linked disparate areas, creating organizational links across the entire area within which Malayalam is spoken—including jurisdictions directly—ruled by the British and Princely States as well. Hunger songs of K.P.R. Gopalan and K.A. Keraleeyan became popular in the villages.[84] Dramatic presentations carried the theme of the evils of landlordism (*Pattabakki* [Arrears of Rent] and *Raktapanam* [Drinking Blood]), but also alternative visions of a new organization of agriculture (*Koottukrishi* or Collective Farming).[85] Social oppression was attacked symbolically through large inter-caste dinners and programmatically through demands for temple entry and access to government jobs and education. Social oppression and decadence were presented as symptomatic of the decaying social system of oppressive landlordism.

Leaders of the peasant mobilization are quite clear on the issue of consciousness. The Mappila rebels had lacked a clear consciousness of class; landlords were perceived more in individual than class terms in local assaults. Activist propaganda and tactics built on this tradition even while linking general misery to systemic causes. Particular *janmis* were attacked as the 'embodiment of all evils', especially when associated with a 'reprehensible lifestyle'[86] increasingly associated with the class as a whole. Landlords were portrayed in propaganda and popular theatre generically as decadent and rapacious parasites, a perception buttressed by the presence of caste reformers from the *janmi* station among Congress radicals.

If the Mappila rebellions were clearly 'against lord and state', so too were the subsequent mobilizations buttressed by the concrete fusions between colonial state and agrarian system. Fallow land belonging to both lords and state was an affront to the landless; fallows were forcibly occupied and tilled. Failure of official channels to cope with famine in 1942–3 led to confiscations of grain at locally determined fair prices and distribution through peoples' committees. Black market sales of rice were collectively opposed. Government sales of forest land in Malabar, to non-local capitalists followed by restrictions placed on traditional rights to gather green manure and wood were opposed militantly. More important for future politics, responsibility for agricultural development was placed squarely on the state; failure to drain or irrigate potentially cultivable land, distribute fertilizers, provide credit for land clearing and cultivation, or assure food distribution were the occasions for mass meetings, protest marches and direct action, often leading to violent official reaction, death, and imprisonment.[87]

Repression creates martyrs. Opposition to landlords evoked retaliation in the form of evictions, harassment through police and courts, social boycott, and physical coercion.[88] Just as the Mappilas were memorialized by the naming of mosques after martyrs[89] and care for their dependants, martyrs in later struggles were memorialized in song and by providing for their families. Young E.K. Nayanar (later Chief Minister of Kerala) recalled that one of his early exposures to leftist discussions and literature was in a reading room named for Sri Harshan, a Harijan who died in the Cannanore jail.[90] The Kayoor martyrs (1943) were memorialized not only in legend and song,[91] but through celebration of March 29, the date of their death, as All-India Kisan Day. The All-India Kisan Sabha organized relief for their families; British trade unionists raised the then princely sum of Rs 61,600 for the effort as well.[92]

The movement's aims had moved beyond security of tenure. As early as 1935, the slogan of 'death to landlordism' had joined demands for representative government and extension of security downwards in the class structure. The movement had to retain support from superior tenants as it extended the movement down the social and tenurial structure. At the Chirakkal Taluk Peasants' Conference in November 1936, it was resolved that landlords were entitled not to rent, but to the residual: that portion of gross produce (if any) left after the subsistence needs of peasants working the land had been met. As interim measures, the Conference demanded rental limits at one-fourth the gross produce, abolition of extra-rental payment obligations (*kazhcha*, *kankani*, *seelakkasu*, etc.), security of tenure, cancellation of arrears of rent, price supports for agricultural commodities, and fixation of wages for agricultural laborers.[93]

The open split which created the communist party was presaged by division on these measures. The Congress Party, which was then the umbrella under which radical rural organizations operated, won the elections of 1937 and formed a ministry in Madras. When this government failed to pursue even those limited remedial measures within its power, peasant organizations launched a movement against both landlords and the government. As usual the tactics included social boycott and *jathas* to the homes of prominent and especially obnoxious landlords.[94] British concern with the social boycott (e.g. by barbers and washermen) was twofold: that a 'law and order situation' could result and that the withholding of rent could jeopardize the fiscal imperative which was the centre of colonial rule. A dispatch from a confidential report to the Home Ministry in Madras noted in 1938:

> The District Magistrate of Malabar reports that a no-rent campaign . . . which has been carried on for some time . . . is achieving considerable success, and that in the absence of any organized opposition is in some parts undermining the authority of Government. He fears that, if the jenmies are unable to collect their rents, it will have a serious effect on the land revenue collections. . . .[95]

The alliance between superior and inferior tenants began to show strains during the debates on amendments to the Malabar Tenancy Act.[96] Maintenance of the coalition was aided by agreement to focus agitations on the refusal of the Congress Government of Madras to reduce statutory rents or waive the advance deposit of one year's rent for tenants-at-will (*verumpatakar*).

Communist theoretician E.M.S. Namboodiripad raised in his dissenting opinion to the report the question of whether landlordism serves 'any useful social function'. Namboodiripad later explained his conclusion that landlordism was 'parasitic' under modern conditions: 'In mediaeval days, landlordism was a social, political and cultural institution, as well as economic. But shorn of all these functions, the Malabar *janmis* today are only dead corpses of their own forefathers.'[97] The vast sums hitherto collected by landlords was calculated by E.M.S. Namboodiripad.[98] In social contract terms, if this sum were matched by performance of services (specifically analogous to the entrepreneur of industry, including advancing of working capital, construction of irrigation works, research into scientific agriculture, etc.), it would be justified. Since dead corpses 'as a class' had ceased to perform traditional functions, and had taken up no modern ones, the institution of landlordism could not withstand scrutiny.

Focus on the aggregate rent collected by landlords created the coalition-building notion of a 'rent fund'.[99] The move to abolish landlords *as a class*, whether decadent or not, was a tactical ratchet which permitted the party to promise that distribution of a rent fund would satisfy the disparate claimants (whose class positions were objectively opposed to one another) in the coalition.[100]

Independence did not change a great deal for those at the bottom of the agrarian structure. Demonstrations on the issue of food availability and prices, as well as militant intervention in food distribution, continued. Slogans escalated to reflect the Calcutta motto of the communist party: 'land to the tiller and power to the people'.[101] Unemployment and near-famine conditions continued to produce militant confrontations, deaths, and martyrs. The Munayan Kunnu incident in north Malabar in April of 1948 was held by Malabar activists to have the 'same place in Kerala politics as that of Vayalar (in Travancore)',[102] though with much less loss of life. After a period under ban during the 'left adventurist' (armed insurrectionary) period of early Independence, the Communist Party re-emerged as an electoral force; the peasant movement 'rose up from its own ashes'.[103] Unification with peasant organizations of the Congress and the Indian Socialist Party (Kisan Congress and Kisan Panchayat respectively) was attempted but failed.[104] The party's

Malabar wing gained great prestige in hosting the Eleventh All-India Kisan Sammelan in Malabar in 1953. The conference site was significantly named 'Kayyoor Nagar' in memory of the Kayoor martyrs.[105]

Until its final amendment in 1954, the Malabar Tenancy Act remained the centerpiece of struggles specifically focused on land. The 1951 amendment prompted more of the agitations and petitions which had begun around the turn of the century. Significantly, the 1954 Amendment granted most of the minimalist claims of the tenantry (falling short of 'death to landlordism'), including new fair rent provisions, strengthening protection from evictions, and abolishing the payment-in-advance provisions for *verumpattakar*.[106] The rent fund remained in the hands of landlords, though reduced in size (*de jure*) and with fewer levers to control tenants. What remained was the final abolition of landlordism altogether.

Beyond Malabar: The Importance of Political Space

Extensive connection to international trade (coir, rubber, cardamom, pepper, ginger, etc.) made the depression of the 1930s especially catastrophic for Kerala's masses.[107] From 1931 onwards, landless or virtually landless agricultural labourers increased dramatically in number both in absolute terms and as a percentage of agriculturalists, concretely linking the non-agricultural distress to pressure on the agrarian structure.[108]

Early and penetrating commercialization was coupled with a settlement pattern which differentiates Kerala from much of India; rather than discrete villages of the modal sort, Kerala presents a continuous gradient of urban to peri-urban to rural communities. The agrarian poor often had one foot in economic activities associated with trade, simple agro-industrial processing (coir is archetypal), and small-scale industrial activities. The familiar leftist exhortation to form a 'worker-peasant alliance' was achieved in part by the very structure of settlement patterns, physical ecology, economic activity and occupations.

In contrast to Malabar, organized peasant revolts were largely absent in the princely states of Travancore and Cochin; T.K. Oommen correctly characterizes the major uprisings (the Kundara

Declaration of Velu Thampi [1810–19] and the Malayalee Memorial of 1891) as anti-imperialist struggles in which peasants participated, though their specific demands were not primary.[109] Travancore led in tenurial reforms, essentially as a part of the struggle to establish royal authority over local chiefs and stimulate commercial development. New regulations beginning in 1818 promoted recovery of 'waste' lands for commercial crops. Pro-tenant regulations began in 1829 and were strengthened (*de jure*) in episodes of reforms that ratcheted down the tenurial ladder. Land was concentrated under royal control and tenants in effect became tenants of the state, with permanent occupancy rights and low rents. Ownership was conferred on tenants of state lands in 1865, laying the base for what is usually considered a 'peasant-proprietor' system, in stark contrast to Malabar.[110] In line with academic theory of the productivity consequences of tenurial systems, the government hoped through this arrangement to promote commercial agriculture, and succeeded.

The Travancore land reforms were top-down, not a response to peasant pressure, but an exercise in state formation and creation of property rights conducive to commercial development. Likewise, slavery was abolished in 1855 in Travancore, though most agricultural labourers continued to be attached to landowners in a 'semi-slave status'.[111] As the site of intensive commercialization and early capitalist development, Travancore witnessed extraordinary social mobility (both up and down) that disrupted the traditional caste occupational structure and intensified the process of proletarianization.[112]

Like Travancore, regulations in Cochin (Kochi) offered nominal protection for the upper stratum of tenants in the nineteenth century, though with minimal implementation. T.K. Oommen argues that these protections help explain relatively quiescent agrarian relations.[113] To this explanation must be added relative economic opportunity, particularly in Travancore; new commercial development of lands claimed by the state provided outlets for surplus mercantile capital and some employment for labour. Moreover, the extraordinary outbreak of evictions noted in Malabar was muted in the southern regions. Certainly landlordism as a social system was neither so dominant nor oppressive as in Malabar.

Reforms in Travancore and Cochin reinforced demands for reform in Malabar. This spread effect was fortified by the activities of the Congress, which connected Malabar activists not only with their counterparts in other Malayalam-speaking areas, but with those with all-India perspective and experience. Finally, and most important for mobilization on the Left, protections in the southern regions were poorly enforced, creating the need for popular militancy to secure nominal benefits. Such protections also did not reach down the tenurial and social ladder; land to the tiller remained an attractive mobilizing force. Finally, limited reforms did not prevent increased proletarianization over time, nor general immiserization during economic crises. Rural radicalism in Travancore and Cochin was in any event more integrated with working class militancy and anti-authoritarian demands for popular rule.

Agrarian radicalism was thus more pronounced in Malabar, but leftist strength built in the rest of what was to become Kerala State. Leftist success in an exploitative agrarian structure is not inevitable, but not unexpected; similar dynamics characterized Thanjavur (Tanjore) district as well.[114] Under colonial rule, Malabar was but one district of the Madras Presidency, distant from the capital in Madras (Chennai), and from Thanjavur. Malabar was easy for the Presidency to ignore. After Independence, Malabar was joined to Kerala State, uniting Left movements over the entire area in which Malayalam is spoken and adding a more militant agrarian base to Kerala's populace. Thanjavur remained an isolated outpost of agrarian radicalism in the state of Tamil Nadu. This conjunctural reorganization of political space explains much of the success of radical mobilization in Kerala and its failure in neighboring Tamil Nadu.

Origins of a Radical Exceptionalism As Party

Much of Kerala's exceptionalism rests on competition between a successful Communist Party and a Congress Party that must respond.[115] Why did the Congress fail to smother, with its umbrella and patronage, those radical impulses as it did in much of India?

The Left succeeded in large part because the Right failed. Differences in the ability to address expressed grievances and organize around radical programmes reflect both the social theories and social bases of the contending groups which later became the Congress Party and the Communist Party. The split between radicals and conservatives in the Congress movement began early. The Moplah rebels were branded indelibly with the mark of violence and class conflict, tactics repeatedly disavowed by All-India Congress leadership and by Mahatma Gandhi in particular. The Congress connection with local notables rendered an alliance with peasant radicalism practically impossible. Gandhi's theory of exploitation was palatable, if not universally acceptable, to landed elites: landlordism *as usually practised* was indeed exploitative, Gandhi argued, not from any 'inherent necessity', but rather because of the moral defects of certain landlords (defects which were corrigible through suasion and enlightenment). Gandhi's theory of 'trusteeship' explicitly allowed for maintenance of traditional class divisions and privileges, though optimally with reforms in the moral economy of the overlords.[116] In the developing leftist analysis, the abuses of landlordism were not simply manifestations of aberrant, morally-deficient landowners. Rather, landlordism was perceived in structural, systemic terms: a social system sustained by colonial rule and ultimately guaranteed by force. In this analysis, landlordism was a multi-faceted institution inextricably intertwined with caste indignities (which were more severe and extreme in Kerala than elsewhere), economic exploitation, political inequality, and imperialism: a social system which neither tenure reform nor independence alone could dissolve.[117]

Leftists did fight for land-tenure reform (security of use-rights and rental controls), but not as end in itself. Their strategy resembled a ratchet. As the colonial government made minimal concessions (such as the Malabar Tenancy Act of 1930), leftists mobilized for an extension of the concessions to lower layers of the peasantry and simultaneously organized both for effective implementation of the limited relief provisions and against the multifaceted social manifestations of landlordism.[118] A lever in ratcheting up was extensive moral outrage.

Moral outrage was generated about extreme exploitation—

debt-bondage, slavery, and serfdom—and the deterioration of traditional security and economic rights of middle sectors, exacerbated by the world depression of the 1930s. Subordinate orders were degraded and humiliated by such practices as untouchability, which prevented certain groups from using public roads, entering temples, approaching 'clean caste' members, covering certain parts of their bodies with clothing, using certain water supplies, etc. The rural poor were subjected to sexual exploitation and beatings, as well as to petty significations of inferior status, such as not being allowed to wear shoes or long wraps or to use the same language to refer to themselves or their possessions.[119]

Solutions proposed by the Congress to the social indignities of the depressed castes/classes did not address the multi-faceted nature of the exploitation, and thus sometimes boomeranged. Communist leader E.K. Nayanar recounted a formative experience as a youth active in the Congress movement. Congress workers promoting the liquor-prohibition movement asked an elderly peasant not to drink. He responded:

> You sons of rich landlords need no liquor. Those like me who work hard from morning to evening do need it. Only then can we prepare ourselves for work the next day. What we earn by such hard work, you drain from us as rent and other payments. . . . Even after this perpetual hard work we are poor. Our only enjoyment is toddy. Won't you let us enjoy this humble refreshment? We don't want your Congress. Will you let us draw drinking water from your wells. No. . . . You will not let us live on this earth.[120]

Nayanar's experience with the Congress prohibition campaign is symptomatic of the confrontations of leftists with the Congress in several ways. Reformist agitations not only brought him into contact with peasants as individuals, but exposed the hypocrisy within the reformist movement: 'Many who joined us to picket the [toddy] shops would have liquor brought to them in the evening and drink. This nauseated me. I hated these hypocrites.'[121] Even those who hated the communists acknowledged their sincerity, self-denial, and personal integrity—all values central to the Congress movement ideologically. Leftist leaders acknowledged the extraordinary impact of Gandhi and the

Gandhians in introducing new forms of public protest and legitimating idealism, generating enthusiasm and nurturing activism. The conflict with the Gandhian position concerned limits on the scope of organization, tactics, and substantive issues important to the people with whom they were encouraged to work.

Ratchet Tactics

Sustaining the agrarian coalition—divided by community, class, individual identities and interests[122]—necessitated tactical wisdom. Land reform was central to the solution of collective action problems among 'the peasantry' of Kerala historically. The peasantry did not exist; it was formed.

The failure of state-level elites affiliated with the Congress to redistribute rural assets and opportunities raised the concern, explicitly articulated by Indira Gandhi, that failure of land reforms produces political instability and the opportunity for radical parties to mobilize the rural poor.[123] In Kerala, Indira Gandhi's fears—echoing the concerns of William Logan as Collector of Malabar—have been born out by history. Clearly there were conflicts other than land, but questions of the forms of landed property and its relation to market forces generated the organizational base without which communist electoral power would have been impossible. That the land issue was central, is buttressed by the astounding electoral performance of the communists after their first ministry was dismissed by Delhi, when issues of colonialism were long passed.[124]

But promising and delivering land reform are no mean tasks. There are always too many claimants with powerful claims. 'Peasants' have both other interests and competitive relations to one another. Tactics on the Left deployed a combination of ratchet and inclusionary elements. For those nominally protected by legislation won through popular struggles (e.g. the *kanakkar*), the movement offered the means to benefit from legislative victories; tenure reform is universally recognized as vulnerable to landed power at the local level: laws are never self-enforcing.[125] T.K. Oommen notes that the legal victories of tenants in

Travancore and Cochin were frequently rendered infructuous by 'the class character of the state bureaucracy—particularly the revenue administration and judiciary'.[126] Full protection of even limited gains required continuous activism to spread the weight of society against the local state and recalcitrant elites. An interest in politics of the Left was thus created for tenants regardless of the despotic benevolence of Travancore and (to a lesser extent) Cochin.[127]

Contingent rights thus married objective interests of many layers of tenants who were in competition with one another for security and land to a Left programme. As ratchets gave additional security and retained incentives for superior tenants to stay with the Left, expansion gave incentives for lower social classes to join the struggle: the unemployed, the socially despised, the landless. Their interests in objective economic restructuring were paralleled by a cultural interest in abolishing the disabilities and indignities imposed by social superiors enabled by economic super-ordination. A necessary condition for these politics was a disentangling of land as a 'bundle of rights'.[128] Colonial land policy had collapsed the bundle and concentrated rights in a simple commodity called land, which could be owned and subjected to market principles like any other factor of production. Yet the specific strands of that bundle—to evict tenants, to prevent collection of forest materials, to hoard the land's product, to brutalize labor—were disputed in the moral economy of subordinates on the land.

The Left linked general economic disaster to visible symbols of the old order; distributive issues took on targets outside the coalition—fallow lands of lord and state. Without lord and (colonial) state there would be land and wages to go around, as in the mythic reign of Mahabeli.

The uprisings of the Mappilas were ultimately suicidal, and left no organizational residues, but taught both the colonial state and peasant leaders lessons. Though tenurial grievances figured in their outrage, participants were a disparate collection cast off by a society undergoing profound change, reflecting neither a coherent class position nor a political programme. Yet subsequent movements built on the core of outrage and tactics established by the Mappilas—from targeting the most reprehensible landlords to memorialization of martyrs. As the state rejected petitions for redress, and backed landlord power concretely, the uprisings illustrated the fusion of landed power and state policy that became the target of decades of organized politics.

The subsequent progression of the Malabar peasantry's organizational and programmatic struggle from *jacquerie* to coalitional strategy is encapsulated in the changes of the name of the first newspaper of the movement founded in the 1920s. *Kudiyan*, meaning 'tenant', gave way to *Krishikaran*, meaning 'farmer' or 'agriculturalist', launched in 1952. The specifically 'tenant' origins of the movement had expanded to a claim to represent the interests of agricultural communities *in toto*: debt relief, government aid to agriculture, traditional commons rights for gathering fuel and timber, rural unemployment, control of food prices and black marketeering and a host of subsidiary issues. The radical content of 'land to the tiller and power to the people' was paralleled by a more conservative politics, in which concessions wrung from the government were expanded both to make meaningful the previous concessions granted and to extend the agitation to a broader base.

Thus the Malabar Tenancy Act of 1930 was a measure for 'superior tenants', but realization of its benefits required measures of debt relief, taxation limits, and social curbs on the effective power of landlords on the ground: a hemming in of the market. Simultaneously, agitations for amendments to the Act created new collective interests (those of *verumpattakar*) while retaining a core of previous beneficiaries—whose *de facto* benefits depended on continued mobilization of local countervailing power. As slogans radicalized, most clearly in the very first years of Independence, the promise to strata below the tenants was more implied and general than specific: abolition of landlordism would provide new lands even as attacks on hoarders and black marketeers promised that a moral economy other than the market would govern distribution. The bloody uprising at Punnapra-Vayalar was neither tenant-led nor based, but rather a broad attack on state- and market-driven determinations of want and privilege.[129]

By the 1950s, revolution had receded to a rhetorical flourish superimposed on electoral politics appealing to the agrarian poor, working class, and radical intelligentsia.[130] The legacies of the agrarian mobilization I have described, before and just after the first communist electoral victory in 1957, are social and ideological. To an extent unmatched in the rest of the subcontinent, political elites learned that agrarian grievances must be answered; the rural poor would not accept inaction or a retrenchment of hard-won rights. Parties of the Right learned the value of rural mobilization and of at least symbolic commitment to redistribution. Perhaps the most extraordinary feature of debates on land reform in the Legislative Assembly in the 1960s and 1970s was the consensus that appearing to be on the side of reform was a political asset. Political parties across the ideological spectrum followed the communists in establishing peasant associations and then agricultural workers' unions.[131]

As a consequence of these organizational developments, the Left in rural Kerala became a persistent social force. The cultural effect of this force was that the very bottom of society began to believe that in combination, and with sufficient militancy, they could exercise power, both defensively and progressively. Later generations of politicians attempted to answer the rural underclasses with a shift from the agrarian question to agricultural development, from redistribution to distribution, from moral economy to growth, but understood that they could not be ignored.

Collective Action of 'the Peasantry'

Agrarian mobilization of such duration and persistent strength presents a nested problem of collective action. There is no such thing as the 'peasantry' of organicist social theory.[132] The peasantry is not only class-stratified, but composed of individuals with multiple identifications, all of which are potentially important for political action. For mobilization to succeed, individuals in large numbers must determine that identification of interests as 'peasants' overrides, at least temporarily, other class interests; that these aggregate identifications are relevant to political action; that sufficient others will so identify; that some specific representation of collective interests is consonant with identified interests; and that the extraordinary risks of confrontation should be borne.[133]

Failure to win periodic victories threatens disintegration of the collective project; winning victories threatens withdrawal of winners. How did the Left in Kerala avoid that outcome? A structural feature of landlordism—the massive 'rent fund' collected by landlords as a class—provided a mechanism to facilitate collective action in face-to-face communities. First, redistribution of the rent fund offered selective incentives to inferior tenants and laborers whose interests were in conflict with those of the superior tenants—who would get the land. Second, the rent fund presupposed and symbolically stood for landlordism as a social system; targeting of multi-dimensionally egregious behavior of landlords knit together stratified layers of the unprivileged. These efforts at collective action cannot be understood without the historical conjunctures that drove them—the great depression and colonial rule in particular—or the political theory and practice of the insurgent Congress leftists who turned communists.

The solution of the collective action problem for 'the peasantry' thus required both long-standing structural fact—the 'rent fund'—and the conjunctural evolution of a political party rooted organically in the villages with both appropriate theory and tactical space. Consider the contrast to the villagers of Malaysia as described by James Scott. An important reason for resort to 'weapons of the weak' was the absence of a political party that proposed land reform as a credible political project.[134] Tenants and landless workers in Sedaka desired land reform, but would have been foolish to believe that either political party would deliver even if they promised.[135]

Redistribution of land rights is a prominent strand of the argument that peasant mobilization depends on selective incentives in the rational-choice tradition.[136] But that perspective naively assumes that political entrepreneurs are free to choose maximizing strategies with no reference to their social base or (consequent) credibility. Here Popkin's view of political entrepreneurs is decidedly superior:[137] credible proposals that have some probability of solving the assurance problem derive from demonstrated political wisdom, derived from practice, and bolstered by resonance with cultural norms of integrity.

The ratchet tactics Kerala's agrarian Left came undone with was the final abolition of landlordism in the 1970s. Further redistribution of land was tactically impossible; the landless could be answered only at the cost of alienation of their former (and dominant) allies—tenants, now proprietors. That new proprietors proved not eager to share the rent fund via higher wages to the landless workers is not surprising, but did raise a fundamental challenge to continuation of the agrarian coalition that abolished landlordism. A concession to the numerically dominant class of laborers—the Agricultural Workers Act that granted permanency of employment and other anomalous benefits—created for a time a stalemated class. Whether or not new solutions to the collective action problem in the form of pie-expanding social democracy can be found will determine the future of the Left and the fate of the economy.[138]

If there is a lesson here for theories of collective action, it is that parsimony may not be an unalloyed good. The long experience of peasant mobilization in Kerala depended not only on central facets of agrarian structure but on broader social ecology and political structure as well. A solution to the collective action problem could not depend on selective incentives, but did require organic political theory derived from praxis. Choice presupposes structure; structure in turn depends for its effect on a double cognitive filter—what is right, what will work—which has an irreducibly contextual element. 'Moral outrage' was as important as material interest in motivating powerless people to face a repressive social order: the Mappila paradox remains.

Notes

1. William Logan, *A Malabar Manual*, Madras: Government Press, 1887 (reprint Trivandrum: Charithram, 1981), p. 667.
2. Ladejinsky's article was entitled: 'The Plow Outbids the Sword in Asia: How General MacArthur Stole Communist Thunder with Democratic Land Reforms, Our Most Potent Weapon for Peace', *Country Gentleman* (now *Farm Journal*), June 1951. A year later came a companion piece, 'Too Late to Save Asia?' For more on the

theme, see Al McCoy, 'Land Reform as Counter-Revolution: U.S. Foreign Policy and the Tenant', *Bulletin of Concerned Asian Scholars*, vol. 3, no. 1, winter/spring 1971, pp. 14–49.

3. Henry C. Hart and Ronald J. Herring, 'Political Conditions of Land Reform: Kerala and Maharashtra', in R.E. Frykenberg, ed., *Land Tenure and Peasant in South Asia*, Delhi: Orient Longman, 1977. On the failure of reforms after the partially successful abolition of 'intermediaries', see Ronald J. Herring, *Land to Tiller: The Political Economy of Agrarian Reform in South Asia*, New Haven: Yale University Press, 1983, chap. 5. A crucial distinction between '*zamindari* abolition' and the Kerala reforms is the elimination of the institution of tenancy in the latter.
4. Ronald J. Herring, 'Contesting the "Great Transformation": Local Struggles with the Market in South India', in James C. Scott and Nina Bhatt, eds., *Agrarian Studies: Synthetic Work at the Cutting Edge*, New Haven: Yale University Press, 2001; K.P. Kannan, *Of Rural Proletarian Struggles*, Delhi: Oxford University Press, 1988.
5. See Herring, *Land to the Tiller*, chaps. 3 and 6; Mridula Mukherjee, *Peasants in India's Non-Violent Revolution: Practice and Theory*, New Delhi: Sage, 2004, pp. 507, 510. On the empirical case for land reform, Michael Lipton, 'Land Reform as Commenced Business: The Evidence Against Stopping', *World Development*, vol. 21, no. 4, 1993, pp. 641-58. On West Bengal, Ross Mallick, *Development Policy of a Communist Government: West Bengal Since 1977*, Cambridge: Cambridge University Press, 1993; Sanjib Baruah, 'The End of the Road in Land Reform? Limits to Redistribution in West Bengal', *Development and Change*, vol. 21, 1990, pp. 119-46.
6. Samuel P. Huntington, *Political Order in Changing Societies*, New Haven: Yale University Press, 1968, p. 375.
7. Roy L. Prosterman and Jeffrey M. Riedinger, *Land Reform and Democratic Development*, Baltimore: Johns Hopkins University Press, 1987, chaps. 5 and 6; McCoy, 'Land Reform as Counter-Revolution.'
8. Herring, *Land to Tiller*, chap. 2.
9. 'Nationalism' was in effect anti-imperialism, or more specifically, moral outrage against specific connections between the colonial state and individual life-chances. Sub-nationalism—states' reorganization on linguistic grounds—was a source of communist success, potentiated by the niche provided by the peculiar organization of political space which was a residue of colonial rule. For careful analysis of historical reasons for success, see E.M.S. Namboodiripad, *A Short History of the Peasant Movement in Kerala*, Bombay:

People's Publishing House, 1943, *The National Question in Kerala*, Bombay: People's Publishing House, 1952, and *Reminiscences of an Indian Communist*, New Delhi: National Book Centre, 1987.

10. Contrary to Mark Lichbach, 'What Makes Rational Peasants Revolutionary? Dilemma, Paradox and Irony in Peasant Collective Action', *World Politics*, April 1994, pp. 383-418; Samuel L. Popkin, *The Rational Peasant*, Berkeley: University of California Press, 1979, chap. 6.
11. Herring, op. cit., 2003.
12. Eric R. Wolf, *Peasants*, Englewood Cliffs: Prentice Hall, 1966; Eric R. Wolf, *Peasant Wars of the Twentieth Century*, New York: Harper and Row, 1969.
13. Ronald J. Herring, 'Rational Actors, Structure and Culture', paper presented at the American Political Science Association meetings, Atlanta 1989.
14. Karl Polanyi, *The Great Transformation*, Boston: Beacon, 1957.
15. Herring, op. cit., 2001.
16. W. Booth, 'On the Idea of the Moral Economy', *American Political Science Review*, vol. 88, no. 3, 1994, pp. 653-67.
17. P. Radhakrishnan, *Peasant Struggles, Land Reforms and Social Change: Malabar 1836-1982*, London: Sage, 1989; for the general argument, see James C. Scott, *The Moral Economy of the Peasant*, New Haven: Yale University Press, 1976. On Malabar specifically, K. N. Panikkar, 'Peasant Revolts in Malabar in the Nineteenth and Twentieth Centuries', in A. R. Desai, ed., *Peasant Struggles in India*, Bombay: Oxford University Press, 1979; Prakash Karat, 'Agrarian Relations in Malabar, 1925-1948', *Social Scientist*, vol. 2, nos. 2-3, September-October 1973; Thomas Paulini, *Agrarian Movements and Reforms in India: The Case of Kerala*, Saarbrucken: Verlag Breitenbach, 1979.
18. Polanyi, *The Great Transformation*.
19. 'Feudalism' outside the European context is always contested. The Kerala system clearly contained core elements of political decay and decentralization implied by the usage of Marc Bloch, as well as the 'unfreedom' and 'personal dependence' stressed by Marx. Variations within European feudalism in any case prevent any strict derivation of necessary components to define the concept.
20. Logan, op. cit. argues that the derivation of *pattam*, which has come to mean 'rent', lies in the combination of *padu* (authority's) and *varam* (share). In any event, what is clearly true is that the *kanakkar*'s appropriation of *pattam* as rent was tantamount to expropriation of public revenue, only a part of which was

traditionally due the Nairs as payment for their supervisory and executive functions under feudal arrangements.

21. D.N. Dhanagare, 'Agrarian Conflict, Religion and Politics: the Moplah Rebellions in Malabar in the Nineteenth and Early Twentieth Centuries', *Past and Present*, vol. 74, February 1977, pp. 112-41.
22. Logan, op. cit., p. 670
23. B.H. Baden-Powell, *The Land Systems of British India*, Oxford: Clarendon Press, 1892, vol. III, p. 121.
24. 'Moplah' is also rendered *Mapilla*, *Mappilla*, *Mappila*, *Moplai* and other variants in transliteration. The term refers to descendants of Arab men and Malayali women and has generically meant Muslims of Malabar. It is derived from the Malayalam *ma* 'great' [from *maha*] and *pilla* 'child' connoting an honorific for son-in-law: i.e. descendants of Muslim traders.
25. A brief summary is available in Hart and Herring, 'Political Conditions of Land Reform, pp. 256-59. K.N. Panikkar's *Against Lord and State: Religion and Peasant Uprisings in Malabar, 1836-1921*, Delhi: Oxford University Press, 1989, is especially searching and authoritative. See also Radhakrishnan, *Peasant Struggles, Land Reforms and Social Change*, pp. 42-82; P. Radhakrishnan, 'Peasant Struggles and Land Reforms in Malabar', *Economic and Political Weekly*, vol. XV, no. 50, 1980; Robert Hardgrave, Jr., 'The Mappilla Rebellion, 1921: Peasant Revolt in Malabar', *Modern Asian* Studies, vol. 11, no. 1, 1977; K.N. Panikkar, 'Peasant Revolts in Malabar in the Nineteenth and Twentieth Centuries'; E.K.G. Nambiar, ed., *Agrarian India: Problems and Perspectives*, Kozhikode: University of Calicut, 1999, pp. 56-63; D.N. Dhanagare, 'Agrarian Conflict, Religion and Politics' and other sources in text.
26. *Jacquerie* connotes a spontaneous combustion of peasant anger, derived from the uprisings which began in Beauvais, north of Paris, in 1358. The name itself originally meant a collection of Jacques, which is, like Jacques Bonhomme, patois for a French peasant.
27. Panikkar, *Against Lord and State*, p. 190.
28. Literally, 'holders of a naked lease'. *Verumpattakar* were closer in the traditional system to tenants-at-will than were *kanakkar*, who had expectations about heritability and assured renewal (at twelve-year intervals) of leases. The British recognized *kanakkar* as tenants rather than as holders of usufructuary mortgages.
29. Dhanagare, 'Agrarian Conflict, Religion and Politics', p. 118.
30. Logan, op. cit., pp. 1, 672.

31. Karat, 'Agrarian Relations in Malabar, 1925-1948'; Dhanagare, op. cit., pp. 118-19.
32. Panikkar, *Against Lord and State*, p. 7.
33. Ibid., p. 11.
34. Ibid., pp. 12-16. It is important to note that a destruction of non-agricultural jobs creates the same effects as population increases, but engenders a greater sense of deprivation.
35. Calculations from Table 1.2 in Panikkar, op. cit., p. 16. The absolute level of land revenue collections was fairly constant despite fluctuations in yields.
36. Panikkar, op. cit., p. 17.
37. Quoted in Panikkar, op. cit. p. 17. By mid-nineteenth century, these taxes amounted to a fourth of the land revenue and 15 per cent of district revenue.
38. In Panikkar, op. cit., p. 16. It should not be assumed that the 'lower orders' which concerned Graeme were well off in the pre-colonial period; agrestic slavery offered little more than bare subsistence. The destruction of jobs and survival niches such as handicrafts certainly made poverty more open and observable, and probably more extensive.
39. Stephen Dale, *Islamic Society on the South Asian Frontier: The Mappilas of Malabar, 1498-1922*, Oxford: Clarendon Press, 1980; David Arnold, 'Islam, the Mappilas and Peasant Revolt in Malabar', *Journal of Peasant Studies*, vol. 9, no. 4, July 1982, pp. 255-65.
40. 'Frenzy' (*hal illakkam* in Malayalam) was the frequently used official prose.
41. Conrad Wood, 'Peasant Revolt: Interpretation of Moplah Violence in the Nineteenth and Twentieth Centuries', in Clive Dewey and A. G. Hopkins, eds., *The Imperial Impact: Studies in the Economic History of Africa and India*, London: Athlone Press, 1978, p. 133.
42. William Logan, op. cit., p. 692.
43. R.H. Hitchcock, *A History of the Malabar Rebellion, 1921*, Madras: Government Press, 1925, p. 10.
44. An excellent summary is available in Robert Hardgrave, Jr., 'The Mappilla Rebellion, 1921: Peasant Revolt in Malabar', *Modern Asian Studies*, vol. 11, no. 1, 1977. Contrast the treatments of Dale, *Islamic Society on the South Asian Frontier*, and Arnold, 'Islam, the Mappilas and Peasant Revolt in Malabar'.
45. For example, three participants in the 1852 outbreak were officially classified as 'day labourers', but their father was a *vermupattakkaran* who had been evicted 'from a plot he had held for many years'

(Wood, 'Peasant Revolt', p. 146). Wood (p. 133) summarizes the status of participants as 'wage-workers [field laborers, porters, timber-floaters], poor tenants, . . . *mullas* of barely-distinguishable economic standing, criminals on the point of having their careers cut short by authority, the chronically diseased, and men who were rather more comfortably-off but who, often, had experienced economic decline.' Official accounts add 'mendicants and others of the lowest class, living from hand to mouth'.

46. David Arnold, op. cit., 1982, pp. 262-3.
47. Cited in Wood, 'Peasant Revolt', p. 140. A 'parrah' (*para*) is a unit of volume (about 2000 cc.) of paddy weighing about 7.5 kg. The area of rice fields is frequently measured by the volume of seed necessary to plant it; the area referred to in the text is probably about one-half an acre, though actual sizes of *paras* and planting ratios varied locally.
48. James C. Scott, *Weapons of the Weak*, New Haven: Yale University Press, 1985.
49. Ronald J. Herring, 'Stealing Congress Thunder: The Rise to Power of a Communist Movement in South India', in Peter Merkl and Kay Lawson, eds., *When Parties Fail*, Princeton: Princeton University Press, 1988.
50. Hussain Randathani, 'Mappila Peasant Revolts: The Role of Religious Ideal' in Nambiar, ed., *Agrarian India,* pp. 46-55.
51. Wood, 'Peasant Revolt', p. 151.
52. On the 1921 rebellion, see S. M. Mohamed Koya, 'Peasant Masses in Revolt: The Tragic Episode in Malabar, 1921', in Nambiar, ed., *Agrarian India*, pp 56-63; Hardgrave op. cit.; Hitchcock, op. cit.; Panikkar op. cit., pp. 131-90.
53. Hitchcock op. cit., p. 20.
54. The term is Hobsbawm's. Conrad Wood uses the example of Athan Gurikal to illustrate. His 'gang' supported itself by levies on rich landlords; Gurikal 'set himself up as champion of the oppressed Moplahs, among whom he enjoyed great prestige' (Wood, 'Peasant Revolt', pp. 143-4). Social banditry is redistributive and hostile to property relations established by the state (and thus to the state), but is 'pre-political' in the sense that no positive political project is entailed.
55. For example, 'the outcome of early efforts to restore law and order in Ernad resulted in fanatical outbursts among the ignorant Mappillas' (Hitchcock, op. cit., p. 16). Government policy from the mid-nineteenth century had been to fine whole areas for disorder,

spreading discontent from activists to the general population, to disarm and deport activists and to impose stiff jail sentences.

56. Hitchcock, op. cit., p. 17.
57. Ibid., p. 15.
58. Conrad Wood, 'Peasant Revolt', p. 151.
59. Contemporary accounts of Palestinian martyrs exhibit exactly the same dynamics as those in the text. Suicide assures community support of the family of the martyr, who enjoys empirically unverifiable benefits after death.
60. This account does not deny Menon's emphasis on the expansion of opportunities in Malabar in the late nineteenth and early twentieth centuries until the Depression. The moral economy of winners is always more plastic than that of losers—a major conclusion of Jim Scott's 1985 study of the 'green revolution' in Malaysia (Dilip M. Menon, *Caste, Nationalism and Communism in South India: Malabar, 1900-1948*, Cambridge: Cambridge University Press, 1994).
61. Donald S. Zagoria, 'The Ecology of Peasant Communism in India', *The American Political Science Review*, vol. LXV, no. 1, March 1971.
62. Herring, op. cit., 1988.
63. E.M.S. Namboodiripad, *How I Became A Communist*, trans. P. K. Nair, Trivandrum: Chinta Publ., 1976, p. 183.
64. Robin Jeffrey argues that the success of communism in Kerala is driven by the dissolution of the Nair joint family. But it takes more than disaffected elites to accomplish mobilization; moreover, much of the discontent of Nairs had precisely to do with land relations, with or without dissolution of joint families (Robin Jeffrey, 1978, 'Matriliny, Marxism, and the Birth of the Communist Party in Kerala, 1930-1940', *Journal of Asian Studies*, vol. XXXVIII, no. I, November 1978, pp. 77-98).
65. Namboodiripad, *A Short History of the Peasant Movement in Kerala*, p. 4.
66. T.V. Krishnan, *Kerala's First Communist: Life of 'Sakhavu' Krishna Pillai*, New Delhi: Communist Party of India, 1971, p. 32.
67. A. K. Gopalan, *In the Cause of the People: Reminiscences*, Bombay: Orient Longman, 1973, chaps. 8, 9; Prakash Karat, 'Peasant Movement in Malabar, 1934-1940', *Social Scientist*, vol. 5, no. 2, September 1976.
68. Robin Jeffrey, 'Destroy Capitalism! Growing Solidarity of Alleppey's Coir Workers, 1930-1940', *EPW*, vol. XXIII, July 21, 1984, pp. 1159-65.

69. Radhakrishnan, op. cit., 1989, pp. 78, 79.
70. Ibid., pp. 79-81.
71. Ibid., p. 85.
72. Ibid., p. 86.
73. Ibid., pp. 87-8.
74. Jeffrey, op. cit., 1978.
75. Namboodiripad, op. cit., 1943, p. 12.
76. Paulini, op. cit., 1978, p. 160.
77. See K. Gopalan Kutty, 'Songs of Freedom, Unity and Strength: Peasant Mobilization in Malabar, 1934-47' in Nambiar, ed., *Agrarian India*, pp. 156-63; Paulini, op. cit., 1978, p. 168; Victor M. Fic, *Kerala, Yenan of India: Rise of Communist Power, 1937-1969*, Bombay: Nachiketa Publ., 1970, chap. 2; Gopalan, op. cit., 1973, chap. 8; Radhakrishnan, op. cit., 1989, pp. 75-94; Karat, op. cit., 1976.
78. Gopalan, op. cit., 1973; compare the position of 'Master' in the incident of the Kayoor martyrs Tejaswini Niranjana trans., *The Stars Shine Brightly: Saga of the Kayoor Martyrs*, New Delhi: People's Publishing House, 1977).
79. E.M.S. Namboodiripad, *Kerala: Past, Present and Future*, Calcutta: National Book Agency, 1968, p. 156.
80. Radhakrishnan , op. cit., 1989, p. 77.
81. Hart and Herring, 'Political Conditions of Land Reform', p. 200.
82. Kannan, op. cit., 1988.
83. Karat, op. cit., 1976; Kannan, op. cit., 1988, pp. 82-7; Radhakrishnan, op. cit., 1989, p. 89.
84. On hunger marches, see the work of one of the major organizers, A.K. Gopalan (op. cit., 1973). Also, Kutty, 'Songs of Freedom'; Radhakrishnan, op. cit., 1989, pp. 94-5.
85. The first two were written by K. Damodaran, the latter by Edasseri.
86. T.K. Oommen, *From Mobilization to Institutionalization: The Dynamics of Agrarian Movement in Twentieth Century Kerala*, Bombay: Popular Prakashan, 1985, p. 46.
87. Namboodiripad, op. cit., 1943; Kannan, op. cit., 1988, pp. 117, 121; Oommen, op. cit., 1985, pp. 50-3.
88. Oommen, op. cit., 1985, p. 48.
89. Logan, op. cit., 1887, p. 648.
90. E. K. Nayanar, *My Struggles: An Autobiography*, New Delhi: Vikas, 1982, p. 8.
91. Niranjana, op. cit., 1977.
92. M.A. Rasul, *A History of the All India Kisan Sabha*, Calcutta: National Book Agency, 1974, p. 97. The incident involved the

death of a policeman who was believed to have molested a peasant woman. Though identification of culprits was virtually impossible, as admitted by the trial judge, four young *karshaka sangham* activists were accused and executed. As in the Mappila uprisings, authorities of the Cannanore jail refused to release the bodies as demanded by 3,000 peasants assembled. Corpses were 'disposed of' on jail grounds. In terms of contemporary wage rates for agricultural laborers, the British trade unionist contribution would exceed Rs. one lakh (1,00,000).

93. Gopalan, op. cit., 1973; Radhakrishnan, op. cit., 1989, p. 94.
94. Radhakrishnan, op. cit., 1989, p. 96.
95. Ibid.
96. Ibid., p. 99.
97. Namboodiripad, *The National Question in Kerala*, pp. 19-20.
98. Namboodiripad, op. cit., 1943, pp. 19-20.
99. Wolf, *Peasants*.
100. See Ronald J. Herring, 'Dilemmas of Agrarian Communism', *Third World Quarterly*, vol. 11, no. 1, January 1989, pp. 89-115, for field evidence of the bitterness of landless laborers when the promised distribution of the rent fund was prevented by the superior power of former tenants (now landowners) in the party.
101. See the discussion in Radhakrishnan, op. cit., 1989, pp. 102-5; Nayanar, op. cit., 1982, pp. 77-84.
102. Nayanar, op. cit., 1982, p. 80.
103. Ibid., p. 81.
104. Ibid., p. 81. The competing organizations retained their symbolic attachment to Congress symbolism by employing the Hindi word *kisan* rather than the Malayalam *karshaka* used by the communists.
105. Ibid., p. 82.
106. On the history of the Malabar Tenancy Act, see T.C. Varghese, *Agrarian Change and Economic Consequences: Land Tenure in Kerala, 1850-1960*, Bombay: Allied, 1970; M.A. Oommen, 1975, *A Study of Land Reforms in Kerala*, New Delhi: Oxford and IBH, 1975; Radhakrishnan, op. cit., 1989, pp. 75-105.
107. Paulini, op. cit., 1978, p. 195; Kannan, op. cit., 1988, pp. 81-7; Menon, op. cit., 1994, pp. 25-6.
108. K.N. Raj and Michael Tharakan, 'Agrarian Reform in Kerala and its Impact on the Rural Economy—A Preliminary Assessment', in Ajit K. Ghose ed., *Agrarian Reform in Contemporary Developing Countries*, London: Croom Helm, 1983, pp. 31–90.
109. T.K. Oommen, op. cit., 1985, p. 54.

110. This perception is not altogether accurate, at least by the 1950s; see Herring, op. cit., 1983, chap. 6.
111. T.K. Oommen, op. cit., 1985, pp. 55.
112. Kannan, op. cit., 1988, pp. 38-88.
113. T.K. Oommen, op. cit., 1985, 58.
114. Marshall Bouton, *Agrarian Radicalism in South India*, Princeton: Princeton University Press, 1985.
115. Herring, op. cit., l983, Ch. 7.
116. D.N. Dhanagare, 1975, *Agrarian Movements and Gandhian Politics*, Agra: Institute of Social Sciences, Agra University, 1975; on landlords, M.K. Gandhi, *Socialism of My Conception*, ed. Anand T. Hingorani, Bombay: Bharatiya Vidya Bhavan, 1966, pp. 233-40, 248-50; on 'trusteeship', see M. K. Gandhi, *My Theory of Trusteeship*, ed. Anand T. Hingorani, Bombay: Bharatiya Vidya Bhavan, 1970. Bhabani Sen Gupta, *Communism in Indian Politics*, New York: Columbia University Press, 1972, p. 289, notes the importance of Gandhi's retreats from peasant militancy, and documents the weakness of the movement nationally (Chap. 8). On the political culture of strategic agrarian violence, see Walter Hauser, 1993, 'Violence, Agrarian Radicalism and Electoral Politics: Reflections on the Indian People's Front', *Journal of Peasant Studies,* vol. 21, no. 1, October 1993, pp. 85-126.
117. This account depends on works of early communist activists and party leaders: Gopalan, op. cit., 1973, chaps. 8, 9; Krishnan, op. cit., 1971, pp. 44; Namboodiripad, op. cit., 1968, p. 97; Nayanar, op. cit., 1982, as well as the author's interviews in Kerala. On social disabilities and indignities of 'lower' orders, K. Saradamoni, *Emergence of a Slave Caste: Pulayas of Kerala*, New Delhi: People's Publishing House, 1980.
118. Radhakrishnan, op. cit., 1980; V. C. Koshy, 'The Politics of Land Reforms in Kerala', PhD Thesis, New Delhi 1976, pp. 110-16.
119. Menon, op. cit., 1994, pp. 2, 18-19; Saradamoni, op. cit., 1980; K. C. George, *Immortal Punnapra-Vayalar*, New Delhi: Communist Party of India, 1975, p. 16; G. Rajendran, *The Ezhava Community and Kerala Politics*, Trivandrum: Kerala Academy of Political Science, 1974, p. 829; P. Thomas, *The Death of a Harijan*, Trichur: Horizon Publ., 1984. Accounts by activists in the labor movement in Padoor provide more concrete local examples see Herring, op. cit., 2001.
120. Nayanar, op. cit., 1982, p. 7.
121. Ibid., p. 8.

122. Menon , op. cit., 1994.
123. Herring, op. cit., 1983, pp. 4-8, 125-52.
124. Ibid., chap. 6.
125. Ibid., chap. 2.
126. T.K. Oommen, op. cit., 1985, pp. 56-7.
127. For a correction to the common misperception that Travancore and Cochin had healthy agrarian structures, see the data in Herring 1983, op. cit., p. 160.
128. Baden-Powell, *Land Systems of British India.*
129. George, op. cit., 1975.
130. T.V. Sathyamurthy, *India Since Independence: Studies in the Development of the Power of the State*, Volume I, *Centre-State Relations: The Case of Kerala*, Delhi: Ajanta, 1985.
131. Herring, op. cit., 1983, chap. 7.
132. Dilip Menon's (op. cit., 1994) treatment of Malabar takes as its central problematic the conjunctural nature of 'community' formation from divergent individual interests.
133. Jon Elster, *Making Sense of Marx*, Cambridge: Cambridge University Press, 1985.
134. Scott, op. cit., 1985, p. 81.
135. This is not the only difference of course; in Sedaka, an economy that is rich and growing softens the edge of capitalism in a setting of difficult but not disastrous land-person ratios. Largesse from patronage channels reaches the poor via the dominant (UMNO) party (Scott, op. cit., 1985, pp. 52-4). Moreover, ethnic politics mitigates market deprivation perceived in class terms.
136. Mark Lichbach, 'What Makes Rational Peasants Revolutionary? Dilemma, Paradox and Irony in Peasant Collective Action', *World Politics*, April 1994, pp. 383-418.
137. Popkin, op. cit., 1979, chap. 6.
138. Patrick Heller, 'From Class Struggle to Class Compromise: Redistribution and Growth in a South Indian State', *Journal of Development Studies*, vol. 31, no. 5, June 1995, pp. 645-72.

Cultures of Resistance or Commerce? Re-examining Timber Use in the Himalayan Punjab, 1850–1925*

Ruhi Grover

> Do you mean to tell me that if I grow *deodars* on land for which I pay land revenue, I cannot dispose these trees as I please? As a zamindar [peasant] I am entitled to as many trees as I need at zamindari rate, you don't encourage me or any body else to grow trees for sale. . . .[1]

> The villagers do not divulge each other's secrets. They steal timber from the riverbank at night and send it to their relatives and friends living at a distance from the river. And when stolen timber is found in the possession of any one of them they can easily obtain false receipts from petty retailers of timber that they produce in courts in their defence.[2]

These statements accent the plurality of local response to the commodification of timber in mid-nineteenth century colonial north India. Most reports on forest administration detail the forest rights enjoyed by the local communities and give the impression of a seeming largesse. However, the large number of petitions and forest offences recorded in the very same reports make such an assessment seem incongruous. This seeming incongruity forms the subject of this inquiry. This essay examines the local response—from the petitioning by local landholders to colonial officials for sale of timber in the market, to timber

* This essay was previously published in the *New Zealand Journal of Asian Studies* 1, 2 (1999), and is reproduced here with permission.

thefts from rivers—to suggest that local communities contested state spaces not only for their livelihood but also for the benefits that accrued from the commodification of timber. The objectives are to delineate the varied nature of local response beyond issues of subsistence, and to relate them (at least in part) to the political economy of commerce.

Mid-nineteenth century colonial India witnessed a tremendous rise of demand for timber. Railway lines and cantonment towns were only two manifestations of an imperial state with needs of an ever-growing administrative infrastructure. This was to be soon followed by forest policies which delineated distinct spaces for forest management in general and for timber regeneration in particular. The colonial state imbued forests with new notions of space and authority—expressed through laws and territorial boundaries—and separated the rights to use forest resources from the rights to market them. The manner in which the commodification of timber developed increased the vulnerability of many local communities that were dependent on forests. However, it did not impoverish equally, and certainly not everyone. Just as it undermined the economic means of livelihood for some communities, it also provided opportunities for other groups who contested the newly defined forest space for economic benefits. In other words, the response of local communities was not just one of negation or the inversion of state policies; their interests were also ones of inclusion. Thus the commodification of timber should not be treated as alien to an inhabited world however regional or local its existence and reach.[3]

The categories through which we choose to understand the plurality of social response have to be carefully constructed. Resistance, as a trope, has been useful to understand social opposition to state policies. Many issues have been raised and several questions posed even as the trope of resistance has come under scrutiny. Is resistance passive and devoid of any agency (Gramsci)? Does resistance entail the agency and 'consciousness' of the community or group involved (Subalternists)? Does resistance of the subordinate privilege the dominant group? Does resistance have to be understood within one mode of production (Marx) or resource use (Gadgil and Guha)?[4] Does resistance appear as an overtly articulate moment of contradiction

(Subalternists) or is it also a strategic choice of the subalterns to act invisibly and silently (James Scott)? The relationship between coercion (domination) and consent (hegemony) in colonial South Asia has been discussed at great length by many, including the scholars of the Subaltern Studies project from the early 1980s.[5] These works have, quite succinctly and tellingly, shown how dominance under colonial conditions was exercised without hegemony.[6] They have argued for an autonomous domain of peasant politics exemplified by peasant insurgency in which there was a common notion of resistance to elite domination.[7] Although they have on the whole succeeded in highlighting the essential nature of domination and subordination permeating power relationships, they provide a binary opposition between the categories of the elite and the subaltern even as the categories themselves remain unpacked. Furthermore, resistance also gets defined in moments of great historical visibility, i.e. rebellion, with periods of quiet resistance and ordinary opposition completely overlooked. This is a lacuna which has been addressed by scholars such as James Scott who reject the assumption that subordinate groups acquiesce in economic systems that are manifestly against their interests because they come to believe in a dominant ideology that legitimates or naturalises the power of ruling elite.[8] Scott asserts that there is more resistance to dominant ideologies than is acknowledged, since resistance is expressed at hidden social sites where transcripts are created and acted out. The appearance of consent is produced in the public realm, given the practical and material pressure on subordinates to refrain from speaking the truth. Undoubtedly a useful distinction, this not only flattens out the range of power relations between the dominant and the subordinate but also inflates the distinction between the public and the private transcripts. Furthermore, it overlooks the fact that different forms of domination produce different configurations of response, including configurations of language use in politics.[9]

In the context of forest history, Ramachandra Guha's work on peasant protests in the Kumaon and Garhwal hills has indeed been pioneering.[10] He has examined the links between structures of domination and the idioms of social protest, and has shown how peasant communities drew legitimacy from custom while protesting against the raja, adopting a different strategy while protesting against the colonial state. However, in presenting societies as generally egalitarian and bound by strong communal ties, resistance to the state is read in the context of the contrast between pre-colonial subsistence and colonial commercial economy. This, in turn, presupposes an idyllic pre-colonial society untouched by commercial transactions and not only imposes the mantra of resistance to capitalism but also, in fact, reifies it. Similarly, Sumit Sarkar has treated conflicts over forest claims within the context of the development of a bourgeois concept of property that posed a threat to the customary rights of forest lands.[11] This approach not only obfuscates the dynamics which arose in the course of interaction between the state and the local communities, but also overlooks the manner in which opposition to state policies was constituted by the very nature of those policies. For instance, the manner in which some local communities resorted to marketing stolen timber was a direct result of policies that created a demand for timber in the first place. And while the state is distinguished in its colonial and local context, the local community is not—a drawback that has been taken care of in much of the recent literature on forest history.[12]

Nancy Peluso's work on Indonesia highlights the inadequacy of employing a single opposition between the dominant and the subordinate to explain the plurality of responses in a society which in itself was complex and diverse in its making.[13] She suggests that different forms of forest resistance parallel different forms of forest access control:

> Forest peasants resist forest land control by reappropriating forest lands for cultivation; they resist species control by 'counter-appropriating' species claimed by the state (or other enterprise) and by damaging mature species or sabotaging newly planted species; they resist labor control by strikes, slowdowns or migration; and they resist ideological control by developing or maintaining cultures of resistance (ideology, local social structure, and history).[14]

Following Peluso I propose here an inquiry into alternate perceptions of forests and use of timber. This is not to discard the trope of resistance or to repackage it into something entirely different and new. Rather, it is to suggest that while the local contest of state notions of timber use and timber control may constitute resistance, it does not tell us anything about alternate ways of using that timber. As Sherry Ortner points out, one can only appreciate the ways in which resistance can be more than opposition if one appreciates the multiplicity of projects in which social beings are always engaged, and the various ways in which these projects feed on and collide with one another.[15] This essay provides another way of looking through the lens of timber that does not romanticise local communities or treat them as being always at the receiving end. Without sanitizing the issue of contestation or domination, I highlight the resilience of indigenous life, and its varied responses, albeit influenced by state laws. I also suggest that the local communities and the colonial state did not represent two different and conflicting domains of forest use, but shared the same contested domain.[16] The culture of commerce or the culture of countermarket—as Braudel terms it—was not entirely independent of the state economy.[17] I have labelled the economy of the local as a 'shadow economy', an economy that emerges in light of the timber demand generated by a colonial state.[18]

The area of study is broadly the trans-Dhauladhar region of the Ravi, Beas and Sutlej divisions, which form part of present-day Himachal Pradesh. While this essay is based on the hill states of Chamba and Bashahr in which commercial timbering gained considerable significance, and the Kangra district (which includes the Kulu division) that the British acquired directly from the Sikhs in 1849, examples are also taken from other districts in the Punjab region.[19] The species of timber identified by the British for commercial purposes were deodar (*Cedrus deodara*) which, along with blue pine (*Pinus excelsa*), silver fir (*Abies pindrow*) and spruce (*Picea smithiana*) grew between the altitude of 5,000 and 8,000 ft in the Chamba, Bashahr and Kulu regions. Chil (*Pinus longifolia*) occupied the lower portions of Bashahr and Kangra region between 2,500 and 5,000 ft. The bamboo (*Dendrocalamus strictus*) forests were the most important in the Kangra region below 3000 ft.[20] The topography of the region necessitated a mixed economy which linked forestry, agriculture and husbandry practice.

PEOPLES AND FORESTS

Village society in the Himalayan Punjab was rather small, usually located close to terraced cultivated fields and, notwithstanding the physiographic diversity of the region, largely egalitarian in nature.[21] In general, pre-colonial society had its own circuit of commercial exchange; *hats* (local markets) exemplified a vibrant local economy. Trading contacts between the hills and the plains had existed since ancient times, and had even influenced state formation in various micro-regions.[22] Forest products such as gum lac, turpentine, and Indian incense (*jalap*) formed an integral circuit of commodity exchange.[23] Boat-building industries flourished at various places in Punjab and Wazirabad was an important boat-building centre.[24] While the main occupation remained agriculture and grazing, forests and pastures formed an integral component of the village economy and boundaries between villages evolved to demarcate their access to resources.[25] In general, village society in Himalayan Punjab was not isolated, topographically marked, or bounded by maps, but fluid with adaptable social complexes that harvested trees, collected forest products, grazed livestock, and lopped trees.[26] It used timber for domestic and agricultural purposes (cut branches, collected leaves and fallen wood for fodder and fuel, and harvested honey), grazed its livestock in 'wasteland' for manure, meat and wool, and used local herbs and flowers for fodder and general use.[27] Local artisans made ropes from *bagar* grass, brushwood, and the bark of small elm trees. They earned revenue by selling fruits (walnut, apricot and peach), medicinal roots (*karu, patis*), and incense (*bethar, gugal, dhup*) in the market.[28] They also sold honey and *ghee*. It is clear that non-agricultural alternatives for monetary benefit existed during the pre-colonial period. Thus, it was not the presence or the absence of money, of markets, or of cash transactions that differentiated a pre-colonial from a colonial forest economy, but the manner in which these different economies came to operate.

Forests, in general, were the private reserves of local rajas in the pre-colonial days, but had not been widely tapped as a revenue-based resource. Rather they were retreats for royalty and tracts for hunting. They not only provided natural political boundaries for local states but were also cleared during periods of war.[29] Access to forest products was, even before the advent of the British, somewhat restricted. Local rajas controlled distributive rights to land and forests from which they derived most of their revenue. The hereditary right to cultivation (*warisi*) was conferred by a raja in the form of a deed or a grant (*patta*), which was never granted for a whole village or even a hamlet, but to individuals. Zamindars did not have free access to forests; for instance green trees could not be felled without permission. In certain forest regions in most principalities, the raja imposed a prohibition on grazing for three months during the monsoon (*thak*).[30] Owing to relatively undeveloped communication, limited demand and modest state requirements, the use of timber had not attained the proportions it did under the British. The relative contrast between timber production for sale and for local use was precisely that—a relative and not an absolute contrast.

Forests and Rights

Once the British annexed Punjab in 1849, forests came to be tapped on a much larger scale for their commercial use. What grew on land became significantly relevant to its legal identity.[31] Forests were defined as distinctly separate from cultivated land;[32] they were meant for timber regeneration and not for grazing or shifting agriculture.[33] Forests were divided into reserved, protected, and civil categories, each with different access rights to produces for commercial and domestic use. The state drew upon a complex ideology of conservation, commercial extraction of timber, and an economy of use to justify the curtailment of local user-rights.[34] It constructed physical barriers and imposed high fines on forest offenders to regulate forest management. However, the colonial state was by no means the only claimant to forest resources. Given the multifaceted resource base, local rajas, landlords, zamindars and grazers also used forests extensively. Said an official in 1872:

> . . . this question of rights in the forest is one not easy of adjustment, especially when it assumes a political bearing from the fact that the greater portion of the people belong to those classes who inhabit the forests, and as it were, live in them. . . . It will be both possible and

advisable, by gradually and judiciously asserting the claims of government, and avoiding any sudden enquiry into the question of prescriptive rights, to accustom the minds of the people to our presence in the forests, and to dispel their pre-conceived ideas of quiet and undisturbed rights to the brushwood and jungle.[35]

By 1874, two years after this report, the Forest Department took steps to clearly regulate local access to forest resources.[36] The colonial state recorded local user-rights based on *wajib-ul-arz* (local deeds) and attempted to codify what appeared to it as a rather diverse congeries of localized customs. Local communities were entitled to forest use, but the nature of these rights depended on the recently established British land-tenure systems that were partly based on pre-colonial patterns of use.[37] These rights were not only codified, but also fixed and enforced by law. The Kulu and Kangra forest settlements, completed in 1894 and 1897 respectively, capped the process of demarcating and delineating local access to forests.[38] In general, rightholders received 23 per cent of the total outturn of timber, 74 per cent of firewood, and 77 per cent of minor produce.[39] Given that the average size of a land-holding was three acres in the Kangra district, with smaller holdings in the Chamba and Bashahr region, the importance of forest produce per household per annum in the Kangra district, tabulated in a report in the early 1930s,

TABLE 1

Cost per Family of Forest Products (by category of use): Haripur and Mangarh Taluqas, Kangra District, early 1930s

Item	State Forests			Privately owned Forests or Trees		
	Rs.	A.	P.	Rs.	A.	P.
Buildings	10	0	0	—	—	—
Roofing	—	—	—	5	0	0
Fuel	51	0	0	—	—	—
Fences & Hedges	25	0	0	—	—	—
Baskets	—	—	—	1	4	0
Agricultural Implements	2	0	0	—	—	—
Fodder Leaves	45	8	0	45	8	0

Source: see endnote 40.

shows the extent to which the local economy was dependent on forests.[40] It is clear from the Table 1 that the greatest reliance of local communities on forests was for fuel and fodder leaves in both state administered and private forests.[41]

Empirically, the rights enjoyed by the local communities were considerable. However, it was not always a matter of the number of rights conferred by the British; the place, the timing and the manner in which they were accorded were of considerable significance as well. For instance, the zamindars in Kulu were given rights to fell timber, but they had to walk several miles to collect it. They also witnessed an official transformation of their area into 'forest', with the exception of their homesteads and cultivated area.[42] They were allowed to cultivate their land, but given the proximity of forests to populated agricultural areas, the moment they stepped outside their homesteads, they were in a 'forest' where even carrying an axe was considered to be a crime.

The Forest Department secured a monopoly over the commercial value of forests by making itself the chief beneficiary of the timber trade, and by prohibiting forest harvesting for sale or monetary profit. For instance, the Department listed 62 species of trees that it considered suitable for use in building, to be given for local consumption only on payment.[43] The zamindars could not sell *deodar*—which was marked by the Forest Department as a commercial species—on their private zamindari forest land without official permission. If they did, they forfeited the privilege of obtaining timber for subsistence needs at favourable rates.

The issue of grazing occupied considerable ground in the debates over forestry. Since the overwhelming view in the Forest Department was that grazing undermined forestry, the grazing community of the Gaddis, who had been frequenting the Kangra region from the alpine regions prior to the advent of the British, experienced a regulation of their pastoral movements.[44] They had to pay a higher grazing tax, and since they were treated as tenants of the state they were subjected to detailed inventories of their pasture area and their grazing runs. For example, the Gaddis could not halt in one place for more than one night without permission of the Assistant Commissioner, and they had to travel at least five miles a day irrespective of altitude, climate, and sick or injured animals. Their access to grazing lands in demarcated forests near villages during their halts was another cause for concern.[45] The biggest problem for the grazers was the enormous change taking place around them. Their relationship to their environment was even more complicated because they were simultaneously dependent on arable land, forest, and pasture as they moved from one region to another according to the rhythms of the seasons. But by the beginning of the twentieth century, as grasslands gave way to pastures, and pastures to feedlots, their network of social and economic relations was greatly undermined.

The zamindars in other regions of Chamba and Bashahr divisions were also subjected to similar restrictions in the exercise of their rights. A code of forest laws was always appended to a lease that included, among other things, restrictions for zamindars to cut down forests for purposes of cultivation. They were not allowed even to carry any implements for cutting wood without authorization or license.[46] In sum, local rights, in the absence of a formal legal precedence, were conferred by the colonial state. Forest law, as it developed, was a colonial invention that eventually effaced local custom.

Peoples and Markets

Railways largely determined the agenda of the Forest Department in the Punjab from their inception in 1865. Starting with forest revenue of approximately half a million rupees in the 1880s, the Forest Department's earnings increased to approximately five million rupees by the early 1920s.[47] In the all-India context, the revenue generated by the Forest Department increased from 5.6 million rupees in 1874 to approximately 56.7 million rupees by 1924.[48] When the issue of 'who benefited and who lost in the commodification of timber' is translated in the local context, the beneficiaries emerge in a different light. Chetan Singh explains this process quite lucidly.[49] He asserts that the greatest involvement with the market was found either amongst people from the most accessible and well-cultivated parts of the region or the agriculturally poorer areas of the trans-Himalaya. Territories with a mixed pastoral-agricultural economy were inclined to restrict their engagement with the market. In keeping with this argument, it becomes clear that local communities in the Kangra region—one of the most accessible and well-cultivated parts of the region—experienced a greater change than in the Chamba and Bashahr regions.

A section of zamindars in Kangra was able to side-step colonial laws by diversifying its economic interests. For instance, once a market developed for livestock products by the third quarter of the nineteenth century, cattle farming became popular there.[50] Between the years 1890 and 1894, livestock had increased by 12 per cent. The villagers were largely paying their revenue from the proceeds of surplus stock, and making money by supplying the local wool industry and the Shimla meat market.[51] In his 1897 Settlement, Anderson noted that grazing dues on the Gaddis could not be further enhanced, since zamindars were keeping more goats in villages near scrub for the meat markets in Dharamsala, Pathankot, and the cantonments of Bakloh and Dalhousie. The Amritsar butchers also drew a considerable amount of their meat supply from Kangra proper. Many of the zamindars in the Kangra region also began to keep buffaloes in order to produce *ghee* for sale in the nearby towns.[52]

At the same time, a substantial section of the zamindari community also benefited from the increase of irrigation and the contraction of grazing lands. The 'rush' of prosperity and unaccustomed wealth to a people, whose outlets for the display of wealth were jewellery and cattle, resulted in an increase by 50 per cent in the total number of animals in the Kangra district alone.[53] The first Financial Commissioner, J.M. Douie, tabulated the livestock figures for various *tahsils* in the Kangra district at the time of O'Brien's settlement, presented in the Table 2. The numbers represent the total animals owned by residents wherever

TABLE 2
Livestock Figures for Kangra District, 1910[54]

Year	*Bulls and Cows*	*Buffaloes*	*Young Stock*	*Sheep*	*Goats*
1894	342,697	88,678	137,444	110,181	262,404
1904	439,544	110,250	163,671	146,462	473,642
1909	440,360	117,919	174,564	172,564	445,560

they happened to be at the time of the enumeration, and also include the small number of animals belonging to non-right-holders, but not animals owned by the *Gaddis*.[55]

Clearly, by the early twentieth-century livestock wealth had increased significantly, and grazing had entered a new phase of revenue generation. Due to the forest laws, the tenurial system of zamindari did not encourage the growth or the protection of trees. But then, just as maintaining large livestock holdings became commonplace, one can argue that a similarly enterprising system of harvesting trees on private forest plantations for the market could have also evolved under favourable colonial laws.[56]

As far as airing grievances against the Forest Department is concerned, zamindars resorted to both formal and informal devices. Formally, they invoked the responsibility of the government through petitions. For instance, in a rather detailed appeal made to the Lieutenant-Governor of Punjab, Charles Montgomery Rivaz, the zamindars of Kangra expressed their dissatisfaction with Anderson's Settlement Report of 1897. They listed twenty grievances and made appeals to stop the public sale of dry trees from all demarcated and undemarcated forests, to increase the number of *chil* trees to be cut for local building purposes, and to extend the number of nights the Gaddis could stay for their livestock to manure the fields.[57] Several rightholders also objected to the fact that although they were entitled to timber at concessional rates, there were repeated delays in giving timber, and often the timber was to be collected from distant localities. For instance, in Rupi and Seraj, all trees marked for grants were only distributed after three to six months which made everyday living, especially in the winter, difficult.[58] The Lieutenant-Governor forwarded these and several other complaints to the Deputy Commissioner of Kangra who responded in a rather dismissive manner.[59] He concluded his reply by stating that had these complaints been addressed directly to him, he would have taken steps to redress any legitimate grievances consistent with scientific forest management. Given the fact that they were addressed to a visiting official showed that the 'petitions were largely the work of a few "irreconcilable malcontents" who wished to give everybody as much trouble as possible'.[60]

TABLE 3
Violations of Forest Regulations, 1880–1

Province	*Prosecuted*	*Convicted*
Bengal	143	112
C. Provinces	1,008	824
Coorg	7	3
Ajmere	285	122
Assam	121	105
Punjab	2,188	1,131

The fact that these were not just a few displeased individuals is evident from the colonial documents that abound with instances of non-compliance of rules with forest offences classified as 'minor' and 'major'. Many zamindars, especially in the Punjab, were involved in the breach of forest rules.

The nature of 'offences' in forests varied: Injury to state-controlled reserve forests by fire,[61] unauthorized felling, and appropriation of wood or minor produce (numbered the highest). The increase in the number of forest offences related directly to state policies such as increase in the area of cultivated land that resulted in a simultaneous decrease of forest area.[62] For instance, forest offences in illegal felling increased by 9 per cent in the years 1906–7 due to an extension of cultivation.[63] Grazing without permission, another offence listed in forest records, varied according to the monsoon.[64] Attacks on state symbols such as forest guards, guard huts and boundary lines were not infrequent just as the sense of being wronged was expressed in popular songs and verses.[65] What was once seen as custom or could have been regarded as the entrepreneurial spirit of the local populace now began to be treated as a crime by the state. Neither the formality of the law nor the threat of its enforcement seemed entirely effective.[66] Most of these 'offences' seemed to be the assertion of either pre-existing rights or for the benefits from an emerging economy. Although the rate of convictions was high, the number of breaches increased significantly as evident in Table 4.[67]

A large number of timber thefts also occurred *en route* to the plains. Timber trade, in general, was segmented and specialized in nature. Forest areas were auctioned and timber was felled

TABLE 4
Forest Crimes in Chamba, Bashahr, and Kangra Districts, 1873–1915

Year	Chamba				Bashahr				Kangra			
	Prose-cution		Convic-tion		Prose-cution		Convic-tion		Prose-cution		Convic-tion	
	C	P	C	P	C	P	C	P	C	P	C	P
1873–4	17	19	16	17	4	—	4	—	—	—	—	—
1879–80	44	78	32	56	—	—	—	—	121	284	116	274
1884–5	25	—	21	36	101	27	63	—	—	—	—	—
1888–9	41	—	21	—	330	—	121	171	68	—	60	126
1898–9	91	—	53	106	242	—	192	385	936	—	859	1586
1914–15	—	—	—	—	478	—	375	871	2623	—	2412	3344

C—Cases P—Persons

into logs or sawn into railway sleepers; marked and registered as the private property of an individual or of a firm, the felled timber was then transported to river-heads with the aid of slides and labour; it was floated to the nearest collecting outlets at the foothills where it was collected, hoarded, dried and stacked in timber and sale depots; it was inspected for its quality and dimensions and auctioned for its final journey to its myriad destinations such as railway depots, barrack towns, sports factories and furniture shops. Large-scale theft of timber from forests was difficult for several reasons. First, the demand for timber in the higher reaches of Chamba and Bashahr was lower than in the neighboring lower regions of Kangra, Jhelum, and Chenab that had pressures of a relatively dense population. For instance, the average density per square mile of cultivated land in Kangra was 984, which was quite high when compared to an average of 460 for the rural population of Punjab.[68] Second, transporting timber from forests to a site of habitation was harder for villagers than transporting it from rivers to nearby villages, given the relatively less hospitable land terrain. And last, state supervision of rivers was rather difficult compared to the forests.

The Forest Department report of 1902–3 showed a loss of 32 per cent of government scantlings on the Chenab River and 18 per cent on the Sutlej for the same years. Even private companies suffered losses. During the four years ending 1909, the private British trading firm of Spedding and Company alone lost more than Rs. 100,000 worth of scantlings to theft.[69] A letter by the Inspector-General of Police, Punjab is indicative of the scale of theft: '. . . Practically the whole of the villages along the rivers obtain their wood from the rivers, and, were a special body of Police appointed, the fact of their deputation would at once become known, and the people would suspend their thieving operations until they went away again.'[70]

While a few individuals were involved in these acts, many more people were involved, in their protection of the actual takers when entire logs were targeted. It is clear that timber brought into villages in log form would have been bulky enough to attract the attention of many people. This expression of village solidarity created what Peluso terms a culture of conspiracy.[71] Without acknowledging crime as defined by the colonial state, peasant resistance attracted allies and sympathizers from within its own quarters.[72]

If one follows the course of the stolen timber, two things become apparent. First, timber was not stolen only for local subsistence needs. Second, its final destination was different from the public timber markets in north India where state timber was auctioned. Thirty per cent of timber thefts were for local markets, especially along the Chenab and Jhelum rivers.[73] Rather than interpreting these acts of theft as crimes, one can also treat them as a sector that thrived in the shadow of the timber economy of the state. The villagers had devised ingenious ways to use timber. Some would stamp timber with forged 'sold' marks and then sell it in the open market. Local communities always needed some timber for agricultural implements, firewood and charcoal.[74] Some villagers sawed the wood and sold it at the nearest market at a much cheaper rate, or concealed it in the ground for a few months before it was considered safe to dispose of it. Sometimes the villagers put two or three roofs on their houses in an attempt to conceal as much wood as possible. After a year or two, when the timber was sufficiently weathered to avoid detection, the villagers sold entire houses, roofs, and posts to outsiders for considerable sums.[75] They also carried timber to small market towns and sold it to petty shopkeepers who could easily remove the ownership marks and saw them up with other timber. The more enterprising ones, whom the British referred to as 'the bolder spirits', bought a little wood from Wazirabad or Sialkot, brought it to their villagers, and opened small shops which acted as a cover for the owner to sell stolen produce. The timber the owner had purchased legally was produced whenever any official came to question him.[76] What becomes clear is that these markets were neither traditional nor transitional and contained a considerable degree of heterogeneity and complexity.

In fact, forest officials admitted that 'organized thefts' of timber on the Punjab rivers—especially on the Chenab and Jhelum—were so widespread that they had to call for special measures that were outside the ambit of the prevailing Forest Act.[77] Suggestions had been forwarded to empower forest officers with judicial authority. This implied that forest officers could enter residential premises to search for stolen timber, since it was felt that the time taken by the police in searches was always too long, which gave the 'offenders' time to dispose of the stolen timber.[78] But the Punjab government did not accept these suggestions. The Forest Department continued to face the difficulty of proving that it was government property, that it was stolen, and that the possessor knew or had reason to believe that it was stolen. Concerns over timber theft continued to dominate official debates, including the Punjab Forest Conference held at Lahore in 1909.[79] The issue was not only to control the surface transit of timber but it was also recognized that the control of its transit by river was imperative.

The Punjab Legislative Council subsequently passed specific legislation in 1911 to control theft while wood was in transit down the rivers.[80] Villagers were not allowed to saw up timber at places within a distance of three miles from the bank of a river. The procedure for applying to do otherwise was detailed and so tedious as to dissuade most from applying. Also, all sale depots had to be registered and had to be at least ten miles from the banks of a river. However, as the subsequent forest report indicates, this was a problem that the Forest Department had to deal with for a long period of time:[81] '. . . . It has been reported that six carpentry shops have been erected near Bilaspur some

50 yards above the river. I am of genuine suspicion that these shops have been erected and a notice board erected, prohibiting entrance, in order to conceal the cutting up of stolen government timber.'

CONCLUSION

Much of the historiography on forests has treated the commodification of timber within the colonial logic. The primary actors remain the state in its various incarnations and those local communities who are regarded as 'marginal' or as 'victims', since most writings emphasize the manner in which colonial laws shaped the imagining of forests, and the way local access was linked to colonial logic of property ownership. Rather than focus on the marginality of local communities, I have traced the variety of local responses based on the rationale of commerce. This is not to suggest that every peasant in a local community was a rational actor shrewdly adjusting to the market economy of timber.[82] Rather, it is to show the multiplicity of local responses that included the circumvention of laws, and to highlight what Migdal calls the 'dispersed domination' of the state.[83]

The more mobile, concealable and fungible the property at stake, the more extensive the social organization and markets that developed around it. The proliferation of informal timber markets clearly indicates that certain local communities created autonomous spaces, circumvented forest policies, and reworked the colonial understanding of forest resources as distinct, separate and legible. These communities used the market and along with local traders and timber dealers, created a widespread and active network to partake in the benefits from the commodification of timber.

I have argued that timber was a metaphor of resistance, and much more. Resistance somehow presupposes a reactive and defensive stance targeted against an all-powerful state. But many of the local responses cannot be read simply as acts of resistance, for that implies an attempt to revert to a pre-colonial culture of timber use. It also somehow implies that local communities were static or closed groups, far removed from the market. It is only in examining the manner in which relations of domination were actually contested that one can arrive at a more nuanced understanding of the plurality of local response. The prevalence of this shadow economy was another form of commodification. The conflict was not about commodification *per se*; it was about the people who benefited from the revenue which timber generated. Howsoever subsumed and fugitive its nature, this economy was about commerce.

NOTES

1. Himachal Pradesh State Archives (HPSA), Shimla, D.C. Kangra, file no. 81, 'Preservation of Trees Growing on Private Lands in Kulu,' remark by a Kulu *zamindar* to the Deputy Commissioner of Kangra District (1908). The presence of a landholding elite was far less of a presence in the Himalayan Punjab than in other parts of lowland India; thus the translation of the term zamindar as a peasant rather than a landholder.
2. Oriental and India Office Collection (OIOC), London, Rev. & Agr. Proceedings (Forests), A, nos. 4-12, file 26, letter from the Extra-Deputy Conservator of Forests, Chenab Division, to the Deputy Commissioner, Gujranwala (1914) p. 10.
3. Brad Weiss, *The Making and Unmaking of the Haya Lived World: Consumption, Commoditization, and Everyday Practice*, Durham: Duke University Press, 1996, p. 8.
4. Madhav Gadgil and Ramachandra Guha, *This Fissured Land: An Ecological History of India*, Delhi: Oxford University Press, 1992.
5. This was under the stewardship of Ranajit Guha who edited *Subaltern Studies: Writings on South Asian History and Society,* Delhi: Oxford University Press, 1982-9. There have been three more volumes that have come out subsequently under the editorship of other subaltern scholars.
6. For a comprehensive view see K. Sivaramakrishnan, 'Schools and Scholars: Situating the Subaltern: History and Anthropology in the Subaltern Studies Project', *Journal of Historical Sociology*, vol. 8, no. 4, 1995, pp. 395-429. Also Vinay Bahl, 'Relevance (or Irrelevance) of Subaltern Studies', *Economic and Political Weekly*, vol. 32, no. 23, 1997, pp. 1333-44.
7. Ranajit Guha, *Subaltern Studies: Writings on South Asian History and Society,* Delhi: Oxford University Press, 1982-89, volume I, pp. 3-4.
8. James C. Scott, *Domination and the Art of Resistance: Hidden Transcripts*, New Haven: Yale University Press, 1990; Also see

Susan Gal Language and the 'Arts of Resistance', *Cultural Anthropology: Journal of the Society for Cultural Anthropology*, vol. 10, no. 3, 1995, pp. 407-24.

9. Susan Gal, op. cit., p. 416.
10. Ramachandra Guha, *The Unquiet Woods: Ecological Change and Peasant Resistance in the Western Himalaya*, Delhi: Oxford University Press, 1989; also see Gadgil and Guha *This Fissured Land.*
11. Sumit Sarkar, 'Primitive Rebellion and Modern Nationalism: A Note on Forest Satyagraha in the Non-Cooperation and Civil Disobedience Movements' in K.N. Pannikar, ed., *National and Left Movements in India*, New Delhi: Vikas, 1980, pp. 14-26.
12. For instance see K. Sivaramakrishnan, 'Forests, politics and governance in Bengal, 1794-1994', PhD Dissertation, Yale University (1996); Atluri Murali 'Whose Trees? Forest Practices and Local Communities in Andhra, 1600-1992', in David Arnold and Ramachandra Guha, eds., *Nature, Culture and Imperialism: Essays on the Environmental History of South Asia,* New Delhi: Oxford University Press 1995, pp. 86-122.
13. Nancy Lee Peluso, *Rich Forests, Poor People: Resource Control and Resistance in Java,* Berkeley: University of California Press, 1992.
14. Ibid., p. 19.
15. Sherry B. Ortner, 'Resistance and the Problem of Ethnographic Refusal', *Comparative Studies in Society and History*, vol. 37 no. 1, 1995, pp. 173-93.
16. Akhileshwar Pathak, *Contested Domains: The State, Peasants and Forests in Contemporary India,* New Delhi: Sage Publications, 1994.
17. Ferdinand Braudel, *Afterthoughts on Material Civilization and Capitalism,* Baltimore: Johns Hopkins University Press, 1977, pp. 27-8, pp. 51-63.
18. This economy has been variously interpreted as an informal or an uncaptured economy. In our present-day parlance it is referred to as smuggling, Janet MacGaffey, ed., *The Real Economy of Zaire: The Contribution of Smuggling and other Unofficial Activities to National Wealth*, Philadelphia: University of Pennsylvania Press, 1991. For an insightful discussion of informal trading networks in Africa see Michael Bratton 'Peasant-State Relations in Postcolonial Africa: Patterns of Engagement and Disengagement' in Joel S. Migdal, Atul Kohli and Vivenne Shue, eds., *State Power and Social Forces: Domination and Transformation in the Third World*, Cambridge: Cambridge University Press, 1994, pp. 231-54.

19. Since Chamba and Bashahr were under the control of local rajas, the British could not introduce new land and forest settlements although forest rights were restricted and specified in appendices of forest leases between the rajas and the British.
20. *Imperial Gazetteer of India, Punjab*, vol. I, New Delhi: Atlantic Publishers and Distributors, 1991 reprint, 1908, p. 73.
21. Both Ramachandra Guha and Chetan Singh emphasize this in their studies of Uttar Pradesh and Himachal Pradesh respectively.
22. D.N. Jha, 'State Formation in Early Medieval Chamba' in D.N. Jha, ed., *Society and Ideology in India: Essays in Honour of Professor R.S. Sharma*, Delhi: Munshiram Manoharlal, 1995, pp. 125-34.
23. Irfan Habib, *The Agrarian System of Mughal India, 1556-1707,* London: Asia Publishing House, 1963.
24. Chetan Singh, *Natural Premises: Ecology and Peasant Life in the Western Himalaya 1800-1950,* Delhi: Oxford University Press, 1998.
25. *Census of India 1911*, Lahore: 1912, p. 529.
26. For an excellent overview of the economy in the region see Singh, *Natural Premises*.
27. In the pre-colonial period, the term 'wasteland' applied to uncultivated (including long fallow land), and unmeasured land. It was land that did not yield any tax; see Irfan Habib, *The Agrarian System*, pp. 16-17.
28. Punjab State Archives (PSA), Patiala, 'Kulu Forest Settlement', *Selections from the Records of the Office of the Financial Commissioner, Punjab*, New Series 25, vol. I, Lahore, 1910, p. 34.
29. Rapid and extensive ecological transition was frequently a feature of pre-colonial landscapes and states, either as a consequence of the development of agriculture or, as indicated here for purposes of war; see Richard Grove, *Green Imperialism: Colonial Expansion, Tropical Island Edens and the Origins of Environmentalism, 1600-1860,* Cambridge: Cambridge University Press, 1995, p. 7.
30. *Gazetteer of the Kangra District: Kangra Proper*, vol. I, Calcutta: Punjab Government Press, 1883-4, p. 110.
31. V. K. Gidwani, 'Waste and the Permanent Settlement in Bengal', *Economic and Political Weekly*, vol. 27, no. 4, 1992, pp. 39-46.
32. By the 1878 Forest Act which proposed to ascertain, control, limit, or extinguish private rights in forest lands which interfered with the promotion of better forestry; see OIOC, Rev., Agr., & Commerce Proc., (Forests), A, no. 5, 'Draft of a General Forest Bill' (1877), p. 7.

33. For a succinct account of the tensions between the Forest and the Land Revenue Departments, see Vasant K. Saberwal, *Pastoral Politics: Shepherds, Bureaucrats, and Conservation in the Western Himalaya*, Delhi: Oxford University Press, 1999.
34. This is reminiscent of the Enclosure Movement in England that was designed to give greater scope to improved methods of arable farming and sometimes to convert arable land into pasture. It made farming subservient to the needs of the markets in which merchant capital dominated the scene.
35. Lieutenant-Colonel G.F. Pearson, *Report on the Administration of the Forest Department in the Several Provinces under the Government of India, 1870-71*, Calcutta: Government Press, 1872, p. 27.
36. For instance, many species of timber such as *deodar* and *chil*, could not be cut for building or for other purposes without official permission, which was only given once every five years. Furthermore, there were fixed zamindari rates that depended on the revenue paid to the state. No wasteland could be brought under cultivation without the permission of the Deputy Commissioner in undemarcated forests. Of course, the extension of land for cultivation was prohibited in demarcated forests; PSA, Patiala, Selections, New Series 26 'Kangra Forest Settlement', p. 22.
37. For instance, there were several revised land revenue settlements introduced in the Kangra district. See G.C. Barnes, *Report on the Settlement in the district of Kangra in the Trans-Sutlej States*, Lahore: Chronicle Press, 1855; J.B. Lyall, *Report of the Land Revenue Settlement of the Kangra District, Punjab*, Lahore: Central Jail Press, 1874; A. Anderson, *Final Report of the Revised Settlement of the Kangra District, Punjab*, Lahore: Civil and Military Gazette, 1897.
38. Punjab State Archives (PSA), Patiala, 'Kulu Forest Settlement' *Selections from the Records of the Office of the Financial Commissioner, Punjab*, New Series 25, vol. I, Lahore 1910; PSA, Patiala, *Selections*, New Series 26 'Kangra Forest Settlement', 1910.
39. PSA, *Progress Report on Forest Administration in the Punjab for the year 1926-27*, Lahore, 1928, p. 4.
40. Bhai Mul Raj, 'An Economic Survey of the Haripur and Mangarh Taluqas of the Kangra District of the Punjab', *The Board of Economic Inquiry,* Lahore, 1933, p. 101. If one compares this to the cost of living, an average land owner, after paying his rent, earned approximately Rs. 10 per month in 1908; See *Imperial Gazetteer of India, Punjab*, p. 70.
41. The Forest Department systematically inspected all forest products

for their economic potential. For instance in Kulu, it inspected the wood of the yew (*Taxus baccata*), walnut (*Juglans regia*) and ash (*Fraxinus floribunda*), to conclude that *deodar* was the most important article of trade from Kulu; see D. Brandis, B.H. Baden-Powell and Lieut-Colonel W. Stenhouse, *Suggestions Regarding the Demarcation and Management of the Forests in Kulu,* Calcutta: Government Press, 1877 pp. 10-11.

42. PSA, *Selections from the Records of the Office of the Financial Commissioner*, 1911, pp. 49-85.
43. PSA, Patiala, *Selections*, n.s. 26, 'Kangra Forest Settlement', p. 24.
44. See Neeladri Bhattacharya, 'Pastoralists in a Colonial World' in Arnold and Guha, eds., *Nature, Culture and Imperialism,* pp. 49-85; also see Saberwal, *Pastoral Politics.*
45. Messrs Lace and McIntire, *Revised Working-Plan for the Upper Ravi Forests, Chamba Division, Punjab,* Lahore, 1895, p. 2.
46. OIOC, Rev. & Agr. Proc., (Forests), A, pp. 21-7.
47. National Archives of India (NAI), Home Dept. (Forests), A, nos. 8-9, June 1884.
48. E.P. Stebbing, *The Forests of India*, vol. III, New Delhi: A.J. Reprints, 1982, p. 620. In fact, by the early 1890s, the Indian Forest Department had surpassed the annual revenue of the French Forest Department, and even the Prussian Forest Department, both of which had been in existence for centuries.
49. Singh, *Natural Premises*, p. 178.
50. NAI, Delhi, Rev. & Agr. Proceedings, (Forests), B, nos. 36-7, Appendix A, 1875.
51. HPSA, D.C. Kangra, File no. 10(46), 'letter from Lieutenant Colonel C.F. Massey, Commissioner & Superintendent Jalandhar Division, to the Senior Secretary to Financial Commissioner', Punjab, 1896.
52. This was apart from the Gujars who traded in milk and *ghee*; see Lyall, *Report of the Land Revenue Settlement of the Kangra District, Punjab*, p. 44.
53. OIOC, Rev. & Agr. (Forests), A, 40-1, February 1911, 'The Progress Report of the Forest Administration in the Punjab for the year 1909-1910.'
54. NAI, Rev. & Agr. (Forests), A, nos. 1-22, April 1913.
55. D.C. Kangra, file no. 10 (31), 'Forest Conservancy', 1906.
56. Haripriya Rangan makes a similar point in the context of the Garhwal forests in Uttar Pradesh 'Property vs. Control: The State and Forest Management in the Indian Himalaya', *Development and Change* vol. 28, no. 1, 1997, pp. 71-94.

57. HPSA, D.C. Kangra, file no. 114, 'Forest Bartan Rights of Zamindars', 1904.
58. The stance of the Forest Department over the collection of timber from remote areas was that trees could not be felled from the nearest line of forest; instead trees had to be felled evenly throughout the forest.
59. HPSA, D.C. Kangra, file no. 108 (1), 'Timber Supply and Arrangements in Kulu', 1882.
60. HPSA, D.C. Kangra, file no. 13, 1920.
61. The average annual number of fire outbreaks in the 1880s was 12.5 which burnt 2,314 acres, in the 1890s, the number increased to 45.3 burning 10,471 acres; see NAI, Rev. & Agr. Proceedings, (Forests), A, no. 105, 30, letter from the Deputy Conservator of Forests, Kangra Division to the Deputy Commissioner, Kangra, June 1898.
62. OIOC, Rev & Agr. (Forests), A, nos. 51-2, February, 1908.
63. NAI, Home Dept. (Forests), A, nos. 6-9; NAI, Rev. & Agr. Proc., (Forests), A, nos. 4-7, 1886. There is striking similarity between eighteenth-century Britain and nineteenth-century colonial India with regard to conflict over forest resources. See Douglas Hay and E.P. Thompson, *Albion: Fatal Tree*, Harmondsworth: Penguin, 1976; E.P. Thompson, *Whigs and Hunters*, Harmondsworth: Penguin, 1977.
64. For instance, there was a marked decrease in the number of cases of illicit grazing and forest fires when the region had a good monsoon. The years 1916-17 produced an abundant supply of fodder outside the forest due to the monsoon, and the region witnessed a marked decrease in the number of cases of illicit grazing and forest fires. OIOC, Rev. & Agr (Forests), A, 36-8, February 1918, p. 1.
65. See Neeladri Bhattacharya 'Colonial State and Agrarian Society' in Burton Stein, ed., *The Making of Agrarian Policy in British Raj 1770-1900,* Delhi: Oxford University Press, 1992, pp. 113-49.
66. Peluso, *Rich Forests, Poor People*, p. 11.
67. Relevant *Progress Reports on Forest Administration in the Punjab.*
68. *Report of the Punjab Government Forest Commission, 1937-38*, 1938, p. 65.
69. NAI, Rev. & Agr. (Forests), B, nos. 8-9, file 110, Appendix P, 'Extract from the Abstract of the Proceedings of a meeting of the Legislative Council of the Punjab held at Govt. House, Lahore', 10 April, 1912.

70. OIOC, Rev. & Agr. Proceedings (Forests), A, nos. 12-20, file no. 10, letter from E. Lee French, Inspector-General of Police, Punjab to the Under-Secretary to Govt., Punjab, Rev. Dept., 1912.
71. Peluso, *Rich Forests, Poor People*, p. 236.
72. As Marx wrote, 'If popular customary rights are suppressed, the attempt to exercise them can only be treated as the simple contravention of a police regulation, but never punished as a crime. . . . The punishment must not inspire more repugnance than the offence, the ignominy of crime must not be turned into the ignominy of law. The basis of the state is undermined if misfortune becomes a crime or crime becomes a misfortune', Karl Marx and F. Engels, *Collected Works I*, Moscow: International Publishers, 1975, p. 235.
73. Forest Research Institute (FRI), Dehradun, *Punjab Forest Conference*, Feb., 8-13, Appendix A, 1909.
74. See C.G. Trevor, *Revised Working Plan for the Kulu Forests 1919-20 to 1943-47*, Lahore: Civil and Military Gazette Press, 1920, p. 31.
75. OIOC, Rev. & Agr. Proceedings (Forests), A, no. 362, Jan. 1911, p. 44.
76. OIOC, Rev. & Agr. Proceedings (Forests), A, no. 51, 1912.
77. OIOC, Rev. & Agr. Proceedings (Forests), A, nos. 35-67, letter from J. Copeland, Conservator of Forests, Punjab, to the Revenue Secretary to Govt., Punjab, 1912.
78. OIOC, PWD, Proceedings (Forests), A, nos. 22-3, 'Thefts of Wood in Forests', 1867, p. 17.
79. FRI, *Punjab Forest Conference*, Lahore, 1909.
80. OIOC, *Proceedings of the Legislative Council of the Lieutenant-Governor of the Punjab*, 1913.
81. PSA, letter from G.D. Kitchingman, Deputy Conservator of Forests, Lower Bashahr Forest Division, to the Wazir, Bilaspur State, Simla: 11 December 1924.
82. Samuel L. Popkin, *The Rational Peasant: Political Economy of Rural Society in Vietnam*, Los Angeles: University of California Press, 1979, in response to James C. Scott, *The Moral Economy of the Peasant: Rebellion and Subsistence in Southeast Asia*, New Haven: Yale University Press, 1976.
83. Migdal, Kohli, and Shue eds., *State Power and Social Forces*.

Homeless in Gujarat and India: On the Curious Love of Indulal Yagnik*

Ajay Skaria

In the 1920s, the writer Ramanlal Desai (father of the Marxist sociologist A.R. Desai) drew a comparison between two Gujarati figures whom he considered amongst the most prominent in the post-Gandhian generation—K.M. Munshi and Indulal Yagnik. He described them as symptomatic of two strands of Gujarat: Munshi was a *pratibashaali siddh purush*, a resolute and accomplished man, and Yagnik as an *asthir man na fakir*, a mendicant of unstable mind.[1]

That remark is reproduced by Yagnik—without too much comment—in the preface to the first volume of his *Atmakatha* or autobiography. Indeed, the six volume autobiography is structured almost as an analogy to the remark. It draws heavily on the trope of homelessness—a state which is often associated with fakirs. But this is a distinctive kind of homelessness—it is

* This paper—begun for a conference in May 1997 at the University of Virginia, Charlottesville in honour of Walter Hauser—is dedicated to the memory of Rosemary Hauser (1928-2001). In the long period of its making, it has benefited from many conversations, and for these I thank Arun Agrawal, Shahid Amin, Dipesh Chakrabarty, Sudhir Chandra, Partha Chatterjee, Alon Confino, David Hardiman, Walter Hauser, Qadri Ismail, Pradeep Jegannathan, Priya Kumar, Allan Megill, Parita Mukta, Gyan Prakash, Gloria Goodwin Raheja, Tridip Suhrud, and Babu Suthar. The essay was previously published in the *Indian Economic and Social History Review* 38, 3 (2001), and is reproduced here with permission.

accompanied by love of having a home. There was the homelessness produced by his vow to remain celibate—first made in 1914–15 when he was 23, broken briefly a few years later because of family pressure to accept the marriage performed when he was a child. In 1923–4, just before he decided to separate from his wife, and renew his vow, 'the deep, inchoate thirst for love continued to harass me. . . . A yearning for a life filled with love in its many colors started burning in my heart.'[2] Finally, after the advice of an unnamed friend, he decided that he 'should leave the *maya* of a home (*ghar*) and remain a sacrificing person without a home—the attraction of even the dearest person should be reduced to ashes, that is all'.[3]

There was also the homelessness that accompanied his love for the khedut or farmer, and mazdoor or worker. Indeed, he differentiated himself from Munshi primarily in terms of this love: 'He [Munshi] was a great admirer of leaders like Caesar and Napolean, of Dayanand Saraswati and Aurobindo Ghosh, whereas I was wedded to the common people'.[4] He loved the 'common people', of course. Visiting Panchmahals in Gujarat in 1918, he reported that he saw that 'yesterday's miserable looking Bhils had worn good clothes, and were moving about joyously. . . . As evening fell, the Bhil people's merrymaking increased. When, in all the large open grounds around town, I saw hundreds of young boys and girls holding each other's hand, singing and dancing in circles to the rhythms of the drum, my heart swelled with love and pleasure. An enthusiasm rose in my heart to serve such innocent children of mankind all my life.'[5]

And yet this love for common people too led to homelessness in relation both to people and to mainstream political parties and projects. He began with Gokhale's Servants of India Society, went on to a more radical wing of the Congress, then to Gandhi, and then left politics for journalism. He then turned to organizing peasants, and with the founding of the Kisan Sabha arguably emerged as amongst the three most prominent leaders of peasant struggles in early and mid-twentieth-century India. He again came back to the Congress briefly after Independence before leaving it again, and started the movement for a separate state of Gujarat. During this period and later, he also ran an ashram on the banks of the Vatrak river, and became involved with trade unions in Ahmedabad. Reflecting on his life in one particularly dispirited moment in 1956, he wrote:

> I feel upset with myself. I have chosen to lead only unsuccessful fights. Now, I have reached the final point. . . . I am regarded as unintelligent and unfaithful. When I cast my glance on 64 years the result is a big nothing. I go to meet several friends but rarely do they come here [to the ashram in Nenpur, near Ahmedabad] to meet me. It is as though nobody thinks of me at all. Because of this, I sometimes feel tired of life. It affects one's self-respect to go aimlessly to the city (Ahmedabad), knocking over and again on people's doors. When nobody has any need for me, why should I keep moving back and forth. . . .[6]

Even if not usually stated in such dispirited terms, this theme was repeated in his *Atmakatha*: that he had never been quite at home in any of the major political parties.

If we begin—as we surely must as historians—with the assumption that homelessness does not mean the same thing in all times and places, that metaphors too have history, then the question follows: how was Yagnik's homelessness produced? Within what conceptual field, more precisely, were Yagnik's simultaneous love of home and homelessness conceived? I shall situate Yagnik's simultaneous love of home and homelessness in relationship to two other sets of practices of home and homelessness—those involved in the logic of transcendence and the politics of neighborliness.

The logic of transcendence, I would like to argue, was characteristic of mainstream nationalism. In one of the most often quoted passages in *Discovery of India*, Nehru remarks:

> Sometimes as I reached a gathering, a great roar of welcome would greet me: Bharat Mata ki Jai—'Victory to Mother India'. I would ask them unexpectedly who was this Bharat Mata, Mother India, whose victory they wanted? My question would amuse them and surprise them, and then, not knowing exactly what to answer, they would look at each other and at me. I persisted in my questioning. At last a vigorous Jat, wedded to the the soil from immemorial generations, would say that it was the *dharti*, the good earth of India, that they meant. What earth? Their particular village patch, or all the patches in the district or province, or in the whole of India? And so question and answer went on, till they would ask me impatiently to tell them all about it. I would endeavour to do so and explain that India was all

this that they had thought, but it was much more. The mountains and the rivers, and the forests and the broad fields, which gave us food, were all dear to us, but what counted ultimately were the people of India, people like them and me, who were spread out all over this vast land. Bharat Mata, Mother India, was essentially these millions of people, and victory to her meant victory to these people. You are parts of this Bharat Mata, I told them, you are in a manner yourselves Bharat Mata, and as this idea slowly soaked into their brains, their eyes would light up as if they had made a great discovery.[7]

Notice the way that India as a nation-home is configured in this argument. On the one hand, there is the vigorous Jat wedded to the soil for generations. This Jat already is India; he already is the nation-home; it is this fact which makes India possible. On the other hand, there is also a gap between this Jat and Bharat Mata; the two have to be constantly brought together in a fusion; the Jat has to realize himself by transcending his Jatness, so to speak, by subsuming it within Bharat Mata. Much of the work that nationalist thought set itself involved bringing about this transcendence; hence, of course, the repeated emphasis on building patriotism and national awareness.

This logic of transcendence does not reject or disregard the very local and particular homes represented by the Jat, the peasant, and other such figures. Rather, it affirms them in a particular way: by focusing on how they transcend into higher levels of generality and abstraction; the insistence is that it is only through such transcendence that the true meanings of the local home are realized. It is in this fairly precise sense of transcendence that mainstream nationalist thought can be described as cosmopolitan. This is not so in the sense that nationalist thought seeks to embrace or subsume humanity within it (quite the contrary, obviously); it is so, rather, in the sense that it is constituted by a logic which subsumes identities designated as local, contingent or particular within more general identities. This process created both the nation-home and a certain homelessness in relation to those particular identities—the Jat and the peasant—which had been transcended.

Much scholarship on nationalism has been characterized by the same logic of transcendence. Thus, for instance, one crucial innovation of Anderson's *Imagined Communities* lay in specifying, very precisely, the way in which such transcendence occurred. For Anderson, this transcendence occurs through an emphasis on the 'homogeneous empty' time of history that allows all the different parts of nation to exist all at once in some nationalist imaginary of simultaneity.[8] In this analysis, the characteristic technologies of nationalism—the map, the museum, the census, and of course print capitalism—are precisely efforts to translate the nation-home into the terms of abstract time and space.

Another kind of home and homelessness was produced by the politics of neighborliness. Gandhi was one of the most articulate practitioners of this politics in the twentieth century. This politics too claimed India as a home, but it was in a tense and even perhaps conceptually incommensurable relationship with the nation-home constituted by a logic of transcendence. It claimed the immediate neighbour or *padoshi* as home, and insisted that the nation was constituted not by transcending the singularity of the immediate neighbour, but by serving that singularity. I do not wish to suggest that this politics affirmed some authentic local identity, some substantive modern ethnographic space autonomous of or prior to mainstream nationalism. Such modern spaces or identities do not exist, and any attempt to describe or recuperate such them would only reinscribe those practices that constitute mainstream nationalism. Rather, I wish to argue that the politics of neighborliness—and especially Gandhi's version of it, which was dominant in early twentieth-century India—susbsists in an intimate and yet agonistic relationship with mainstream nationalism. By exploring Gandhi's concept of *swadeshi*, I hope to point to how this politics, denying as it did the very necessity of a sovereign state, worked to question mainstream nationalism, how it subverted the latter in the very process of sustaining it. Accompanying this neighborliness was also a distinctive homelessness, one created by discipline required for *swadeshi*.

Like Gandhi, Yagnik in his more interesting moments rejected mainstream nationalism. (My focus is only on such moments, since he made many other deeply problematic political moves. This paper makes no claims to reconciling various strands of his politics or evaluating them as a whole: indeed, this paper is possible only because it sets aside the possibility of any such evaluation.) In his rejection, he drew on the problematic of a politics of neighborliness. But this was a Gandhian politics directed against Gandhi himself. Gandhi, in his insistence on neighborliness, had been unable to deal seriously or systematically with questions of marginality. His politics effectively evaded such questions by presuming that neighborliness, practised seriously enough, would ensure that nobody was marginal. Yagnik, in contrast, insisted that the question of marginality could not be resolved this quickly. By bringing questions of marginality into systematic engagement with neighbourliness, Yagnik not only transformed the latter, he also rendered himself homeless in the nation constituted even by Gandhi's politics of neighbourliness.

The best place to begin is not the life of Yagnik (1892–1970), but that of the writer Kanaiyalal Munshi (1887–1971)—the figure with whom Desai had chosen to compare Yagnik.[9] Munshi was deeply involved with producing a distinctive love, simultaneously, for India and Gujarat. He saw his widely read historical novels as part of the process of regenerating India, remarking: 'Bankim revived the memory of the heroism of the samnyas rebellion. Both he and Dwijendralal Roy resurrected Rajput heroism. Not that such authors intentionally set out to foster national or regional pride. They became the spontaneous voices of the coming spring. The same was perhaps the case with me.'[10]

His novel *Gujarat no Nath* (The Lord of Gujarat) is quite characteristic of his concerns. First published in 1917, and translated into several Indian languages, it was set in the twelfth-century Patan (Gujarat), and described confrontations amongst the Rajput kings of Avanti (Malwa), Patan, and Junagadh (Saurashtra).[11] One theme in the book is the love of Gujarat. The policy of Munjal Mehta, the Prime Minister of Patan, had been 'very clear': it was to produce a love of Gujarat that rose above parochial concerns. In the novel, Gujarat itself is centered in what is now central and north Gujarat. The regions of Saurashtra, Kutch, and Lat (modern south Gujarat) are outside it; in other words, the task of constructing Gujarat remains.

This is a task that is assigned by Munjal Mehta to Kak (the Brahman warrior who is the central figure in the novel) as the book draws to a close: 'Remember, your aim is not to conquer Lat (modern South Gujarat) but to make it Gujarat'.[12] Involved here was something quite different from the rapid constructivism involved in the usual invocation of imagined communities. Here, the imagination of the nation as an abstract time and space was supplemented by the emphasis on love and active making; it is such a practice of imagination that Dipesh Chakrabarty has referred to as *darshan*.

It was also a statist love. Though himself a Jain, Munjal had managed to keep religious disputes apart from the consolidation of state power (formerly, the state had been debilitated by disputes between Jains and Shaivites). 'His main objective was the growth of the kingdom and the establishment of a strong empire in Gujarat, and he considered philosophical and religious disputes utterly futile'.[13] This concern with producing a statist love for Gujarat recurs not only in many of his other novels, but also in his social commentaries and histories, including *Gujaratni asmita* (The identity of Gujarat), and the *The Glory that was Gurjararashtra* (1954).

To understand this sentiment better, let us also consider the tension between the love of Gujarat and another register of the same kind of love: that involved in making Bharat or India. Munjal, being a figure of the older generation, could not appreciate the need for this task of unity amongst the various states. For him, the transcendent love that rejected parochial identities stopped at Gujarat; it did not transcend Gujarat to include Bharat. The unity of Bharat that Munshi envisioned was of course of a particular kind, directed against the Muslim, or the 'ravaging Yavan hordes (that) are advancing steadily year by year'. The figure who articulated the need for unity against Muslims was young Kirtidev, an associate of the Avanti commander who had successfully laid siege to Patan and forced it to agree to a peace treaty. Pleading for a more extensive peace than the treaty would have provided, he argued, 'I pray to almighty god that the peace should prevail forever. Look, Patan and Avanti are like our country's two eyes. Doesn't it pain you when the two fight'.[14] In other words, while Patan and Avanti may retain their identities, there should also be a non-antagonistic unity between them. To ensure a longer peace treaty, Kirtidev proposes that the Avanti king's daughter marry the king of Patan. However, Munjal, who despite his appreciation of Kirtidev's vision, fears that any alliance will give Malwa ascendancy over Patan, ensures that this plan is foiled. By refusing to spell out the consequences of this failure, Munshi produced a commonsensical knowledge amongst his readers: the 'knowledge' that it was the failure of Hindu kings to stay united which led to Muslim rule in Bharat.

As this suggests, Munshi of course envisioned a particular kind of Bharat. Kirtidev appeals to Kak on the basis of his caste: 'You are a brahman, captain. This country has been blessed and sanctified by you and your ancestors. If you do not come to her help, who will?'[15] This emphasis on the making of a Hindu Bharat was pervasive in Munshi's writings. Here, the emergence of the Indian nation is located in a historical past, specifically the Vedic and immediate post Vedic period which he located in the first and second millennia BC. Tracing the development of this already constituted subject, Bharat, was for Munshi the task that Indian historians had to set themselves. One of the most major projects undertaken by the Bharatiya Vidya Bhavan, the powerful educational institution that he founded in 1938, was the writing of a multi-volume history of India in precisely this spirit.[16]

But I do not wish here to dwell on the exclusionary upper caste martial and male Hinduism that constituted Munshi's Bharat. For now, I wish only to stress that this statist love—a love that authorized the subsumption of various regions within Gujarat, and of Gujarat within India—was constituted by a particular kind of emphasis on having a history. In the remarkably early 'Swadeshabhiman' (1856) (pride in/respect for one's own country), the poet Narmad, for instance, argued that while in India there was considerable *abhiman* or pride in the accomplishment of one's family or caste, an *abhiman* for the *desh* or country was not visible.[17] Nor was *swadeshabhiman* simply about having knowledge of or pride in the past of the *desh*—that kind of pride already existed amongst Hindus, and the genealogical accounts of Bhats and Charans were that form of knowledge. Rather, it was about a particular kind of relationship with the past: it involved judging the past in moral terms (which the Charans did not do, hence the inadequacy of their histories), and building, in the present, on a moral pride in the past. This was what countries like Britain and France had done; it was what Hindustan needed to do. To acquire *swadeshabhiman* in this sense was crucially a matter of studying the past to establish the proper relationship with it: he had recently heard, he said, that a writer called Macaulay had written a two-volume history of England: though expensive, a first edition of 25,000 had sold out in a few days, as had a second edition of another 20,000. In later essays in the book, he turned to writing this kind of history—providing a history of Gujarati literature and poetry, of his city Surat, of Gujarat, of the Rajput kings of Mewar, and of the *Ramayana* and *Mahabharata*.

As Narmad's argument suggests, to have a history was to love the country in a specific way: one where local affiliations like those involved in the family or caste were, rather than being rejected, subsumed into or transcended for a higher identity. To have a history created through such transcendence was to create a stable object—be it Bharat or Hindustan or Gujarat—which could then be loved, and which could then shape the present. The nation-home had precisely the stability and resoluteness that Ramanlal Desai approved of in Munshi—it had a vision of India produced through history, and it worked to achieve this. It was this resoluteness that Narmad sought to foreground through his emphasis on *abhiman* or pride; indeed, for a later generation of Gujarati nationalists, *desh-prem* or love of country was to become synonymous with *desh-abhiman*. That very Nehruvian book, Khilnani's *Idea of India*, recognizes and celebrates a similar resoluteness in Nehru: he, it says, 'rejected Jacobin notions of popular sovereignty . . . in favour of the idea of an abstract, historically durable 'people' or nation'; in contrast, the book laments, later generations 'preferred to invoke the immediate, volatile authority of electoral majorities'.[18] This logic of transcendence, then, requires a stable object, usually created through history.

This logic of transcendence also produces the distinctive relationship between Gujarat and Bharat. Though both are constituted by the same logic—that of having a history—the relationship between them is one where Gujarat is subsumed under Bharat. Nationalist thought even had a name—regionalism, Munjal's crime for those moments when this hierarchy was not accepted: to be regional was to refuse transcendence, and to become parochial. Munshi was worried by the spectre of regionalism. Thus his ambivalence towards the creation of the separate state of Gujarat. Munshi's own books were part of the early twentieth-century movement for such a state. In 1948, on the occasion of the establishment of Saurashtra as a state, Vallabhbhai Patel had suggested that all the states in Gujarat be merged under one administration. Later, Munshi organized a Mahagujarat conference, which again called for such a state. Yet, Munshi perhaps felt constrained by the prospect of losing the city of Bombay to Maharashtra, which he felt was inevitable if a state of Gujarat was formed. Also, he saw the movement for a separate state of Gujarat as potentially undermining the broader identity of India. Ironically, when the Mahagujarat agitation for such a state started, Munshi kept out of the struggle.

And as the spectre of regionalism or volatile electoral majorities suggests, while the logic of transcendence sustained the nation-home, it also produced homelessness. The affirmation of a home is also undercut by their subsumption within a higher level of generality; regional loyalties and electoral majorities cannot really be a home. This was the curious sense in which Munshi was homeless within Gujarat: to affirm India was, within this logic, necessarily to not affirm Gujarat beyond a point. This kind of cosmopolitan homelessness was pervasive within the nationalist movement; it was the modality by which mainstream nationalists affirmed their loyalty to India. It was also the modality by which some of the most consistent nationalist thinkers affirmed a universal civilization over the nation. Thus it was that Nehru sometimes felt stifled by the idea of being an Indian, or that Tagore insisted that nationalism was a destructive force because it was so parochial. Liberal cosmopolitanism not only produces the modern nation-home; it also produces the homelessness, perpetual exile, and even alienation of the citizen of the world-citizen who is also a citizen nowhere.

In Yagnik's writings too, there is certainly a similar cosmopolitan logic which creates both modern homes and homelessness by subsuming these homes under higher levels of generality. As we saw, one kind of home that Yagnik claimed was amongst peasants and marginal groups, and indeed amongst the 'common people'. When he stayed in their midst in 1918, when he travelled in villages, his 'love for natural, outdoor beauty, for the farms and trees, which had remained suppressed in Bombay, was aroused'. And yet, this affirmation of peasants went hand in hand with a distancing from them. 'While my heart swelled with my love for the village, my intelligence and imagination were constrained. I was like the lover of an illiterate but beautiful woman.'[19]

The subsumption and even subordination of the popular to Gujarat is most evident in his account of the Mahagujarat movement, to which the sixth volume of his *Atmakatha* is dedicated.[20] As chairman of the Mahagujarat Parishad, Yagnik was perhaps the most important leader of the movement, which sought, in the 1950s, to carve out a separate state of Gujarat from the colonial administrative division, Bombay Presidency.[21] Partly as a result of the movement, Bombay Presidency was divided in 1960 into the states of Maharashtra and Gujarat. In Yagnik's account, the opposition to the Mahagujarat movement came only from a government and ruling party that was out of touch with the people. The identity of the people of Gujarat, in his account, is constituted by that long history of shared literature and culture; the movement is only about realizing this identity through a linguistically unified state. The invocation of the linguistic community of Gujaratis, then, glossed over the politically charged fissures in the everyday use of the language, and over the relations of class, region, and gender that so differentiated the region. In the subsumption of the various regions within Gujarat, it practised a violence in no way different from that involved in Munshi's subsumption of Gujarat within India.

This is perhaps most strikingly evident in Yagnik's account of the eventually successful struggle to make the Dangs region part of Gujarat rather than Maharashtra.[22] The region was inhabited by forest communities, largely Bhils and Koknis. It clearly did not fit—in political, cultural or linguistic terms—the schema envisioned in partitioning Bombay into two linguistically homogeneous states. Even more clearly than most other groups, Dangis were neither Marathi nor Gujarati; most were little involved in the issue of linguistic states. Despite (or perhaps because of) this, as the struggle for the creation of Gujarat and Maharashtra heated up, the question of which state Dangs should be part of became one of the most contentious issues. Yagnik devoted much energy to mobilize the Gujarati moneylenders and timber merchants working in the region in order to ensure that the Dangs became part of Gujarat. There was a deep irony in this, since both were amongst the groups who were most exploitative of Dangis. The creation of Gujarat involved the marginalization of precisely the Bhils for whom his heart had swelled with love. Yet, it would be a mistake to treat this as a contradiction within Yagnik's practices, or as a case of bad faith. Rather, precisely because the nation—whether Gujarat or Bharat—could only be made by subsuming within it more particular identities, there were contexts in which moneylenders and merchants and adivasis had to join hands; the violence practised on adivasis was justified on the grounds that it enabled them to affirm a less parochial identity.

Indeed, the *Atmakatha* itself was cast in part as an affirmation of Gujarat. As a shy person, he said, it was not that he wanted to write about himself, or that he thought his life important. But he had been repeatedly asked to write his *Atmakatha* since he had been such a crucial actor in, and witness to, the making of modern Gujarat over the previous fifty years.[23] It is thus as a history of Gujarat that he casts his *Atmakatha*—he is one of the major makers of that history of which Gujarat would appear the natural subject and object.

Even his marriage was subsumed within Gujarat and Bharat. For Yagnik, as for many other middle class Indian nationalists, conjugal homes could only be created by companionate marriages.[24] And in his view his own marriage was not companionate—he had been engaged to his future wife when a child, and did not wish to get married at the time he was in college in Bombay. He even wrote a letter breaking off the engagement. But under intense pressure from his mother, he gave in and married his betrothed, Kumud Tripathi. In ensuing decades, he invoked his commitment to a companionate marriage to practise a distinctively nationalist violence against Kumud. On the grounds that he had discovered that Kumud could not be educated to become the kind of nationalist-reformist wife he desired, he refused to stay with her. Finally, when he moved to Ahmedabad, he was persuaded to have her stay with him. But his refusal to have much to do with her drove her to attempt suicide. After this, her family in Nadiad took her away, and the two never stayed together again, though she repeatedly wrote to him requesting that they try being together again. She died in 1929, and Yagnik remained single.[25]

The mirror image of this violence towards his wife in the name of the nation was Yagnik's concern with *stri-kelavni* (women's education). Here, as for many other nationalists, *kelavni* carried the connotations of education, improvement, and training directed not so much at personal advancement or objective knowledge as at edifying the self and the nation. *Stri-kelavni*, amongst other things, educated women for companionate marriages—in other words, for making nationalist homes. Such women—those with *kelavni*—came to symbolize the nation as a whole. It was these 'home goddesses' he had met, Yagnik wrote, who came to mind when he tried to think of Gujarat. It was the households that they adorned, he said, which were his homes.

As this suggests, his celibacy did not always imply homelessness. It was also part of the embracing of another home—the nation-home. In choosing celibacy, Yagnik was acting within a longstanding nationalist tradition: recall, for instance, Aurobindo's famous call to youth to dedicate their lives to the nation. And less than two years after Yagnik chose celibacy for a second time, Hedgewar had founded the Rashtriya Swayamsevak Sangh (RSS), with its demand that all followers be celibate—that they be committed, in other words, to only one home.

That celibacy was so often enjoined on nationalists is indicative of how the nation was seen to require the same kind of loyalties as the household did: they were organized on identical principles. When the committed male nationalist deployed the language of kinship, even though his form of address (where women became mothers or sisters, and men became brothers) was scarcely new, the logic on which it was based—that the nation was a household-home organized on the principle of identity—was novel. It was as such a male that Yagnik had access to the households of other middle-class Gujarati nationalists. And precisely because he had access to these households as a figure committed exclusively to the nation-home, he felt that developing a romantic relationship would have violated the sanctity of the nation home, and that therefore celibacy was almost enjoined upon him. He realized, he writes, that had he not taken a vow of celibacy, all the places that were open to him as refuge would be closed. 'I would be obliged to fly away from them'.[26]

Gujarat, in turn, was subsumed under Bharat. From around 1907, the 'ideals of social service and national freedom continued to grow in my mind. *Hind maiya* (Mother India) became the highest Goddess to be worshipped, the whole of Bharat a vast temple of the Goddess; now the uppermost goal for me became service to its 33 crore children, and the struggle for their freedom.'[27] Yagnik insisted repeatedly that the Mahagujarat movement was deeply committed to, and finally subsumed under, the idea of Bharat: he claimed legitimacy for the movement by invoking major Gujarati nationalist leaders such as Gandhi and Vallabhbhai Patel. And he felt homeless at times even within Bharat. This was especially so in the 1920s, when he insisted that India had a lot to learn from Western civilization, but the theme was present in later years too.

Such cosmopolitanism was, in the case of Yagnik, always accompanied and undermined by another modality of being homeless: that produced by the marginality of a politics that affirmed the peasant, that which questioned the logic of transcendence. Consider, for a start, his ambivalent relationship with the Congress. In 1917 and 1919, he had been involved in providing relief to the Bhils and other communities in Panchmahals, which was reeling from a famine. By 1921, he felt that these relief works should be made permanent, and in 1921 he and Amritlal V. Thakkar (better known by his later name—Thakkar Bapa) went ahead and started a 'Rashtriya Bhil Ashram' at Mirakhedi village. Yagnik also started a school for untouchables, and, to meet the expenses, made a budget for Rs 5000 and submitted it to the Congress Provincial committee. Vallabhbhai however refused to approve this: while the Congress was committed to a campaign against untouchability, he said, it had to direct its financial resources to the struggle against the British. Yagnik argued,

> How long can we watch as the defenceless and half-naked Bhils are looted by government and *sahukars*, and are hurled into starvation with every failure of the rains? . . . If the present destitution and misery of the Bhils continues, does swaraj mean anything for them? . . . If our fight for *swaraj* is not for a fistful of *bhadra* people but for the *daridranarayan* (poorest of the poor, God in the poor) then even in the course of our struggle we should establish ideal institutions to demonstrate our unity with those backward people, and to show them the governance of the future.[28]

When Yagnik's arguments had little effect with the committee, he approached Gandhi directly and secured his approval. This upset Vallabhbhai, who remarked, 'How long will you go over our heads and get your work done through Gandhiji?'[29] Feeling that there was little point staying in the Congress in the face of such hostility, Yagnik submitted his resignation, which Gandhi promptly accepted.

Note how the trope of the 'common people' figures in the debate. Vallabhbhai and others within the Congress did not question the centrality of the people, or of working for them. But theirs was the abstract, historically durable people constituted by having a history. Their arguments were the traditional ones made by mainstream nationalists: that the money did not exist for the purpose, that swaraj was for the moment the more important goal, and that projects such as this should ideally be undertaken after swaraj. Indeed, Vallabhbhai saw himself as committed to the people, but as subsuming that commitment into its realization within the nation. Yagnik's resignation was for him about the refusal to accept the discipline needed to serve the people *by* serving the nation: 'To resign, and to free oneself— it is more painful than that to remain inside without resigning. Indulal is my younger brother. We have lived together as brothers till today, and now matters have come to this. What can I say?

Words fail me. I cannot speak further. Saying this, the brave Patidar leader, the *naik* (leader) of Gujarat, sat down, trying to hold back the tears in his eyes.'[30] The nation in whose name Patel defers the setting up of ashrams for Bhils and untouchables, is of course the nation constituted through the claim that it had a history.

Similarly, though marginal groups are virtually never actors or significant presences in their writings, Munshi and Nehru claim to speak for them by subsuming them in the imaginary of the popular. This imaginary of the popular is inseparable from the logic of transcendence associated with nationalist history. It is in this sense that nationalist history was part of a mediatory project: it claimed to be Indian modernity, and to thus know and subsume the popular within it. The task that nationalist thought set itself therefore was that of mediating between the popular and the modern, of making the popular into the modern nation or, more precisely, in the image of the nation already provided in and by history. By situating Indian identity not in the consequences of contemporary politics involving peasants or other marginal groups but in the imaginary of the popular, the implications of this politics could be circumscribed: it was legitimate to the extent that it affirmed a people—Khilnani's abstract, historically durable 'people'—already provided through history.

Yagnik, in contrast, was skeptical of this understanding of 'common people' through history. He felt that his fellow Congress members 'continued to look at the rural people of Gujarat from an urban point of view'. As for him, 'the conviction that my identity with this different rural world, with its miserable and oppressed people . . . would become permanent—this conviction grew within me'.[31] Here, then, the people come to have a different connotation: rather than having the solidity given by having a history, they are characterized by a marginality. And this is a marginality that explicitly challenges the notion of the popular constituted through history. Thus, not only are he and Vallabhbhai different from the marginal 'rural people', but it is the latter, in their marginality, who constitute the nation.[32]

In the 1930s, around the time that he had just started publishing a periodical called *Khedut Patrika* (Peasant Newsletter),

Yagnik's sense of identity with the kisans was almost literal. 'I would remember the thousands of naked hungry Bhils that I had seen at Meerakhedi. I would imagine their incarnation as one immense, powerful, world-father kisan, and, becoming one with them, I assumed the form of that huge kisan, with my head reaching the sky and my feet going deep down in the soil. In this mood, I would take long strides to my host's place and draw everybody into stories of kisans. In this fashion, turning into a proper kisan, I got ready to work for the kisans'.[33]

True, there was often a seeming convergence between the kisan and the nationalist trope of the popular. Consider how he characterizes the rule of Vanraj Chavda, one of the Hindu rulers of Gujarat. Speaking at a school, he characterized Vanraj Chavda as a *gurjarvir*, or a warrior of Gujarat, rather than simply a king, because he said, despite being a king, Vanraj Chavda had lived with the Bhils; Champa Vaniya (a prominent merchant) had helped him so much that that Vanraj named the fort of Champaner after him; that the Jain *muni* Shilgunisuri (an important priest) had instructed him; that the Bharvad Anhil (head of the powerful Bharvad community) had helped him so much that Anhilwad Patan was named after him. Thus, Yagnik argued, it was through the support of a range of groups that Vanraj Chavda established rule over Gujarat.[34]

But the argument is not that Vanraj is a people's king, that he represents the popular. It is a subtly different one: it insists that there is a distance between the ruled and the king, that the forging of a relationship across this distance cannot be taken for granted. It is after Vanraj forges such a relationship that he becomes a king. Thus, in contrast to the claim to have a history—which constitutes the nation as an already known entity—this account rests on the inadequacy of Vanraj, the absence at the centre of the nation. This absence has to be filled by an engagement with various groups, but the question whether it has been filled can never quite be settled. The presence of kisans and rural people does quite a different work from the imaginary of the popular—by emphasizing the need for active affirmation from marginal groups, it introduces a fundamental instability in the nation. To ally with 'rural people' in this sense was indeed to become an *asthir man na fakir*.

The prominence of figures like Yagnik—and they are legion through the twentieth century—may suggest a need to revisit our usual understandings of Indian politics and nationalism. We have often been misled by the prominence of figures like Bankim, or Nehru for the later period, into presuming the hegemony of a cosmopolitan historical vision. We presume that the mainstream nationalist discourses of history, citizenship, or secularism, with all their exclusions, have been constitutive of the modern Indian state. And it is certainly true that both the Nehruvian Congress and the Bharatiya Janata Party (BJP) have shared the emphasis on having a history, though of course in very different ways. This is also why many of us have sought to criticize these discourses. Through our criticisms, we seek to criticize the modern Indian state, to argue that the historical, the secular, and the citizenly are not simply means of liberation or empowerment but are also forms of domination.

Still, while these discourses are a crucial part of modernity's self-representation, surely it is in the failure of this cosmopolitan vision to hegemonize the polity that an understanding has to be sought for many of the forms of everyday politics in colonial and post-colonial India. Without a fairly restrictive and pre-Foucauldian understanding of the state, it would be difficult to sustain the argument that a Nehru–Patel–Munshi vision—which shared an emphasis, despite differences, on secularism, history, and citizenship—constituted the state. True, it did constitute what could in an unhappy phrase be described as the formal apparatus of the state. But what of those myriad spaces of government—and, even more, of politics—outside that state, where other practices of power, no less modern if less symbolic of the modern, were influential? These practices are what we sometimes describe, suggestively but inadequately, as plebiscitary and populist politics; these forms are what occasion the laments of those like Khilnani who are committed to the historical vision that is more resolutely cosmopolitan. It is in understanding the politics involved here—the politics of the ahistorical, asecular, and acitizenly (neither pre, nor anti)—that figures like Gandhi, Yagnik, and a myriad others who had a troubled and even sometimes antagonistic relationship with mainstream nationalism are of particular significance. Indeed, tracing and accentuating the tension of such politics with the mainstream nationalism that remains dominant is perhaps one of our most pressing tasks as subaltern historians.

But how do we conceptualize this politics—the politics that rejected the logic of transcendence and affirmed instead the ahistorical, asecular, and acitizenly? In his rejection of mainstream nationalism, Yagnik worked his way through the thought and politics of Gandhi, whose own questioning of nationalism was at the time particularly influential in the country. The centrality of ashrams in Gandhi's politics is symptomatic of such questioning. As we know, he stayed more or less continuously in ashram or ashram-like institutions from around 1904—the Phoenix settlement and Tolstoy Farm in South Africa; the Satyagraha Ashram in Ahmedabad from around 1915 to 1931, and Wardha and Sevagram ashrams in later years. Mainstream nationalists such as Nehru were often frustrated by the amount of time Gandhi spent in and on the tiny institution of the ashram—they regarded this as a wasteful eccentricity in a man who was after all the principal leader of the nationalist movement. Gandhi, obviously, did not feel this way. He said of the Satyagraha Ashram that it 'set out to remedy what it thought were defects in our national life'. It was in the ashram that he tried to think about and develop practices for an alternative politics. This politics is most explicitly spelt out in two books which deal with the vows or observances (as he interchangeably translated the Gujarati words *vrat* and *yama*) involved in ashram life. The first book, *Mangal Prabhat* (Tuesday Dawn/Auspicious Dawn, translated into English as *From Yeravada Mandir*) focused on the vows involved in ashram life, heading each chapter after the vow it discussed. The second book, *Satyagraha Ashramno Itihas* (A History of the Satyagraha Ashram, translated into English as *Ashram Observances in Action*), shared many of the same chapter headings, but now dealt more directly with what these vows meant for everyday life in the ashram.[35]

Between them, these approximately eleven vows—the precise number kept changing, but they usually included the vows of Truth, ahimsa or love, celibacy or brahmacharya, control of the palate, poverty, swadeshi, fearlessness, and removal of untouchability—articulated a very precise alternative politics. I have elsewhere explored the politics involved in many of these concepts. Here I limit myself to the vow of swadeshi (lit. of one's own desh, or country), where Gandhi's distance from the logic of transendence is perhaps articulated most forcefully. As we know, swadeshi was a concept which was already in place before Gandhian politics became influential in India—a swadeshi which involved the use only of locally made goods, and the boycott of British goods, was already practised during the 1905 agitation against the Partition of Bengal. Gandhi too repeatedly called for swadeshi, and urged in particular that everybody take a vow to wear only swadeshi clothes (he felt that a swadeshi vow that was inclusive of other items would be too ambitious). But his was a distinctive concept of swadeshi, as different from the earlier swadeshi as his ashram was from those it acknowledged as its precursors. Considering the matter in his characteristically careful fashion, he made the concept of swadeshi an occasion for specifying what was local or native, what foreign, and what universal.

> To use foreign articles rejecting those produced or manufactured in India is to be untrue to India, it is an unwarranted indulgence. To use foreign articles because we do not like indigenous ones is to be a foreigner. It is obvious that we cannot reject indigenous articles even as we cannot reject the native air and the native soil because they are inferior to foreign air and soil.[36]

This invocation of native air and soil may, on a quick reading, seem redolent of that nationalism associated with Herder or Mazzini, which treats the nation as a natural fact constituted by blood, soil, race, and language. Such nationalism has been questioned in our times by the emphasis on an imagined community. Yet, despite rendering as contingent constructions what the former had presented as natural facts, this shift in emphasis operates with the same elements. In contrast, Gandhi's invocation of native air and soil involved a radically different move. Here, the native had nothing to do with a shared culture, history, or political experience. Thus swadeshi never seemed to refer to any finite, clearly mapped boundaries. Rather, swadeshi was that which was insistently local in a way that turned its back on transcendence. 'The purest swadeshi vow will be to use cloth made out of yarn spun by one's wife, sisters, and children in the home.'[37] Addressing a group of women at Nadiad, similarly, Gandhi emphasized that the focus should be on weaving khadi cloth primarily to meet Nadiad's own needs, and then that of surrounding areas.

Swadeshi thus centred around the neighbor or *padosi*—a concept that could not be identified with nation produced by history, culture or the people, a concept that had very clear obligations but no clear boundaries. In 1915, when Gandhi had made swadeshi one of the vows of ashram life, he invoked the logic of neighbourliness to explain swadeshi: 'Man is not omnipotent. He therefore serves the world best by first serving his neighbour. This is Swadeshi, a principle which is broken when one professes to serve those who are more remote in preference to those who are near.'[38]

The neighbor or *padosi* is a crucial concept in Gandhi's writings. Indeed, neighbourliness might be one of the best possible renderings into English of *ahimsa*, one of Gandhi's most important vows. In the English translations of his writings (which Gandhi himself usually supervised or revised, and which he occasionally undertook himself), Gandhi avoided translating *ahimsa* as 'non-violence'; his preferred translation was 'love'. Thus, for instance, the chapter on *ahimsa* in the English versions of *Satyagraha Ashramno Itihas* and *Mangal Prabhat* is titled, 'ahimsa or love'; in the Gujarati version, the title is simply 'ahimsa'. Gandhi's addition of the word love changed the connotations of the English equivalents. *Ahimsa*, when translated simply as non-violence, was quite consonant with the liberal notion of civil society (which is constituted, after all, by the absence of violence—hence its civility); the emphasis on love, rather than the neutrality or negativity of non-violence, foregrounded Gandhi's distance from liberalism. That emphasis on love, of course, has created its own problems (especially because scholarship has been so surprisingly dependent on the English translations of his writings rather than using these along with his Gujarati writings): Gandhi's politics has often been understood as some form of spiritual universalism.

To understand *ahimsa* as neighborliness, instead, entirely avoids this connotation of spiritual universalism, and is in keeping with the spirit of Gandhi's rendering of ahimsa. The concept of the *padosi* or neighbor was a familiar one in Gujarat. Babu Suthar has pointed out that *padosi dharma* (it is possible that when Gandhi used the English phrase 'law of love'—and in most places his Gujarati originals don't seem to have a parallel for this phrase—he was referring to this) is a very common phrase in Gujarat. It has usually referred to the moral principles which guide relationships with neighbours. As a *padosi*, one had certain claims on neighbours—hence the common phrase '*padosi pahelo*' or neighbor first.[39]

I have explored elsewhere how this neighborliness led, for Gandhi, to two ways of relating to the neighbor—friendship and service.[40] For now, suffice to note three implications of this emphasis on neighborliness that are particularly salient to understanding the distance and tension between it and the logic of transcendence. First, there was the question of the relationship to that which was being rejected—the foreign. Because the foreigner too was a neighbor, even if a more distant one, Gandhi insisted on the difference between swadeshi and boycott. A boycott of British goods and cloth would have been 'a purely worldly and political weapon . . . rooted in ill-will and the desire for punishment'. In contrast, swadeshi was 'the natural duty imposed upon every man'.[41] He sought a 'swadeshi in a religious and true spirit without even a suspicion of boycott', a swadeshi in which even the British Viceroy would be able to take part.[42] Put differently, the logic of boycott was that of mainstream nationalism. While it contested that imperialist argument that the interests of the colony had to be subsumed to those of the empire, it did so because of its claim that the Indian nation was the true culmination of the logic of transcendence. As such a culmination, the relationship of the Indian nation to that which was foreign was necessarily one of antagonism: hence the possibility of a boycott. Because Gandhi's 'native' was constituted by a neighbourliness rather than transcendence, it did not have this relationship of antagonism with that which lay outside it. Thus, the vow of swadeshi did not seek, necessarily, to end British rule, but rather to transform it: if this was followed, 'even British rule will cease to be foreign rule and will become swadeshi rule'.[43]

Second, there was Gandhi's rendering of the universal. In 1930, revisiting the question of swadeshi as an ashram vow again, he again opposed this principle of serving one's immediate neighbour to that of serving the world in more general terms.

. . . a man who allows himself to be lured by 'the distant scene' and runs to the ends of the earth is not only foiled in his ambition but also fails in his duty towards his neighbours. Take a concrete instance. In the particular place where I live, I have certain persons as my neighbours, some relations and dependeants. Naturally, they all feel, as they have a right to, that they have a claim on me, and look to me for help and support. Suppose now I leave them all at once, and set out to serve people in a distant place. My decision would throw my little world of neighbours and dependants out of gear, while my gratuitous knight errantry would, more likely than not, disturb the atmosphere in the new place. Thus a culpable neglect of my immediate neighbours, and an unintended disservice to the people whom I wish to serve, would be the first fruits of my violation of the principles of Swadeshi.[44]

Running through these arguments is a concern with how neighbourliness allows one to 'serve the world'. But rather than seeing a tension between the two, Gandhi insisted that pure service of the neigbour was also service of the world:

At the Ashram we hold that Swadeshi is a universal law. A man's first duty is to his neighbour. This does not imply hatred for the foreigner or partiality for the fellow-countryman. Our capacity for service has obvious limits. We can serve even our neighbour with some difficulty. If everyone of us duly performed his duty to his neighbour, no one in the world who needed assistance would be left unattended. Therefore one who serves his neighbour serves all the world. To serve one's neighbour is to serve the world. Indeed it is the only way open to us of serving the world.[45]

Indeed, he argued that the 'votary of swadesh' should become indistiguishable from those who live with us through sevice to them. This may make it appear as if there could be exclusion and even sacrifice of the rest. But it is not so. Pure service of our neighbors is also necessarily service of the foreigner. 'As with the individual [from *pind*] so with the universe [*brahmand*].'[46]

Involved here is a radical reworking of the concerns that characterized the logic of transcendence. Like the latter, *swadeshi*, too, claims to provide a 'universal law', But this universal law, one which cannot be arrived at by subsuming the particular under ever higher levels of generality. The concept of the neighbor is constituted by singularity rather than particularity, and it is only through service of this singular that the universal can be reached.[47]

There was also the relationship of *swadeshi* with sovereignty. In mainstream nationalist understanding, to become a nation-state was to become a sovereign community. This sovereignty, in its nationalist form, involved a distinctive relationship with the logic of transcendence. While the logic of transcendence provided the norm by which the nation-state constituted itself, the latter's sovereignty also had to be constituted by the latter's sovereign denial of that very norm. On the one hand, thus, sovereignty over the components of the nation—its various localities—was claimed precisely on the basis of transcending them. And yet, to claim sovereignty was also to break with this logic; it was to insist that there could be no further subsumption, that the nation-state was sovereign. It was this very claim to sovereignty which authorized the nation-state to impose a logic of transcendence on its various localities, and which authorized also the nationalist paradigm of development, where violence was practised against people in the name of the people.

In contrast, neighborliness did not as a concept allow for the sovereign nation-state. Gandhi's hostility to such a state is of course well known. As early as *Hind Swaraj*, he had remarked to his liberal nationalist interlocutor who wanted such a state: '(You) want English rule without the Englishman. You want the tiger's nature, but not the tiger; that is to say, you would make India English. And when it becomes English, it will be called not Hindustan but Englistan. This is not the Swaraj that I want.'[48] For him, especially by and after the mid-1920s, freedom from British rule was sought not in order to establish a post-Independence nation-state to replace the British state, but rather because the British state hindered the pursuit of swaraj, as he feared that even an Indian nation-state committed to 'modern civilization' might. This is the sense in which Gandhi's homelessness was radically different from that conceivable from within a cosmopolitan vision.

As these three implications of *swadeshi* indicate, Gandhi's homelessness was not the cosmopolitan one possible within the terms of the mainstream nationalist problematic; it was outside the very problematic that produced the nationalist home and homelessness. At the same time, the practices of the ashram and of neighborliness produced their own home, but they used a very different set of procedures for thinking of home and homelessness. Indeed, Gandhi was on several occasions to refer to Gujarat and India as his home, and in doing so he was deploying the politics of neighborliness to constitute the home. For him, to make a place a home was to be neighborly; any other way of claiming a home was to create Englistan.

This home had its own discipline, just as the nationalist home had a discipline where the particular was subordinated to the general (and it is this discipline which authorizes development as a nationalist project).[49] The ashram was the principal site for this discipline that produced neighborliness. It is because of the centrality of discipline in creating the nation as a neighborly home that Gandhi was never quite able to describe swaraj (self-rule) as a birthright or any sort of right; he famously insisted, as we know, on the duties and restraint involved in swaraj. Indeed, as early as 1908, he insisted on the centrality of neighborliness in the making of the nation: arguing that America, France or England did not have 'real swarajya', which was enjoyed only by the man who 'does his duty' to his family, 'his servant, and his neighbour'. This swarajya was independent of and even prior to the creation of an autonomous nation state. 'Such a man will enjoy swarajya wherever he may happen to live'.[50]

Of course, as with the logic of transcendence, the neighbor too needed to be transformed; despite his celebration of villages, he remarked that they needed to 'shed their laziness and make a corporate effort to live'.[51] But unlike the discipline involved in development, discipline involved in bringing about this transformation was directed entirely at the self. This was so not in the severe nationalist sense familiar to us from the celibacy of the RSS, where self-discipline authorized the disciplining of the neighbour. In Gandhi's argument, nothing could authorize the direct disciplining of the neighbour. Rather, it was through a discipline of the self that a non-coercive dialogue with the neighbour could begin. Thus, while he described 'the Bhils, the Pindaris, the Assamese, and the Thugs' as 'jungli', he insisted that they are 'our own countrymen' and that effort had to be made to 'win them over'.[52] Here, then, the tribes and villagers in Gandhian discipline were not converted into backward groups requiring that historicist staple—development; and there was no conceptual space for Vallabhbhai's tearful subsumption of the peasants within the nation's long-term interests. It was in principle (though a principle more often observed in the breach in the various ashrams set up amongst such groups by Gandhi's followers), a mutual conversation, one in which the interlocutor could also transform the Gandhian. Gandhi's support for figures like Nehru or Patel is best understood in these terms: neither as a contradiction that reveals the true class character of his politics nor as an anomaly that should be ignored, but rather as an attempt to transform the dominant logic of transcendence through the practice of neighborliness, to supplement the nationalist home with the neighborly home.

The discipline that produced neighborliness also created its own homelessness. 'Ashram here means a community living religiously together. . . . As soon as I set up house, my home was like an ashram in two senses, for *grahasth-ashram* is not about pleasure (*bhog*) but duty (*dharma*), and. . . .'[53] Because neighborliness itself was constituted by duty, there was no place in it for the kind of attachment and immediate personal ties that usually constituted home. This was the sense in which true neighborliness was also simultaneously about a homelessness. Gandhi admired this kind of homelessness. Clarifying a misunderstanding once, he wrote: 'I paid you a compliment by summing up your life as of a homeless wanderer. I connected you with *aniketa* (the state of being without a home) of the *Gita* and envied you. Your home was nowhere and everywhere. How could you mistake all this for a reflection on you. It shows what a sorry thing foreign speech is.'[54] The practice of this kind of *aniketa* led, strikingly, to the *niketan*. For many early twentieth-century Indian thinkers, the niketan was the home constituted by the practice of spiritual disicipline: thus Shantiniketan and

Anandniketan amongst others. But the spiritual discipline of the niketan was often identified with the logic of transcendence (as with the Arya Samaji ashrams), and what Gandhi attempted was to constitute the niketan instead through a politics of neighborliness. A different home and homelessness, then, existed together within the politics of neighborliness.

Yagnik's homelessness was produced by engagement with Gandhi's politics of neighborliness. He was, of course, a close associate of Gandhi. He had been associated with Gandhi almost since the latter's arrival in Gujarat from South Africa. Indeed, the Gujarati weekly, *Navjivan*, had been initially started by Yagnik in 1915 quite independently of Gandhi. Later, on Gandhi's request, the weekly was effectively turned over to him, with Yagnik carrying out most of the editorial work in the early years. Yagnik was also in Yeravada jail with Gandhi; during this time, he took extensive dictation from Gandhi.

In the early years, when a staunch follower of Gandhi, he had played a crucial role in setting up ashrams in Panchmahals and Kheda. When he set-up an ashram for untouchables in Panchmahals, he secured a building away from their locality, 'for only then could we impart sound cultural influences to their children'. Working with the Bariya-Kshatriya community of the region, he remarked that they had been given a bad name and harassed on charges of drinking and theft. It was not enough to provide them with the spinning wheel, and with ideas of prohibition; there was rather a need to 'colour them with new cultural influences like other backward communities'.[55] Yagnik's early ashrams thus performed tasks quite congruent with those that Gandhi emphasized: they provided discipline, especially important in the context their attempt to reform Bhils and untouchables *kelavni*. It is symptomatic of Yagnik's closeness to the Gandhian paradigm that he was to write, while imprisoned in Yeravada, that if nothing else in the world suited him, then he would go to the Mirakhedi Bhil Ashram, which would always welcome the 'homeless traveller' and spread his mattress there.[56]

By the 1940s, however, when Yagnik set-up his ashram at Nenpur near Mehemedabad, just a short train ride away from Ahmedabad (this is the ashram most closely associated with him), it was quite unlike the Gandhian ashram. Though he remained single, the conventional Gandhian emphasis on discipline disappeared. There was *kelavni* here too, not only through schools, but also training for agriculture. Nevertheless, the position that it occupied was different. The emphasis was less on how this *kelavni* would transform the 'harijans' as on the confrontations that this created with the ashram's neighbors—upper-caste orthodox Hindus. On learning that not only were there harijans at the ashram, but that they ate and drank with other village students, Bansiwala Maharaj, the powerful upper-caste religious leader in the area who had permitted him to use land for the ashram, led a large procession of villagers to the ashram, and demanded that they vacate the spot immediately. Yagnik consented by moving to another site, but threatened legal steps. Indeed, the tensions between the upper castes and the ashram remained high, with Yagnik making few conciliatory moves. Yagnik's actions in this case were early indicators of the growing transformation of his ashram into primarily a locus for the organization of peasants and workers.

Involved here was not only a rejection of the logic of transcendence (to organize peasants and workers for a radical politics was effectively, after all, to question the independent Indian nation-state that was constituted by this logic) but also, more interestingly, a questioning and radicalization of Gandhi's politics of neighborliness. Two lines of questioning are particularly salient here. Gandhi's emphasis on service and love of the neighbor was not attentive to the political relations that constituted the neighbour. True, one of the vows of the ashram was for the removal of untouchability, and Gandhi campaigned ceaselessly for it. Similarly, Gandhi sought to serve the *daridranarayan*, as we saw Yagnik reminding Congress members. But neighborliness as a form of love did not systematically take account of such matters. In this sense, there was a serious tension and even perhaps contradiction between the Gandhian vow for the removal of untouchability—which broached the question of the marginal—and that of *swadeshi*. The agonized playing out of this tension in Gandhi's writings and politics is so complex that it needs to be addressed separately rather than in passing here. For now, suffice to note the first question that Yagnik's politics effectively posed: what when the neighbor to be loved and served was constituted not only by singularity but by singularity *and* marginality?

Even in his early days, Yagnik had been skeptical of the Gandhian deployment of the concept of neighborliness.

> I had written to Thakkarbapa even from jail that if nothing would suit me in the world, finally, I would spread my mattress in the Bhil ashram of Meerakhedi. Still, within a short while of going to such places and seeing the oppression by government departments of the poor peasants, a fire would flare within me, and I would become impatient to fight it and awaken the peasants. But usually in such ashrams, there was a tradition of keeping one's head down and looking after the needs of students, concentrating only on education, without confronting the government. This I could not accept. Without some vision about the future of the entire peasant community, without doing some daily activity, I could not be part of such an institution.[57]

The love involved in neighborliness, in other words, did not seem to deal seriously enough with the antagonisms constituted the everyday lives of marginal groups.

This reservation about the love involved in Gandhi's neighborliness was one that Yagnik returned to repeatedly. When Gandhi was upset in early 1920s about the violence in the national level satyagraha movement, Yagnik insisted that love was not the criterion by which to judge 'ordinary people'; their anger should be regarded as natural and just.[58] Later, he wrote an article attacking Gandhi's focus on love, partly on the grounds the latter did not allow for a scientific world-view. Nevertheless, Yagnik's politics (always far more sophisticated than his analyses and writings) through most of this period drew heavily on the trope of love. And this was a particular kind of love—love for the 'ordinary people', where ordinariness signaled marginality. To love ordinary people in this sense, however, turned out, in Yagnik's politics, to be forcefully confrontational of other neighbours. This unresolvable antinomy between the politics of neighbourliness and marginality may perhaps also help us understand the profound irresoluteness of Yagnik's politics.

Yagnik had been critical of the ashram's self-discipline from quite early on. After 1918, as the editor of *Navjivan*, he used to go to Sabarmati Ashram regularly to have proofs corrected, and sometimes stayed overnight. But the daily routine of the ashram chafed on him—his taste for reading late at night could not be fulfilled since the family with whom he stayed got up at 4.00 a.m. Also, he was in the habit of drinking several cups of tea in the morning, and this was not possible. Finally, he gave up and stayed in the city overnight, cycling over to meet Gandhi in the morning.[59] Some of this irritation surely came from a sense that such discipline was irrelevant to the task of securing independence.

But in its more interesting moments (and I do not wish to claim that these moments were dominant in his politics), the question that was involved in Yagnik's irritation was also this: what when the emphasis on loving the neighbor blurred the distinction between the self and the neighbor, not in the transcendent sense where the self subsumed the neighbor, but rather in the sense that the self itself becomes fragmented or suffused by the neighbor? (In its simultaneous emphasis on affinity and difference, Gandhi's concept of the neighbor covered, in a strikingly different manner, some of the same territory as that covered in European philosophical thought by the concept of the other.) Again, the possibility for this question was created by Gandhi's politics of neighborliness, but his emphasis on self-discipline defused many of its radical implications. Two implications of the austerities of self-discipline are particularly relevant to us here. First, these austerities were meant to make possible conversation with the *daridranarayan*—the neighbor who was most common in India—by becoming more like the *daridranararayan* to be served. Second, and this has not yet been emphasized enough in this paper, the austerities were also meant to create a physical space for the neighbor—and here the neighbor included all living things—by reducing wants. Thus Gandhi insisted: 'If I save the food I eat or the clothes I wear or the space I occupy, these can clearly be used by those poor whose need is greater than mine. Since my selfishness prevents him from using these things, my pleasure (*bhog*) involves violence to my poorer neighbor. When I eat cereals and vegetables in order to support life, that means violence done to vegetable life.'[60] Some violence was thus unavoidable for the sustenance of human life, but by reducing it one created more space for others, Gandhi insisted.

Nevertheless, this communication and space was produced by insisting on the integrity of the self; it was this integrity which made self-discipline possible. In contrast, though Yagnik's politics sought the same conversation, the intensity of his engagement with the kisan often (though obviously not always, as his involvement with the Mahagujarat agitation indicates) rendered uncertain the distinction between him and the kisan. In this sense, self-discipline as a way of communicating with the neighbor became less important. And yet, not quite. For, once again, this tension between self-discipline and a love for the neighbour that went so far as to render uncertain the distinction from the neighbor was an antinomic one. Self-discipline was important, within the politics of neighborliness, for creating, if nothing else, the physical space for neighbor. To reject self-discipline without rejecting the politics of neighborliness: this was the concern that drove Yagnik's politics in its most interesting moments. It was a concern that he never quite managed to address adequately, and the consequent constant shuttling between self-discipline and its rejection was yet another irresoluteness that marked Yagnik's politics.

Yagnik's questioning of self-discipline, despite its almost necessary irresoluteness, had one distinct consequence. It was self-discipline that constituted both home and homelessness within the politics of neighborliness; to reject self-discipline was to refuse the ashram as a home as well as to refuse the detatchment of aniketa as homelessness. In this sense, Yagnik's homelessness was not only outside the nationalist problematic (as was Gandhi's); it was also almost inconceivable within the problematic of the politics of neighborliness.

Homeless in the nation and homeless in the ashram: why did this homelessness not lead to an affirmation of the figure of the subaltern and the marginal as a home—to a home, say, in an affirmation of the *daridranarayan*, or of kisan or *khedut* lifestyles? Such a home, we know, is claimed by many forms of radical political romanticism; it is the desire for and claim to such a home that has produced some of the most thought-provoking of our radical ethnographies and histories. Yet, Yagnik never quite claimed such a home. He was heavily involved with the everyday lives of the peasants, and the *Atmakatha* does provide accounts of these struggles. Even so, there is little that is written about the kisans' everyday lives, save in the context of the oppression they faced.

We would certainly not be incorrect in treating this as a symptom of nationalist or Gandhian affiliations: perhaps Yagnik claimed no home amongst them because of his distance from them, because he was not interested in them save as objects to be reformed and awakened. But in his more interesting moments at least, his homelessness amongst the kisans pursued a politics that sought to both reject the logic of transcendence, and to dramatically radicalize the politics of neighborliness. Perhaps Yagnik suspected (like many others involved in radical politics, including his associate Swami Sahajanand) that the marginal and the subaltern could not ever be a home, that marginality and subalternity involved a homelessness that yearned for a home. To produce an ethnography or history of everyday subaltern lives, to claim that such history and ethnography constituted their homes, and to claim residence in these homes: such acts would have been to be more faithful to history and ethnography than to the marginality of the subaltern. Barred by his politics from claiming a home, Yagnik became homeless. By being carefully attentive to the modalities and registers of such homelessness, perhaps we can engage more seriously with the subaltern politics that we have often failed to even recognize in our midst.

NOTES

1. *Atmakatha*, vol. 1, 'Jivanvikas', Ahmedabad: Ravani Prakashan Grha, 1955, p. 8. I thank Babu Suthar for suggesting how this complex formulation should be translated.
2. *Atmakatha*, vol. 3, 'Karavas', Mehemedabad: Vatrak Khedut Vidyalaya, 1956, p. 263.
3. *Atmakatha*, vol. 3, p. 265.

4. *Atmakatha*, vol. 1, p. 179.
5. *Atmakatha*, vol. 3. Both here and in other extended quotations, I have depended greatly on the 1986 typescript translation of Yagnik's *Atmakatha* by Devavrat Pathak, Howard Spodek, and John R. Wood, deposited at the University of Pennsylvania Library.
6. Dhanvant Oza, ed., *Atmakatha*, vol. 6, *Chhela Vehan*, Ahmedabad: Ravani Prakashan Grha, 1973, p. 18-19.
7. Jawaharlal Nehru, *The Discovery of India*, Delhi: Oxford University Press, 1981, p. 60.
8. Benedict Anderson, *Imagined Communities: Reflections on the Origins and Spread of Nationalism*, revised and extended, London: Verso, 1991, see pp. 22-36.
9. Munshi and Yagnik were fairly close in the 1910s, and even founded and ran a journal, *Navjivan ane Satya* (New Life and Truth) together. There was almost a contrapuntal element to the ways their personal and political careers intertwined and diverged. Munshi was a key figure in the nationalist movement, though far more part of the mainstream. Like Yagnik, he had trained to be a lawyer, but unlike Yagnik, he was extremely successful. Both were deeply committed to the idea of companionate marriages, and regarded themselves as confined in their initial years to traditional marriages that did not meet their ideals. The wives of both died in the twenties; Munshi then married Leelavatiben, a reformist widow from Ahmedabad. Yagnik remained single. In the 1930s, as Yagnik, having left the Congress, was getting more deeply involved in kisan and trade union activities, Munshi joined the Congress government in Bombay. As Home Minister, he was in the forefront of efforts to put down strikes by trade unionists. In the 1940s, Munshi went on to be a key assistant to Sardar Vallabhbhai Patel, and directed the 'police' operations that led to Hyderabad becoming part of the Indian state despite the Nizam's opposition; around this time, Yagnik was involved in organizing the peasants of the princely states against landlords. In the years immediately after Independence, Munshi went on to become the Food Minister in the central government, and to play a key role in ensuring that Hindi was the official Indian language; Yagnik languished in his ashram, fretting at his political irrelevance. When the movement for a separate state of Gujarat started, Munshi remained aloof; Yagnik, in contrast, was the principal leader of the Mahagujarat agitation.
10. Jayana Sheth, *Munshi: Self-sculptor*, Bombay: Bharatiya Vidya Bhavan, 1979, p. 33f.

11. K.M. Munshi, *Gujarat no Nath*, Ahmedabad: Gurjar, 1952 (1917). The novel was part of a trilogy which focused on the rule of the twelfth century Gujarati king Jaysimha Solanki. The first volume in the trilogy, *Patanni Prabhuta*, Ahmedabad: Gurjar, 1991, (1916) is set in the time when Jaysimha was still very young; in *Gujarat no Nath* , Jaysimha is beginning to assert himself; and in *Rajdhiraj*, Ahmedabad: Gurjar, 1981 (1922), Jaysimha is near the height of his powers. In the quotations from the text that follow below, I depend on the translation by N.D. Jotwani of K.M. Munshi, *The Master of Gujarat: A Historical Novel*, Bombay: Bharatiya Vidya Bhavan, 1995.
12. *Master of Gujarat*, p. 496.
13. Ibid., p. 81.
14. Ibid., p. 153.
15. Ibid., p. 204.
16. For some of Munshi's remarks on history, see his *Sparks from a Governor's Anvil*, Lucknow: Publications Bureau, Information Directorate, 1956, pp. 519-26; also V.B. Kulkarni, *K.M. Munshi*, New Delhi: Publications Division, Ministry of Information and Broadcasting, 1983, p. 261.
17. Narmadshankar Dave, *Narmagadhya*, Baroda 1975 (1874). This is a collection of a series of essays by Narmad written between the 1850s and 1870s.
18. Sunil Khilnani, *The Idea of India*, New York: Penguin, 1997, p. 41.
19. *Atmakatha*, vol. 2, 'Gujaratma Navjivan', Gurjar Granthratnak Karyalaya, 1970 (1955), p. 140.
20. *Atmakatha*, vol. 6. Yagnik died in 1971, at which time he was still writing the sixth volume, and had reached only as far as the Mahagujarat movement. The volume is thus incomplete. The writer Dhanvant Oza, who prepared the volume for publication, has included in it a selection of Yagnik's writings from later years in order to indicate the range of issues that Yagnik was involved with.
21. The remarks in this paragraph and the next are based on the *Atmakatha*, vol. 6; and also on Brahmakumar Bhatt, *Le ke rahenge Mahagujarat*, Ahmedabad 1994.
22. Yagnik discusses developments in the Dangs in *Atmakatha*, vol. 5, 'Kisankatha', Ahmedabad: Gurjar Granthratnak Karyalaya, 1971, pp. 346-8, 462-5, and 478-9.
23. *Atmakatha*, vol. 1, pp. 7-13.
24. See for instance his discussion of the marriage between Mansukhlal

Master and Taraben Master in *Atmakatha*, vol. 1, p. 139f. Hansaben Mehta, Leelavati Munshi, Premleela Khandvala, Sharadaben Mehta, amongst others, are presented in his *Atmakatha* as other women capable of companionate marriage. See especially vol.6, chapter 9.

25. Yagnik discusses his marriage at length in *Atmakatha*, vol. 2, chapter 13, partially in response to those who had criticized the first volume for not saying much about it. 'Why did a sincere worshipper of women like me commit this sinful deed?' Once he had married, he 'had no right to refuse it (the marriage) unilaterally', he should at least have given her a place in heart as lifetime companion. 'This ... analysis is not my defence but a confession of my mistake, my secret sin. I hope the reader will accept it as such'.
26. *Atmakatha*, vol. 3, p. 265. It is a different matter that Yagnik may not actually have been literally celibate. According to David Hardiman, 'In Ahmedabad, it is often said that Indulal was distrusted because he committed the two greatest of sins for a 'Gujarati' (read: for a person having to operate within a Gujarati *baniya* culture), namely he was sexually loose (there were numerous rumours about his dallyings with the wives of prominent men) and also could not be trusted with money (he 'squandered' it, did not keep careful accounts). He lacked that careful, calculating and moralistic approach to institution building which was so conspicuous a feature of the nationalist movement in Gujarat' (personal communication, 14 July 1999). Certainly, the allusions in his *Atmakatha* must have contributed to these rumours.
27. *Atmakatha*, vol. 1, p. 130.
28. *Atmakatha*, vol 3, p. 14. Yagnik's earlier efforts at helping advasis, and the tensions that these caused with Vallabhbhai, are the subject of *Atmakatha*, vol. 2, chapter 12.
29. *Atmakatha*, vol. 3, p. 21.
30. *Atmakatha*, vol. 3, p. 25.
31. *Atmakatha*, vol. 3, p. 26.
32. The tension between these two very different renderings of the popular is particularly forceful in the writings of Swami Sahajanand, a figure with whom Yagnik was closely allied. See, for instance, his *Mera Jivan Sangharsh* (*My Life Struggle*), published by Sitaramashram at Bihta in Patna district in 1952, two years after the Swami's death. Walter Hauser is at present completing an edited translation of *Mera Jivan* (forthcoming, New Delhi). See also Hauser's 'Swami Sahajanand and the Politics of Social Reform, 1907-1950', *Indian Historical Review*, vol. 18, nos. 1-2, July 1991

and January 1992, pp. 59-75. Yagnik was a great admirer of Sahajanand, and dedicated the fifth volume of his *Atmakatha* to the Swami. The dedication described the 'danda swami' as a fighter against zamindari, and as a figure who had lavished unparalleled *prem* or love on the kisans or peasants. Yagnik and Sahajanand were key figures setting up of the All India Kisan Sabha, the premier organization that lead peasant struggles through the thirties and forties.

33. *Atmakatha*, vol. 5, p. 43.
34. *Atmakatha*, vol. 5. p. 13.
35. For arguments regarding the ashram, see Ajay Skaria, 'Gandhi's Politics: Liberalism and the Question of the Ashram', *South Atlantic Quarterly*, vol. 101, no. 4, fall 2002, pp. 955-986; and Alon Confino and Ajay Skaria, 'The Local Life of Nationhood', *National Identities*, vol. 4, no. 1, 2002, pp. 7-24.
36. *Collected Works of Mahatma Gandhi* (henceforth *CWMG*), Publications Division, Government of India, vol. 18, p. 43; 'The swadeshi vow', *Young India*, 17 May 1919.
37. *CWMG*, vol. 18, p.117, Gujarati, 22 June 1919.
38. 14 June 1928, *CWMG*, vol. 42, p. 109.
39. Personal communication Babu Suthar, July 2001.
40. For a more extended discussion of these two modalities of neighborliness, and of Gandhi's practices of translation between Gujarati and English, see my 'Gandhi's Politics'.
41. *CWMG*, vol. 17, p. 396, 'The Swadeshi vow-I', *Bombay Chronicle*, 17 April 1919.
42. 'The Duty of Satyagrahis', *Young India*, 9 July 1919, *CWMG*, vol. 18, p. 184f.
43. 'Speech on Swadeshi', Gujarati, 22 June 1919, *CWMG*, vol. 18, p. 116.
44. From *Yeravda Mandir*, Ahmedabad: Navjivan, 1932, p. 62f.
45. 'Satyagrahaashramno itihas', *Akshardeha*, vol. 50, p. 213; *CWMG*, vol. 56, p. 172.
46. 'Swadeshi vrat', *Navjivan*, 31 May 1931; *Akshardeha*, vol. 46, p. 266; vol. 52, p. 209: 'The Law of Swadeshi'; *Young India*, 18 June 1931 (translation modified).
47. I thank Qadri Ismail for pointing out to me the importance and stakes of this question of singularity.
48. *CWMG*, vol. 10, p. 255.
49. Ajay Skaria, 'Development, Nationalism, and the Time of the Primitive,' in K. Sivaramakrishnan and Arun Agrawal, eds.,

Regional Modernities: The Cultural Politics of Development in South Asia, Oxford: Oxford University Press, 2003.

50. *CWMG*, vol. 8, p. 458, 'Sarvodaya-IX', *Indian Opinion*, 18 July 1908.
51. *CWMG*, vol. 66, p. 29, letter to Sahebji Maharaj.
52. M.K. Gandhi, *Hind Swaraj and Other Writings*, ed., Antony Parel, Cambridge: Cambridge University Press, 1997, p. 45.
53. 'Satyagrahaashramno itihas', *Akshardeha*, vol. 50, p. 186; *CWMG*, vol. 56, p. 142, translation modified.
54. *CWMG*, vol. 85, p 35, Letter to A.N. Sharma, 12 October 1944.
55. The work done in these ashrams is described at length in *Atmakatha*, vol. 3, chapter 1.
56. Letter from Indulal Yagnik to Amritlal Thakkar, published in *Navjivan*, 4 November 1923; reproduced in *Atmakatha*, vol. 3, pp. 346-51; see also p. 317.
57. *Atmakatha*, vol. 3, p. 317.
58. *Atmakatha*, vol. 2, chap. 7.
59. For an account, see *Atmakatha*, vol. 2, chap. 9.
60. *CWMG*, vol. 56, p 160, 'A History of the Satyagraha Ashram', translation modified.

PART IV

Into the Present: Social and Political Development in Bihar and Beyond

Competing Inequalities: The Scheduled Tribes and the Reservations System in Jharkhand*

Stuart Corbridge

This paper discusses the economic and political consequences of reserving government and public-sector jobs for members of the Scheduled Tribes in Bihar. It also contributes to a more general debate on the system of compensatory discrimination that has existed in India since the 1940s, and which was made tangible for middle-class Indians by the decision of the government of V.P. Singh (1989-90) to adopt some of the recommendations of the Second Backward Classes Commission (1979-80: chairman B.P. Mandal). The Mandal Commission report advised that a system of reserved jobs in central government could usefully be extended from the Scheduled Castes and Tribes of India (roughly 15 and 7.5 per cent of the population, respectively) to embrace a broader collection of Socially and Economically Backward Classes.[1] In August 1990 V.P. Singh found it expedient to act upon Mandal's suggestion that up to 49.5 per cent of all jobs in central government services and public undertakings should be reserved for the Scheduled Castes (SCs), Scheduled Tribes (STs), and Other Backward Classes (OBCs).[2] In 1989 Singh's Janata Dal party had gained votes disproportionately from the 3,743 castes, tribes or communities (52.4 per cent of the Indian population) that the Mandal Commission Report identified as Backward.[3]

* This essay was previously published in the *Journal of Asian Studies*, 59, 1 (2000), and is reproduced here with permission.

The fury unleashed by various high-caste communities in the wake of V.P. Singh's decision was predictable. Public-sector jobs in India are much sought after and are regarded by many high-caste men, and some women, as a bulwark against the uncertainties that can be induced by economic 'development'. Public-sector steel plants, for example, have long provided their workers with dearness allowances, sick pay, and guaranteed holidays in addition to quite reasonable wages.[4] As one respondent told the anthropologist Jonathan Parry when he has working at Bhilai steel plant in Madhya Pradesh, there was 'no mother or father like it'.[5] Much the same can be said of India's banks, which were nationalized by Indira Gandhi in 1971. The proposals of Mandal and V.P. Singh threatened high-caste Indians with increased competition for jobs and university places, and this competition came from communities more powerful than the Scheduled Castes or Tribes. Violent responses were par for the course.

But what of the initial reservations system and its supposed beneficiaries? What lessons can we learn from a study of its functioning, both in terms of the workings of local labour markets and the formation of political attitudes? We need to ask if the reservations system empowered members of the scheduled communities in terms of livelihood strategies or access to government agencies, and if this can be linked to the formation of political groupings that seek to further the interests of particular scheduled communities. Kanchan Chandra argues that the rise of the Bahujan Samaj Party (BSP) in Punjab and Uttar Pradesh is linked to the emergence of a class of government officers drawn from the ranks of the Scheduled Castes. Affirmative action has helped to pave the way to political empowerment. This paper offers a further perspective on present concerns by reviewing the system of compensatory discrimination as it has applied to the Scheduled Tribes.

The paper takes shape along three axes. The core is an empirical study of the system of reserved jobs (and to a lesser extent that of educational support) that has operated on behalf of ST communities in south Bihar. This study is linked to an account of the changing position of tribal communities in independent India. The Government of India maintains that tribal society is egalitarian and undifferentiated. It offers compensatory discrimination to STs on this basis. I dispute this view. I critique the ideology of tribal economy and society upon which this suggestion rests, and consider how and why the formation of a tribal middle class has been encouraged (but not initiated) by the reservations system. A third strand of the paper reflects more generally on accounts of development and anti-development in India, particularly as these apply to tribal communities. Although I dispute static and stereotypical accounts of 'tribalness' in India, I do not accept that the category of tribe is entirely fictive or a simple by-product of official categories. Nor do I accept that state-sponsored development in India has worked entirely or exclusively to the disadvantage of tribal households. The evidence from Bihar suggests that many poor tribals have accessed jobs in the public sector and have garnered cultural capital on that basis. In addition, it seems clear that the reservations system in Bihar has served as an important site for the production of a tribal elite or petty bourgeoisie.

The paper is organized as follows. The first section is concerned with what Marc Galanter has described as a system of 'competing equalities',[6] or what we might describe, following Foucault, as attempts by the state to create a new class of 'modern (ex)-Backwards' by virtue of economic and legal interventions apparently designed to reposition India's troublesome 'marginal' groups (SCs and STs). It sets the scene for the empirical analysis that follows. I also comment on work by Ronald Inden which suggests that the normalizing voice in 'modern India' is a unitary voice, and damaging to many of India's marginal communities as a result.[7] The third strand of the paper can be read as a critical engagement with Inden's work.

The next section of the paper mines a more empirical vein. On the basis of fieldwork data collected through the 1980s and 1990s in tribal South Bihar (the Bihar Jharkhand), I seek to answer two sets of questions. First, what evidence is there to suggest that a system of reservations of government and public-sector jobs has worked to the advantage of Scheduled Tribe households? If such an advantage has been secured, to whom has it accrued and by what means? Have the benefits of a reservations system been monopolized by particular groups within the ST community? If so, what implications might this hold for the category 'ST' and the state's ideology of an undifferentiated tribal economy and society? Second, what, if any, are the political consequences of the reservations system, in terms of 'tribal' political identities, aspirations, and activities? Is it the case, as Crispin Bates has argued recently,[8] and much in line with Inden, that India's so-called original or *adivasi* (ST) populations were invented by such acts of classification/reservation, and that this has harmed those communities called into existence as supplicants of the state?

In my conclusion I suggest that the reservations system in Bihar has been captured in part by well-to-do tribals, the vast majority of whom are male and many of whom now reside in urban areas. But this is not because of the reservations system itself. The reservations system has not brought a tribal middle class into existence; rather it has been captured by a tribal elite, the existence of which the framers of the Constitution chose not to acknowledge. This elite is building its stock of cultural (or social) capital in and through its efforts to access (funded) places in state educational institution.[9] A tribal elite is also using its success in the educational arena to access positions of (relative) economic and political power in Jharkhand.

It is not only members of a pre-existing tribal elite who are using state patronage for their own ends, nor are these 'ends' entirely private. The reservations system has served to expand the size of the tribal middle class, particularly where jobs are linked to educational qualifications rather than social background. It has also forced government officers to pay more than just lip-service to the idea of compensatory discrimination by instituting, for example, roster systems of job advertisement and allocation such that each service job has a serial number and an indication of whether it is reserved for a particular community.[10] The reservations system has even helped to crystallize a conception of *adivasi* identity that recognizes the exploitation and marginalization of many tribal communities, and which demands compensation from the authorities. To the extent that this identity can be mobilized by advocates of a separate

Jharkhand State, it may yet be that compensatory discrimination will have positive, if unintended, effects upon the broader target population of STs. The sting in the tail is that these positive effects depend upon the ST populations of the Jharkhand refusing various programmes of political and cultural 'normalization' proposed on their behalf by the framers of the Constitution. Their strength lies in exploiting the politics of difference/protection, not the politics of homogeneity or inclusion.

'NORMALIZING' THE 'OTHER'

The Constitution of 1950 and India's Scheduled Communities

In a perceptive recent paper, Ronald Inden has argued that the discourse of nation-building that India committed itself to in the 1950s was a discourse of high modernism which failed to register its similarities to earlier conceptions of imperial progress and religious procession.[11] Inden takes up a common observation about India's commitment to 'development' after Independence and carefully subverts it. Inden agrees that a key to understanding post-Independence India is the idea (or imperative) of modernization. India in the 1950s sought to invent itself anew as the opposite of the society that had been pushed towards famine and Partition/parturition ten years earlier. Strength would be found in the founding myths of socialism, secularism, federalism, and democracy.[12] India would throw off the shackles of tradition and imperialism and would embrace reason and the agencies of modernization (including industrialization, education, time discipline, urbanization, and family planning).

All this is well known. But Inden subverts this account by insisting that Reason and Planning have taken the place of Religion and Imperial Progress in the 'new India' only to end up imitating them. He contends that development in modern India has been established by courtesy of a concept of reason—embodied in planning, the Planning Commission, and in Nehru himself—that is every bit as transcendental as the religious progresses that endowed the medieval king of kings with the 'luminous will' of Vishnu.[13] In each case, *particular* pilgrimages or progresses (or small-scale developments) are sublimated into a grander idea of Progress or Modernity, a grander idea that turns its back on the lives and wishes of a majority of Indians who are expected to heed their master's voice and respond dutifully.

The conclusion that Inden draws from all this is a controversial one, and one that I share only in part. The luminous will that stands behind Inden is Foucault, and Inden shares (the early) Foucault's taste for seeing power as damaging rather than as disabling-and-enabling. Inden wants to celebrate the voices of those he believes to have been damaged by India's imperious march towards Development. He wants to resist the idea that development as represented by large dams and heavy industrialization is development in a deeper sense. For Inden, as for Escobar,[14] it is a sham development that should be and is resisted by the less transcendent processions of the poor and marginalized; by *gheraos* or blockades, by *andolans* (protest movements) like Chipko, and even by Hindu nationalism (a political project that refuses the myth of secularism.[15]

But there are problems with this view. Even as Inden highlights one set of contradictions in the discourse of modernization, he fails to notice another.[16]

Inden chooses not to acknowledge that many of India's 'marginal' groups, its Scheduled Castes and Tribes, might welcome some aspects of the new order of Development and the jobs and education it brings with it; he chooses not to see that development with a capital D can be reshaped and reclaimed by 'marginal Other' groups without ditching the idea in its entirety or the claims that can be made on the state in its name. Inden is also inattentive to the contradictions that he himself highlights in the state's attitude towards dissenting voices. It is true that 'political leaders have policed, banned, patrolled, regulated, monitored and marginalized processions as best they can',[17] but so also has the state had to 'tolerate them and even appropriate them',[18] as it did with the Chipko *andolan*. In sum, the discourse of modernization that Inden rightly spotlights was always more fractured than he later suggests. Nowhere was this more true than in the state's debate with itself, and with some concerned community leaders, over integration and isolation as two possible means of dealing with India's Scheduled populations after Independence.

The Constitution of India was framed after a four-year period of debate by various groups involved in the making of a modern India. The Constituent Assembly debates of 1946–9 give a remarkable insight into the founding of a post-colonial polity, as indeed does the Constitution proposed for adoption by the Assembly on 'this twenty-sixth day of November, 1949'. The Fundamental Rights of the Constitution commit India to a Western model of societal relations, whereby a sovereign democratic republic resolves to secure for all its citizens Justice, Liberty, Equality, and Fraternity.[19] Article 15 maintains that 'The State shall not discriminate against any citizen on grounds only of religion, race, caste, sex, place of birth or any of them.' New Indian bodies will be produced that are not scarred by the primordial markings of caste and communalism. Education and the law will see to it. Untouchability, indeed, is 'abolished and its practice in any form is forbidden'. In addition to these Fundamental Rights, the makers of modern India provided various nonjusticiable Directive Principles of State Policy which cut against the grain of equal treatment for all by the state. The Directive Principles embody a Fabian conception of the state as redeemer/provider. Economic and social groups unable to look after themselves, or which might be thought to suffer from residual forms of exploitation/discrimination as the old India withers away, should qualify for active state support/protection for a limited period.

The five key Articles of the Constitution embodying this view are:

Article 46: The State shall promote with special care the educational and economic interests of the weaker sections of the people, and, in particular, of the Scheduled Castes and Scheduled Tribes, and shall protect them from social injustice and all forms of exploitation.

Articles 330, 332, 334: Provision of Reserved Seats for Scheduled Castes and Tribes in the House of the People for ten years (since extended by Constitutional Amendment Acts in 1959, 1969, 1980, and 1990).

Article 335: The claims of the members of the Scheduled Castes and the Scheduled Tribes shall be taken into consideration, consistently with the maintenance of efficiency of administration, in the making of appointments to services and posts in connection with the affairs of the Union or of a State.

Article 338: There shall be a Special Officer (later Commissioner) for the Scheduled Castes and Scheduled Tribes to be appointed by the President.

Articles 341 and 342: Allow the President, by public notification, to specify the castes, races, or tribes which shall for the purposes of the Constitution be deemed to be Scheduled Castes or Tribes, and to consult with the Governor of a State where the Schedule is to apply at State level.

It would be folly to assume that these provisions were not welcomed by representatives of the Scheduled Castes and Scheduled Tribes. In the Constituent Assembly debates, speaking against Gandhian notions of village self-rule, the Untouchable leader Dr. B.R. Ambedkar denounced Indian villages as 'dens of ignorance, narrow-mindedness and communalism'.[20] As Galanter points out, Ambedkar

> ardently supported machine technology which would provide leisure, cultural advancement, and finally equality. To the same end, he rejected Gandhi's ideal of trusteeship by the rich in favour of a kind of state socialism which would promote rapid industrialization. And in spite of his suspicion that India might require benevolent autocracy, he was a supporter of centralized parliamentary government rather than of village autonomy. In all of this Ambedkar stood closer to the left wing of the Congress than either stood to Gandhi.[21]

In contemporary terms, we might say that Ambedkar was not an advocate of alternative development, of a model of (anti-) development that he would have dismissed as romantic and likely to be captured by the forces of reaction.

Nor was it the case that India's elite groups were always impressed by the model of compensatory discrimination embodied in the Directive Principles of State Policy. Masani warned in December 1946, 'Either the nation absorbs these minorities or, in course of time, it breaks up'.[22] Likewise, Sharma declared that 'it is in the interests of the tribal classes not to be told again and again that because they are inferior people, because they are weaker people, therefore such and such facilities are provided for them'.[23] I would also cite the more forceful complaints of Assembly Members B.R. Singh from Bihar and B. Das from Orissa. According to Singh, 'it must be paining everybody in this country to find that we have begun to do things now against which we have so long protested during the British rule'.[24] And Das:

> Though it has been thought wisdom for over a century to keep these tribal people and these Scheduled Areas as museums for purposes of demonstration and exhibition before the world to justify their existence [British rule] in India, what is the purpose today to perpetuate this evil? . . . I must frankly state that I am not at all happy for the way in which we have been proceeding, copying in most cases important portions of the Act of 1935.[25]

Das's complaint was not without merit. The Constitution of 1950 did replicate many of the provisions of the (Imperial) Act of 1935, and his reference to tribal museums and exhibitions spoke directly to a policy of isolation that many colonial officers pursued without question. The arrogance of this view had been perfectly expressed by a Colonel Wedgwood, speaking in the U.K. Parliamentary Debates of 1935.

> The only chance for these [tribal] people, is to protect them from a civilization which will destroy them and for that purpose, I believe, direct British control is the best. . . . Unless you have our experience of the last fifty or even one hundred and fifty years in dealing with this problem, it is impossible to say that any other race on earth can look after them so well.[26]

It is hardly surprising that many Congressmen—and members of the Rashtriya Swayamsevak Sangh (RSS)[27]—resisted this 'isolationism' and demanded the assimilation into mainstream Indian life of communities that G.S. Ghurye referred to as 'degraded Hindus' or 'so-called aborigines'.[28] Modernization as 'normalization' had many supporters in the Indian nationalist and social scientific communities. The (post)-colonial Other had to be tied into the body politic of the new nation.

Intriguingly, though, the Constitution refuses this blunt view, urging that the integration of India's Depressed or Backward

Classes has to be worked for by a state that in the short-run will have to recognize differences, if only to erase them later. This attitude was further complicated in relation to the Scheduled Tribes by Nehru's willingness to respect tribal claims to 'develop according to their own genius'.[29] The tribal Other was exoticized as well as patronized, protected as well as offered development.[30] In this respect, the makers of modern India treated the SCs and the STs differently. In the case of the Scheduled Castes, the state has taken the view that economic deprivation and low ritual status are interlinked, and that government actions on both fronts can rapidly speed the integration of SCs into a modern polity organized around class and merit rather than caste and status.[31] The main difficulty the state has faced in regard to the SCs is in the matter of notification. The framers of the Constitution discovered, as the Simon Commission and the 1931 Census Commissioner, J. Hutton, had discovered earlier, that 'untouchability' meant different things in south and north India, so much so that untouchables in one state might not be treated as untouchable in a neighboring state. The notification of communities as SC has been a controversial, and heavily litigated, issue in Indian political life since 1950.[32]

But not so the Scheduled Tribes. Notwithstanding a tautological definition of just who the tribals are—in 1951 the Commissioner for Scheduled Castes and Scheduled Tribes proposed as common elements 'tribal origin, primitive way of life, remote habitation and general backwardness in all respects' the state has faced few legal challenges to its lists of Scheduled Tribes. Since 1950, India's Scheduled Tribes have been the recipients of a range of governmental programmes that have been both protective and developmental in inspiration.[33] These programmes have at once claimed to respect the cultural and geographical distinctiveness of the STs while at the same time providing then opportunities for 'advancement' through educational scholarships, reserved jobs (in centre and state government positions since 1950, and in public sector enterprises since the late 1960s), and reserved seats in Parliament and Legislative Assemblies. It is to the rhetoric and reality of these claims on behalf of 'tribal (protective) modernization' that I now turn.

Mining the Seams of Compensatory Discrimination

A common complaint against forms of positive discrimination or affirmative action or compensatory discrimination is that the benefits on offer are monopolized by elite groups within the target constituencies (what is called the 'creamy layer' in India).[34] It is further suggested that cultures of dependency are created by such actions. Set against these claims, the proponents of compensatory discrimination in India have pointed to the range of existing discriminations faced by these vulnerable (target) groups; they have also insisted that such compensation as is on offer should be for a limited period only. Proponents of reservations in respect of the Scheduled Tribes further maintain that elite sections are unlikely to capture the benefits of compensatory discrimination because elite groups do not exist in India's tribal communities. This point is important and I will return to it later. The Indian state claims to treat Scheduled Tribal communities and areas on the basis that they are outside the caste system and in key respects are undivided and unaffected by processes of economic modernization. This is why a system of reservations has to be balanced by legislation that protects tribal communities from land sales and money contracts that seek to exploit their ignorance or innocence. India's Scheduled Castes, by contrast, are not assumed to be landowners, and the state has no interest in maintaining their cultural and economic traditions; advancement and change are necessary and desirable for these communities.

I have argued elsewhere that India's ideology of tribal economy and society has long been at odds with the realities of tribal life in parts of central India.[35] The discovery of coal and iron ore and other minerals in Jharkhand in the nineteenth and early-twentieth centuries ensured that this 'unspoilt' tribal homeland would be spoiled soon enough to meet the demands of industry and for profit in a slowly modernizing India. Outsiders, or *dikus*, poured into the Jharkhand from north Bihar and eastern Uttar Pradesh in the 1930s, 1940s, and 1950s, in the process changing the ethnic composition of the region.[36] At the same time, many 'aborigines' and 'semi-aborigines', as the British styled the tribals of this region before the 1930s, were inducted into the mining labour force.[37] Although hundreds of tribal people died in the mines, many thousands more earned incomes far in excess of anything they could have earned in their villages. By the 1940s, as mining or ex-mining tribal families acquired land from less fortunate tribal families, a tribal middle class emerged in rural Jharkhand.[38] Such land transactions were not outlawed by the Chota Nagpur Tenancy Act of 1908, which assumed that landed tribal persons needed only to be protected against unregulated land transfers to nontribals. Another middle class of sorts was emerging in the 1940s among educated Christian tribal families, some of whom were already resident in towns such as Ranchi and Chaibasa.[39] In sum, a tribal elite was already in place when a system of reserved jobs in government service was introduced in 'tribal Jharkhand' in 1950. Its ranks had swollen further by the time this system of reservation was extended to public sector jobs in the late 1960s. A certain amount of 'elite capture' of reserved jobs was inevitable in many parts of 'tribal' central India, whatever the rhetoric of government claims to the contrary.

But how much capture has there been, and how damaging is such capture for the state's ideologies of compensatory discrimination and tribal unity? Most of the information we have on this topic comes from the Annual Reports of the Commissioner for Scheduled Castes and Tribes and various Reports of the Committee on the Welfare of the Scheduled Castes and Scheduled Tribes (CWSCST). In both cases, publication became less assured in the 1980s than it was previously, so much so that the data sets we have are now hideously dated and incomplete. (There is another story to be told here, about the willingness of the Indian government to collect and publish information for certain purposes but not for others, but it is a story that will have to be told elsewhere.) What emerges from these reports is a tale of promises unfulfilled and of government duplicity. In Bihar, as elsewhere in India, Scheduled Tribals failed for many years to fill their complements of government service jobs, and most of the jobs they filled were in Class III and (more so) Class IV. The failure of STs to gain Class I and Class II jobs is explained away by the government in terms of its statutory obligation to balance the claims of compensation against those of 'efficiency'.[40] The following statement, made by the Ministry of Finance on behalf of the State Bank of India, is by no means exceptional:

> The Bank stated that it is not in a position to adopt the recommendation (of reservation) in view of the fact that having regard to the need to preserve certain minimum standards of efficiency and in view of the fact that the clerks in the State Bank of India are considered for promotion as officers at early stages in their career, the waiving of the minimum qualifying standard in the written test will not be in the interest of the institution.[41]

Beyond this official data we have surprisingly little evidence on local patterns of uptake of job reservations in tribal communities. In part, this reflects the difficulties inherent in designing a study that would investigate such patterns. One way of going about the task is to visit the workplace to interview a representative sample of Scheduled Tribe persons who have achieved their jobs by means of the reservations system. Thus, one might visit, as I did in 1980, 1983, and 1993, government offices and public sector companies in Ranchi-Hatia, Chaibasa, Noamundi, Gua, Dhanbad, and Jamshedpur, and questioned tribal respondents on their wages bonuses, qualifications, social and geographical background, political affiliations, and so on. (In 1980 and 1983 the questionnaire was administered in the course of a much broader project that was concerned to understand the dynamics of economic and political change in India's Jharkhand; the data I collected in 1993 were gathered while I was employed on a project concerned principally with forestry and migration in the region.)

This approach commends itself because it is easy to make contact with STs who have gained jobs via the reservations system. I was able to interview men and women who worked in various government departments, in 'service', and for companies including the Indian Iron and Steel Company (as was), Indian Railways, Indian Airlines, State Bank of India, and the Heavy Engineering Corporation. I also interviewed tribals working for private sector companies such as Tata Iron and Steel Company and Bata Shoes, but this was for comparative purposes that are not always relevant here. Interviews with STs in the workplace (or in tea shops and nearby residences) also proved useful for assessing the political aspirations and affiliations of respondents. Overall, I have collected data from 132 interviews conducted in this manner. Most were conducted in 1980 and 1993, but in the tables that follow I have aggregated the data except where there are compelling reasons not to do so.[42]

I have also approached the matter of data collection from a source-of-respondent perspective. The main drawback of the workplace-based questionnaire is that it is difficult to assess the 'initial social standing' of a respondent. Specifically, it is hard to test the proposition that reserved jobs are captured by elite groups within the Scheduled communities. Respondents might be persuaded to say how many acres of land their family owns in a village where they may or may not maintain a residence, but the reliability of their answers is open to question (even if one assumes that the question is meaningful). Similar difficulties arise when one is interviewing a tribal worker who comes from an urban background. If one is properly to test the 'elite monopolization' thesis, one needs to conduct a certain amount of fieldwork in the villages/mohallas/chowks from which respondents hail. But this is easier said than done. For obvious reasons, it is not practical to move backwards from a respondent's workplace to his or her residence. Respondents will rarely have the time or inclination for such journeys, and even if ten willing respondents can be found, the interviewer would likely be dragged to ten different villages or urban areas. The fieldwork has, then, to be approached the other way around. The interviewer must somehow gain familiarity with a sample of villages from within whose ranks men and women emerge who have gained reserved posts. Such men and women can then be interviewed *in situ* or at their workplace, and some quite robust data can be collected on the family's economic and social standing in the (stratified) host community.

As chance would have it, my research career since 1979 has allowed me to live for long periods in three 'tribal' villages in Singhbhum and Ranchi Districts of Bihar—three villages dominated by members of the Ho, Munda, and Oraon communities—and I have visited a large number of villages close-by for various 'control' purposes. In the course of these extended periods of residence (most notably in 1980, 1983, and 1993), I was able to collect data on the compensatory discrimination/ reservations issue, having become interested in it when researching for a doctoral dissertation on the 'tribal question' and the movement for a separate Jharkhand State. Less extended research trips in 1981, 1986, 1994, 1996, and 1997 have allowed me to add to my core data sets, so that I now have information relating to 72 men and women from more than a dozen locations who are, or have been, in reserved jobs or who have gained jobs in the public sector having first received special educational assistance from the state.

In the discussion that follows I draw upon a total of 204 interviews. It should be noted straight away that a total of 204 interviews is not the same as a total of 204 households. The 204 interviewees came from 185 households. Of these households, fifteen contained two members who had at one time been employed in jobs reserved for Scheduled Tribes, and two households contained three members who had been successful in gaining public sector employment. According to the criteria I develop below, 13 of these 17 'multiple' households belonged to a recognizable tribal elite. Of these, 8 were also firmly urban-based, in the sense that family members did not at any time in the calendar year contribute labour to farms that might or might not be maintained in an ancestral village. To put this in context, only 31 of the remaining 168 households can be described as 'urban' in this restricted sense (although more than half of the sample population is urban-based in the more usual sense of working or being ordinarily resident in a town or city).

I will argue shortly that a good many reserved jobs in tribal south Bihar have been captured by members of the tribal middle class or petty bourgeoisie, if not so disproportionately as to invite the word 'monopolization'. Some clarification is in order. Proponents of what I have called the ideology of tribal economy and society in India maintain that tribal communities are undivided almost by definition. Tribal communities reside in the remote hilly interiors of India (or at its north-eastern frontiers) and survive by means of shifting cultivation or a primitive plough agriculture that combines paddy cultivation with local forest dependency. Tribal communities have their own languages and dialects and are unused to the ways of the modern world. Their survival depends upon their continuing isolation, aided by careful government actions on their behalf. More generally, 'There is no functional differentiation in the tribal community as yet even in relation to such basic aspects like the religious, social, economic and political. The tribal is not yet used to the sectoralized approach which is the distinguishing characteristic of modern advanced communities. For example, he cannot distinguish between a loan for consumption or for production purposes'.[43] Or, again, in the words of two noted American commentators: 'to speak of levels of functions in tribal organization is hardly possible because of pervasive egalitarian patterns'.[44] Says Mandelbaum:

> In tribal life the principal links for the whole society are based on kinship. Individual equality as kinsman is assumed; dependency and subordination among men are minimized. Agnatic bonds form the fundamental web, affinal ties are of lesser significance. Lineages or clans tend to be the chief corporate units; they are often the principal units for land ownership, for defense, for economic production and consumption. Each man considers himself entitled to equal rights with every other.[45]

Mandelbaum further maintains that whilst 'tribesmen are not averse to accumulating food stores, to deferring consumption [and] to maximizing productivity . . . they characteristically feel that these worthy pursuits should not be pressed so hard as to interfere with the prompt prospect of pleasure.'[46] In short, tribal society is different (Myron Weiner suggested that tribal people look different and are a 'distinctive racial type'[47]). Its dominant cultural principles are reflected in its economic organization in ways that emphasize an attitude towards life and the future which is extremely contingent and which may be described as 'exotic'. On this reading, the essence of tribal life is its all-night dances and its *dhumkarias* (youth dormitories). As the 1962 (Dhebar) Report of the Scheduled Castes and Scheduled Tribes Commission puts it: 'It is difficult in the dry pages of an official report to convey to the reader the zest for life expressed in tribal poetry and dancing, the instinct for colour and pattern . . . (nevertheless) above all things, the tribal people are intensely lovable and have fascinated most of those who have had anything to do with them.'[48]

A fascination for things 'tribal' may or may not be worthwhile, but this construction of 'the tribal' is radically at odds with the life-stories of many members of Scheduled Tribes in central India. Andre Beteille hinted at this in the mid-1970s, when he wrote of his first field visit to an Oraon village in Ranchi District, Bihar: 'I clearly remember my initial disappointment in discovering that, although we had come to investigate proper tribals, the people who confronted us were outwardly no different from the poorer villagers one might find anywhere in rural Bihar or West Bengal.'[49]

I will take issue later on with the idea that 'tribalness' is merely conventional (and so unimportant or uninstructive), but many of the qualities routinely attributed to the Scheduled Tribes of Bihar are fictional. In villages throughout Jharkhand tribal men and women survive as peasants and even as agricultural labourers. Not all tribal families own land in Jharkhand, although most do, and private property is everywhere the norm. Some tribal families own and operate quite large landholdings (by the standards of dryland central India); others own and operate much smaller landholdings. In each of the three villages where I have lived for extended periods, I was able to detect and report a tribal landed elite. In the western fringes of Singhbhum District, there is evidence to suggest that a landed elite had emerged in part because some tribal families had gained remunerative employment in the region's iron mines in the 1940s, 1950s, and 1960s. Many tribal men in the Jharkhand have sweated hard in the region's mines and quarries, notwithstanding stereotypical views to the contrary. Most of them are also mobile. Tribal men and women migrate to survive or to accumulate. They come into contact with non-tribal individuals on a daily basis; indeed, it is rare to find villages in Jharkhand that are exclusively tribal. The *adivasis* are not living in a splendid or primitive isolation. Moreover, the range of tribal contact with 'the outside world' is fast expanding. Despite government rhetoric about the need to protect tribal people from a corrupting (anti)-civilization, the truth is that the push for development since 1950 has brought factories, roads, and outsiders to Jharkhand in huge numbers.[50]

Tribal people have tried to get a slice of the action, and tribal society has doubtless changed in the process—not that it was ever timeless in the way that it is sometimes portrayed in the ideology of tribal economy and society.

In short, a tribal middle class exists in Jharkhand. It is not a unitary middle class and it takes on different colours in different parts of Jharkhand. In rural areas of Ranchi District, land and service occupations are the best indicators of class. In Ranchi City levels of income and education may be better indicators, along with religion. When I refer to a tribal middle class in this study I refer to a diverse group of men and women who share a lifestyle markedly superior to the majority of Jharkhandis (non-tribal and tribal), and who very often employ others as labourers. Looking, then, at the evidence I have collected from Jharkhand (which suffers no doubt from being collected over a long period of time, and in the lee of other research projects), I would make the following observations. First, there is a significant number of nil returns (see Table 1). This is because reliable information on 'class' was more readily obtained from the source-based sample of 72 respondents than it was from the work-based sample of 132. Second, 69 of the 124 respondents for whom data is available can be defined as belonging to a tribal middle class (55.6 per cent). This compares with a tribal middle class that I would put at 10 to 15 per cent of the tribal population in Ranchi and Singhbhum Districts. Obviously, middle class STs are gaining reserved jobs disproportionately: they are generally better educated and qualified than other tribals and they have the contacts and social skills (and sometimes money) required to

TABLE 1

Scheduled Tribals in Reserved Jobs, By Class and Origin in Jharkhand, 1980-93

	Source-Based	*Work-Based*	*Total*
Elite	40	29	69
Non-elite	26	29	55
Nil Returns	6	74	80
Total	72	132	204

Source: Author interviews, 1980, 1983, 1993.

gain access to reserved employment, particularly in public sector undertakings. Several respondents told me how they had acquired reserved jobs through extended kin networks or by forged paperwork and outright bribery. Although reserved jobs in Bihar have to be advertised by means of a notification order, this information is not readily available to rural Jharkhandis. Word of mouth and personal contacts matter greatly, and not least for Class III jobs such as office clerks, foresters, and assistant sub-inspectors of police.[51]

This imbalance in respect of class is even more marked when it comes to gender. Only 36 of my 204 ST respondents were women (17.6 per cent). This is an interesting and worrying finding. Evidence from three 'tribal' villages suggests that the percentage of ST girls going to college is only slightly less than the percentage of ST boys going to college (12 versus 15 per cent). College principals have also confirmed this broad picture in interviews. The bias against tribal women would seem to emanate less from tribal society (which is often less male-dominated than caste Hindu society[52]), than from gatekeepers to the society of reserved jobs.[53]

Next, the capture of reserved jobs by middle class STs has not been so pervasive that less affluent tribals have no hope of landing a reserved job. To the contrary: almost half the jobs available seem to be going to less affluent tribal men (and women), and my interviews suggest that for such individuals success in education and competitive examinations is the key. Several informants told me that they had gained quite well-paid and secure government jobs having first been the beneficiaries of postmatriculation scholarships in local colleges. Many of these informants had started life in rural areas and had since moved to towns and cities for work or permanent residence. Most of them owed their success to a state-sponsored system of compensatory discrimination that was and is working reasonably well, notwithstanding the existence of a tribal middle class. Indeed, and perhaps surprisingly, poorer but well-educated tribals from amongst my sample populations are relatively more represented in Class II jobs than in Class IV jobs. Given small sample sizes it is perhaps unwise to read too much into this finding, but the qualitative data I have collected seem to confirm the view that members of middle class tribal families are more easily placed in Class IV jobs (constables, forest guards, drivers, sweepers, gardeners, and the like) than in Class II jobs (Block Development Officers, head of a police station) where educational achievements are more closely scrutinized. To the (limited) extent that children from poor ST (and SC[54]) families can access government or (more rarely) private/mission-sponsored education, so also can they hope to gain access to reasonably well-paid government jobs in later years.[55]

The suggestion that some (mainly male) STs have benefited from state educational or employment policies will surprise some observers. In recent years, the critique of tribal essentialism that began with the work of Béteille and others has been taken much further by contemporary historians like Crispin Bates[56] and Ajay Skaria.[57] Bates contends not so much that tribal communities are internally divided or subject to different mechanisms of counting/scheduling by the state, but rather that the nineteenth-century term tribal and the twentieth-century term adivasi are each recent inventions. These words created 'aboriginal'/ 'indigenous' populations as convenient fictions that have 'over the generations . . . remade [India) in the image invented for it by European colonialists'.[58] Less opaquely, we are faced in Bates's work with a powerful reworking of some of the same ideas mobilized by Ronald Inden. Just as Inden refuses the suggestion that the state has sponsored real development in independent India, so does Bates refuse the suggestion that India's tribal populations correspond to some authentic autochthonous populations that were later displaced from the plains by the Aryan invaders. Bates argues that: 'In reality the majority of adivasis lived comfortable lives, at least until the colonial period, having control over large areas of land, having armies, an aristocracy, tax collection, and judicial systems of one sort or another'.[59]

The modern poverty of tribal populations is thus a recent creation; there is nothing primordial or primitive about the backwardness of many tribal populations. It then follows, for Bates, that post-1950 attempts to uplift tribal communities are inattentive to the ebb and flow of tribal fortunes over time and across space. Particular social and economic communities get listed as 'tribal' because they are poor, and a series of stock characteristics are attributed to them so that a tribal identity is created, shaped by the state and set in aspic. Bates concludes by making two key points. He argues, first, that the state's attempts at 'positive discrimination (as with most "instrumental" efforts at social engineering) have not solved but merely aggregated the problem of . . . prejudice within Indian society.'[60] Second, and more generally, Bates argues that the casual use of words like tribe and *adivasi*: 'would not be (of) any harm but for the fact that many of the prejudices and misconceptions associated with the origins of the terms have persisted as well'. Further, 'It is arguable that *adivasi* leaders and ideologues are not innocent of this, and that the very form of their identification and the trajectory of their political struggle serve to reinforce rather than contradict the prejudices directed against them.'[61]

These are powerful arguments and they bear directly on the issues under discussion here. Bates is right to direct our attention to the possibility that tribal political movements should seek empowerment by deconstructing and disavowing the categories of tribal and adivasi that are instrumental in reproducing patterns of discrimination against them. This act of deconstruction/disavowal would be akin to calls from Inden and others for a discourse of alternative development that eschews the category of Development (as modernization) and the conceptual frameworks that sustain it. But herein also lies the weakness of Bates's position, as I see it. Bates's argument is sustained empirically with reference to recently affluent tribal kingdoms in Bastar and the Nilgiri Hills. Having once suggested that tribal fortunes have waxed and waned within historical memory, Bates is able to argue against the fixity of categories like adivasi and ST in the present.

I am not convinced, however, that such an argument can be extended to Bihar, where patterns of community exploitation and discrimination seem to be more entrenched. There is a danger in Bates's work, as in Inden's, that one form of essentialism substitutes for another.[62] I am also not persuaded by the political logic that Bates deploys, although I am sympathetic to some aspects of his wider political project. Bates clearly takes the part of India's 'tribals' to the extent that they suffer from institutionalized patterns of discrimination and exploitation. But

Bates suggests, or seems to suggest, that adivasi leaders (and their followers) are being disingenuous when they seek empowerment as adivasis or tribals. I doubt they have much choice. I would contend not only that a significant number of tribals have gained from the policies of compensatory discrimination on offer from the state (albeit a second-best system of job allocation and creation), but also that many have been successful in mounting a broader critique of development programmes in the Jharkhand—if not of Development itself—in part on the basis of a tribal political identity. Significantly, this tribal political identity is far from fixed in Jharkhand, but is regularly reinvented by local political leaders as circumstances require. In the 1950s Jaipal Singh's Jharkhand Party was largely uncritical of the developmental ambitions of the Nehruvian state. The Jharkhand Party wanted a separate state within which tribes would more easily appropriate the benefits of industrial development. In the 1980s and 1990s, a less unitary Jharkhand movement has sought to build Jharkhand as a state for tribal and non-tribal Jharkhandis (against post-1950/55 *dikus*). To this extent it has refused a neat tribal/nontribal boundary. At the same time, some in the Jharkhand movement have campaigned for a more inclusive Jharkhand state by suggesting that all Jharkhandis might want to draw upon the ecological and cultural traditions of local tribal communities.[63]

It is not possible to say much in detail here about Jharkhandi politics.[64] On the specific point of tribal identities and political activities, however, the empirical materials I have collected seem to refute the suggestion that tribal participation in the reservations system dulls the capacity for a more sustained critique of the causes of poverty and exploitation. Table 2 suggests that the opposite is more likely to be the case. Of 204 respondents, 124 (60.8 per cent) from my 'reserved ST' sample said they had either voted for or campaigned for activists within the Jharkhand movement. (Most respondents claimed to be supporters of the Jharkhand cause, but this tells us very little. It is important in studies of political affiliation and identity to seek out evidence of active or committed support for a political cause.) This compares to just 42 per cent of a control group of tribals not

TABLE 2

Reserved Jobs and Political Attitudes in Jharkhand, 1980-93

	STs in reserved jobs (total = 204) (Percentage)	*STs not in reserved jobs (total = 100) (Percentage)*
Supported Jharkhand Cause	189 (92.65)	81 (81.00)
Campaigned for Jharkhand	124 (60.78)	42 (42.00)
Voted for Jharkhandi Politicians	75 (36.76)	25 (25.00)
Jharkhandi activist (electoral)	21 (10.29)	5 (5.00)
Jharkhandi activist (non-electoral)	11 (5.39)	3 (3.00)
Opposed to Jharkhand cause	8 (3.92)	11 (11.00)
Nil returns	7 (3.43)	8 (8.00)

Source: Author interviews, 1980, 1983, 1993.

working in reserved jobs (the data being accumulated over the same time period).

This is a very crude way of measuring political support, but the broad conclusions that might be drawn from Table 2 were also confirmed in the course of a large number of extended interviews. Several respondents told me that their active support for the Jharkhand cause followed their induction into a reserved job. Most also made it clear that they see the Jharkhand movement, still, as a tribal movement, even if it has the support of some non-tribal people. Some respondents even advanced the view that the state (or the state as a territorial unit) had to be captured politically in the same way that STs had captured some labour markets. In almost all cases I gained the strong impression that success in the sphere of reservations had encouraged both a sense that other (private) labour markets remained out of ST control, and that STs could and should join together to seek control over these labour markets. The preferred vehicle for this politics was and is the Jharkhand movement, a movement that seeks to validate local political identities against Bihar and the *dikus*, but which also draws upon state programmes for the 'protection' of STs.

In sum, my respondents wanted it both ways. Many of them would first describe themselves as Oraon or Munda or Ho, then as STs or as adivasis. The government-inspired acronym is sticking and is worn with pride. At the same time, many of these very people wanted more than just to be the beneficiaries of state largesse. They understood very well that well-paid jobs in the private sector are generally denied to STs, and that real power in Jharkhand lies in non-tribal hands. They wanted not just to colonize the lower reaches of the state, but to take command of a territorial state, Jharkhand, for their more general empowerment. As one respondent put it: 'I am happy to have a job as a (. . . Class III job). Tatas will not hire us except as sweepers [not true, but a widely held view in Singhbhum], so I am pleased to work for (the) government. Government takes care of me. Government gives me *chutti* (leave). But it is not my government; it is the *dikus*' government. Government jobs should not be [the] only option. This is my land and it is tribals who should be giving out jobs. That is why I now campaign for Jharkhand. The government owes us wealth, not just jobs.'

Conclusion

This paper has advanced two main arguments. Empirically, I have tried to show that the reservations system in tribal Bihar has worked more successfully than some commentators have deemed likely. In its own terms, the present system of reserved jobs is flawed in three respects: it is not working to the advantage of tribal women, it is working to the disproportionate advantage of members of the tribal middle class, and it is still failing to deliver Class I or even Class II jobs to STs in the manner desired by the framers of the Constitution (although certain improvements have been made since the mid- to late-1970s). Nevertheless, large numbers of STs in Bihar have gained reasonably well-paid and secure jobs through the reservations system, and it is significant that members of non-tribal communities like the Nayaks have on occasions sought to pass themselves off as 'tribal' to gain access to reserved jobs. It is also the case that educated tribals from a rural background have made progress—and do make progress—through the reserved jobs system.[65] ST men and women can and do progress from Class IV to Class III jobs, the more so now that there is an effective system of rostering. Galanter is right to describe the reservations system in India as a system of 'competing equalities' that weighs the constitutional rights of equal and sovereign individuals against the very real inequalities that exist between social groups. Galanter himself is inclined to endorse the compromise that results and to defend it against criticism from political sympathizers of both the Left and Right. For my part, I am inclined to support Galanter. The reservations system in India can be defended in liberal or Rawlsian terms without its defenders turning a blind eye to the deficiencies of the system as it exists. Some inequalities are reproduced within target constituencies by the system of compensatory discrimination, but this needs to be weighed against the direct (employment) and indirect (political identity) effects of reservation on the competing inequalities between target and non-target populations. Striking a balance is no easy matter, but the increasingly loud protests against reservation coming from India's high-caste communities tell their own story.

A second argument has threaded its way through the paper and concerns what I will call the 'deconstructionist turn' in writings about modern Indian politics. The focus of this argument is the work of Ronald Inden and Crispin Bates. Both authors have produced telling critiques of the modernizing ambitions of the post-Independence state in India, and both draw heavily on the work of Foucault. Inden suggests that India's attachments to a transcendental conception of Development has ridden rough-shod over the legitimate voices and aspirations of its dispossessed. The Scheduled Tribes have been emptied out of many of their native lands to make way for the false god of Development, for factories and dams (and not least in Jharkhand). The STs have also been worked upon by various agencies of the state to secure their docile integration into the supposed mainstream of Indian life. Bates, for his part, being more of a student of tribes, has paid rather less attention to the normalizing instincts of the Indian state, and rather more attention to the state's capacity to invent 'tribal' communities and thus (inadvertently?) secure their continuing domination within discursive practices which for the most part despise tribal ways of life. For Bates, a deconstruction of 'tribalness' is a precondition for so-called tribal peoples securing their real freedom and equality with other social groups.

These are powerful arguments but at the same time, I find them each to be deficient to the extent that they essentialize the powers of the state and the innocence/incapacity of the tribes. The empirical work discussed in this paper suggests a more complex set of state/tribal relationships than is offered by Inden or Bates. Inden's work reinforces existing views of tribal societies as undivided and as somehow opposed to both the joys and the pain of modernity. Within this explanatory system the state must inevitably be seen as an agent of destruction; the state destroys the (assumed) oneness and integrity of the indigenous populations, and imposes on them a model of development which seemingly offers nothing to them. It is a model that is inattentive to the formation of a tribal middle class in areas like Jharkhand, largely as a result of an earlier round of mining and industrialization, and which fails to consider that many tribal families have been inclined to seize the opportunities made available to them by public- and private-sector sponsored industrialization. (This is not to suggest, of course, that tribal people are pleased to see their lands acquired for dams or factories, but nor are most non-tribal people in the same circumstances).

As regards Bates, although the detail of his work demands a different set of empirical responses, at a deeper level it invokes for me several of the misgivings I have outlined in respect of Inden. Specifically, there is within Bates's work a tendency to assume that because the categories of 'tribe' and '*adivasi*' are socially constructed and temporally fluid (in some parts of India), so it must follow that attempts to mobilize politically around these fictions are both innocent and disabling. On balance, I disagree. I would rather argue two points that cut against the grain of some aspects of Bates's argument. First, the construction of tribal communities as STs in the Constitution of India, 1950, and thereafter, has made this category rather less fluid than Bates suggests. Second, my reading of the Jharkhand movement suggests that many STs are well informed as to the bases of their domination, and have mobilized politically in ways that offer them a realistic chance of lessening this domination. Crudely put (and *contra* Inden), the key to Jharkhandi politics has been a willingness to contest the state by colonizing the state. Jharkhandi political leaders and their (ST) supporters have had some success, through the reservations system, in accessing some of the benefits of modernization in the resource triangle. Contra Bates, it is hard to see that giving up ST status would have heaped greater rewards upon the region's poor.

In the early 1990s the Jharkhand movement pushed once more for the central government to declare a separate Jharkhand State within the federal Republic of India. It is a measure of the movement's success that the government agreed to the setting up of a Jharkhand Autonomous Area Council in August 1995. The state of Jharkhand finally came into being in 2000. The new State was carved exclusively from the state of Bihar. It does not embody the demands for Greater Jharkhand that were pushed by Jaipal Singh and many other Jharkhandi activists, and certainly it has not yet resolved continuing tensions around the meanings of Tribalness, Development, and Compensatory Discrimination in the region. The formation of Jharkhand has not ended the forms of politics that sustained the wider Jharkhand movement.

Acknowledgements

I thank Ashutosh Varshney for his encouragement, and Paul Brass for his detailed comments on a version of the paper that was read at the 50th Annual Meeting of the Association for Asian Studies (Washington D.C., March 1998). I am also grateful to Craig Jeffrey, Sanjay Kumar, and Manoj Srivastava for their helpful advice, and to the anonymous readers for the *JAS* for their comments and suggestions.

NOTES

1. Legislation on behalf of India's Scheduled Castes was first enacted in 1943; similar legislation for the Scheduled Tribes was passed in 1950. A system of compensatory discrimination was meant to last until 1960 and no longer. By that time, or so the founders of Independent India supposed, the economic uplift of the country's poorest and most backward communities would be complete. A

nation of sovereign individuals equal before the law would be fused together by planned modernization. But this is not how things turned out. The accommodative landscapes of Indian politics have not encouraged a transfer of private assets to the Scheduled communities, and these communities have put pressure on successive governments to renew a framework of positive discrimination. The enabling legislation was duly reenacted at the end of the 1950s, 1960s, 1970s, and 1980s, in part, no doubt, because India's major political parties (and not least the Congress Party) were keen to corner the votes of the Scheduled communities.

2. Of all such jobs, 22.5 per cent were already reserved for members of the Scheduled communities. Singh's proposal was for a further 27 per cent tranche of reserved jobs for members of the Other Backward Classes. Most Hindu OBCs come from rural Sudra communities. India's political landscapes were transformed in the 1980s and 1990s by the rise to power of political parties representing them. The phenomenon is most apparent in states like Uttar Pradesh and Bihar, but it is not confined to the Hindi-speaking heartland: see Paul Brass, *The Politics of India Since Independence*, 2nd edn. Cambridge: Cambridge University Press, 1994; Kanchan Chandra, 'The Transformation of Ethnic Politics in India: The Decline of Congress, and the Rise of the Bahujan Samaj in Hoshiarpur', *The Journal of Asian Studies*, vol. 59, no. 1, February 2000, pp. 26-61; Christophe Jaffrelot, 'The Rise of the Other Backward Classes in the Hindi Belt', *The Journal of Asian Studies*, vol. 59, no. 1, February 2000, pp. 86-108; Yogendra Yadav, 'Reconfiguration in Indian Politics: State Assembly Elections 1993-1995', in Partha Chatterjee, ed., *State and Politics in India*, Delhi: Oxford University Press, 1997, pp. 177-207; see also G. Shah, 'Social Backwardness and the Politics of Reservations', *Economic and Political Weekly*, vol. 26, nos. 11 and 12, 1991 pp. 601-10. In south India substantial reservations for BCs in state government services have been common since the 1960s. It is also worth noting that: 'Educational concessions (but not reserved posts) for Other Backward Classes began in UP in 1948' (Marc Galanter, *Competing Equalities: Law and the Backward Classes in India*, Delhi: Oxford University Press, 1991, p. 161), and that the Government of Bihar issued a list of Backward Classes as early as 1951.
3. B. Sivaramayya, 'The Mandal Judgement: A Brief Description and Critique', in M.N. Srinivas, ed., *Caste: Its Twentieth Century Avatar*, New Delhi: Viking, 1996, p. 222; see also Brass, *The Politics of India Since Independence*.

4. Vijay Joshi and I.M.D. Little, *India: Macroeconomics and Political Economy, 1964-1991*, Washington, D.C.: World Bank, 1994.
5. J. Parry, 'No Mother or Father Like it: The Bhilai Steel Plant in Central India', Department of Anthropology, London School of Economics, Mimeographed, 1996.
6. Galanter, *Competing Equalities*.
7. Ronald Inden, 'Imperial Progresses to National Progresses in India', *Economy and Society*, vol. 24, 1995, pp. 245-78.
8. Crispin Bates, "'Lost Innocents and the Loss of Innocence": Interpreting Adivasi Movements in South Asia' in R.H. Barnes, A. Gray, and B. Kingsbury, eds., *Indigenous Peoples of Asia*, Ann Arbor: Association for Asian Studies, 1994.
9. The reference to cultural capital is indebted to the work of Pierre Bourdieu (Pierre Bourdieu, *Distinction: A Social Critique of the Judgement of Taste*, London: Routledge & Kegan Paul, 1984); the reference to social capital refers more specifically to the building up of networks of interaction with and trust in government and non-government agencies.
10. Notification of a job by means of a roster does not ensure that all jobs are filled; the employer can invoke the criterion of efficiency to block the employment of a member of a Scheduled or Notified community. Notwithstanding this provision, the serial number of the job is not lost (at least not for government jobs in Bihar). The post remains open, ostensibly to be filled by a suitable candidate at a later date. The act of notification may also caution state officers against visibly unfair hiring practices because of the threat of litigation that now hangs over them. It could reasonably be argued that the macroeconomic efficiency of Bihar's labour market—public and private—is not helped by such 'tentative bureaucratization' (a phrase much loved by a bureaucrat friend of mine), but that is not my concern here.
11. Inden, 'Imperial Progresses to National Progresses in India'; see also Ronald Inden, *Imagining India*, Oxford: Blackwell, 1990, chap. 5; on high modernism, see James Scott, *Seeing Like a State: How Certain Schemes to Improve the Human Condition Have Failed*, New Haven: Yale University Press, 1998, and Inden, 'Imperial Progresses to National Progresses in India'.
12. Stuart Corbridge and John Hariss, *Reinventing India: Liberalization, Hindu Nationalism and Popular Democracy*, Cambridge: Polity Press, 2000.
13. Inden, 'Imperial Progresses to National Progresses in India', p. 271.

14. A. Escobar, *Encountering Development: The Making and Unmaking of the Third World*, Princeton: Princeton University Press, 1995.
15. See S. Kaviraj, 'On State, Society and Discourse in India' in J. Manor, ed., *Rethinking Third World Politics*, Harlow: Longman, 1991, chapter 4; and Thomas Blom Hansen, *The Saffron Wave: Democracy and Hindu Nationalism in Modern India*, Princeton: Princeton University Press, 1999.
16. On the dangers of essentialism within the anti- or post-development paradigm, see M. Berger, 'Post-War Capitalism: Modernization and Modes of Resistance after the Fall', *Third World Quarterly*, vol. 16, no. 7, 1995, pp. 17-28; M. Cowen and R. Shenton, *Doctrines of Development*, London: Routledge, 1996; Stuart Corbridge, 'The Ideology of Tribal Economy and Society: Politics in the Jharkhand, 1950-1 980', *Modern Asian Studies*, vol. 22, 1988, pp. 1-42. For two very different, but illuminating accounts of the dilemmas of development, or the Faustian tragedy of modernization, see J. Toye, *Dilemmas of Development: Rejections on the Counter-Revolution in Development Theory and Policy*, 2nd edn. Oxford: Blackwell, 1993 and Marshall Berman, *All That Is Solid Melts into Air: The Experience of Modernity*, London: Verso, 1982.
17. Inden, 'Imperial Progresses to National Progresses in India', p. 273.
18. Ibid., p. 273.
19. On the Indian Constitution and nation-building, see G. Austin, 'The Constitution, Society, and Law', in Philip Oldenburg, ed., *India Briefing 1993*, Boulder: Westview, 1993; Ayesha Jalal, *Democracy and Authoritarianism in South Asia: A Comparative Perspective*, Cambridge: Cambridge University Press, 1995; U. Phadnis, *Ethnicity and Nation-Building in South Asia*, Delhi: Sage, 1989; R. Sudarshan, 'The Political Consequences of Constitutional Discourse', in *State and Nation in the Context of Social Change*, vol. 1, edited by T. Sathyamurthy, Delhi: Oxford University Press, 1994, and A. Vanaik, *The Painful Transition: Bourgeois Democracy in India*, London: Verso, 1990. On constitutional conventions in comparative perspective, see L. Spillman, '"Neither the Same Nation nor Different Nations": Constitutional Conventions in the US and Australia', *Comparative Studies in Society and History*, vol. 38, 1996, pp. 149-81.
20. CAD (Constituent Assembly Debates), Government of India, 1946-49. Debates of the Constituent Assembly of India, 1-9. New Delhi, 6: p. 39.

21. Galanter, *Competing Equalities*, p. 39; see also B. R. Ambedkar, *Annihilation of Castes, with a Reply to Mahatma Gandhi*, Bombay: Bharat Bhushan Press, 1945.
22. CAD 1: p. 91.
23. CAD 8: pp. 515-16.
24. CAD 9: pp. 984-5 (that is, Scheduling Castes, Tribes, and Areas for special treatment).
25. CAD 9: p. 994.
26. Government of the United Kingdom, Parliamentary Debates: Official Report, 5th Series, Volumes 299-301. London 1935, House of Commons Debates, 5s, cols. 1548-49.
27. The Hindu nationalist RSS continues to be very active in Jharkhand, where it enjoys a formidable reputation for providing high quality educational and health-care facilities. RSS members also helped to lay the foundations of the rise to power of the Bharatiya Janata Party (BJP) in the region in the 1990s.
28. G.S. Ghurye, *The Scheduled Tribes*, New Brunswick: Transaction, 1980.
29. J. Nehru, 'The Tribal Folk' In *The Adivasis*, New Delhi: Government of India, 1955.
30. See V. Elwin, 'Beating a Dead Horse', *Seminar* 14, 1960, pp. 25-8; also Ramachandra Guha, *Savaging the Civilized: Verrier Elwin, His Tribals and India*, Chicago: University of Chicago Press, 1999.
31. André Béteille, *Caste, Class and Power: Changing Patterns of Stratification in a Tanjore Village*, Berkeley: University of California Press, 1965.
32. See Galanter, *Competing Equalities*, chap. 5 for a discussion; see also C.J. Fuller, ed., *Caste Today*, Delhi: Oxford University Press 1996.
33. Galanter, *Competing Equalities*, p. 153.
34. On affirmative action in the U.S., see J. Skrentny, *The Ironies of Affirmative Action*, Chicago: University of Chicago Press, 1995; in India, see S. Mitra, ed., *Politics of Positive Discrimination: A Cross National Perspective*, Bombay; Popular, 1990 and A. Shah, 'Job Reservation and Efficiency', in M.N. Srinivas, ed., *Caste: Its Twentieth Century Avatar*, New Delhi: Penguin, 1996. For more general reflections, see A. Sen, *Inequality Reexamined*, Oxford: Oxford University Press, 1992.
35. Corbridge, 'The Ideology of Tribal Economy and Society'.
36. N. Sengupta, ed., *Fourth World Dynamics: Jharkhand*, Delhi: Authors Guild, 1982.
37. V. Bahl, *The Making of the Indian Working Class: The Case of the Tata Iron and Steel Co., 1880-1946*, Delhi: Sage, 1995; C. Simmons,

'Recruiting and organising an industrial labour force in colonial India: the case of the coal mining industry, *c.* 1880-1939', *Indian Economic and Social History Review*, vol. 13, no. 45, 1976, pp. 5-85.

38. Stuart Corbridge, 'Ousting Singbonga: the Struggle for India's Jharkhand', in P. Robb, ed., *Dalit Movements and the Meanings of Labour in India*, Delhi: Oxford University Press, 1993.
39. M. Lal, *The Munda Elite*, New Delhi: Harnam, 1983.
40. The situation in the 1990s is probably not as bleak as it was in the 1960s and 1970s, at least not in Bihar. The data I have collected in Jharkhand, and which I discuss shortly, suggest: (a) that most Class II jobs for STs are now being filled in the first round (although the number of such reserved posts that has been advertised recently is low, notwithstanding the fact that senior government personnel still refer to a shortage of suitable candidates for higher level reserved posts); (b) that many holders of Class II jobs are proceeding to Class I jobs in due course (and much earlier in their careers than people in nonreserved posts: given the 'shortage' of candidates for Class I jobs, it is not uncommon for the civil surgeon in a District, for example, to be younger than a civil assistant surgeon where the former but not the latter has gained employment within a reserved category); and (c) that more STs are presenting themselves for Class I (including Indian Administrative Service, Indian Police Service, and Indian Forest Service posts) and Class II posts as schooling and college systems have improved locally. It should further be noted that in central public sector undertakings in Bihar, Classes I-IV of employment are listed as Groups A-D.
41. Government of India. Reports of the Committee on the Welfare of Scheduled Castes and Scheduled Tribes (CWSCST), (various), New Delhi 1973, 18th Report, 1.
42. Disaggregation of the data sets will be necessary for a planned second stage of this research project, which will focus rather more on employment histories and the possible conversion of educational qualifications into reserved jobs and positions of political influence.
43. B.D. Sharma, 'Administration for Tribal Development', *Indian Journal of Public Administration*, vol. 23, no. 5, 1978, p. 531.
44. R.A. Schermerhorn, *Ethnic Plurality in India*, Tucson: University of Arizona Press, 1978, p. 71.
45. D.G. Mandelbaum, *Society in India* (2 volumes), Berkeley: University of California Press, 1970, p. 576.
46. Ibid., p. 581.

47. Myron Weiner, *Sons of the Soil*, Princeton: Princeton University Press, 1980, p. 155.
48. U.N. Dhebar, *Report of the Scheduled Castes and Scheduled Tribes Commission*, New Delhi: Government of India, 1962, p. 20.
49. André Béteille, *Six Essays in Comparative Sociology*, Delhi: Oxford University Press, 1974, p. 64; see also Amita Baviskar, *In the Belly of the River: Tribal Conflicts over Development in the Narmada Valley*, Delhi: Oxford University Press, 1995.
50. A. Das, *The Republic of Bihar*, Delhi: Penguin, 1992.
51. Craig Jeffrey has uncovered bribes of up to 60,000 rupees for Class III jobs in the reserved category in Meerut District, Uttar Pradesh (personal communication and Craig Jeffrey, 'Reproducing Difference: The Investment Decisions of Richer Jat Farmers in Meerut District, Uttar Pradesh, India', PhD Dissertation, Cambridge University 1999). I have yet to hear of bribes in excess of 15,000 rupees in Jharkhand, but I have not pressed on this issue as carefully or as insistently as Jeffrey. It is clear that there is an active 'market' in Reserved Jobs in Jharkhand. It is also clear that the returns to holders of Reserved Jobs (for example, forest guards or police constables) can warrant sizeable initial payments for access to the society of reserved jobs. I cannot estimate with any degree of accuracy what percentage of reserved posts are allocated through a system which James Scott once described as 'market corruption', but I would note that not all jobs are allocated on this basis. Although I did not push all or even most of my respondents on how they gained their posts, and while it is true that one would need to treat any replies with caution (will people admit to offering a bribe?), several of my respondents insisted that they had not had to pay a bribe or commission to acquire a post in government service, or, more especially, in a public sector undertaking. In this regard, at least, my findings (or suspicions) tally with those of Jonathan Parry in respect of reserved jobs in Bhilai, Madhya Pradesh. Parry reports that, while it would 'be rash to deny that retail corruption has grown over the past thirty years, I am nevertheless struck by a certain disjunction between the belief in, and the actual evidence for, its all- pervasiveness. Even where it is reputedly most rampant there are those who resist it; and even though it is an article of faith that you cannot get a job with the largest public sector employer in the area without paying for it, there is reason to suppose that most of those who have such jobs did not do so' (J. Parry, 'The "Crisis of Corruption" and "the Idea

of India": A Worm's Eye View', Department of Anthropology, London School of Economics 1999, Mimeographed, p. 28).

52. Govind Kelkar and Dev Nathan, *Gender and Tribe: Women, Land and Forests in Jharkhand*, New Delhi: Kali for Women, 1991.
53. Again, further research is needed here. It might be argued that the high levels of gender equality associated with ST communities is a myth, and/or that tribal societies are less 'tribal' than they have commonly been portrayed. An observed gender imbalance in the society of reserved jobs might then reflect significant shifts within tribal society. It might be, for example, that a tribal middle class is keen to promote the marriageability and not employability of females as a way of boosting household status. But I doubt this is the case. What evidence I have suggests that tribal women are better represented in Class III jobs than in Class IV jobs. This reflects the fact that Class IV jobs-gardeners, cooks, clerks, peons, and the like-are still coded as 'male' jobs; ironically, perhaps, jobs demanding more qualifications are coded as more gender-neutral. Tribal women certainly find it hard to get their feet on the employment ladder.
54. G. Nambissan, 'Equity in Education? Schooling of Dalit Children in India', *Economic and Political Weekly*, 31, 20-7 April 1996, pp. 1011-24.
55. I have not collected data systematically on this issue, but recent fieldwork inclines me to the view that ST households who have gained access to government or public sector jobs are also in a stronger position to deal with other government agencies. I am currently reviewing this issue (with Sanjay Kumar) in relation to a selection of villages that are part of the U.K.-funded Eastern India Rainfed Farming Project (EIRFP). Initial evidence suggests that there are strong networks of association between STs who hold government jobs and panchayat sevaks, forest guards, or even bank officials. Quite a number of the young men or women who act as *jankars* (volunteers or link-persons) for the EIRFP come from families where a household member holds a government job.
56. Crispin Bates, 'Lost Innocents and the loss of Innocence'.
57. Ajay Skaria, 'A Forest Policy in Western India: The Dangs, 1800s-1920s', PhD Dissertation, Cambridge University, 1992.
58. Bates, 'Lost Innocents and the Loss of Innocence', p. 104.
59. Ibid., p. 109.
60. Ibid., p. 106.
61. Ibid., p. 103.
62. I am reminded here of Nicholas Dirks' comments on the threatened

birth of a new orientalism that is ahistorical or even antihistorical. Dirks states that: 'Said writes about orientalism as if it transcends the exigencies of history, exempting it of its necessarily contingent relations to histories of nationalism and colonialism, rendering it as a totalizing monolith' (Nicholas Dirks, 'Castes of Mind', *Representations*, vol. 37, 1992, p. 74). As for orientalism, so also for development and the colonial mind. For a recent account of colonialism's culture(s) which refuses such (hard) essentialism, see Nicholas Thomas, *Colonialism's Culture: Anthropology, Travel and Government*. Cambridge: Polity Press, 1994. For an interesting defense of a 'soft essentialism' in the social sciences, and for a critique of an essentialized anti-essentialism, see Sayer 1997.

63. Susana B.C. Devalle, *Discourses of Ethnicity: Culture and Protest in Jharkhand*, Delhi: Sage, 1992; P. Parajuli, 'Ecological Ethnicity in the Making: Developmentalist Hegemonies and Emergent Identities in India', Department of Anthropology, Syracuse University, Mimeographed 1996.
64. See R.D. Munda, 'The Jharkhand Movement: Retrospect and Prospect', *Social Change*, vol. 18, 1988; B.P. Keshari, *Jharkhand Andolan Ki Vastuvikta*, Ranchi: Prakash, 1983.
65. It is not my intention in this paper to suggest that a sufficiently large number of STs have gained reserved jobs so as fundamentally to alter the nature of labour markets and community relations in Jharkhand. Of course not: for every 1,000 STs in reserved jobs there must be almost 100,000 not so employed. But this is not what is at issue here. In this paper I am not arguing that the reservations system is a panacea for STs excluded from private labor markets or locked into the so-called informal sector of employment; I am rather arguing that public sector jobs in India are greatly sought after and that more tribal people are gaining access to reserved public sector/government service jobs in Bihar than some critics of the system of reservations might think likely. I am further arguing that tribals from a nonelite background have been able to access a significant number of these jobs where they have first acquired a formal education. In this respect it is interesting to compare my findings in Bihar with those of Jan Breman in Gujarat. Although Breman is well known for arguing that proletarianized tribal Halpatis in Gujarat are systematically frozen out of local labour market opportunities by employers keen to bring in migrant labour to the Surat region, he also acknowledges that members of the partially proletarianized Dhodhiya (tribal) community have fared rather better, using their remaining land

rights to access educational opportunities and jobs for some children. Breman writes that 'one element of this programme [of positive discrimination] is the reservation of jobs in the public sector in order to help the target group to make up for their social backwardness. During the last few decades the series of measures taken in the framework of this attempt at positive discrimination have enabled younger Dhodhiyas from Chikhligam [village] in particular to become upwardly mobile. Their advance has invariably been preceded by some years of education. Equipped with school-leaving certificates they have been able to penetrate into the lower ranks of government bureaucracy and the teaching profession, to become bank clerks and work for the railways or post office. Education has also helped the Dhodhiyas to qualify for permanent employment in the large-scale industries which have sprung up in the region.' (Jan Breman, *Footloose Labour: Working in India's Informal Economy*, Cambridge: Cambridge University Press, 1996, p. 179.)

Success and Failure in Rural Development: Bihar, Bangladesh and Maharashtra in the Late 1980s

Harry Blair

This paper is offered to Walter Hauser as an effort to promote and provoke dialogue on what I consider to be his lifetime research project: what makes rural Bihar the fascinatingly and exasperatingly backward place that it has been and continues to be? The paper represents the last stage of a research project that has occupied me from the early 1970s to the late 1980s, tracing rural development first in Bangladesh, then Bihar, and finally Maharashtra.[1] The three regions offered a nice set of contrasts in rural development—the relatively successful track record in Maharashtra, particularly the sugar-growing area in the western part of the state, as against the abysmal failures experienced in Bihar and the mostly (though not completely) bleak course established by Bangladesh. My hope is that this comparative inquiry can provide some understanding of how rural development was progressing and stalling in these three parts of the subcontinent in the 1980s, and in the process contribute a bit to Walter Hauser's main research enterprise.[2]

Here I rough out a set of ideas as to why rural development had become been more or less successful in western India by the 1980s, while it unquestionably continued to fail in most of the eastern part of the subcontinent. Specifically, I concentrate on western Maharashtra as a relative success story, though the concepts to be sketched out here in many ways apply to Maharashtra as a whole and within broad limits to Gujarat as well. As cases of failure in rural development, I discuss Bihar and Bangladesh, though much of the reasoning would apply with equal force to eastern Uttar Pradesh and Madhya Pradesh. Between the two cases of failed development, Bihar clearly appeared the more intractable, though perhaps not absolutely and hopelessly so, while in Bangladesh silver linings on the dark clouds of reality seemed somewhat brighter.[3]

Before getting on with things, a few definitions and terms are in order. 'Rural development' is used here in a fairly wide sense; it encompasses economic growth and distributional equity (across lines of class, ethnicity and sex) in the countryside, as well as advances in such 'life quality' measures as literacy, infant mortality, and life expectancy. Political and institutional development are also a part of rural development, but more as means than as ends. In particular, popular participation in decision-making is treated here as instrumental to such ends as better public health or social welfare. As a shorthand, I shall refer to western Maharashtra as WM, and to Bihar/Bangladesh as BB.

The Political Economy of Rural Development in Bihar and Bangladesh

The story of Bihar and Bangladesh is a depressingly familiar one to students of the Indian subcontinent,[4] and can be summed up in Figure 1, which can be taken to represent that wide swathe of territory running from eastern Uttar Pradesh though Bihar, Madhya Pradesh and Orissa, as well as including Bangladesh,[5] whether one is viewing the scene as an academic researcher or a rural development practitioner. Its only redeeming virtue is an elegant simplicity which makes it dismayingly easy to lay out in a few words. There were three groups of significance here in this semi-feudal[6] rural political economy, connected together by an age-old binding of patronage, support and exploitation. The first level comprised the state, lying uneasy at the apex of the structure, concerned principally to maintain itself in power.[7] Its primary objective with respect to the countryside was to assure a relative peace and to prevent serious disorder from breaking out (previously, an additional objective was to extract rents, but this revenue function had attenuated virtually to the vanishing point not long after Partition). The state attained this goal by forming and keeping a *de facto* alliance with village-level landowning elites, guaranteeing property rights (despite periodic rhetorical fusillades fired off promising land reform) and provided patronage in the form of rural development programme spending, in return for which rural elites kept local order and supported the regime.

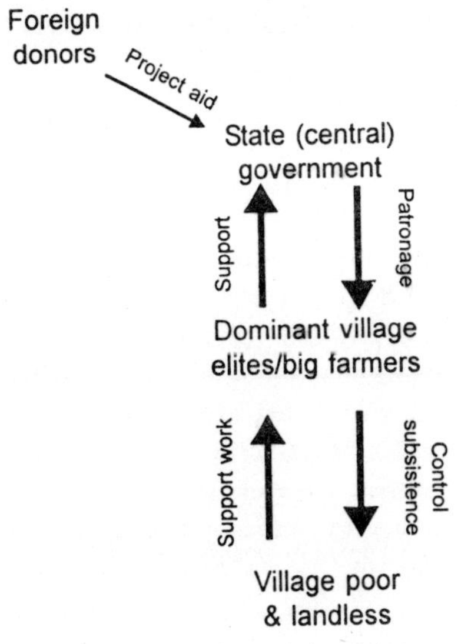

Figure 1: Political-Economic Development Linkages in Bihar & Bangladesh Mid-1980s

Village elites in their turn exercised a control over the lower orders through the customary machineries of patron-client relationships, moneylending, sharecropping, wage labour, dominance over institutions of local self-government, and of course the traditional *goondas, lathials* (or in Bangladesh *mastaans*) kept on retainer to enforce elite authority. The objects of these attentions were of course the remainder of the village population, the small and marginal farmers, the artisan families and those who without either land or traditional craft skills, i.e.

the landless agricultural workers and their families, who formed the residual occupational category. In return for the subsistence that was provided to them and in consequence of the control that was exercised over them, these poor and landless worked for their patrons and provided support to them by accepting the *status quo* in the countryside. At times, things would wear too thin and protest would reach a magnitude that could not be easily subdued by village thugs; on these occasions, the state would send in sufficient armed constabulary to subdue whatever trouble had arisen. But such outbreaks were relatively rare and isolated, such that the usual systems of control generally sufficed to keep things in order.

Whatever resources came into this system, whether from foreign donors or the central government's development budget, fit easily into it and even reinforced it. Thus funds for agricultural credit or irrigation equipment or small-scale rural industries were diverted into the hands of local elites. But this pattern of rural development perversion should not, as Keith Griffin[8] among others has pointed out, be viewed as 'failure', but rather should be seen as evidence of a successful attempt to maintain the *status quo* in the countryside. The overall rural economy, then, was an impressively homeostatic structure, into which an independence movement could come, political parties could flourish (even competitively for much of the time), a zamindari system could be abolished, sizeable infusions of development funding could be poured, hordes of development administration personnel could be deployed, and a 'Green Revolution' in agricultural technology could be introduced, all without producing much more than ephemeral change. Indeed, in the years after the Green Revolution began transforming the rural scene in the Punjab, Haryana, and western Uttar Pradesh, the annual rate of growth in Bihar's agricultural production sank to the lowest among all the major Indian states save Kerala.[9]

That all these developments served primarily to reinforce an enduring reality can be explained in large part by the overall orientation of the landed class, which was essentially to preserve its position and to maintain control over the lower orders, rather than to maximize income or wealth. For their part, the rural poor found that their most pressing need in an environment of steadily increasing pressure on the land and surplus labour eking out a living from that land was simple survival. If acceptance of elite dominance was the price to be paid for survival, then the bargain was not a bad one, and in any event, the alternative was most likely not to survive.[10]

The picture presented here is certainly a greatly simplified one. There were other classes or strata in the countryside beside elites and the poor. One significant group here was a 'middle farmer' segment of the peasantry attracted by the prospect of increasing income through raising productivity, thereby offering a way out of the semi-feudal economy. This was the heart of the middle-caste Lok Dal constituency that at the onset of the 1980s seemed on the verge of consolidating a breakthrough in Bihar, but which then succumbed to a restoration of high-caste, large farmer control (in Bangladesh there has not as yet appeared any political party to champion the interests of this stratum, though the 'progressive farmer' spirit certainly existed to some extent). And there was a pattern of increasing unrest at the bottom of the class/caste spectrum, particularly in Bihar, which saw a growing activism among landless Harijans, met often by brutal repression.

There was also, it should be conceded, some evidence of rural development efforts achieving a modest success. A new bridge across the Ganga at Patna at the end of the 1970s, for instance, connected a large swathe of previously isolated north Bihar with the larger economy and brought a more rapid economic growth to the area. In Bangladesh, fertilizer and tubewell use grew substantially over the late 1970s and 1980s. Rural electrification made some progress in both areas. But these qualifications are comparatively minor, indicative perhaps of social transformations slowly and even glacially emerging, but as of the end of the 1980s, they seemed small currents and isolated eddies set in a huge and essentially stagnant backwater. *Plus ça change, plus c'est la même chose.*

Rural Development in Western Maharashtra

On the other side of the ledger, there is the sugar economy of western Maharashtra in the later 1980s,[11] as shown in Figure 2.

The institutions and linkages portrayed in Figure 2 apply to Ahmednagar District in particular, which might be said to be the central or core region of the sugar belt, but *mutatis mutandis* the analysis here would apply to the remainder of western Maharashtra as well and, in a somewhat modified fashion, to the state as a whole.[12]

The first thing to note is that the structures of Figure 1 are also present in Figure 2. Village level elites (here labelled 'big and middle farmer', noted as A in the figure) and the rural poor and landless (B) are still there, as is the state government, though the latter is renamed 'representative political system (D)', for reasons which will become apparent as the discussion proceeds. But there are a good number of other institutions present as well.

What is important here is not only the institutions but also the linkages connecting them. Both aspects were far more highly developed in WM than in BB by the mid-1980s. In general terms, the institutions of WM were also present in BB, but in the former case, they had become functionally specific, in the Parsonian sense, such that they could and did perform the tasks they were nominally assigned, whereas in BB the rural political economy virtually ensured that whatever the formal purpose of an institution, its true function was simply to grease the machinery supporting the *status quo*. Thus development projects like the Mula irrigation scheme in WM (J in Figure 2) did in fact provide water to farmers in timely fashion, sugar cooperatives (E) had become immensely powerful engines of rural development, and the Employment Guarantee Scheme (K) established a welfare 'floor' which guarantees a wage to all in the rural areas of the state.

Several features of Figure 2 deserve mention, even in a treatment as brief as this one. The sugar co-operatives have been an outstanding success story in the annals of rural development. Begun in the early 1950s, by the mid-1980s they were processing the overwhelming majority of a steadily increasing sugar crop in the state, providing immense direct benefits to their members, and exercising a large (some would

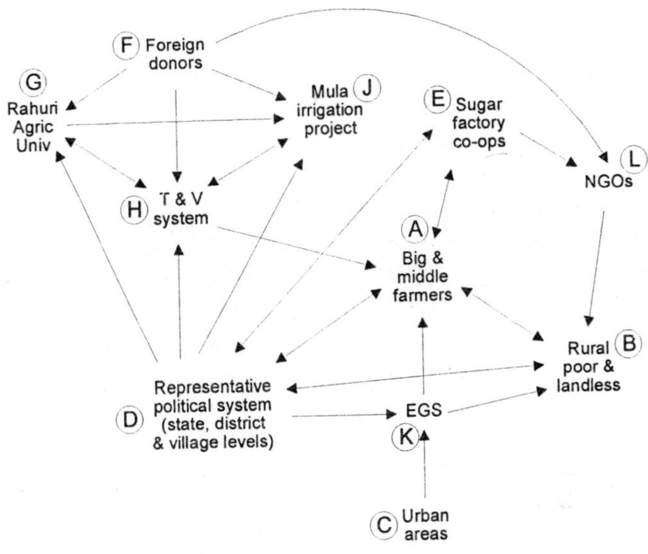

Figure 2: Political-Economic Development Linkages in Rural Western Maharashtra: Ahmednagar District, Mid-1980s

say inordinate) influence in the state as a whole. Various reasons can be cited for their success, perhaps chief among them the several peculiarities of sugar cane production which make it relatively easy for cooperatives to maintain a close linkage to their growers. To begin with, sugar is a crop that, unlike food grains, needs significant processing before it can be used by consumers. Some variations on that processing can be fairly rudimentary, such as *gur* (crude brown sugar) making, which consists essentially of squeezing the juice from the cane and boiling it down in large vats.[13] But by the 1980s the major demand was for refined white sugar which sold at a considerably higher price. Refining had become a highly sophisticated technology, necessitating a very large outlay in terms of investment. The point is that before sugar can be sold retail, it must be processed by organizations standing between producer and consumer.

•

It was this need for processing that gave the cooperative its leverage, for growers found they had to sell (at least most of) their crop to the cooperative, and when they delivered it, the cooperative could deduct from the price the cost of whatever loans had been made. There was in other words a built-in mechanism for recovering loans, a feature which allowed the coop to remain solvent, thereby avoiding the problems of loan default that so devastated coops elsewhere. A second quality of sugar here is that it is highly perishable. After cutting, the cane begins immediately to lose its sucrose content; it 'spoils as rapidly as milk,' in the local aphorism. Accordingly, long storage to wait for a price rise or transport to distant processors who might offer a better price is just not feasible. And third, sugar is an extremely thirsty crop; its need for water is far in excess of any other crop grown in the region, which means in semi-arid WM that sugar is dependent on reliable irrigation.

But these were far from the only reasons for sugar's success. In addition to these factors of crop production and processing technology, there was a very strong connection to the *political sector* (D in Figure 2) in the form of massive subsidies bestowed on the sugar cooperatives. These subsidies came in several forms. First, the state government provided large-scale loans to sugar cooperatives to help them raise the sizeable start-up capital required. Second, the water supplied through the various irrigation schemes was priced to farmers at a fraction of its true cost.[14] Third, electricity used to lift water for sugar was heavily underwritten by the Maharashtra State Electricity Board.[15] And last, government provided cane price supports that mean the domestic price of sugar in India has been a multiple of several times the world price.[16] Thus water was a massively subsidized input provided by the state at high cost, to be wastefully used in growing and processing a crop to be sold at a very handsome price and profit in lieu of what would have been a rather cheap imported commodity.

The mechanism involved in securing this bounty to the cooperative sugar sector was one that would be very familiar indeed to North Americans or Europeans. Simply put, the cooperatives used a portion of their profits to back candidates for political office, and then put pressure on those elected to obtain and maintain massive subsidies to sugar. The story sounds strikingly like the saga of Florida and Louisiana cane sugar and western beet sugar growers in the United States, who have also been able through political pressure to push the domestic price of sugar in the United States up to three or four times world levels.

The *Employment Guarantee Scheme* (K in Figure 2, known throughout the state by its English acronym, EGS) has been another remarkable institution in Maharashtra.[17] Begun in the early 1970s, by the mid-1980s it virtually assured a daily job in unskilled labour at minimum wages to anyone who asked for one, subject to the stipulations that there can be no unmet demand for agricultural labour in the area and that the wages paid by EGS should not be higher than those prevailing in the local agricultural sector. In the early 1980s, EGS provided annually about 150 million person-days of work, at a cost of about Rs 140 crore (US $115 million) a year. There were a number of problems, to be sure. Much of the rural works constructed, for instance, turned out to be land improvements such as bunding and levelling on land belonging to richer rural households, rather than community assets. Second, in some areas (particularly the drought-prone districts of WM), officials were at the point of running out of projects that could be taken up through EGS. Just about all the work that could be done had been done, leaving less and less for future years. Third, the EGS itself could be seen in a cynical light as a device perpetrated by urban elites (C in Figure 2) for keeping rural hordes in the countryside (bribing them to stay out of Bombay). It was funded mainly through a combination of urban professional taxes, sales taxes and general state revenues, most of which came from Bombay. And last, there was considerable political pressure on elected officials to implement the programme to nurse their constituencies. But the long and short of it is that the EGS built a rural social safety net that at the time did not exist in like form anywhere else in the country.[18]

It is of course true that similar institutions existed in BB. There were cooperatives, representative political institutions, and rural works schemes in both regions. But in this environment, rather than to raise agricultural production, the entire cooperative structure served mainly to channel state funds into the hands of rural elites by allowing and even encouraging them to take over cooperative units, steer loan monies to themselves, and then default on their overdues. Institutions of local and state government were dominated by these same elites, who were thereby able to abet in perverting the cooperative structure, while doing nothing for the rural poor and landless. Likewise, programmes specifically aimed at such groups were also swept into the politics of patronage and corruption, yielding little but further rewards for the rural rich.

Needless to say, I have exaggerated the picture somewhat here. It would be hard to find many successful coops in BB, but there was some evidence that the political system was having to pay some attention to the middle class/caste farmers in Bihar that formed the backbone of the Lok Dal, if only by buying their allegiance to the Congress Party.[19] In Bangladesh, the Rural Works Programme that began under Ayub Khan in the early 1960s was a case study in all the abuses outlined above, but later efforts emerged that developed better management, such as the CARE Food for Work Scheme, which by the mid-1980s was generating some 20 million days of work annually in Bangladesh and had become a model of development administration.[20]

But the overall tenor of the rural development experience in WM and BB could scarcely be more different. In WM there was some corruption and considerable public waste offset against a pattern of steady and significant rural development that has had a real effect in raising income and living standards across the entire spectrum.[21] In BB on the other hand, there was some indication of development here and there, but the overall pattern was one of stagnation and decay. The question, then, is *why* should things be so different in the two regions? It is to this issue that the discussion turns in the next section.

Explanations: Why Are the Two Regions So Different?

As might be expected with anything so complex as success and failure in rural development over the past four decades, possible explanations abound. For convenience, they are grouped here in terms of history, demography, socio-economic and cultural dimensions, and political style, an ordering which in a very loose sense constitutes a spectrum between what is more causal and what is more consequential. Some of my thinking here is well supported in the literature, but a good part of it is inferential, based on my experiences in these places from the late 1960s up to the present. I hope that some of my conjecture here might contribute to future research agendas.

History

1. *Land tenure systems.* The basic outlines of the differences between the ryotwari and zamindari systems of land revenue and tenure are sufficiently well known (certainly so to students and colleagues of Walter Hauser) that I need not spend time on them here.[22] Their consequences are also well appreciated by those who have worked in the vineyard of the subcontinent's rural economy. In many, many ways the former zamindari areas of India and Bangladesh still labour under the historical weight of a system that discouraged husbandry and land improvement among the peasantry while rewarding indolence and parasitism among the landlord class. On the other hand the relatively freehold tenure enjoyed by the peasantry of the Bombay Presidency in the British period gave it a head start as a class producing independently for a market. For the former, the feudal/semi-feudal concerns of status and control were paramount, while for the latter, landowners were more concerned with maximizing income.

2. *Urban-rural linkages.* The *mofussil* of the Bengal Presidency constituted a hinterland supporting with its rents a cosmopolitan elite in Calcutta, whereas the rural areas of Bombay Presidency, though in many ways a hinterland of Bombay city, did have a cultural self-sufficiency and self-identity with centres of culture and economic dynamism like Pune, Ahmedabad and Vadodara that were lacking in the Bengal hinterland (Dhaka, Patna, and Cuttack, were just not on a par with the western towns). When the various segments of territory from the Bombay Presidency, Central Provinces, Hyderabad, and a wide scattering of smaller princely states all joined together in the states reorganization of

the 1950s to make up the Maharashtra that emerged in 1960, Nagpur and Aurangabad replaced the Ahmedabad and Vadodara that went to Gujarat state. In sum, Maharashtra developed a relatively integrated regional culture and economy.

In BB, on the other hand, an urban regional infrastructure did not develop after the 1912 splitting off of Bihar and Orissa. The new province continued to be dominated by Calcutta down through the partition in 1947. Even at the end of the 1980s, as shown in Table 1, its population remained barely more than 10 per cent urban, among the very lowest in all India.[23] Bihar had nothing like a developed urban regional economy, as is clear in Table 2, where it will be observed that this area of more than 53 million could support just one city—Patna—with (barely) over one million in population. The second largest municipality was Gaya, which in 1991 had fewer than 300,000 souls, making a revealing comparison with Maharashtra, where Pune as the second city had about 2.5 million inhabitants in 1991. Perhaps most strikingly, to the north of the Ganga, the largest urban agglomeration that the Tirhut division with more than 20 million people could support was the headquarters at Muzaffarpur with just over 250,000 population.

TABLE 1
Urbanization in Bihar, Bangladesh and Maharashtra, 1981-2001

(Figures in per cent, boundaries as of 2001)

	Bihar	*Bangladesh*	*Maharashtra*
1981	9.8	15.1	35.0
1991	10.4	19.6	38.7
2001	10.5	23.1	42.4

For Bangladesh, the story in East Pakistan days was one of even less urbanization, as East Pakistan became cut-off from its Calcutta metropolis in 1947, leaving the new province of 40 million people with its capital Dhaka a mere 200,000 inhabitants. Even in 1961 Dhaka still had less than 600,000 people, though its growth as the capital of independent Bangladesh has been quite rapid indeed, so that by 1981 it boasted almost 3.5 million

TABLE 2
Five largest cities of Bihar, Bangladesh and Maharashtra, 1981-2001
(Figures in millions of inhabitants, boundaries as of 2001)

	Largest city	*2nd largest*	*3rd largest*	*4th largest*	*5th largest*
Bihar 1981	0.92	0.26	0.22	0.19	0.18
Bihar 1991	1.10	0.29	0.26	0.24	0.22
Bihar 2001	1.71	0.39	0.35	0.31	0.27
B'desh 1981	3.44	1.39	0.62	0.17	0.16
B'desh 1991	6.95	2.35	1.00	0.54	0.21
B'desh 2001	10.71	3.39	1.31	0.70	0.32
Maha 1981	8.23	1.69	1.55	0.65	0.52
Maha 1991	12.57	2.49	1.66	0.72	0.62
Maha 2001	16.37	3.76	2.12	1.15	0.89

Notes: *Boundaries*. Bihar's territory shrunk in the year 2000 when 18 of its 55 districts in the south were hived off to form Jharkhand State. Census figures shown above were readjusted to correspond to the reduced area remaining in Bihar after 2000.

Sources for data: *Census of India* (2001c and 2001d); BBS (2003).

people and ten years later it had virtually doubled in size. The drop-off in the rank-size listing in Table 2 remains remarkable, however. After the first two cities (Dhaka and Chittagong), number three (Khulna) had only a million, and the fourth highest was less than 200,000.

By contrast, Bombay had become a mega-city even in the British period, and continued as the leading financial and industrial centre of the country through the 1980s. By the 1980s, the state's second (Pune) and third (Nagpur) cities had also become financial and industrial centres with substantial populations.

In these respective processes of urban growth and non-growth, the linkages that tie city to countryside progressed quite differently. Calcuttta had (and to some extent Patna still has, though by now in Dhaka the situation is rather different, I believe) an essentially exploitative relationship with its *mofussil*, extracting rural rents to maintain a sophisticated urban lifestyle.

Bombay, Nagpur, and Pune are scarcely innocent of exploiting their hinterlands, but in the bargain they provide an array of developmental assistance (state services, finance, trade, etc.) that has actually promoted economic growth in the countryside.

3. *Martial history*. WM was the base of Shivaji's operations in the eighteenth century, when the Maratha Confederacy began to push out the Mughal Empire and then gave a fair challenge to the East India Company for dominance of western India, before its final collapse in 1818. There is thus a legacy of martial self-assertion in WM that contrasts markedly with the experience of BB, which has been under the sway of 'foreign' (though some of them indigenized themselves quite well) rulers for the last thousand years or so. One obvious manifestation of this is the equestrian statues of Shivaji that one sees all over WM (almost always in a traffic circle fenced in by wickets shaped like military shields with crossed spears), proclaiming the martial legacy of the citizenry. Self-assertion *vs* subjugation by foreigners is the theme here.

Demography

The social makeup of WM has one clearly dominant caste, as indicated in Table 3. The Marathas constitute about 35 per cent of total population in Maharashtra (people commonly say 40 per cent, but as best as I can tell from the 1931 census[24] it seems to be about 35 per cent, assuming population growth *pari passu* among all the state's communities). The next largest group are the Mahars, a Scheduled Caste community with about 10 per cent of the population. They do have some political clout (the Nava Buddhist movement and the Dalit Panthers, for instance, are mainly Mahar in their leadership and composition), but they are not in any serious way rivals to the Marathas for dominance. The result is that Marathas determine the political leadership of the state. They do have factions among themselves, to be sure, but this has not been enough to allow other groups to move into control. Even when a non-Maratha has been in charge, e.g. V. P. Naik as Chief Minister in the 1960s, his sitting on the *gaddi* was possible only because a substantial segment of Maratha political chieftains agreed to it.

TABLE 3
Principal Ethnic/Religious Groups in Bihar, Maharashtra and Bangladesh
(groups with >2% of population in the 1980s)

	Bihar		*Maharashtra*		*Bangladesh*
All Hindu Castes	84		88		14
'Twice-borns'	Brahman	5	Brahman	4	
	Bhumihar	3	Maratha	32	
	Rajput	4			
'Backwards'	Yadav	11	Mali	3	
	Kurmi	4			
	Koiri	4			
	Teli	3			
Harijans	All castes	14	All castes	13	
	Chamar	4	Mahar	9	
	Dusadh	4			
	Musahar	2			
All Muslims		14		8	85
All other groups		3		4	1
Grand total		100		100	100

Notes: Boundaries for Bihar are those extant in the 1970s (i.e. including present-day Jharkhand State).
Adivasis can be any religion, and so are not included here.
Mahars in Maharashtra include both Hindus and Buddhists.

Sources: Mainly 1931 census for Hindu castes, with boundaries adjusted to conform with 1981 areas; 1971 census for Muslims (1974 for Bangladesh). See Blair (1980, 1981) for more details on the Bihar data.

In Bihar the largest Hindu community with about 11 per cent of total population (again making the same assumptions on growth of different groups at the same pace since the 1931 census) is the middle ('backward' in the Bihar lexicon) caste of Yadavas. Then there are three major upper caste ('forward') communities in contention (Brahmans at 5 per cent, Bhumihars at 3 per cent and Rajputs at 4 per cent), as well as two other prominent 'backward' caste groups (Kurmis and Koiris, both at 4 per cent). The consequence in Bihar is that since the first Congress government in the late 1930s there has been intense caste rivalry over gaining control of the state's politics. It is not indulging in hyperbole to say that an incredible amount of time and energy was squandered ever since the 1930s on fights for caste dominance in state politics, leaving very little of either available for leading serious development efforts.

Bangladesh of course is 90 per cent Muslim and so caste conflict is really not an issue there. The implication is an interesting one. In so far as Bihar and Bangladesh are similar cases, and given that caste conflict is not present in the latter, then that same caste conflict cannot explain more than a part of the backwardness of the former. Obviously, the two are not the same, and so caste can carry some of the explanatory freight for one of them, but the similarities in most other respects of their histories, cultures, and economies are so striking that the explanations of their backwardness must be similar in many ways as well.

Social Relations in the 1980s

1. *Interpersonal relations* were generally less harsh in WM than in BB. In a palpable sense, people were nicer to each other. This manifested itself in all sorts of ways. For one thing, the *superior/subordinate relationship* in BB was characterized by arbitrary arrogance from above and a fawning sycophancy from below—the '*ji huzoor*' mentality pervaded all hierarchical organizations. While WM was scarcely egalitarian, the relations between higher and lower status levels seemed significantly less rigid and exploitative. Secondly, *social behaviour* was more public-regarding. People in BB hardly ever stood in queues in public places like bus stops and post offices, they had virtually no civic consciousness in throwing out refuse, they drove and parked vehicles with no regard to convenience of pedestrians.[25] In WM people were much more socially conscious on these counts.

2. The *status of women* was much higher in WM. Women were more conspicuous in public and less restricted in habits of dress and movement. The whole milieu of *purdah*, which was so pervasive in BB was hard to discern in WM. In Pune women

wearing dresses were so common in the 1980s as to be ordinary, while in Bihar and Bangladesh dresses were only for small girls. In WM women riding bicycles or motorscooters by themselves were piloting perhaps 15-20 per cent of the two-wheeled vehicles on the roads, whereas in BB they were almost never seen doing so. Women were also better represented in the professions in WM—as doctors, professors, lawyers, etc. 'Eve teasing' (the public abuse of adolescent females by males of the same age, including verbal harassment, pinching, punching, etc., but very rarely rape) had become a growing pandemic in north India. In WM, on the other hand, it seemed exceedingly rare. It was not part of the culture there.

Perhaps the most telling statistics are those for *female literacy*, as can be seen in Table 4. The effort to educate females began

TABLE 4

Literacy in Bihar, Bangladesh and Maharashtra, 1981-2001

(Figures in percentage, boundaries as of 2001)

	Bihar	*Bangladesh*	*Maharashtra*
Male literacy			
1981	47.1	33.8	70
1991	51.4	38.9	77
2001	60.3	49.6	86
Female literacy			
1981	16.6	17.5	44
1991	22.0	25.5	52
2001	33.6	40.8	68

Notes: *Boundaries*. Bihar's territory shrunk in the year 2000 when 18 of its 55 districts in the south were hived off to form Jharkhand State. Census figures shown above were readjusted to correspond to the reduced area remaining in Bihar after 2000.

Definitions. For 1991, the Indian Census changed the definition of literacy to apply to persons seven years of age and older (previously the cut-off had been five years). Figures shown above were readjusted for 1981 but not for earlier years. For Bangladesh only those seven and older were canvassed for literacy for all years shown above.

Sources for data: *Census of India* (2001a and 2001b); BBS (2003).

in modern times in Maharashtra with Mahatma Phule (see a below), but in terms of literacy things geared up only after the Partition. By 1981, literacy among females in Maharashtra was getting close to levels for Bihar males and well ahead of Bangladesh males. Ten years later female literacy in Maharashtra had pulled significantly ahead of the male figures in Bangladesh (which had even retrogressed somewhat in the 1970s) and was just about even with Bihar in this respect.

3. There is a *tradition of social reform* movements in WM, stretching back into the nineteenth century if not earlier. Mahatma Jyotirao Phule was the first of the great social reformers, responsible in large part for displacing the small Brahman community from their traditional dominance in the Bombay Presidency and for beginning efforts at uplift of women. Dr. B.R. Ambedkar is undoubtedly the premier social reformer of the twentieth century and his statue is probably second or third in popularity in public places. But there are many less well-known leaders as well. One way to put this tradition in perspective is to note that it is considered a worthy and respectable avocation for successful men in their later years to involve themselves in social uplift activities (or perhaps more important, there seems some social pressure on them to appear to be doing so, even if in fact they are not).

By contrast, the leading social reformer in Bihar up through the 1970s was generally regarded to be Sachchidānand Sinha, whose great contribution was to lead the movement for a Bihar Province separate from the Bengal Presidency. This was 'social reform' in a sense, but it was also very much and mainly an effort to set-up a Bihar for his caste brethren, the Kayasthas, to administer and manage, independent of the *bhadrolok* Bengalis who had all the good jobs in running the Bengal Presidency. Similarly, the great hero of modern times in Bangladesh was A.K. Fazlul Huq, the *Sher-e-Bangla* ('Tiger of Bengāl'), whose main contribution was perceived to have been establishing the political dominance of the Muslim majority in undivided Bengal during the brief popular governments of the late 1930s, thereby displacing Hindu control.[26]

In more recent times, of course, there was Jayaprakash Narayan in Bihar, whose credentials as a genuine social reformer were very high indeed, while on the other hand Y.B. Chavan might have taken Sachchidanand Sinha as his role model in making his early career as a politician by masterminding the bifurcation of Bombay state into present-day Maharashtra and Gujarat, thereby establishing a state where Marathas could manage things (acting in the name of Maharashtrians generally, of course). But these are exceptions, I would argue. The impulse to social reform has not been unknown in Bihar, but it has been certainly rare. Political opportunism is definitely found in Maharashtra, and it is scarcely rare, but it is not so overpoweringly the motif that one finds in BB.

Political Culture

1. There was a kind of *accommodational approach* in the politics of Maharashtra absent in the more vicious 'winner take all' politics of BB. In Maharashtra political winners were expected to reserve some share of rewards for losers, or at least to keep the losers working within the system. Winners in Congress Party factional struggles did not try to purge losers of all rewards of political life, for today's losers were expected to stay in the game, maybe even to win later on. In my time in 1985, the main political issue of the day centered on Sharad Pawar, a former chief minister who had left the Congress to form his own party, a splinter group which had lost badly in the parliamentary and assembly polls earlier. Instead of trying to eliminate him completely from political life (which is what the winners would have done in Bihar), the winners in Maharashtra were dickering with him on the terms of his readmission to the Congress Party (a move that eventually occurred in late 1987). This mellowness no doubt reflected the Congress' leadership's assessment of Pawar's own real strength, but what was most interesting was the mentality that says 'let's make a deal' rather than 'let's liquidate the other side while we can'. By contrast, politics in BB tended to follow what might be called a *spoils approach*, in which winners took all the benefits of office they could lay their hands on, completely excluding losers.

2. *Rural violence* offers much evidence, but it tends to be contradictory. To begin with, even though it is hard to measure

in any valid way (people killed is a concrete gauge, sure enough, but beatings, rapes, or intimidations are much more elusive), there can be no doubt that violence in Bihar increased greatly in the 1980s, with the advent of the various rural Marxist movements and *senas* (armies) organized by castes of all levels in rural Bihar.[27] In Bangladesh, to the contrary, rural violence, though far from absent, appeared much attenuated over what it had been in the early 1970s, when the well-armed remnants of various freedom fighter groups roamed the countryside. So while agrarian violence was obviously a critical matter in Bihar, it did not figure that much in Bangladesh.

On the other side of the ledger, *communal violence* was probably no higher in Bihar than in Maharashtra during the 1980s.[28] In Bangladesh, communal violence did not come so much in large scale outbursts of atrocity as in slow harassment of the Hindu minority, which steadily diminished during the decades after partition from 28.0 per cent of the population in 1941 to 10.5 per cent in 1991 as Hindus left (or fled) to India. Just during the 1980s, their numbers diminished from 12.1 per cent in 1981 to 10.5 per cent ten years later.[29]

3. The *standards of judgement for officeholders*. The ways in which the culture evaluates political leadership was quite different in the two regions. In Maharashtra the principal criterion seemed to be *performance*, with integrity in a strong second place. It was expected that there will be some corruption, leakage, lobbying for special interests, or nursing of constituencies, but it was also expected that government deliver something concrete in promoting rural development (and development in general, for that matter). Programmes intended to raise agricultural production had to deliver inputs so that they would be used to improve irrigation, get fertilizer onto the fields, make credit available to those who would use it to increase crop production, and so on. In WM's archetypal example, the Employment Guarantee Scheme had to provide unemployment relief for the rural poor (though it would also be beneficial to local politicians in the process, there would be some bungling and embezzling, etc.).

In BB *patronage* seemed the main criterion for judging officeholders. It wasn't really expected that inputs would ever be used as intended, that irrigation projects would actually deliver much water to farmers, that roads would be built to handle the traffic load for which they were designed. The first purpose of government development activity was to provide patronage and build allegiance for those who can deliver the patronage. A second and allied purpose was to maintain the rural gentry's *control* over the lower strata at village level by diverting the loot that comes down from higher level to reinforcing their own positions, as per the earlier discussion of Figure 1.

The 'upazila' development scheme undertaken under Ershad in the 1980s provides an excellent illustration of patronage masquerading as development. This massive decentralization initiative put elected officials in charge at the thana (renamed upazila) level in non-partisan elections, for the ostensible purpose of creating local decision-making unencumbered by party affiliation. But it soon became evident that the underlying purpose was to put in place a cohort of local office holders who could then be enticed into supporting Ershad's Jatiyo Party in exchange for gaining control over development funds coming into their areas.[30]

It probably goes too far to say that the local power structure in BB was *hostile* to any significant economic growth on the grounds that such growth might encourage the lower orders to be more demanding, for there were some (albeit feeble) signs of the beginnings of an agricultural transformation to a market-oriented agriculture. But there was certainly a massive reluctance on the part of the gentry to see any benefits go to the rural poor. To sum up, one could ask: was an effective EGS even remotely conceivable in rural Bihar during the 1980s? To ask such a question, regrettably, was to know the answer.

A good illustration of the difference in standards of judgment of officeholders can be seen in the resignations of chief ministers A.R. Antulay and Shivajirao Patil-Nilangekar in Maharashtra. Both were forced out because of corruption scandals aired and publicized in the media—Antulay in a cement allocation scam (awarding allocations of this perennially scarce commodity in return for contributions to a political fund) and Patil-Nilangekar in medical examination fixing scheme (getting the marks adjusted on the state gynecological exams so that his twice-failed daughter could pass).[31] By contrast, at about the same time as Patil-Nilangekar was resigning in Maharashtra, a medical scandal was emerging in Bihar in which Chief Minister Bindeshwari Dubey was trying to 'regularize' the appointments of (i.e. give permanent civil service status to) the one-third of the state's health service cadre who had been given their jobs on various ad hoc schemes over the previous eight years. Needless to say, more than a few of these appointments had been made on the basis of qualifications other than medical, but there was no threat to the chief minister on this ground.

Indeed, in Bihar it was inconceivable that a chief minister would be sacked on grounds of corruption or incompetence. There were forced departures and even hints of scandal connected with them, but the ousters had always been mainly concerned with factional intrigues and power bases. The most notable example in the 1980s was chief minister Jagannath Mishra, who had been strongly implicated in massive corruption at the state fertilizer cooperative. He was dismissed by Prime Minister Rajiv Gandhi, but no one interpreted the departure as seriously related to the fertilizer scandal. Rather, it was because of factional shifts against Mishra in the Bihar Congress and because the personal dynamic between Rajiv Gandhi and Mishra was highly negative (by contrast, Indira Gandhi, who had a well-known 'soft corner' for Mishra, had kept him in office no matter what the aroma of misdeeds surrounding him). Perhaps the best way to put it is to observe that a chief minister in Bihar would have been judged wanting if he were *not* fiddling with medical exams and cement allocations on behalf of relatives, caste-fellows and cronies.

4. *The styles of politics*. Politics in Maharashtra was characterized in the 1980s by what might be called a *transactional style*, in which people involved themselves in the political arena to exchange benefits. Trading and deal-making were the modes of participation. In BB, the dominant pattern was an *allegiant style,* whereby one played politics to build-up and nurture a support base. Goods and services did change hands, but they did so as a means of buying and selling support, whereas in Maharashtra the exchanges were made with a view to using the

goods and services to produce and build things. True, transactional politicians needed their support bases too, and the goods and services traded by allegiance-oriented politicians did sometimes serve to increase economic and/or social productivity. But in the main, there is a meaningful distinction here. The sugar nexus in WM is illustrative of the transactional style, for all the vote-trading, surreptitious candidate-funding and so on really did lead to more investment in rural infrastructure, while in BB, the horsetrading that goes on was designed to build or destroy patronage empires.

This makes Maharashtra sound more like an idealized Western political system than perhaps it should. It was not, after all, pluralist in quite the sense that the US claims to be (though it may have more resemblance to the US system as it in fact is—somewhat pluralist but not all that far away from the elite-domination end of the spectrum). Furthermore, the EGS did not prove to be a panacea for rural poverty. The point is that it may have put a floor under rural incomes, in total contrast to BB. There real income for agricultural labour appeared to fall for most of the 1970s and 1980s, as this pool of residual rural labour grew. The EGS may even have raised rural incomes slightly in Maharashtra. The social/economic/political infrastructure of Maharashtra thus, provided a kind of security for the rural poor that was simply nowhere in sight in BB, and it also provided an integrated dynamic of rural development absent in BB.

A Developmental Bottom Line

For some years now, the United Nations Development Programme (UNDP) has compiled a 'Human Development Index' (HDI), that has become widely accepted in the world as an standard measure usable across countries to gauge attainment and (by comparing across years) progress in promoting human welfare. The HDI comprises a combination of gross domestic product per capita, literacy and schooling rates, and life expectancy. A number of countries including India have carried the idea down below the national level, and so it is possible (with some manipulation[32]) to compare Indian states with

Bangladesh, as is done in Table 5. Here Bihar and Bangladesh show up roughly even in 1980 and almost exactly even for 1990. The gap between them and Maharashtra widened from 160–180 points in 1980 to almost 200 points in 1990. In this latter year, Maharashtra at .610 compared in HDI with countries like Bolivia (.603) and Indonesia (.623), while BB at .416 and .417 were on a level with Tanzania (.413) and Zaire (later Congo, at .414). Little prospect for catching up seemed to be in the cards for either Bangladesh or Bihar at that point.

TABLE 5
Human Development Index for Maharashtra, Bihar and Bangladesh, 1980–1990

	Maharashtra	*Bihar*	*All-India*	*Bangladesh*
1980-UNDP	*525*	*342*	437	363
1981-GOI	363	237	302	
1990-UNDP	*610*	*416*	514	417
1991-GOI	452	308	381	

Notes: Italicized figures imputed from UNDP calculations (note that GOI uses a much more rigorous standard in calculating the HDI than does the UNDP; the italicized figures have been adjusted to the UNDP standard to facilitate comparison with Bangladesh).

Sources: UNDP (2005) for India and Bangladesh 1980 and 1990 data; GOI (2002) for 1981 and 1991 figures for Bihar, Maharashtra and All-India.

Implications for Rural Development Policy

In Maharashtra, or certainly WM, the themes of rural development in the 1980s appeared to be capitalist agriculture, cooperative-based politics, interlinked institutional infrastructure to support development and (to a more modest extent) social responsibility. In BB, the predominant themes were a semi-feudal agriculture, a predatory politics reinforced by a functionally diffuse institutional infrastructure, and a lack of social responsibility. The key difference in terms of rural development strategy would seem to be the emergence of an infrastructure of (more or less) functionally discrete institutions in WM that did not get sucked into or perverted by the maelstrom of patronage politics but instead could actually deliver goods and services to promote rural development. What then were the prospects for rural development policy changes at the end of the 1980s that might improve things in BB?

In Bihar there had been some indications of an agricultural transformation and the mobilization of a constituency to support it (with Karpoori Thakur and the Lok Dal being the premier case in point), but the process was at best slow and seemed to have stalled indefinitely after the brief Lok Dal surge to power in the late 1970s.[33] Would it have been possible to regain the momentum, whether with the Lok Dal or with a reoriented Congress Party that sought to mobilize 'progressive farmer' strata? A case might be made in counterfactual history, but in reality the beginning of the 1990s saw the rise to power of Laloo Prasad Yadav as chief minister of Bihar and the onset of his long dominance of the state's politics, which continued into the new millennium. Under him, backward caste men gained the spoils of office but so far as rural development was concerned, little changed. Corruption continued as the principal theme of government programmes (reaching a high point in 1997 when he was forced to resign office in the wake of a fodder scandal[34]), rural violence continued to roil the countryside, and agricultural production continued to stagnate. Any semblance of a state accountable to its citizens for fostering rural development remained far from view. Elections continued to be held, but Laloo's tactical success, at least until the last state elections in 2005, in rendering them into what amounted to caste referenda on the Backwards' right to dominate the polity, made them useless as occasions for parties to put programmatic policy platforms before the voters.

In Bangladesh on the other hand there was considerably more room for policy maneuvre. Unlike Bihar, where rural elites with large landholdings linked directly into the upper echelons of state power, in Bangladesh the dominant elements in the countryside have been smaller in scale—in Bihar they would be middle peasants, a situation partly due to land pressure fragmenting holdings and partly to the departure of so many Hindu zamindars after the partition of 1947, thereby leaving the field to the smaller fry. Thus while the state has needed local elites to help maintain order, it never became beholden to them in quite the same way as in Bihar, for they themselves did not loom so large as a class on the wider scene of state politics.

One of the consequences of this relative separation is that the state has had somewhat more autonomy to pursue reformist rural development policies. Nothing on the order of land reform has been on the cards, to be sure, but the state has had more latitude to support policy reforms in the agricultural sector. Probably of equal importance, it has also had a good deal of direct pressure from its donors to pursue such changes (and when those same donors were pumping in US $1-2 billion annually, as they were throughout the 1980s and early 1990s, the pressures were hard to ignore). Thus it was that over the later 1980s and 1990s, the state privatized the fertilizer trade, and then tubewells and pumps, allowed private international trade in grain (basically with West Bengal), and invested heavily in such infrastructural needs as electricity and roads. In effect, the state traded in the *dirigiste* policies it had been following since gaining independence in 1971 for a variant of the 'Washington consensus' on agricultural policy. The early steps came under the dictatorship of H. M. Ershad, but the trajectory carried over into the democratic era that began with his overthrow at the beginning of the 1990s. The result has been an annual growth rate in foodgrain production of 3.3 per cent during the 1990s, a trend that has led to falling rice prices and higher consumption, increasing agricultural wages, and even switching from *bargadar* (sharecropper) status to rent tenancy as cultivators have been able to gain better terms from landowners—altogether an amazing set of developments.[35]

Will these changes enable Bangladesh to restore the *Sonar Bangla* ('Golden Bengal') of mythical antiquity? Probably not, but the changes do seem to have provided a significant improvement over the 1970s and 1980s. At the same time, the Bangladesh trajectory represents quite a different path from that taken in western Maharashtra, with its combination of government-subsidized production, wasteful allocation of resources (to sugar), and political culture demanding that those in office have to deliver a modicum of developmental goods.

To close, it could be said that western Maharashtra has followed a state-subsidized path to rural development, and Bangladesh has pursued a donor-induced market path; both have led to increased rural welfare in terms of steady or rising wages and higher food consumption, albeit at the expense of the environment in Maharashtra and precariously balanced on continued good monsoons in Bangladesh.[36] In contrast, Bihar has taken a counterproductive path of casteism, corruption and violence that scholars like Walter Hauser have charted all too well.

NOTES

1. I thank the American Institute of Indian Studies, the Fulbright research programme, the Social Science Research Council, the Rural Development Committee at Cornell University, Bucknell University, and the A.N. Sinha Institute for Social Studies in Patna for their support at various stages along the way.
2. After writing the first version of the paper in 1988, my own research trajectory changed markedly, first narrowing to a largely exclusive focus on Bangladesh, and then broadening away from the subcontinent to the global democratization support initiative then being undertaken by the international donor community, an enterprise that still engages the largest part of my research attention. The experience has been an exciting one, but a part of the opportunity cost has been an almost total neglect of the subcontinental research that attracted me for so long. The Hauserfest offers an excellent opportunity to return to those earlier ruminations, to see if they still make sense.
3. As things turned out, Bangladesh did experience significant agricultural growth in the 1990s and on into the new century, while Bihar has continued to stagnate. See Raisuddin Ahmed, Steven Haggeblade and Tawfiq-e-elahi Choudhry, *Out of the Shadow of Famine: Evolving Food Markets and Food Policy in Bangladesh*, Baltimore: Johns Hopkins University Press, 2000, also Harry Blair, 'Civil Society and Pro-poor Initiatives at the Local Level in Bangladesh: Finding a Workable Strategy', *World Development*, vol. 33, no. 6, June 2005, pp. 921-36.
4. The literature on both Bihar and Bangladesh is immense. For Bihar see, e.g., Arun Sinha, *Against the Few: Struggles of India's Rural Poor*, London: Zed Press, 1991, Arvind N. Das, *State of Bihar: An*

Economic History Without Footnotes, Amsterdam: Vu University Press, 1992; Pradhan H. Prasad, *Lopsided Growth: Political Economy of Indian Development*, Bombay: Oxford University Press, 1989; Pradhan H. Prasad, *India: Dilemma of Development*, edited by Meeta Krishna, New Delhi: Mittal Publ., 2000; also Harry Blair, 'Rising Kulaks and Backward Classes in Bihar: Social Change in the Late 1970s', *Economic and Political Weekly*, vol. 15, no. 12, January 1980, pp. 64-74. For Bangladesh, Betsy Hartmann and James Boyce, *A Quiet Violence: View from a Bangladesh Village*, London: Zed Press, 1983 remains an outstanding account; see also Harry Blair, 'Rural Development, Class Structure and Bureaucracy in Bangladesh', *World Development*, vol. 6, January 1978, pp. 65-82; and Harry Blair, *The Political Economy of Participation in Local Development Programs: Shortterm Impasse and Longterm Change in South Asia and the United States from the 1950s to the 1980s*, Ithaca: Rural Development Committee, Center for International Studies, Cornell University, 1982.

5. West Bengal belongs geographically in this same area, and before the Partition in 1947 belonged in many ways socio-economically as well. But by the 1980s it had diverged markedly onto a different path, charted largely by the Marxist government then in power. So I omit it from the present analysis.
6. I take refuge in this term, which is I believe reasonably accurate, but at the same time sufficiently vague that it is possible to avoid the 'mode of production' debate that bedevilled much analysis of the subcontinent in the 1970s and 1980s.
7. For Bihar the government is a state which is part of a larger central government, whereas in Bangladesh the state is of course a national government in its own right. In terms of the rural political economy, however, the state has virtually the same relationship to the countryside for both cases. The maintenance of state power in the late 1980s means continuation of a Congress ministry in Patna and of the Ershad regime in Dhaka.
8. Keith Griffin, *The Political Economy of Agrarian Change: An Essay on the Green Revolution*, Cambridge: Harvard University Press, 1974.
9. From 1969-70 through 1983-4, reports Prasad (*India: Dilemma of Development*, p. 135), Bihar's growth rate in agricultural production was 0.49 per cent. Maharashtra, by contrast, clocked in at 5.50 per cent over the same period.

10. Geof Wood, a longtime observer of both Bihar and Bangladesh, has elaborated on this 'Faustian bargain' in 'Staying Secure, Staying Poor: The Faustian Bargain', *World Development*, vol. 31, March 2003, pp. 455-71.
11. Literature on the political economy of sugar in western Maharashtra is not as rich as for rural Bihar and Bangladesh, but fortunately it has had two exemplary analysts explaining it. See B.S. Baviskar, *The Politics of Development: Sugar Co-operatives in Rural Maharashtra*, Delhi: Oxford University Press, 1980; Donald W. Attwood, 'Social and Political Pre-conditions for Successful Co-operatives: The Co-operative Sugar Factories of Western India', in D. W. Attwood and B. S. Baviskar, eds., *Who Shares? Co-operatives and Rural Development*, Delhi: Oxford University Press, 1988, pp. 69-90; Donald W. Attwood, *Raising Cane: The Political Economy of Sugar in Western India,* Boulder: Westview Press, 1992. For a simpler account, see Harry Blair and Charles Mann, 'Assisting Indian Agriculture, 1940s to 1980s', unpublished essay, 1986.
12. It is more difficult to deal with regions in Maharashtra than for Bihar and Bangladesh, in large part because while the latter have been more or less identifiable since the division of the Bengal Presidency in 1912 (and in many ways date back long before that), Maharashtra is a much more recent creation, having been formed in its present shape only in 1960. The focus of this essay is on the western Deccan lava of Maharashtra that is the major sugar producing area of the state; this consists of the Pune division's six districts plus three from Bombay division (Nashik, Dhule and Jalgaon), or altogether nine of the state's 27 districts (as of the 1980s), which are collectively often called Western Maharashtra. All of the nine save Kolhapur and a portion of Sangli districts (which were former princely states) were part of the Bombay Presidency during the British period, thus giving them a common history not shared by the Marathwada and Vidarbha regions to their east. For Bihar I should note that the present analysis applies basically to the Gangetic plain region of the state, not to the largely tribal area of Chota Nagpur, which was split off in 2000 along with the old Santal Parganas district to form the new state of Jharkhand.
13. Even *gur*-making is too complex to be done at home. The process requires a huge investment and perhaps a dozen or more employees working at any one time.

14. Some perspective here might be gained from reflecting on the awesomely high subsidies given to water supplied in the western United States by the US Bureau of Reclamation.
15. Much of the irrigation in WM is through gravity flow channels that do not require pumps, but a good part comes from wells, which are charged primarily through underground percolation from unlined channels of the surface water irrigation system, which leak a good deal of their water into the adjacent soil. For the many farmers benefiting from this indirect water supply, electricity for pumps is a major consideration.
16. In the summer of 1987, for example, the world price of sugar was about US 6¢/lb., while inside India it was the equivalent of around US 25¢. At times the world price may have been in excess of the internal Indian price, but for most of the late twentieth century, the international price has tended to stay quite low.
17. The EGS has been the subject of considerable analysis: John Echeverri-Gent, 'Guaranteed Employment in an Indian State: the Maharashtra Experience', *Asian Survey*, vol. 28, no. 12, December 1988, pp. 1294-1310; and Ronald Herring and Rex M. Edwards, 'Guaranteed Employment to the Rural Poor: Social Functions and Class Interests in the Employment Guarantee Scheme in Western India', *World Development*, vol. 11, no. 7, July 1983, pp. 575-92.
18. There are other programmes patterned on EGS that were initiated in the 1980s by the centre, in particular the Rural Landless Employment Guarantee Scheme and the National Rural Employment Programme, but neither proved to be more than a pale imitation of the original.
19. See Harry Blair, 'Electoral Support and Party Institutionalization in Bihar: Congress and the Opposition, 1977-1985', in Richard Sisson and Ramashray Roy, eds., *Diversity and Dominance in Indian Politics: Changing Bases of Congress Support*, vol. I, New Delhi: Sage, 1990, pp. 123-67, for some speculation on this.
20. Altogether the various food for work programs in Bangladesh were estimated to generate upwards of 70 million work days annually around this time.
21. That effect has been uneven, with those better off getting a larger share—but then what place outside of China in the Cultural Revolution has not? The point is that those in the lower income deciles have been getting something tangible from the rural development process, whereas in BB this was evidently not the case.
22. There are many excellent analyses of land tenure and its legacies.

For a good overview, see Lloyd I. Rudolph and Susanne H. Rudolph, *In Pursuit of Lakshmi*, Chicago: University of Chicago Press, 1987. The classic study remains Baden-Powell's 3-volume opus published in 1892 (B.H. Baden-Powell, *The Land-systems of British India: Being a Manual of the Land-tenures and of the Systems of Land-revenue Administration Prevalent in the Several Provinces*, Oxford: Clarendon Press, 1892).

23. This figure applies to the area occupied by the truncated state of Bihar as of 2001, as do all the census data in this essay. But even including the entire state as it existed in 1991, urbanization had reached just over 13.2 per cent, still among the lowest in the country.
24. The 1931 census was the last to provide anything close to a full-scale enumeration of the major Hindu castes. For an assessment of the validity of those old data for present-day uses, see Harry Blair, 'Caste and the British Census in Bihar: Using Old Data to Study Contemporary Political Behavior', in N. Gerald Barrier, ed., *The Census in British India: New Perspectives*, Delhi: Manohar, 1981, pp. 149-75. Updating Bihar's caste distribution is fairly straightforward, but reconstructing the present area of Maharashtra from compilations of the British period is a tedious task, for it involves adding in and subtracting out a number of districts from different British provinces as well as a large group of princely states. Bihar and Bangladesh are a great deal easier to deal with in this respect.
25. To some extent these observations may be more revealing of north-south (or Aryan-Dravidian) differences in India than east-west divisions.
26. Ironically, Huq himself devoted much of his energy to keeping Hindus and Muslims united, but that is not what he is remembered for.
27. See Walter Hauser, 'From Peasant Soldiering to Peasant Activism: Reflections on the Transition of a Martial Tradition in the Flaming Fields of Bihar', *Journal of the Economic and Social History of the Orient*, vol. 47, September 2004, pp. 401-434, for an account of the violence and its origins. Also Prasad, *Lopsided Growth*, Ch. 9.
28. And Bihar largely escaped the communal violence of the 1990s—one of the few real achievements of Laloo Prasad Yadav's time as chief minister.
29. BBS (Bangladesh Bureau of Statistics), *Population Census 2001, National Report (Provisional)*, Dhaka: BBS, Planning Division, Ministry of Planning, 2003, p. 66.

30. See Harry Blair, 'Politics, Civil Society and Governance in Bangladesh', in Rounaq Jahan, ed., *Bangladesh: Promise and Performance,* London: Zed Press, 2000, pp. 181-217, for more on the patronage aspects of the upazila scheme. The initiative did have the potential to become a viable decentralized development mechanism, at least in my view, rather like the zila parishads in Maharashtra, but never grew out of the patronage phase.
31. Rumors at the time focused on the irony that S.B. Chavan, Patil-Nalingekar's Predecessor as chief minister, had engaged in a similar impropriety but had not been caught by the media.
32. The Indian Planning Commission evidently used a considerably more rigorous standard than UNDP, so its all-India calculation for 1981 put HDI at .302 (on a scale running from zero to 1.000) for 1980, whereas the UNDP set India's HDI at .437, compared with .363 for Bangladesh. Table 5 imputes HDI figures for Bihar and Maharashtra for 1980, so that they can be compared with Bangladesh. It should be noted that the data in Table 5 include both urban and rural areas, meaning that Bombay (and to a much lesser extent Pune) pulls up the overall state figures for Maharashtra. Even so, the differences are significant.
33. See Blair, 'Rising Kulaks and Backward Classes in Bihar'.
34. Laloo Prasad Yadav responded to this setback by moving his wife into the chief ministership. See John F. Burns, 'Official in India Sets up a Dynasty of His Own', *New York Times*, 28 July 1997.
35. Raisuddin Ahmed, 'Rice Economy of Bangladesh: Progress and Prospects', *Economic and Political Weekly,* 4 September 2004, pp. 4043-52 gives an account of these policy changes and their effects. See Ahmed et al., *Out of the Shadow of Famine*, for a fuller analysis. For some speculation on potential downstream impact in terms of a widened scope for grassroots civil society advocacy, see Blair, 'Civil Society and Pro-poor Initiatives at the Local Level in Bangladesh'.
36. I do not wish to end this essay with the impression that all is well in Bangladesh. As agricultural production has steadily increased, the political situation has deteriorated rapidly in recent years in an atmosphere of corruption, widespread political gangsterism and self-destructive behavior of the political leadership. For a cogent analysis of the scene as of mid-decade, see inter alia Rehman Sobhan, 'Structural Dimensions of Malgovernance in Bangladesh', *Economic and Political Weekly*, September 2004, vol. 39, no. 36, pp. 4101-8.

Bihar via 'A Virtual Village'

Peter Gottschalk and Mathew N. Schmalz

Perhaps because of its unfavourable reputation among Indians and foreigners alike, Bihar has hardly received the scholarly attention that its diverse cultures deserve. The study of its history has benefitted from the work of such pioneers as Qeyamuddin Ahmad and Walter Hauser and their students. However, the study of religions has suffered a lacuna of interest in Bihar, apart from Buddhist studies centered of such sites as Bodh Gaya, Nalanda, and Rajgir. Scholars of Indian religions also less frequently direct their research to rural field sites, focusing instead of urban, national, and transnational issues. In an effort to devise new and appropriate resources to address these concerns among undergraduate audiences, we turned to developing electronic media.

The rapidly expanding capabilities of educational technology have radically changed the contemporary college classroom. The development of the World Wide Web has not just simply increased the availability and flow of information but also has substantially expanded the space for teaching and learning. Cyberspace then offers an important new dimension for cultural investigation by transforming global boundaries. The potential of using the internet to bridge the confines of time and space is perhaps nowhere more apparent than in the field of South Asian studies in the United States, where the cultural and geographical distance between India and America raises challenging pedagogical issues. To take advantage of advances in educational technology and to address issues in the teaching of South Asian Studies, we have developed an interactive website based upon a contemporary Indian village.[1] The village, which we call by the pseudonym 'Arampur', is located in western Bihar and reflects the cultural richness and complexity of contemporary rural society. With Arampur as a setting, 'A Virtual Village' seeks not only to introduce students to Indian rural culture and society but also to invite a more general discussion of issues of cultural representation and cross-cultural understanding that have developed over the preceding several centuries of Western contact with the peoples of the subcontinent.

HISTORICAL CONTEXT

'A Virtual Village' stands as only the latest in more than 230 years of Western depictions of Arampur. Its designers self-consciously fashioned it in response to the lapses and successes of these previous depictions, with an awareness of post-colonial critiques of 'representations' of South Asia in general. Accordingly, a recognition of the historical context of the specific accounts of Arampur provides both background to the current project and an important pedagogical consideration regarding its use in the undergraduate classroom.

After Jean-Baptiste Tavernier made passing reference to a stop in Arampur in his *Les Six Voyages de Jean Baptiste Tavernier, Ecuyer Baron D'Aubonne, qu'il a fait en Turque, en Perse, et aux Indes* (1676),[2] James Rennell produced the first known depiction of the village with the map he rendered as Surveyor General, *An Actual Survey of the Provinces of Bengal, Bahar &C.*[3] The East India Company had ordered this geographical survey in order to gain a better view of the territories that had fallen suddenly under their control after the Battles of Plassey (1757) and Buxar (1765). Almost forty years later, the Company would command Francis Buchanan (later known as Buchanan Hamilton) to follow Rennell's study with a walking survey intended to record a wide range of information across all of these *zillah*s or districts. In doing so, Buchanan would spend a day in Arampur interviewing residents, recording observations, and executing sketches regarding the antiquities, topography, religions, customs, agriculture, and economics of the area.[4] The notes he made over the years of his expeditions through Bihar and Bengal established a foundation for most of the British investigations—both on site and from afar—that would follow.

Indeed, the Bihar state government in their last gazetteer for Shahabad district, which contained Arampur at the time, includes a reference to Buchanan's observations.[5]

Between Rennell and Buchanan two other British men visited Arampur: Thomas Daniell and his nephew William. These landscape artists would add a number of sketchings and paintings executed in the area in August 1790 to their collection. Their representations of various regions of India, especially those contained in their multiple volume sets entitled *Antiquities of India* (that included two images from the Arampur area), provided perhaps the first mass-produced and popularly embraced depictions of the subcontinent.[6] In particular, their convincing 'on the spot' view prompted British audiences to trust what they saw.

What attracted these early British travelers is not immediately apparent. Rennell depicts a road running through Arampur but offers no other insights why he includes it on his relatively large-scale maps. It appears that the village did once serve as a Suri military centre since a number of impressive funerary monuments remain from that period; its name was lent to the pargana in which it stood, and its name appears a few times in the *Tarikh-i Sher Shahi*. However, those 'glory days' had long faded by the time Rennell arrived. Figuring prominently among British representations are an ancient temple on the Kaimur Range behind the village, a vast Suri-era mausoleum near the village, and an important pilgrimage site inside Arampur. However, considering the relative frequency with which one encounters similar sites throughout Bihar and Bengal, their importance in attracting so much attention remains less than convincing.

Over the remaining 150 years of British imperial rule, an increasing variety of British officials and numbers of Indian authors wrote about Arampur. These included travel writers, revenue collectors, missionaries, and members of the Census of India and the Archæological Survey of India. Historical records include sketches, photographs, sculptures, folklore recordings, revenue maps, and village notes. Following Independence, foreign scholars continued to make stops there, including three dissertators, two art historians, and a historian of religion. Arampur also finds its place in government publications about the folklore and antiquities of the state. All of this attention notwithstanding, Arampur remains relatively unrecognized by Indians, or even Biharis, outside the Bhojpuri-speaking region. This low-profile foreign and indigenous attention to Arampur makes it a well-recorded, but ironically unknown, village. This allows a virtual rendering of it to demonstrate many features common with other villages of its size. Moreover, many portrayals of Arampur reflect common depictions of Indians in general. Concern for the centrality of religion and the pervasiveness of communalism in so much Western-generated literature was the reason for creating this web-based pedagogical tool.

A Virtual Village

'A Virtual Village' takes as its starting point that Hindus and Muslims do not live in separate social, cultural, and religious worlds. The importance of this contention derives from two common assumptions among many Americans, including scholars who study the Indian subcontinent. The first takes religion as the most important criterion in the lives of Indians. As the 'mystical' place of the American imagination, deep with 'spirituality' and full of 'holy people', India is primarily defined by its religious traditions. This leads to the other assumption that Hinduism and Islam are essentially mutually exclusive, if not mutually antagonistic. This perspective emphasizes themes such as 'Muslims eat the meat of the cow that Hindus venerate', and 'Hindus worship the images that Muslims condemn'. Since religion presumably plays such a central role in their lives and their religions operate at the opposite ends of ritual and belief spectrums, Hindus and Muslims must have fashioned entirely different, if not opposing, worlds. With the focus on Hindu-Muslim differences, it is easy to overlook the differences and tensions in what appear to be self-contained 'Hindu' and 'Muslim' communities.

The designers' commitment to challenge these assumptions derives from their experiences in South Asia where they have encountered no small amount of interreligious prejudice along with far more instances of daily coexistence and mutual involvement. Their experience in attempting to teach about the more integrated existence of Indians often proved frustrating because tackling the topic head-on ironically often reinforces the notions of difference. It has proven difficult to directly emphasize interrelations without emphasizing Hindu and Muslim identities. In the discussion of the devotional life demonstrated at the tombs of Sufis (Muslim mystics) for instance, emphasis on Hindus and Muslims worshipping together underscores these two identities as primary for the worshippers when, in fact, they may not be as they venerate the Sufi. Furthermore, focus on religious sites only emphasizes the religious lives of Indians and reinforces the expectation that Indians are first and foremost 'a religious people'.

'A Virtual Village' attempts to demonstrate the more complex social realities of religious lives in India by not directly addressing that topic but instead placing it into the larger context of social and cultural life. So, one meets people of different religions in the shop of a fabric merchant as they sit about looking at cloth while conversing. Across the street they can notice a barber and shoe repairman sitting with one another. When they interview each man they may discern, from the interview answers and surrounding objects, that one is a Muslim and the other a Hindu. In other words, no caption explicitly identifies the barber and shoe repairman as Muslim and Hindu. Instead, their religious identities are implied in their own words and surroundings.

Of course, the user's awareness of religious identity is not accidental either. The designers have still directed, in part, the user's experience by choosing which questions the interview includes, who one meets, and what of the village one sees. The website does not, nor could it ever hope to, capture the experience of innocently walking through Arampur, if that were possible. However, the designers hope that the larger context portrayed by the project and the interactive nature of the interface will provide students a better opportunity to pursue their interests while virtually encountering village residents as they engage the broader field of their everyday lives. 'A Virtual Village' offers a variety of approaches to their exploration of the village. It does so not only in an effort to appeal to the divergent interests of its users but also to portray the multiple facets of rural Indian life.

The structure of the website can be divided into three components: Context, Roam, and Interviews.

Context

The interactive nature of 'A Virtual Village' allows students to choose when and how deeply they would like to explore details of the cultural, religious, social, and economic context of Arampur. To this end, the website includes three sections that allow a diversity of approaches: 'About Arampur', 'Topics', and the interactive 'Glossary'.

The component 'About Arampur' places the village within six sets of geographic interrelations: village, village nexus, state, region, nation, and globe.[7] This nested arrangement responds to recent scholarship which has criticized the manner in which villages have been romanticized as seemingly self-supporting rural communities that live apart from larger social contexts.[8] 'A Virtual Village' works to demonstrate how this is not the case, but it does recognize the centrality of the village in the minds of most of its residents, even as they appreciate the differences between its *muhalla*s (neighborhoods) and their interrelations with neighbouring villages, nearby towns, and distant cities. Through the 'About Arampur' section, students can understand how residents relate to multiple levels of community from the local to the global level.

'Topics', attempts to delineate and address specific themes of interest or question for the user[9]: religion, society, gender, language, and economics. These pages offer some background and prime the awareness of students as they roam the village and interview the villagers. Although the designers primarily had an interest in designing a pedagogical vehicle for learning about religion in India, the breadth of the topics reflects their concern to fully contextualize religious life in the socio-economic realm.

The interactive 'Glossary' represents the final element designed to aid students in what may likely be their first investigation of Indian cultures.[10] This glossary allows students to 'look up' a term that they encounter in most of the text they read. By clicking on any term that is specially marked as so enabled, the user immediately accesses the specific entry in the full glossary that often includes an image when appropriate.

ROAM

The centerpiece of 'A Virtual Village' involves the Roam section and its associated interviews.[11] Although the components outlined above provide useful information about Arampur and rural north-Indian life in general, 'A Virtual Village' relies on the Roam feature as the thread that draws all the other components together. The concept encourages viewers to imagine themselves in Arampur, looking down a street and carefully examining what and who they see.

Roam also allows access to almost all of the features available on the overall website, to navigate through select streets and alleys of Arampur while aided by an interactive map that shows their position and orientation at all times. Users may choose alternative maps that reveal the positions of specific sites connected with specific themes such as healing, narratives, and religious spaces and then manoeuver their way to these places.

With each virtual step that the student takes through Arampur, he has a photograph depicting the view ahead. A short caption offers comment on the image. As the user passes the cursor over specific objects and people, small rollover boxes appear that identify them. Some rollovers offer additional interaction with close-ups and interviews, as discussed in the next section. At certain intersections and viewpoints, the website provides the opportunity to view a 360-degree panorama from the pedestrian's point of view. Just as 'A Virtual Village' uses images and interviews to provide an added dimension to its ethnographic descriptions, so the panoramas add the chance to place the single frame images of the Roam pages into a more sweeping view of the vicinity.

A virtual visitor to Arampur might wish to begin at the bus stand. The area around the bus-stand is represented in a 360-degree panorama, with people seemingly enclosing the viewer. The visitor can then move toward the shrine of Shastri Brahm that stands on a fort over-looking the town at the opposite end of the main road and bazaar that acts as Arampur's spine. By accessing the navigational controls at the bottom of the page, the visitor virtually walks through a series of frames that move along the main road to the fort and the Abode (*dham*) of Shastri Brahm. Along the way, rollovers call the visitor's attention to the workshop of Dukhi Mistri, who makes and sells cooking utensils, and further down the road, another rollover prompts the visitor to investigate a sufi shrine maintained by a Hindu man who lives in the area. As the visitor moves northward, 'pop-up' rollovers identify and explain aspects of rural life seen along the way—from farm tractors to the ubiquitous cow-dung pats that are used as fuel. As the visitor nears the main bazaar, the house of Jnana Singh comes into view and Jnana Singh sits for an interview about life in the village during the Indo-Chinese war in the early 1960s. Further down the road, the visitor can observe P.A. Rahim's roadside tailor shop and then interview Ibrahim Khan in front of a mosque. The visitor can then take a virtual tour of the mosque or of the Shaivite temple opposite it, before proceeding to another intersection that allows a virtual circumambulation of Arampur in addition to moving directly to the fort and temple of Shastri Brahm. In this way, students who become virtual visitors to Arampur have the opportunity to explore the village in variety ways during multiple 'virtual' excursions.

INTERVIEWS

Interviews comprise the central element of the content of 'A Virtual Village'. As the virtual visitor moves through the village, moving the cursor reveals 'hot-spots' that are linked to interviews with Arampur's residents. The interviews are translated into English and transcribed. Select portions are also joined with sound files that allow native speakers or language students to hear the original Hindi and Urdu. There are forty interviews in all, and a conscious effort was made to be comprehensive within the unavoidable constraints and boundaries that circumscribe research. There are interviews with religious leaders such as Kuber Tiwari, the head priest of the Abode of Shastri Brahm, and Syed Farhad, a travelling Islamic preacher. Teachers of the Little Angels School are also represented in the interviews talking about their teaching methods and curriculum. There are interviews with shopkeepers such as the cloth merchant Arvind Jaswar, and interviews with sweet-sellers and *paan-walas*. There are also revealing interviews with those who work by manual labour, such as the cobbler Lacchan Das and the barber Faisal Yacqub. In their interviews, Rukshan and Laila Khan speak of their daily lives and also their Islamic beliefs, while Lakshmi and Saraswati Devi talk about their devotion to Durga as well as the complexity of their familial responsibilities. The inclusion of the full transcripts of the interviews is intended not only to provide a kind of data base when joined with the online glossary, but also to 'demystify' the interviewing process itself. If one listens to the exchanges in their original Hindi and Urdu, or reads the transcripts in their entirety, one can easily hear and see moments when the interviewers and residents are having a difficult time understanding each other. Reflecting upon such disjunctions in communication is an essential part of understanding the potential and limitations of the kind of ethnographic research that informs 'A Virtual Village'.

One of the crucial issues in ethnographic research is authority. Ethnographers can often claim a kind of 'god's-eye' view of the subjects of their research and most obviously control how their research is presented. In spite of the inclusion of the full transcripts of interviews, 'A Virtual Village' as a discrete website is undeniably shaped and controlled by the framework developed by its designers. To this extent, the residents of Arampur do not speak 'for' or 'as' themselves since their comments are already framed by the seemingly authoritative structures of the website. In order to give residents more agency and authority with regard to their portrayals in the website, individuals in Arampur were provided cameras to document their lives in any way they thought appropriate and informative. The resulting section 'My Life', brings together a range of photographs taken by Arampur's residents.[12] The photographs also are coupled with notes—written by residents in both Hindi and English—that explain the portrayals. Indra Jaswar for example chose to write various tongue and cheek notes in Hindi about pictures he took of his friends, while Bhadra Jaswar chose to document her daily household chores and a visit to the Abode of Shastri Brahm.

The school teacher Syed Firdaus elected to document his family life and wrote short captions in English. As a final element in the 'My Life' section, one of the designers is interviewed by one of Arampur's residents—a fitting turning of the tables in a website that is dominated by an agenda shaped by issues concerning pedagogy in an American academic setting.

Hindus and Hinduism

One of the most contentious issues in South Asian studies is how Hinduism can be defined, if at all. While courses on Hinduism have long been staple fare in Comparative Religions curricula in the West, in recent decades the very category Hinduism has been challenged by both Western and Indian academics as a fiction of Orientalist scholarship that sought to define Indian traditions in a manner that would legitimize Western imperialism.[13] In return some Western and Indian scholars have pointed to the coherence of a discrete religious tradition extending from the Vedas while arguing that categories functionally equivalent to 'Hindu' and 'Hinduism' were deployed by Indians themselves before British imperialism began in earnest.[14] Yet even if one posits Hinduism as a definable tradition, there still remains the issue of how it should be characterized and studied.

The issue of how to characterize 'Hinduism' came into sharp relief in a recent controversy over the entry on Hinduism included in the widely available *Encarta Encyclopedia* published by Microsoft. The original entry, written by Wendy Doniger of the University of Chicago, traced the richness of the Hindu tradition from the Vedas onward while also emphasizing the 'contradictions' of Hinduism in practice.[15] True, all religions are inevitably replete with contradictions, both real and apparent, when understood as practised by real and conflicted human beings. But the crucial issue that sparked protest was that this portrayal of Hinduism seemed almost derogatory when compared to descriptions of Christianity and Islam that emphasize these traditions, first and foremost, as coherent systems of belief.[16] In response, *Encarta* chose Arvind Sharma of McGill University to write a new entry on Hinduism that would take the place of Doniger's contribution. While admitting that Hinduism itself is rather difficult to define, Sharma approached Hinduism as a religious tradition with a coherent theology and set of practices.[17] The crucial issue then is how one discusses Hinduism, or any other religion for that matter, as something embodied, or acted out, and reflected upon, or thought through. The emphasis of 'A Virtual Village' is to allow residents the opportunity to engage, or not engage, issues concerning their religious identity on their own terms as much as possible. With regard to Hinduism, responses from residents of Arampur challenge conventional Western understandings of what precisely constitutes religious identity.

THEORIES OF POSSESSION

For students who use the Virtual Village to investigate 'Hinduism', the most explicitly intellectual content comes from what might seem to be a very unlikely source. The centre of religious life in Arampur is the Abode of Shastri Brahm, a Brahman who starved himself to death in defiance of the local king. Kuber Tiwari, the chief priest of the Abode of Shastri Brahm, explains how his family was entrusted with the secret knowledge of how to perform especially powerful rituals that will remove afflictions of the possessed who come to Arampur for healing.[18] This emphasis upon what might be called the 'technology' ritual develops into an extremely sophisticated theory of possession. Kuber Tiwari speaks of a cosmology in which there is a crucial pairing and continuity between the human and ghostly forms of existence. Those who die before their time, without their life wishes being fulfilled, attach themselves to the living and possess them. But not all apparent possessions are 'real', since Kuber Tiwari explains how he discerns various psychological ailments that can often manifest themselves through symptoms resembling possession. For those who are possessed, there is a special process whereby the possessing spirit is finally transferred and 'seated' in a material object called a *pind*. What initially emerges in Kuber Tiwari's discussions is an account of possession that complements the socio-cultural understandings of possession and related phenomena in academic literature.[19] But also crucial to his discussion is that it reveals a sophisticated Hindu psychology and theology that is rarely engaged by textbook or encyclopaedic treatments of belief and practice.

Defining Hinduism

The vast majority of 'Hindu' residents of Arampur do not identify themselves as Hindu. The notable exception to this is Shiv Mistri who speaks of 'Hinduism', although he prefers the term 'eternal faith' (sanatan dharma), as he characterizes Hindus as those who 'worship images'.[20] In addition to repairing bicycles, Shiv Mistri is a leader in the local cadre of the RSS and so his religious identity is crucial to his understanding of his identity as an Indian. If 'Hindu' is not deployed as a marker as much as one would think, neither is caste. At the beginning of their interviews, residents were simply asked 'to give their introduction' —a purposefully open-ended request that was designed not to presume a particular manner of self-identification. Most residents gave their names and their occupations. The only residents who spoke of their caste identity did so in relation to their occupation as Brahman priests. For the typical American college student, who understands Hinduism as dominated by caste or 'Hindu' as indispensable markers of identity, such responses might be unexpected.

In spite of the relative scarcity of explicit references to 'Hindus' and 'Hinduism' there is nonetheless a shared sense of ritual life held by Arampur's residents that would indeed correspond to many scholarly treatments of Hinduism. For example, the Brahman priest Ajay Upadhyay speaks of the centrality of worship (puja) and seeing the deity (*darshan*).[21] After explaining traditional procedures for bring offerings and receiving them back 'infused with grace' as *prashad*, Upadhyay speaks of puja and darshan as fundamentally reflecting a particular attitude or feeling of the heart. His is a vision of Hinduism as fundamentally transactional in nature, a point made perhaps most strongly in the scholarly studies of Hinduism by the ethno-sociologist McKim Marriot.[22] The transactional character of Hinduism becomes clear in relations with deities, as exemplified in the offerings given to the ghost of Shastri Brahm, which, as a shopkeeper near the Abode explains, include wooden sandals and the special sweets that are specifically associated with Brahmans.[23] The transactional character of Hinduism is also clear in the concentric circles of relationships centered upon the Abode of Shastri Brahm, from the prashad that is distributed among Arampur's residents after darshan or puja to the pilgrims who come from all over Bihar, to priests such as Jaganath Pandit.[24] The coherence of Hinduism in Arampur is thus a dynamic and relational coherence based upon a series of deeply meaningful transactions apparent not only in the relationships between human beings and a variety of super-human agents but also in the complex relationships that the residents of Arampur maintain with one another.

MUSLIMS AND ISLAM

As in its portrayal of Hindus and Hinduism, 'A Virtual Village' aims to reflect on larger patterns of Muslim practices, beliefs, and cultures through local examples from Arampur. The balance between local specifics and global generalizations is obviously carried precariously, and the site stresses the diversity in both sets of traditions. Carrying this message across to American students has become particularly important since the turn of the century and the popular fascination with, and media caricatures of, Muslims. Although they often repeat the statistic that 1 in 5 people on the globe today are Muslim (meaning a population of more than a billion Muslims), newspapers and news programs offer little nuance in their depiction of Muslims whether they be in Paris, Pakistan, or Peoria. 'A Virtual Village' attempts to demonstrate differences primarily through three sets of venues: interviews, public and private spaces, and mosques and Sufi shrines.

The interviews allow students the best opportunity to 'hear' Muslim residents reflect on their religious lives in the context of other aspects of their lives. The designers structured the interviews to include questions about the place of Islam in the lives of many of the Muslims interviewed, although the degree of emphasis varied by interviewee.

The roll-over feature of the Roam aspect allows students to explore public and private spaces and discover for themselves the degree to which those who inhabit these spaces fill them with ritual objects and decorate with devotional art. So, for example, an image of a human-headed horse stands above a mirror in the shop of a Muslim barber. When the user rolls his cursor over the image he can read how it portrays Buraq, the steed that bore the Prophet Muhammad aloft to reach Jerusalem from which he ascended to Paradise during his famed 'Night Journey'. On a wall opposite from this image, an Islamic calendar hangs. A rollover informs the user that Muslims time their rituals according to a moon-based calendar. This hopefully prompts the user to wonder about the religious roots of the mainstream Gregorian calendar that dominates American life. Yet shops and homes do not act merely as shrines and so other rollovers allow students to encounter a host of other pieces of material culture including furniture, clothing, and decorations. Overall, these spaces reflect the more personal tastes of individuals and families in all of their variety.

As more formal prayer places, mosques and Sufi shrines reflect the more organized institutional and social aspect of Islam. Even so, they too manifest significant differences among themselves. 'A Virtual Village' allows users to virtually visit three of the many mosques in Arampur. Each differs from the other: a slight mosque wedged into the busy bazaar, a family mosque reputedly built during the era of the Mughal empire, and the large Friday Mosque that the community continues to expand. Students 'enter' the Friday Mosque and can view it through one of the 360-degree panorama movies.[25] They can also 'meet' the muezzin who makes the call to prayer five times daily and a young singer of *nat,* devotional songs to Muhammad.[26]

Although the largest Sufi shrines (*dargahs*) may incorporate a mosque into their devotional space, they represent yet a different aspect of organized Islam. Because a shrine may be only as big as an individual's tomb or large enough to include agricultural land that supports its maintenance, it may be maintained by only one local volunteer or have a broad community of devotees dedicated to its upkeep, or it may be forgotten altogether and allowed to decay. 'A Virtual Village' visits three *dargahs* of varying sizes and importance. One of these, the *dargah* of Asta Auliya, is still run by descendants of the original Sufi whose tomb becomes the centre of an annual festival celebrating his death anniversary and communion with God. Besides interviews with the most recent heir to Asta Auliya's position and his uncle, the website provides views of the attached mosque and a panorama of the tomb with close-ups of the banners, garlands, incense sticks, and bottles of water used by devotees to manifest their regard for the dead Sufi and access his resident powers to heal and help.[27] These shrines represent the space that most obviously expresses the intercommunal nature of shrine devotion as it serves Hindus, Muslims, and Christians equally and without constraint. Meanwhile, students have the opportunity to read one devotee's rendering of the Sufi's miraculous life that proves his power as healer. On the other end of the spectrum, users can view a far smaller shrine under reconstruction and learn of the Hindu man who tends it alone.

The diversity of images and descriptions of the practices and beliefs of resident Muslims and non-Muslims in supposedly Muslim spaces prompts users to wonder about the definitiveness of the adjective 'Muslim'. If certain Hindus participate in the death commemorations of a local Sufi while some Muslims condemn such events as un-Islamic, what does it mean to identify an *'urs* as a Muslim celebration? Meanwhile, when Muslim interviewees discuss the importance of the story of Shastri Brahm—who is, after all, a ghost worshipped in the form of a rock—when discussing their village history, how can this be reconciled with the popular image of the intolerant, monotheistic, aniconic Muslim? Overall, the Virtual Village attempts to infer that while many people describe themselves and their behaviour as Muslim, precisely defining what is Islam presents a far greater challenge.

Conclusion

'A Virtual Village' attempts to challenge students to encounter their assumptions regarding the place of religion in Indian societies by engaging them through a visual medium in recognition of the dominance of the visual in US culture. Use of 'A Virtual Village' in our classrooms has demonstrated the potential of this approach thus far. Students generally enjoy their time engaging the site with its myriad possibilities. As in any exercise, those with the most curiosity gain the most because they engage the material more fully. Some students appear to underestimate the extensiveness of the site: the instructor must outline very clearly what they expect them to do on the site, what they should get out of their experience, and how long they should expect to spend investigating it. Nevertheless, students commonly comment that the degree of interaction among Hindus and Muslims surprised them. They also find the details of religious rituals, beliefs, and spaces very illuminating, especially when encountered in connection with images. In spite of this, a number of pedagogical issues remain unresolved and require attention.

First, because of a predilection among American students to trust images, users must be warned by educators about the limits of the medium. Indeed, it is ironic that the first known Western depictions of Arampur would be on Rennell's maps and the Daniell's pictures and that these would have an enduring impact on their European audiences, while 'A Virtual Village' centrally relies on the interplay between these two image systems. Just as those who enjoy the Daniell's renderings today must engage a scepticism regarding the emphasis of the two artists on the religious and the decadent in their representations of India, so users must query the choice of images and interview subjects in the website. The more successfully an image convinces the viewer that it is 'true', and the interactive quality of the website aims to deepen this impression because of the designers' notions of true depiction, the more difficult to convince an audience to interrogate it. Inevitably this makes for an even more compelling reason to prompt such questioning.

Meanwhile, the import and impact of the 'presence' of the interviewers must be critically examined. Users may read and hear the interviewers' questions, but this does not allow much insight into how the interviewees might have responded had the researchers not been foreigners, or if they had been associated with a particular religious group, or caste, or class. For instance, how would someone's self-description differ had a wealthy Ansari asked, or a poor Dalit? Because the interviewer and the medium connote authority for some users, the interviewer exists as almost a hidden variable in the conversations, apparently transparent when certainly he is not.

Finally, the synchronic character of the current website reflects the ethnographic predilections of its developers. Without attention to the diachronic dimension of Arampur, the project threatens to reinforce popular perceptions of a technologically backward and temporally frozen rural India. Unfortunately, historical materials for a village—even as large and administratively important one as Arampur—remain slight and only sporadically touch on its long history. While a website can never fully capture complexity of an Indian village, 'A Virtual Village' represents an effort to bridge the divide between ethnographic and historical approaches to the study of Bihari society and culture.

NOTES

1. 'A Virtual Village' can be accessed at http://virtualvillage.wesleyan.edu
2. Jean-Baptiste Tavernier, *Travels in India*, trans. V. Ball, Delhi: Orient Reprint Co., 1997.
3. *An Actual Survey of the Provinces of Bengal, Bahar & C., (1776).* Scale British miles, 69 1/2 [= 150 mm].
4. Francis Buchanan, *Journal of Francis Buchanan Kept During the Survey of the District of Shahabad in 1812-1813*, ed. C.E.A.W. Oldham, Patna: Superintendent, Government Printing, 1926.
5. P.C. Roy Chaudhury, *Bihar State Gazetteers: Shahabad,* Patna: Secretariat Press, 1966, p. 699.
6. Thomas Daniell and William Daniell, *Antiquities of India, Part the Second; Consisting of Twelve Views from the Drawings of Thomas Daniell, R.A. F.S.A. Engraved by Himself, and William Daniell, A.R.A. Taken in the Years 1790 and 1793*, London: T. Bensley, 1804.
7. http://learningobjects.wesleyan.edu/virtualvillage/about/index.html
8. See Ronald Inden, *Imagining India,* Cambridge: Blackwell, 1990.
9. http://learningobjects.wesleyan.edu/virtualvillage/topics/index.html
10. http://learningobjects.wesleyan.edu/virtualvillage/cgi-bin/glossarylist.cgi
11. http://virtualvillage.wesleyan.edu/virtualvillage/cgi-bin/loadmovie.cgi?main=true&theme=1
12. http://learningobjects.wesleyan.edu/virtualvillage/mylife/index.html
13. See Richard King, *Orientalism and Religion*, London: Routledge, 1999.
14. See Julius Lipner, *Hindus: Their Religious Beliefs and Practices*, London: Routledge, 1998.

15. Wendy Doniger, 'Hinduism', available: http://www.angelfire.com/realm/shades/ganesh/hinduism.htm
16. For a critique of Doniger's article, see Sankrant Sanu, 'U.S. Hinduism Studies: A Question of Shoddy Scholarship', available: http://www.beliefnet.com/story/146/story_14684_1.html
17. Arvind Sharma, 'Hinduism' , available: http://encarta.msn.com/encyclopedia_761555715/Hinduism.html#s1
18. http://virtualvillage.wesleyan.edu/interviews/transcripts/kuber_tiwari_revised.htm
19. See, for example, Sudhir Kakar, *Shamans, Mystics, and Doctors*, Chicago: University of Chicago Press, 1982; Vincent Crapazano, ed., *Case Studies in Spirit Possession*, New York: Willey and Sons, 1997.
20. http://virtualvillage.wesleyan.edu/interviews/transcripts/shiv_mistri_revised.htm
21. http://virtualvillage.wesleyan.edu/interviews/transcripts/ajay_upandhyay_revised.htm
22. See McKim Marriot, 'Constructing an Indian Ethnosociology', *Contributions to Indian Sociology*, vol. 2, no. 1, 1989, pp. 1-39.
23. http://virtualvillage.wesleyan.edu/interviews/transcripts/arjun_shrivastav_revised.htm
24. http://virtualvillage.wesleyan.edu/interviews/transcripts/jag_pandit_revised.htm
25. http://learningobjects.wesleyan.edu/virtualvillage/cgi-bin/loadmovie.cgi?theme=4
26. http://virtualvillage.wesleyan.edu/interviews/transcripts/azan_revised.htm
    http://virtualvillage.wesleyan.edu/interviews/transcripts/syed_salman_revised.htm
27. http://learningobjects.wesleyan.edu/virtualvillage/cgi-bin/loadmovie.cgi?movieclip=WX1_aa_dargah

PART V

Walter Hauser

South Asian Studies at Virginia

William R. Pinch, with the permission of Walter Hauser

Walter joined the history faculty at the University of Virginia in 1960, at a time when it was regarded as a good regional institution catering primarily to a southern male constituency. By the time he retired, thirty-five years later, Virginia had become one of the top public institutions of higher learning in the United States, in terms of scholarly production, student and faculty recruitment, endowment monies raised, and PhDs awarded. Walter was very much part of this transformation.

True, the transformation of Mr Jefferson's 'academical village'—or any large institution—is not solely the result of any one individual's labour. Without question there are some prominent names that immediately come to mind, such as former deans David Shannon and Ray Nelson, and former presidents Frank Hereford and Edgar Shannon, and current president John Casteen. But there can be no question that the University's rise to national distinction would not have occurred had there not been a cohort of energetic visionaries on the faculty, individuals willing to work long hard hours—and days and months and years—to provide the nuts and bolts, and tools, with which the senior faculty-administrators could reconstruct 'The University'. Walter Hauser was a member of this cohort and one my goals is to communicate precisely what that role entailed over the years. This is done, first and foremost, to record Walter's service to his colleagues at the University, to his many students—both graduate and undergraduate—and to the field of South Asian Studies, between 1960 and 1995. But it is also done to provide a small record of the kind of political skill and intellectual commitment that was required to build the edifice of international 'area studies' in one increasingly prominent corner of higher education.

There are many occasions in my memory of Walter alluding to some curious incident about this or that fundraising moment or grant application, or even Congressional hearing, during the 1960s or 1970s. Invariably those allusions would be cut short by Walter saying that he would 'tell me all about it some time'. It occurred to me last year that that 'time' had now arrived, and so I asked Walter to reflect, in writing, on his career at Virginia with a focus on the creation of the Center as well as its place in the world of emerging area studies programmes, particularly those focused on South Asia. At first, my intention was to use whatever statement Walter drafted as the basis for a brief summary paragraph or two in the context of his wider career. But the level of detail Walter provided in his subsequent note to me, and my realization of the importance to him of the kinds of institution-building activities that are described therein, convinced me that it would stand nicely as an addendum to the present volume. It is also, I believe, a valuable and instructive record of an institution-building process that usually remains hidden.

What follows, then, are the words of Walter Hauser describing his career at Virginia. They were composed as a note to me in early 2006, hence their conversational tone. Needless to say, I am grateful to him for overcoming his discomfort and allowing me to reproduce the bulk of his note here.

*****

I came to the University of Virginia in 1960, fresh from a year of dissertation writing, and teaching in the Introduction to Indian Civilization class in the College at the University of Chicago. I had made my dissertation defence in the summer of 1960 at Chicago (with Barney Cohn and Myron Weiner), and was awarded the degree in 1961. At Virginia I was historian No. 12 in the Department of History (there are now, in September 2006, fifty full-time faculty) and the only non-US, non-Europe historian, although there was in fact, one Latin Americanist. Otherwise in the University, what was then the Department of Government and Foreign Affairs had Tony Leng dealing with China, R.K. Ramazani for the Middle East, and Al Fernbach teaching World Organizations. It was about this time that Fernbach was invited by

Roland Egger, the then chair (who had administrative experience in Pakistan), to teach an occasional South Asia course. It is also the case that there were no Asian or Middle Eastern languages taught in the University at the time. My responsibilities in history included not only India, but also China and Japan, which said something about the academic perception of the world in which we lived in 1960. Essentially, my charge was to teach about a very large part of the human experience. So my first campaign in the department and the University was that we appoint a historian of China. That happened quickly, and in response to China historian No. 1, I agreed to lobby for a second historian of China, namely someone working on classical China.

At the same time, I started leaning on the Dean about the importance of teaching Hindi if we were going to study India seriously, and of the need for having an anthropologist. Both those appointments were also made by 1963. I should point out that at the same time we made the Hindi appointment we made a Chinese language appointment, inasmuch as Tony Leng's wife had taught Chinese at Yale, and was immediately available. Hence, we began the teaching of Hindi, Sanskrit, and Chinese at Virginia in the early 1960s. For India, this meant we then had appointments in History, Anthropology, Hindi, and Sanskrit, which provided the basis for an undergraduate India Civilization course, which was initially housed in the History department.

The then Dean of Arts and Sciences was the political scientist Robert Harris and happily he was responsive to these recommendations, as were all of his successors, in varying degrees to be sure, but they were all positive in supporting the fledgling and developing South Asia project. And this was certainly an element in the decision Rosemary and I made on a number of occasions to stay at Virginia, when there were opportunities at 'Elsewhere-U', as Fritz Mote of Princeton put it, on one of his Charlottesville visits. But that too is not a part of this conversation, though the India appointments that were being made says much about the academic climate the young president Edgar Shannon had created in his efforts to move Virginia from what was then in effect a good Southern men's finishing school, with a strong Law School and a good Medical School attached, to a top flight university with a prominent role for women, from the early 1970s. There had, of course, been prominent Arts and Sciences departments, Mathematics, and also English—but what began happening under Edgar Shannon was an explicit move to the top, and South Asia almost certainly benefited from that effort and certainly contributed to the result.

There was a confluence of other developments in these early years that impinged directly and indirectly on what we were doing. The first and most important of these was the University's participation in the Library of Congress PL-480 India programme. This started in 1961 and Virginia became the eleventh participating member in 1962. John Wiley, the University Librarian at the time, was the American Library Association representative in developing that program with the Library of Congress, as was Horace Poleman, the head of LC's Orientalia Division. We were also accessioning heavily in India materials apart from PL-480, given the warm cooperation of Wiley and Louise Savage, the acquisitions librarian, in that effort. In the process we laid the groundwork for the very substantial South Asia collection we would create in the decades to follow.

There were two other collaborative initiatives in this early period. My friend and senior colleague, the U.S. diplomatic historian Edward Younger had generated $300,000 from the Ford Foundation for the University Center in Virginia, a statewide consortium of Virginia colleges and universities. The idea behind this effort, in which Younger and I collaborated, was to develop Asian Studies. We used those funds to create a series of summer seminars on India and China beginning in 1963 and running for three years through 1965. Each seminar was separately administered but was essentially a sophisticated China and India Civilization course for faculty from the Virginia colleges and universities. These faculty fellows were funded for participating in the summer seminars, and some did both seminars in successive years, and others used the seminars as points of departure in retooling to become China or India 'specialists'. I taught the India seminar in the summer of 1965 on my return from India, and we had invited Bob Crane, then at Duke, to teach in the preceding two summers when I was on leave. There was more than sufficient funding to bring in guest lecturers, which in 1965 included, among others, the anthropologists Milton Singer and Ralph Nicholas from Chicago and the Mughal historian Irfan Habib from Aligarh, who was visiting Chicago at the time.

I used this opportunity also to bring in other sponsored funding from the United States Department of Education (DOE). This was under an act called Title III, which served to supplement the Ford Foundation money and the summer seminar programme, and funded the initial activities of the Virginia Consortium for Asian Studies (VCAS). The VCAS still functions to encourage and support the study of Asia in the colleges and universities of Virginia, with small annual meetings for faculty and students. We included in the initial VCAS proposal a visiting lecture program that brought in outside specialists to speak at member institutions. It was the Asian studies network established by these that then provided the basis for the Teaching Intern Program which we incorporated as a central outreach and training element in the first DOE proposal that created the Center for South Asian Studies at Virginia in 1976. I will return to the Teaching Intern Program in a moment. The VCAS also published a small 'in house' journal, which continues to be edited by Professor Daniel Metraux of Mary Baldwin College in Staunton, Virginia. This is the *Virginia Review of Asian Studies*. Professor Metraux also edits the *Southeast Review of Asian Studies*, the journal of the Southeast Regional Conference of the Association for Asian Studies (SEAAS).

The Southeast Regional Conference, which was similar to the VCAS, but at the regional level, was formed in 1962. The initial idea came from Bob Crane who had come to Duke University from Michigan in 1961. He and I were engaged jointly in that effort, using Duke and Virginia as the institutional bases for this new regional body. The first annual meeting was at Duke, and subsequent meetings have been held in all parts of the Southeast. The SEAAS continues to function in 2006 as one of the regional conferences of the Association for Asian Studies (AAS). Its 46th annual meeting will be held at Belmont University in Nashville, Tennessee, 12-14 January 2007. At one point, in 1973-4, I served as president of the SEAAS, and we hosted the annual meeting on two or three occasions at the University in those early years.

On returning to Charlottesville in 1965 following my first India research leave, we formed the South Asia Committee to coordinate our efforts and to submit proposals to DOE for Title VI South Asia Language and Area Fellowship funding. I served as chair of that coordinating committee. Program funding was then not available because the 1958 legislation creating the Title VI Language and Area scheme, locked such funding in to the initially funded programs, which in the case of South Asia included thirteen American universities. But fellowship applications were not limited in this way. Accordingly, we applied and were immediately funded, if I recall correctly, with one fellowship, and we continued being funded with one, two, and three fellowships in these early years. Then in 1976, under new Title VI legislation permitting open competition, the University of Virginia was funded as a South Asia Language and Area Center. Reflecting the dramatic changes in the intervening years, Virginia received funding for eleven language and area fellowships in the 2005-6 academic year in the amount of $257,210. The Center for South Asian Studies was authorized to offer awards for the study of Hindi, Urdu, Persian, Tibetan, and Sanskrit/ Pali (when taken as a second South Asian language). Fellowship funding for the summer of 2006 was at a level of $42,995, awarding nine language and area fellowships. These levels of fellowship funding are among the highest in the country.

It was in those same early and middle 1960s that the American Institute of Indian Studies (AIIS) took form under the initiative of W. Norman Brown, the eminent American Sanskritist and father of the University of Pennsylvania South Asia program. Penn was the first such program in the U.S. and Brown was the person most directly responsible for introducing the study of modern South Asia into the American academy. He did this in many ways, not least through his role in expanding the Far Eastern Association into the Association for Asian Studies, but significantly through creating the AIIS as the premier facilitating and funding agency for American scholarship in India. Though we were relatively few in South Asia faculty numbers, by this time Virginia was already recognized as conducting a serious program in the field. I don't have the history of the AIIS before me, but if Virginia was not one of the institutions present at the founding, we were there soon after as one of the ten or twelve early Class A institutional members, defining the early purpose and direction of the Institute. This meant a substantial annual membership fee that was initially provided by Dexter Whitehead, the then Dean of Graduate Arts and Sciences at Virginia.

The logic I used with Whitehead was that if we were going to be players in the development of the field, we inevitably needed to be members of the Institute, where the critical decisions would be made, certainly in these early years. And perhaps even more convincing was the demonstrable logic that as our program grew in stature and size, we would, in the end, realize far more support in fellowship funding from the AIIS and other sources than we might pay into the AIIS as membership dues. This was a logic I utilized in subsequent years when Professor David Shannon, our Twentieth-Century US historian, and Provost of the University, assumed the responsibility for the AIIS (and all other institutional dues). Happily David Shannon had had experience with the Ford Foundation, so he understood the issues well.

David Shannon asked for an annual report detailing what we had been doing in terms of teaching, research, and funding, including AIIS and Fulbright awards as well as Title VI Language and Area fellowship dollars we brought into the University. It turned out, of course, that we were always high on the plus side. This pleased Shannon, as it did

Vincent Shea, the University's chief financial officer who was ultimately picking up the AIIS tab. In the meantime, these unofficial annual reports, pounded out on my pre-computer electric typewriter, served several useful purposes. They met the immediate need of generating the AIIS annual dues dollars, but they also met the larger and very important purpose of informing the administration and faculty colleagues, including the several Deans and Chairs whom I plied with these reports, about who we were and what we were achieving. The University at this time was heavily under-administered, so this became an important tool in keeping key people in the loop about the importance of South Asia in the larger academic project.

This process had several critical advantages, but especially to encourage departments to make disciplinary appointments focusing on India, based on their determination, or in response to suggestions coming from the South Asia Committee. This was an ongoing process through the 1960s and 1970s and into the 1980s. I have in mind specifically appointments in History, Anthropology, Government and Foreign Affairs, Religious Studies, Art History, Sociology, Urdu, Persian, and Sanskrit. This included in History the appointment of Tom Kessinger, as our second historian of India in 1970, succeeded in 1974 by Rich Barnett; and so on to Ravindra Khare in 1970 and H.L. Seneviratne in 1971 in Anthropology; Gerald Heeger in Government and Foreign Affairs succeeded by John Echeverri-Gent; Murray Milner in Sociology; a series of appointments in Hinduism, Buddhism, and Islam in Religious Studies, including among others Jeffrey Hopkins, David White, David Germano and Anne Monius, and so too in Persian beginning with Moazzam Siddiqi and culminating with the appointment of Farzaneh Milani, and later, Griff Chaussee in Urdu language and literature.

For me this history was interrupted when I was stricken with the Guillain-Barre Syndrome while in India with a group of architects from the University, in the summer of 1968. Guillain-Barre is a paralysing, neurological syndrome with an international etiology, which happened to strike me while I was in India. I was evacuated by air to Charlottesville in September 1968, hospitalized for most of a year, and fully out of commission for that year. I was back on a part-time teaching schedule in 1969 and resumed full time teaching in 1970. That was the year we appointed Tom Kessinger, which coincided with the first major cluster of South Asia graduate students in History. There had been MA students in the 1960s and two PhD students, but with the arrival of Jim Hagen, Phil McEldowney, and Anand Yang, among others, the programme in history essentially took off, as it would continue in three or four clusters, to the time of my retirement from classroom teaching in 1995.

The primary object of the game for me was always academic and intellectual quality of the highest order whether in History, the related disciplines, or the University project as a whole. I was not content with the suggestion that we could be competitive in 'the Southeast' or 'the South'. We would be competitive with the best, anyplace, with our faculty and graduate students, or not at all. And it turns out, that was equally true of our undergraduates, who, certainly from the middle 1970s with the admission of women, were among the brightest and the best. I make the point in this way because apart from our regular faculty, and new appointments, we also had visiting appointments and guest speakers in our seminar series that were consistently outstanding. I have mentioned the names of Irfan Habib, Milton Singer and Ralph Nicholas as early visitors, and among the historians of India here for a semester or a year while Kessinger, Barnett or I were on leave, were Charles Boxer (1973-4), Ashin Das Gupta (1973-4), Chris Bayly (1974-5), Karen Leonard (1977-78), and David Ludden (1979-80). And while this goes back to the remote past, the first India participant in the Page-Barbour/Richard lecture series was Bernard S. Cohn. This was in 1963-4, and provided Cohn the first opportunity to present his early Banaras research. Cohn's Page-Barbour visit was one of the first recommendations I made at the University following my arrival in 1960. In more recent years the Page-Barbour lectureships have brought to the University Chris Bayly from Cambridge and Wendy Doniger from Chicago.

Apart from these academic guests from the U.K., India, and the United States, we also had a steady stream of Indian political activists at the University. Some of these were prominent politicians from Bihar, whose State Department sponsored tours suggested Virginia as a possible stop-over given our interest in the state and its history; and others came to Charlottesville as a function of my personal research connections in India. There are more names in this list than I can easily recall, but among early visitors was George Fernandes, the Socialist trade union leader at the time, who was in the United States at the invitation of the AFL-CIO to observe the 1972 presidential election. I recall that we pumped Fernandes for hours in a left-politics graduate seminar in Randall Hall 106 at the University. Another name from the political left that comes quickly to mind is that of Shrihansu Acharayya, who visited the University late in the spring semester of 1978 under State Department auspices. Acharayya was the Attorney General of

West Bengal, that is, the chief legal officer in the government of Jyoti Basu. This visit too was the result of a personal connection, but certainly also to expose Acharayya to the idea of Jefferson in the American experience. But I hasten to add that this was not the first time the Marxist Acharayya had encountered Jefferson, though he imbibed fully in the experience of being on Jefferson's home turf. And I should also say that our U.Va. students, graduate and undergraduate, and colleagues, were equally impressed with Shrihansu Acharayya, as much for his warm humour as for the subtlety of his ideas.

The 1970s and continuing to a lesser degree into the 1980s was also the time that I was most actively involved in meeting what I considered to be obligations to the profession beyond the University. In the summer of 1970, I taught in the East Coast South Asia Summer program at the University of Rochester. This was part of a national collaboration among South Asia programs, with similar programs in the Midwest and the West. I have mentioned earlier my involvement with the SEAAS and the University's early membership in the American Institute of Indian Studies (AIIS); and it was now through the Association for Asian Studies (AAS) and the AIIS that I became professionally more active at the national level. In 1971 I was elected to the South Asia Regional Council (SARC) of the AAS for the normal three-year term. And I served the AAS in a number of other capacities, most importantly, I suspect, as programme chair for South Asia at the 1972 meetings in New York City, and then as overall programme chair of the 25th Annual Meeting of the Association in 1973. That meeting was held at the Palmer House in Chicago.

The 25th Annual Meeting also coincided with the 25th year of Indian Independence, that is 1972-3. In any case, the most notable feature of that meeting was the program committee proposal for a series of plenary sessions for each region of the Association to use as they wished. Morris David Morris, the member of the programme committee responsible for South Asia arranged to have a retrospective panel on twenty-five years of Indian Independence. Susanne Rudolph discussed political change, Dick Lambert, the sociologist from Penn considered social change, while the Princeton economist John Lewis examined economic change. L.K. Jha, the Indian Ambassador was the discussant, and the chair was W. Norman Brown. It was certainly one of Norman's last public appearances; he died in 1975. That plenary session was a success in every respect. The panel as such went exceedingly well, and given that there were no competing South Asian panels, we must have had 2,000 people in attendance. This was in the Red Room of the

Palmer House and quite possibly the largest South Asia academic meeting of its kind ever held in the U.S.

Apart from this 1973 program chair responsibility and my involvement with SARC, I served on various other AAS committees in these years, most notably the Institutional Liaison Committee which Hal Gould chaired and which involved us in some serious lobbying on behalf of the profession in Washington. There were many issues, mostly involving funding, and some policy issues as during the Bangladesh war, when we tried, with some moderate degree of success, to lobby the Congress to bring some balance to the Nixon White House and Mr. Kissinger's skewed South Asia position.

And I was similarly involved with the AIIS during these years. As a Class A member institution, the University of Virginia was represented on the Board of Trustees by two trustees, and from the time of our initial membership to the early or middle 1990s I served as one of these trustees. In 1973-4 I served as chair of the AIIS Board of Trustees, which meant that in the following year, in 1974-5, I served as a member of the AIIS Executive Committee. Then in the mid-1980s I also served two terms on the AIIS Fellowship Selection Committee.

You had asked about my testifying before the House Budget Committee, chaired by Congressman Daniel Flood of Pennsylvania. This would have been in the middle to late 1970s, and the issue was rupee funding for the National Science Foundation (NSF) or the Smithsonian Institution, both of which were sources of rupee funds for the AIIS. I was probably asked to testify in my capacity as Chair of the Board of Trustees, but also because a prominent Republican member of that committee, in a Democratically controlled House was J. Kenneth Robinson, from the 7th Congressional District of Virginia, which included Charlottesville. I had gotten to know Robinson when we were applying for Title VI Language and Area fellowship funding, and though a strong fiscal conservative, he had been exceedingly supportive. He knew the University was one of his important constituents. And remember, I had mentioned before that U.Va. was dramatically under-administered in those days, and was just beginning its rise up the academic ladder, and we had no liaison office in Washington. So I effectively functioned as a one-man South Asia liaison committee in Washington.

In any case, on the day that I was testifying, in one of the large House committee rooms, with this outsize committee on its raised podium, and the room jammed, Flood allowed: 'You have five minutes,

Professor'. Robinson intervened, 'Mr. Chairman, with your permission, I would like to introduce my constituent', etc. Congressman Robinson then took five or ten minutes to say nice things about me, about the University, and about our South Asia programme. Flood then allowed, 'Well, Dr. Hauser, that didn't hurt you one bit. Go ahead, you still have five minutes.' In any case, although the rupees had earlier been appropriated as dollars, the process had to be gone through again, and the committee acted favorably. But the Budget Committee's majority action had to be seconded by a minority Republican member. I was asked the next day either by the NSF, the Smithsonian, or AIIS whether Robinson would do this. I allowed that I could only ask, which I did, through Robinson's legislative assistant, who explained that he would get back to me after talking with the Congressman. It seemed a reasonable request because these were not new dollars, but I was nevertheless surprised and pleased when the legislative assistant called back the next day, indicating that Mr. Robinson would indeed second the motion to approve. It was in a very real sense an important moment in our collective lobbying efforts.

In the early 1970s I also served on various fellowship and program selection committees of the US Department of Education (DOE), including among others the Fulbright-Hays program. DOE did a lot of program and fellowship funding in these years, and because the University of Virginia was not a funded South Asia program until 1976, I was often asked to serve as a member of funding selection committees, vetting reapplications of existing Title VI Language and Area programs. It was here that I learned that at least half the thirteen funded South Asia programs had less going for them than we had in place from University sources at Virginia. So I began very soon to apply pressure, wherever I could get a hearing in Washington, for reconfiguring the funding legislation, and I like to think that these efforts, with those of many others, had some small influence in finally opening the competition in 1975 to all comers. And as I have already noted, we were funded as a South Asia Language and Area Center in that first open competition, effective in 1976.

The opening of the application process by DOE, more or less coincided with our having made a key appointment in Religious Studies in Tibetan Buddhism, filled by Jeffrey Hopkins 1973. Given our strengths in supporting disciplines and in the University's Alderman library, it was an appointment that made eminent sense. Hopkins' reputation in the field and his commitment to developing a strong program were certainly important to our success in the 1976 funding cycle and in subsequent achievements of the South Asia program. Hopkins was able to encourage other appointments in Religious Studies, for example, that of David Germano, and he trained a whole generation of graduate students, several of whom have become prominent figures in the field.

Most programme proposals submitted to DOE were fairly standard in what they hoped to achieve, or so at least it seemed to me based on the many proposals I had read as a member of selection committees in the years before 1975. So I have taken great satisfaction in two elements of our initial proposal that I feel have been especially valuable in defining the University of Virginia's South Asia programme. These are the budget line for a Visiting Faculty Enrichment appointment, and the Teaching Intern budget line, which sent one of our most advanced graduate students to teach for a semester in a member institution of the Virginia Consortium for Asian Studies. For example, that programme had some of our best students teaching India courses at the College of William and Mary, James Madison University, Mary Washington College, Sweet Briar College, Randolph-Macon Women's College, Mary Baldwin College, and Emory and Henry College, among others. This was at the same time also one of our most successful outreach efforts.

In my view these two lines were directed at the core of the University's South Asia academic mission: providing teaching experience for some of our best students and achieving and reinforcing faculty range and quality. I will make this point briefly by noting that our first faculty enrichment appointment in the fall semester of 1977 was Joseph Allen Stein in the School of Architecture. Stein was the American architect with a remarkable career of fifty years and more in India, which included the design of the India International Centre in New Delhi, all the other buildings on the Lodi Gardens side of Max Mueller Marg, and the last of his many achievements, in the same neighborhood, the amazing India Habitat Centre at the intersection of Lodi Road and Fourth Avenue. At Virginia, Stein taught a design class and certainly the first class in America on the deterioration of the Himalayan ecosystem. Other Enrichment Visitors over the years whom we placed wherever there might be interest in the University, were Om Prakash of the Delhi School of Economics in Economic History; M. Athar Ali in Mughal history; Amitav Ghosh in Sociology, Anthropology and English; Paul Brass in Political Science; and Daniel Ehnbom, the current Director of the Center, in Art History. This latter visiting appointment turned into a regular tenured position some years after Dan's initial visit, a not unintended consequence.

An important element of the Visiting Enrichment appointments was that we moved the study of South Asia beyond Arts and Sciences to include Architecture, as in the case of Joe Stein, and into other professional schools of the University. For example, there was in the late 1970s or early 1980s a summer visiting appointment in the Darden Graduate School of Business Administration, which we helped fund with Enrichment dollars. That faculty visitor was from the Indian Institute of Management at Ahmedabad, one of the leaders in the field. And we have also had India visitors in the undergraduate McIntire School of Commerce, including most recently the economist and journalist Prem Shankar Jha. In the 1970s and 1980s there were visitors from Dharmashala, the seat of the Dalai Lama, specializing in Tibetan Medicine and interacting with people in the University of Virginia Medical Center. The most fruitful South Asia link with the Medical Center has been the ongoing Virginia Children's Connection, a cleft-lip and burn clinic, organized in the mid-1980s by Dr. John Persing of the departments of Neurosurgery and Plastic Surgery. A team of fifteen to twenty U.Va. surgeons and nurses has gone every two years to the town of Giridih, then in the state of Bihar, and now in Jharkhand State, for this free clinic, which functions with the co-operation of the local Rotary Club, at the Bagaria Clinic, in Giridih. The most recent clinic took place in January 2006, under the direction of Dr. Thomas J. Gampper of the Department of Plastic Surgery in the U.Va. Medical Center.

As I edit final copy of this note in early September 2006, only weeks following the death of the great *shehnai* virtuoso Bismillah Khan, I cannot resist commenting on the appearance of Khan Sahab and his group in the Cabell Hall auditorium at the University in 1990. It was in every sense a magical moment for the overflow audience, and at the same time a metaphor for the kind of musicianship the Center for South Asian Studies has brought to the University through its Performing Arts Program. This was a programme made possible in large part through the generosity of the local Ellen Bayard Weedon Foundation and the cooperation of the departments of Music and Drama, whose venues were always available. I think of the late 1960s appearance of Nikhil Banerjee on *sitar* and Kanai Datta on *tabla* for their first American tour, again performing in Cabell Hall, and Banerjee's return visit in the late 1970s or early 1980s, performing this time on the Culbreth Drama Department stage. Others, among the many groups of performers and musicians who came to the University included the *Kathakali* classical dance troupe from Kerala, and the Dagar family, instrumental and vocal performers in the *dhrupad* tradition, on at least two occasions.

I cannot end this brief performing arts comment without mentioning the name of Cindy Benton-Groner, herself an ethno-musicologist and for many years the assistant director and main administrator of the Center for South Asian Studies. Cindy played a central role in coordinating the Performing Arts Program, as so much else of the Center's activity. And finally, the University has been fortunate in having an active chapter of the Society for the Promotion of Indian Classical Music and Culture Among Youth (SPICMACAY). The group has brought a steady stream of performers to the University, with the cooperation of the Center and the active involvement of student volunteers.

I will wind up with two other institutional observations, the first about the library to which I have referred earlier in this note. But I would be remiss if I didn't mention the names of Skip Martin and Phil McEldowney, our first and current South Asia bibliographers. Each played important roles and both have been critical to the development of a strong South Asia library at Virginia, Martin in developing the Tibetica collection, and McEldowney in marshalling and servicing our broader South Asia needs. And while I have encouraged the library project over the years as a central element of what we do, I hasten to add that the library and the successive librarians from John Wiley, to Ray Frantz, to the current incumbent, Karin Wittenborg, have been consistently supportive of what we do in developing one of the fine South Asia collections in America.

I must also say something about the Friday afternoon South Asia Seminar, which Tom Kessinger and I instituted in 1970 and which has almost certainly been one of the longest running seminar projects of its kind in the country. For six years we ran the seminar on a shoestring and friendship, and then in 1976 made it a regular line item in our Center budget. It has provided, for most members of the South Asia faculty and for many students, a regular forum for thinking collectively about South Asia and exchanging ideas about what it all might mean. That, too, took more organizing and doing than many people realize. But we did it and it worked.

This history suggests something of what we achieved in developing serious academic interests in key departments and schools of the

University, which then took on a life of their own. We had the initial advantage of doing all of this independently, that is without relying on outside funding, and then reinforcing those early beginnings with DOE Title VI Language and Area program funding, beginning in 1976. And the good news is that successive deans have understood who we are, and have been forthcoming in sustaining the South Asia project as an integral element of the University's academic mission. In a sense this has been possible because the Center has from the beginning been a coordinating and facilitating agency and not a degree-granting department. While any academic operation depends heavily on the commitment of the individuals involved, which leaves us with all the advantages and disadvantages of any other institution, we are, in 2006, effectively holding our own.

I have touched on my role in developing the South Asia program at the University of Virginia, and the ways in which I was involved in facilitating the wider study of South Asia at the regional and national levels. But I must emphasize that it was always a collaborative effort at the University and so too beyond the University. It was in every sense, as I have noted earlier, an interactive project, locally and nationally, and most often, warmly congenial in the process. If I were to name some of the key players, the main founder of who we are and what we do in the study of South Asia in the U.S. was clearly W. Norman Brown, the Penn Sanskritist whose vision it was to bring the study of India into the contemporary present. In my view, the anthropologist Robert Redfield at the University of Chicago was another seminal figure, and I am sure there were others, in other parts of the country, with whose roles I am not familiar.

The next generation of mobilizers and organizers included Richard Lambert from Penn, Richard Park from Berkeley and then Michigan, Milton Singer from Chicago, and Robert I. Crane, initially from Michigan, then Duke, then Syracuse. In the next generation were people like Edward Dimock of Chicago, Joseph Elder from Wisconsin, Susanne Rudolph from Chicago, and Hal Gould from Illinois, among others. And I must emphasize that these are only impressions, based on my experience, which almost certainly means that names of persons who did not cross my path are not found here. In other words, this is a personal reflection and however immodest it may appear, it is the image that my mind's eye has produced on this day in response to your queries. Please use it, as you will, in configuring your image of what happened in these years in the study of South Asia.

Bibliography of Walter Hauser

(Prepared by Philip McEldowney)

Books

Culture, Vernacular Politics and the Peasants. Being an edited translation of Sahajanand Saraswati's 1952 memoir, *Mera Jivan Sangharsh* (*My Life Struggle*). New Delhi: Manohar, forthcoming 2008. (With Kailash Chandra Jha).

Sahajanand on Agricultural Labour and the Rural Poor. An edited translation of *Khet Mazdoor,* with the original Hindi text and an Introduction, Endnotes, and Glossary (New Delhi: Manohar, 1994 and Pbk. 2005), xx and xxiii, 239 pp.

Swami Sahajanand and the Peasants of Jharkhand: A View from 1941. An edited translation of *Jharkhand ke Kisan,* with the original Hindi text and an Introduction, Endnotes, and Glossary (New Delhi: Manohar, 1995 and Pbk. 2005), xxvi and xxxiii, 369 pp.

'The Bihar Provincial Kisan Sabha, 1929-1942: A Study of An Indian Peasant Movement'. (University of Chicago Dissertation in History, 1961). 214 pp.

Essays in Books and Journals

'Remembering K.K. Datta', in *Colonial India: A Centenary Tribute to Professor K.K. Datta.* Edited by Professor Surendra Gopal (Arrah: Veer Kunwar Singh University, 2006). Research Publication Series 4, pp. 27-30.

'From the Politics of Culture to the Culture of (Democratic) Politics in Twentieth Century India', in *Colonial India: A Centenary Tribute to Professor K.K. Datta.* Edited by Surendra Gopal (Arrah: Veer Kunwar Singh University, 2006). Research Publication Series 4, pp. 214-31. [A corrected version of this essay is available with the author at <wh2r@virginia.edu>.]

'Sahajanand Saraswati, 1889-2005: Reflections on a Lifetime of Activism', Keynote paper presented at the Ninth Annual Conference of the Economic Association of Bihar, A.N. College, Patna, 2005. Appearing in the Conference Volume of the *Bihar Economic Journal* (2005), pp. 13-24.

'From Peasant Soldiering to Peasant Activism: Reflections on the

Transition of a Martial Tradition in the Flaming Fields of Bihar', *Journal of the Economic and Social History of the Orient,* vol. 47, no. 3, 2004, pp. 401-34. This number is a special issue of *JESHO* honouring Dr. Dirk Kolff of Leiden University on his retirement.

'The Life of a Text and Its Meanings: Reflections on Sahajanand Saraswati's *Mera Jivan Sangharsh*', in *India's Colonial Encounter: Essays in Memory of Eric Stokes.* Second Edition. Edited by Mushirul Hasan and Narayani Gupta (New Delhi: Manohar, 2004), pp. 155-91.

'Peasants, Activists, and Scholars: A Late Twentieth Century Reflection on Definitions', in *Political Economy and Protest in Colonial India: Professor Sunil Kumar Sen Commemoration Volume.* Edited by Chittabrata Palit, Amit Bhattacharya and Ranjan Chakrabarti (Calcutta: Firma KLM, 1997), pp. 251-67.

'The General Elections of 1996 in Bihar: Politics, Administrative Atrophy and Anarchy', *Economic and Political Weekly,* vol. 32, no. 41 (October 11, 1997), pp. 2599-2607.

'Changing Images of Caste and Politics', *Seminar: The Monthly Symposium,* 450. *The State of Bihar: A Symposium on the Legacy of a Troubled State* (February 1997), pp. 47-52.

Foreword for *India Tracts, Major J. Browne's Report on the Jungle Tarai People of South Bihar, during 1774-1779.* Kameshwar Singh Bihar Heritage Series—2. Edited by Chandra Prakash N. Sinha (Darbhanga: Kameshwar Singh Kalyani Foundation, 1996), pp. A3-A6.

'Swami Sahajanand and the Politics of Social Reform, 1907-1950', *The Indian Historical Review,* vol. 18, nos. 1-2 (July 1991 to January 1992), pp. 59-75. A Hindi translation of this *IHR* essay appeared as 'Swami Sahajanand aur Samaj Sudhar ki Rajniti, 1907-1950', in *Itihas*, vol. III (1994), pp. 143-62.

'Violence, Agrarian Radicalism and Electoral Politics: Reflections on the Indian People's Front'. *The Journal of Peasant Studies,* vol. 21, no. 1 (October 1993), pp. 85-126. An earlier version of this *JPS* essay appeared as 'Violence, Agrarian Radicalism and the Audibility of Dissent: Electoral Politics and the Indian People's Front', in *India Votes: Alliance Politics and Minority Governments in the Ninth and Tenth General Elections.* Edited by Harold A. Gould and Sumit Ganguly (Boulder, Colorado: Westview Press, 1993), pp. 341-79.

'The Democratic Rite: Celebration and Participation in the Indian Elections', *Asian Survey,* vol. 26, no. 9 (September 1986), pp. 941-958. (With Wendy Singer).

'Agrarian Conflict and Peasant Movements in Twentieth Century India', in *The Social Anthropology of the Peasantry*. Edited by Joan P. Mencher (Bombay: Somaiya Publications, 1983), pp. 251-61.

'The Political and Social History of a New Nation: A Consideration of Change in Twentieth Century India', in *Problems of Educational Development and Modernization in Asia*. Edited by Peter Hackett (Charlottesville, 1972), pp. 9-29.

'Society and Politics in Modern India', in *Southern Asia*. Edited by Robert I. Crane (Durham: Duke University and the Southern Regional Education Board, 1968), pp. 28-47.

'The Indian National Congress and Land Policy in the Twentieth Century', *The Indian Economic and Social History Review*, vol. 1, no. 1 (July 1963), pp. 57-65.

'The Politics of Co-operative Farming: Will the Peasant Accept It?', *Economic and Political Weekly*, vol. 61, Annual Number (July 1959), pp. 1038-42.

Area Handbook on Jammu and Kashmir State, by Walter Hauser, Belden H. Paulson, Thomas Rusch, Burton Stein, Lester C. Stermer and Robert O. Swan, and edited by Robert I. Crane. Human Relations Area Files, HRAF-24 (Chicago: University of Chicago for the Human Relations Area Files, 1956), 531 pp.

Op Ed Essays

'Is There a Message, Voter? The Bihar Assembly Poll Results Show the Voters Know Their Minds Well', [Reflections on the 2000 Legislative Assembly elections in Bihar], *The Telegraph* (Calcutta), 9 March 2000.

'Fine Balance Sheet: Bihar's Votes May Have Gone For or Against Laloo Yadav, But the Results Confirm National Trends' [Reflections on the 1998 parliamentary elections with specific reference to their meaning in Bihar], *The Telegraph* (Calcutta), 24 March 1998.

'No Longer Sitting Pretty: The Watergate and Fodder Scandals Are Signs That the System Works' [Reflections on the charge-sheeting of Laloo Prasad Yadav, the Bihar chief minister, in the fodder scam], *The Telegraph* (Calcutta), 28 June 1997.

'Peasant Surprise: Bihar's Elections Showed Social Justice Is For the Voter to Define and the Politician to Implement' [Reflections on the meaning of the 1996 parliamentary elections in Bihar], *The Telegraph* (Calcutta), 21 May 1996.

'Peasant Surprise: Warts and All, Indian Elections Are More Meaningful Than Those in Most Democracies' [Reflections on the meaning of the parliamentary elections of 1996 in Bihar], *The Telegraph* (Calcutta), 4 May 1996.

'The Politics of Transition' [Reflections on India's Tenth General Election], in the *Newsletter* of the Center for South Asian Studies, University of Virginia, vol. 4, no. 1 (Fall 1991).

BOOK REVIEWS

Three Statesmen: Gokhale, Gandhi, and Nehru, by B.R. Nanda. New Delhi and Oxford: Oxford University Press, 2004. *The Journal of Asian Studies*, vol. 64, no. 1 (February 2005), pp. 230-2.

Land, Power and Market: a Bihar District Under Colonial Rule, 1860–1947, by Jacques Pouchepadass. New Delhi, Thousand Oaks and London: Sage Publications, 2000. *The Asian Studies Review (Australia)*, vol. 27, no. 4 (December 2003), pp. 522-6.

The Making of Laloo Yadav: The Unmaking of Bihar, by Sankarshan Thakur. New Delhi: Harper Collins Publishers, 2000. *The Telegraph* (Calcutta), 28 July 2000.

India Against Itself: Assam and the Politics of Nationality, by Sanjib Baruah. Philadelphia: University of Pennsylvania Press, 1999. *The Telegraph* (Calcutta), 29 October 1999.

The Agrarian Drama: The Leftists and the Rural Poor in India, 1934-1951, by Amit Kumar Gupta. New Delhi: Manohar Publishers, 1996. *The Journal of Asian Studies*, vol. 57, no. 2 (May 1998), pp. 566-8.

Growth, Stagnation or Decline? Agricultural Productivity in British India. Edited by Sumit Guha. Delhi: Oxford University Press, 1992. *The Journal of Asian Studies*, vol. 55, no. 2 (May 1996), pp. 502-3.

The World of the Rural Labourer in Colonial India. Edited by Gyan Prakash. Delhi: Oxford University Press, 1994. *The Journal of Asian Studies*, vol. 55, no. 2 (May 1996), pp. 502-3.

Bonded Histories: Genealogies of Labour Servitude in Colonial India. by Gyan Prakash. Cambridge: Cambridge University Press, 1989. *The American Historical Review,* vol. 97, no. 4 (October 1992), pp. 1269-71.

Selected Subaltern Studies. Edited by Ranajit Guha and Gayatri Chakravorty Spivak. New York: Oxford University Press, 1988. *The American Historical Review,* vol. 96, no. 1 (February 1991), pp. 241-3.

Subaltern Studies VI: Writings on South Asian History and Society. Edited by Ranajit Guha. Delhi: Oxford University Press, 1989.

The Journal of Asian Studies, vol. 50, no. 4 (November 1991), pp. 968-9.

Weber im Wettbewerb: Das Schicksal des Südindischen Textilhandwerks im 19ten Jahrhundert [Weavers in Competition: The Fate of the South Indian Handloom Weavers in the Nineteenth Century], by Konrad Specker. Wiesbaden: F. Steiner, 1984. *The Journal of Asian Studies,* vol. 47, no. 1 (February 1988), pp. 188-9.

Elementary Aspects of Peasant Insurgency in Colonial India, by Ranajit Guha. Delhi: Oxford University Press, 1983. *The Journal of Asian Studies,* vol. 45, no. 1 (February 1985), pp. 174-7.

The Indian National Congress and the Raj, 1929-1942: The Penultimate Phase, by B.R. Tomlinson. Toronto: Macmillan, 1976. *The American Historical Review,* vol. 83, no. 2 (April 1978), pp. 508-9.

The Indian Army: Its Contribution to the Development of a Nation, by Stephen P. Cohen. Berkeley: University of California Press, 1971. *The American Historical Review,* vol. 77, no. 4 (October 1972), pp. 1171-2.

State Politics in India. Edited by Myron Weiner. Princeton: Princeton University Press, 1968. *The American Historical Review,* vol. 74, no. 4 (April 1969), pp. 1341-2.

Revolution in Pakistan: A Study of the Martial Law Administration, by Herbert Feldman. London: Oxford University Press, 1967. *The American Historical Review,* vol. 73, no. 5 (June 1968), pp. 1607-8.

Die Politische Willensbildung in India, 1900-1960 [The Development of a Political Culture in India, 1900-1960] by Dietmar Rothermund. Wiesbaden: Otto Harrassowitz, 1965. In *The American Historical Review,* vol. 72, no. 3 (April 1967), pp. 1060-1.

The Government and Politics of India, by W.H. Morris-Jones. London: Hutchinson University Library, 1964. *The American Historical Review,* vol. 72, no. 3 (April 1967), pp. 1062-3.

Unteilbare Freiheit: Nehrus Politik Der Selbstbestimmung [Indivisible Freedom: Nehru's Politics of Self Determination], by Wilhelm Wolfgang Schutz. Gottingen: Vandenhoeck & Ruprecht, 1964. *The American Historical Review,* vol. 71, no. 1 (October 1965), pp. 283-4.

REMEMBRANCES

Remembering Kumar Suresh Singh: Scholar, Administrator, and Friend (1935-2006), *Seminar: The Monthly Symposium,* 566 (October 2006). See also the *Seminar* website at <http://ww.india-

seminar.com/>. K.S. Singh was Director General of the Anthropological Survey of India from 1985 to 1992.

Reflections on a Friendship: Samaren Roy of Behala (Samaren Roy, 1919-2006), H-ASIA website for 4 September 2006. See <http://www.h-net.org/~asia/>.

Remembering Jim Hagen, 1941-2006, H-ASIA website for July 7, 2006. See <http://www.h-net.org/~asia/>. James R. Hagen was on the faculty of Frostburg State University in Maryland at the time of his death.

Remembering Barney Cohn (Bernard S. Cohn, 1928-2003), *Newsletter* of the Center for South Asian Studies of the University of Virginia, vol. 18, no. 2 (Spring 2004), pp. 13-14. This reflection also appeared in the book of remembrances prepared by Martha Kaplan for the memorial service held in the Bond Chapel at the University of Chicago, 14 May 2004. See also the H-ASIA website for April 20, 2004 at <http://www.h-net.org/~asia/>.

Joseph Allen Stein, 1912-2001, *Newsletter* of the Center for South Asian Studies of the University of Virginia, vol. 15, no. 1 (Fall 2001), pp. 10 and 13. Among Joe Stein's many notable designs in India are the India International Centre, the Triveni Kala Sangam, and among the last of his major projects, the magnificent Habitat Centre, all in New Delhi.

Remembering Tessa (Tessa Bartholomeusz, 1958-2001), *Newsletter* of the Center for South Asian Studies of the University of Virginia, vol. 15, no. 1 (Fall 2001), p. 11. Tessa was a student of Buddhism and the author of *Women Under the Bo Tree: Buddhist Nuns in Sri Lanka* (Cambridge: Cambridge University Press, 1994). She earned her PhD in Religious Studies at the University of Virginia in 1991, and was on the faculty of Florida State University at the time of her death.

Arvind Narayan Das (1948-2000), *The Journal of Asian Studies*, vol. 59, no. 4 (November 2000), pp. 1103-4. Arvind was an activist historian, journalist and one of the founder-editors of the review journal *Biblio*.

Qeyamuddin Ahmad (1930-98), *The Journal of Asian Studies*, vol. 58, no. 2 (May 1999), pp. 591-2. Qeyamuddin Ahmad was on the history faculty of Patna University throughout his career. He was the author of *The Wahabi Movement in India* initially published in 1966 and reissued in a second revised edition in 1994 by Manohar Publishers, New Delhi.

A. K. Ramanujan (1929-93), *The Independent* (London), Saturday 31 July 1993, Gazette Page, p. 45. Ramanujan was the poet and litterateur *par excellence.* He was Professor of Linguistics and Professor of South Asian Languages and Civilizations at the University of Chicago at the time of his death.

Gordon C. Roadarmel (1932-72), *The Journal of Asian Studies,* vol. 31, no. 4 (August 1972), p. 899. (With Warren F. Ilchman and David Rubin). Gordon had translated Premchand's *Godaan* for the UNESCO edition of the novel in 1968. His edited translation of modern Hindi short stories appeared as *A Death in Delhi* (Berkeley: University of California Press, 1972). Roadarmel was teaching at the University of California, Berkeley at the time of his death.

Index